In Search of the Miraculous

P. D. Ouspensky

IN SEARCH
OF THE
MIRACULOUS

FRAGMENTS
OF AN UNKNOWN TEACHING

A Harvest Book
HARCOURT, BRACE & WORLD, INC.
New York

ISBN 0-15-644508-5

Contents

v

Contents

CHAPTER VII

CHAPTER VIII

CHAPTER XI

"Except a corn of wheat die, it bringeth forth no fruit." A book of aphorisms. To awake, to die, to be born. What prevents a man from being born again? What prevents a man from "dying"? What prevents a man from awakening? Absence of the realization of one's own nothingness. What does the realization of one's own nothingness mean? What prevents this realization? Hypnotic influence of life. The sleep in which men live is hypnotic sleep. The magician and the sheep. "Kundalini." Imagination. Alarm clocks. Organized work. Groups. Is it possible to work in groups without a teacher? Work of self-study in groups. Mirrors. Exchange of observations. General and individual conditions. Rules. "Chief fault." Realization of one's own nothingness. Danger of imitative work. "Barriers." Truth and falsehood. Sincerity with oneself. Efforts. Accumulators. The big accumulator. Intellectual and emotional work. Necessity for feeling. Possibility of understanding through feeling what cannot be understood through the mind. The emotional center is a more subtle apparatus than the intellectual center. Explanation of yawning in connection with accumulators. Role and significance of laughter in life. Absence of laughter in higher centers.

CHAPTER XII

Work in groups becomes more intensive. Each man's limited "repertoire of roles." The choice between work on oneself and a "quiet life." Difficulties of obedience. The place of "tasks." G. gives a definite task. Reaction of friends to the ideas. The system brings out the best or the worst in people. What people can come to the work? Preparation. Disappointment is necessary. Question with which a man aches. Revaluation of friends. A talk about types. G. gives a further task. Attempts to relate the story of one's life. Intonations. "Essence" and "personality." Sincerity. A bad mood. G. promises to answer any question. "Eternal Recurrence." An experiment on separating personality from essence. A talk about sex. The role of sex as the principal motive force of all mechanicalness. Sex as the chief possibility of liberation. New birth. Transmutation of sex energy. Abuses of sex. Is abstinence useful? Right work of centers. A permanent center of gravity.

CHAPTER XIII

Intensity of inner work. Preparation for "facts." A visit to Finland. The "miracle" begins. Mental "conversations" with G. "You are not asleep." Seeing "sleeping people." Impossibility of investigating higher phenomena by ordinary means. A changed outlook on "methods of action." "Chief feature." G. defines people's chief feature. Reorganization of the group. Those who leave the work. Sitting between two stools. Difficulty of coming back. G.'s apartment. Reactions to silence. "Seeing lies." A demonstration. How to awake? How to create the emotional state necessary? Three ways. The necessity of sacrifice. "Sacrificing one's suffering." Expanded table of hydrogens. A "moving diagram." A new discovery. "We have very little time."

THE SEARCH of P. D. Ouspensky in Europe, in Egypt and the Orient for a teaching which would solve for him the problems of Man and the Universe, brought him in 1915 to his meeting in St. Petersburg with Georges Gurdjieff. (It is Gurdjieff who is referred to, throughout the text of this book, as G.) *In Search of the Miraculous: Fragments of an Unknown Teaching* is the record of Ouspensky's eight years of work as Gurdjieff's pupil.

In Search of the Miraculous

Chapter One

I RETURNED to Russia in November, 1914, that is, at the beginning of the first world war, after a rather long journey through Egypt, Ceylon, and India. The war had found me in Colombo and from there I went back through England.

When leaving Petersburg at the start of my journey I had said that I was going to "seek the miraculous." The "miraculous" is very difficult to define. But for me this word had a quite definite meaning. I had come to the conclusion a long time ago that there was no escape from the labyrinth of contradictions in which we live except by an entirely new road, unlike anything hitherto known or used by us. But where this new or forgotten road began I was unable to say. I already knew then as an undoubted fact that beyond the thin film of false reality there existed another reality from which, for some reason, something separated us. The "miraculous" was a penetration into this unknown reality. And it seemed to me that the way to the unknown could be found in the East. Why in the East? It was difficult to answer this. In this idea there was, perhaps, something of romance, but it may have been the absolutely real conviction that, in any case, nothing could be found in Europe.

On the return journey, and during the several weeks I spent in London, everything I had thought about the results of my search was thrown into confusion by the wild absurdity of the war and by all the emotions which filled the air, conversation, and newspapers, and which, against my will, often affected me.

But when I returned to Russia, and again experienced all those thoughts with which I had gone away, I felt that my search, and everything connected with it, was more important than anything that was happening or could happen in a world of "obvious absurdities." [1] I said to myself

[1] That refers to a little book I had as a child. The book was called *Obvious Absurdities*, it belonged to Stupin's "Little Library" and consisted of such pictures as, for instance, a man carrying a house on his back, a carriage with square wheels, and similar things. This book impressed me very much at that time, because there were many pictures in it about which I could not understand what was absurd in them. They looked exactly like ordinary things in life. And later I began to think that the book really gave pictures of real life, because when I continued to grow I became more and more convinced that all life consisted of "obvious absurdities." Later experiences only strengthened this conviction.

3

then that the war must be looked upon as one of those generally catas-
trophic conditions of life in the midst of which we have to live and work,
and seek answers to our questions and doubts. The *war*, the great European war, in the possibility of which I had not wanted to believe and the
reality of which I did not for a long time wish to acknowledge, had become a fact. We *were in it* and I saw that it must be taken as a great
memento mori showing that hurry was necessary and that it was impossible to believe in "life" which led nowhere.

The war could not touch me personally, at any rate not until the final
catastrophe which seemed to me inevitable for Russia, and perhaps for
the whole of Europe, but not yet imminent. Though then, of course, the
approaching catastrophe looked only temporary and no one had as yet
conceived all the disintegration and destruction, both inner and outer,
in which we should have to live in the future.

Summing up the total of my impressions of the East and particularly
of India, I had to admit that, on my return, my problem seemed even
more difficult and complicated than on my departure. India and the East
had not only not lost their glamour of the miraculous; on the contrary,
this glamour had acquired new shades that were absent from it before. I
saw clearly that something could be found there which had long since
ceased to exist in Europe and I considered that the direction I had taken
was the right one. But, at the same time, I was convinced that the secret
was better and more deeply hidden than I could previously have supposed.

When I went away I already knew I was going to look for a *school* or
schools. I had arrived at this long ago. I realized that personal, individual
efforts were insufficient and that it was necessary to come into touch
with the real and living thought which must be in existence somewhere
but with which we had lost contact.

This I understood; but the idea of schools itself changed very much
during my travels and in one way became simpler and more concrete and
in another way became more cold and distant. I want to say that schools
lost much of their fairy-tale character.

On my departure I still admitted much that was fantastic in relation
to schools. "Admitted" is perhaps too strong a word. I should say better
that I dreamed about the possibility of a non-physical contact with schools,
a contact, so to speak, "on another plane." I could not explain it clearly,
but it seemed to me that even the beginning of contact with a school
may have a *miraculous nature*. I imagined, for example, the possibility of
making contact with schools of the distant past, with schools of Pythag-
oras, with schools of Egypt, with the schools of those who built Notre-
Dame, and so on. It seemed to me that the barriers of time and space
should disappear on making such contact. The idea of schools in itself
was fantastic and nothing seemed to me too fantastic in relation to this
idea. And I saw no contradiction between these ideas and my attempts

to find schools in India. It seemed to me that it was precisely in India that it would be possible to establish some kind of contact which would afterwards become permanent and independent of any outside interferences.

On the return voyage, after a whole series of meetings and impressions, the idea of schools became much more real and tangible and lost its fantastic character. This probably took place chiefly because, as I then realized, "school" required not only a search but "selection," or choice—I mean on our side.

That schools existed I did not doubt. But at the same time I became convinced that the schools I heard about and with which I could have come into contact were not for me. They were schools of either a frankly religious nature or of a half-religious character, but definitely devotional in tone. These schools did not attract me, chiefly because if I had been seeking a religious way I could have found it in Russia. Other schools were of a slightly sentimental moral-philosophical type with a shade of asceticism, like the schools of the disciples or followers of Ramakrishna; there were nice people connected with these schools, but I did not feel they had real knowledge. Others which are usually described as "yogi schools" and which are based on the creation of trance states had, in my eyes, something of the nature of "spiritualism." I could not trust them; all their achievements were either self-deception or what the Orthodox mystics (I mean in Russian monastic literature) called "beauty," or allurement.

There was another type of school, with which I was unable to make contact and of which I only heard. These schools promised very much but they also demanded very much. *They demanded everything at once.* It would have been necessary to stay in India and give up thoughts of returning to Europe, to renounce all my own ideas, aims, and plans, and proceed along a road of which I could know nothing beforehand.

These schools interested me very much and the people who had been in touch with them, and who told me about them, stood out distinctly from the common type. But still, it seemed to me that there ought to be schools of a more rational kind and that a man had the right, up to a certain point, to know where he was going.

Simultaneously with this I came to the conclusion that whatever the name of the school: occult, esoteric, or yogi, they should exist on the ordinary earthly plane like any other kind of school: a school of painting, a school of dancing, a school of medicine. I realized that thought of schools "on another plane" was simply a sign of weakness, of dreams taking the place of real search. And I understood then that these dreams were one of the principal obstacles on our possible way to the miraculous.

On the way to India I made plans for further travels. This time I

wanted to begin with the Mohammedan East: chiefly Russian Central
Asia and Persia. But nothing of this was destined to materialize.

From London, through Norway, Sweden, and Finland, I arrived in
Petersburg, already renamed "Petrograd" and full of speculation and patriotism. Soon afterwards I went to Moscow and began editorial work for
the newspaper to which I had written from India. I stayed there about
six weeks, but during that time a little episode occurred which was connected with many things that happened later.

One day in the office of the newspaper I found, while preparing for the
next issue, a notice (in, I think, *The Voice of Moscow*) referring to the
scenario of a ballet, "The Struggle of the Magicians," which belonged, as
it said, to a certain "Hindu." The action of the ballet was to take place
in India and give a complete picture of Oriental magic including fakir
miracles, sacred dances, and so on. I did not like the excessively jaunty
tone of the paragraph, but as Hindu writers of ballet scenarios were, to a
certain extent, rare in Moscow, I cut it out and put it into my paper, with
the slight addition that there would be everything in the ballet that cannot
be found in real India but which travelers go there to see.

Soon after this, for various reasons, I left the paper and went to
Petersburg.

There, in February and March, 1915, I gave public lectures on my
travels in India. The titles of these lectures were "In Search of the Miraculous" and "The Problems of Death." In these lectures, which were to
serve as an introduction to a book on my travels it was my intention to
write, I said that in India the "miraculous" was not sought where it
ought to be sought, that all ordinary ways were useless, and that India
guarded her secrets better than many people supposed; but that the
"miraculous" did exist there and was indicated by many things which
people passed by without realizing their hidden sense and meaning or
without knowing how to approach them. I again had "schools" in mind.

In spite of the war my lectures evoked very considerable interest. There
were more than a thousand people at each in the Alexandrovsky Hall of
the Petersburg Town Duma. I received many letters; people came to see
me; and I felt that on the basis of a "search for the miraculous" it would
be possible to unite together a very large number of people who were
no longer able to swallow the customary forms of lying and living in
lying.

After Easter I went to give these lectures in Moscow. Among people
whom I met during these lectures there were two, one a musician and
the other a sculptor, who very soon began to speak to me about a group
in Moscow which was engaged in various "occult" investigations and
experiments and directed by a certain G., a Caucasian Greek, the very
"Hindu," so I understood, to whom belonged the ballet scenario men-

tioned in the newspaper I had come across three or four months before this. I must confess that what these two people told me about this group and what took place in it: all sorts of self-suggested wonders, interested me very little. I had heard tales exactly like this many times before and I had formed a definite opinion concerning them.

Ladies who suddenly see "eyes" in their rooms which float in the air and fascinate them and which they follow from street to street and at the end arrive at the house of a certain Oriental to whom the eyes belong. Or people who, in the presence of the same Oriental, suddenly feel he is looking right through them, seeing all their feelings, thoughts, and desires; and they have a strange sensation in their legs and cannot move, and then fall into his power to such an extent that he can make them do everything he desires, even from a distance. All this and many other stories of the same sort had always seemed to me to be simply bad fiction. People invent miracles for themselves and invent exactly what is expected from them. It is a mixture of superstition, self-suggestion, and defective thinking, and, according to my observation, these stories never appear without a certain collaboration on the part of the men to whom they refer.

So that, in the light of previous experience, it was only after the persistent efforts of one of my new acquaintances, M., that I agreed to meet G. and have a talk with him.

My first meeting with him entirely changed my opinion of him and of what I might expect from him.

I remember this meeting very well. We arrived at a small café in a noisy though not central street. I saw a man of an oriental type, no longer young, with a black mustache and piercing eyes, who astonished me first of all because he seemed to be disguised and completely out of keeping with the place and its atmosphere. I was still full of impressions of the East. And this man with the face of an Indian raja or an Arab sheik whom I at once seemed to see in a white burnoose or a gilded turban, seated here in this little café, where small dealers and commission agents met together, in a black overcoat with a velvet collar and a black bowler hat, produced the strange, unexpected, and almost alarming impression of a man poorly disguised, the sight of whom embarrasses you because you see he is not what he pretends to be and yet you have to speak and behave as though you did not see it. He spoke Russian incorrectly with a strong Caucasian accent; and this accent, with which we are accustomed to associate anything apart from philosophical ideas, strengthened still further the strangeness and the unexpectedness of this impression.

I do not remember how our talk began; I think we spoke of India, of esotericism, and of yogi schools. I gathered that G. had traveled widely and had been in places of which I had only heard and which I very much wished to visit. Not only did my questions not embarrass him but it seemed to me that he put much more into each answer than I had asked for. I liked his manner of speaking, which was careful and precise. M. soon left us. G. told me of his work in Moscow. I did not fully understand him. It transpired from what he said that in his work, which was chiefly psychological in character, *chemistry* played a big part. Listening to him for the first time I, of course, took his words literally.

"What you say," I said, "reminds me of something I heard about a school in southern India. A Brahmin, an exceptional man in many respects, told a young Englishman in Travancore of a school which studied the chemistry of the human body, and by means of introducing or removing various substances, could change a man's moral and psychological nature. This is very much like what you are saying."

"It may be so," said G., "but, at the same time, it may be quite different. There are schools which appear to make use of similar methods but understand them quite differently. A similarity of methods or even of ideas proves nothing."

"There is another question that interests me very much," I said. "There are substances which yogis take to induce certain states. Might these not be, in certain cases, narcotics? I have myself carried out a number of experiments in this direction and everything I have read about magic proves to me quite clearly that all schools at all times and in all countries have made a very wide use of narcotics for the creation of those states which make 'magic' possible."

"Yes," said G. "In many cases these substances are those which you call 'narcotics.' But they can be used in entirely different ways. There are schools which make use of narcotics in the right way. People in these schools take them for self-study; in order to take a look ahead, to know their possibilities better, to see beforehand, 'in advance,' what can be attained later on as the result of prolonged work. When a man sees this and is convinced that what he has learned theoretically really exists, he then works consciously, he knows where he is going. Sometimes this is the easiest way of being convinced of the real existence of those possibilities which man often suspects in himself. There is a special chemistry relating to this. There are particular substances for each function. Each function can either be strengthened or weakened, awakened or put to sleep. But to do this a great knowledge of the human machine and of this special chemistry is necessary. In all those schools which make use of this method experiments are carried out only when they are really necessary and only under the direction of experienced and competent men who can foresee all results and adopt measures against possible undesirable consequences. The substances used in these schools are not merely 'narcotics' as you call them, although many of them are prepared from such drugs as opium, hashish, and so on. Besides schools in which such experiments are carried out, there are other schools which use these or similar substances, not for experiment or study but to attain definite desired results, if only for a short time. Through a skillful use of such substances a man can be made very clever or very strong, for a certain time. Afterwards, of course, he dies or goes mad, but this is not taken into consideration. Such schools also exist. So you see that we must speak very cautiously about schools. They may do practically the same things but the results will be totally different."

I was deeply interested in everything G. said. I felt in it some new points of view, unlike any I had met with before.

He invited me to go with him to a house where some of his pupils were to forgather.

We took a carriage and went in the direction of Sokolniki.

On the way G. told me how the war had interfered with many of his plans; many of his pupils had gone with the first mobilization; very expensive apparatus and instruments ordered from abroad had been lost. Then he spoke of the heavy expenditure connected with his work, of the expensive apartments he had taken, and to which, I gathered, we were going. He said, further, that his work interested a number of well-known people in Moscow—"professors" and "artists," as he expressed it. But when I asked him who, precisely, they were, he did not give me a single name.

"I ask," I said, "because I am a native of Moscow; and, besides, I have worked on newspapers here for ten years so that I know more or less everybody."

G. said nothing to this.

We came to a large empty flat over a municipal school, evidently belonging to teachers of this school. I think it was in the place of the former Red Pond.

There were several of G.'s pupils in the flat: three or four young men and two ladies both of whom looked like schoolmistresses. I had been in such flats before. Even the absence of furniture confirmed my idea, since municipal schoolmistresses were not given furniture. With this thought it somehow became strange to look at G. Why had he told me that tale about the enormous expenditure connected with this flat? In the first place the flat was not his, in the second place it was rent free, and thirdly it could not have cost more than ten pounds a month. There was something so singular in this obvious bluff that I thought at that time it must mean something.

It is difficult for me to reconstruct the beginning of the conversation with G.'s pupils. Some of the things I heard surprised me. I tried to discover in what their work consisted, but they gave me no direct answers, insisting in some cases on a strange and, to me, unintelligible terminology.

They suggested reading the beginning of a story written, so they told me, by one of G.'s pupils, who was not in Moscow at the time.

Naturally, I agreed to this; and one of them began to read aloud from a manuscript. The author described his meeting and acquaintance with G. My attention was attracted by the fact that the story began with the author coming across the same notice of the ballet, "The Struggle of the Magicians," which I myself had seen in *The Voice of Moscow*, in the winter. Further—this pleased me very much because I expected it—at the first meeting the author certainly felt that G. put him as it were on the palm of his hand, weighed him, and put him back. The story was called "Glimpses of Truth" and was evidently written by a man without any literary experience. But in spite of this it produced an impression, because it contained indications of a system in which I felt something very interesting though I could neither name nor formulate it to myself, and some very strange and unexpected ideas about art which found in me a very strong response.

I learned later on that the author of the story was an imaginary person and that the story had been begun by two of G.'s pupils who were present at the reading, with the object of giving an exposition of his ideas in a literary form. Still later I heard that the idea of the story belonged to G. himself.

The reading of what constituted the first chapter stopped at this point. G. listened attentively the whole time. He sat on a sofa, with one leg tucked beneath him, drinking black coffee from a tumbler, smoking and sometimes glancing at me. I liked his movements, which had a great deal of a kind of feline grace and assurance; even in his silence there was something which distinguished him from others. I felt that I would rather have met him, not in Moscow, not in this flat, but in one of those places from which I had so recently returned, in the court of one of the Cairo mosques, in one of the ruined cities of Ceylon, or in one of the South Indian temples—Tanjore, Trichinopoly, or Madura.

"Well, how do you like the story?" asked G. after a short silence when the reading had ended.

I told him I had found it interesting to listen to, but that, from my point of view, it had the defect of not making clear what exactly it was all about. The story spoke of a very strong impression produced upon the author by a doctrine he had met with, but it gave no adequate idea of the doctrine itself. Those who were present began to argue with me, pointing out that I had missed the most important part of it. G. himself said nothing.

When I asked what was the system they were studying and what were its distinguishing features, I was answered very indefinitely. Then they spoke of "work on oneself," but in what this work consisted they failed to explain. On the whole my conversation with G.'s pupils did not go very well and I felt something calculated and artificial in them as though they were playing a part learned beforehand. Besides, the pupils did not match with the teacher. They all belonged to that particular layer of Moscow rather poor "intelligentsia" which I knew very well and from which I could not expect anything interesting. I even thought that it was very strange to meet them on the way to the miraculous. At the same time they all seemed to me quite nice and decent people. The stories I had heard from M. obviously did not come from them and did not refer to them.

"There is one thing I wanted to ask you," said G. after a pause. "Could this article be published in a paper? We thought that we could acquaint the public in this way with our ideas."

"It is quite impossible," I said. "This is not an article, that is, not anything having a beginning and an end; it is the beginning of a story and it is too long for a newspaper. You see we count material by lines. The reading occupied two hours—it is about three thousand lines. You know what we call a feuilleton in a paper—an ordinary feuilleton is about three hundred lines. So this part of the story will take ten feuilletons. In Moscow papers a feuilleton with continuation is never printed more than once a week, so it will take ten weeks—and it is a conversation of one night. If it can be published it is only in a monthly magazine, but I don't know any one suitable for this now. And in this case they will ask for the whole story, before they say anything."

G. did not say anything and the conversation stopped at that.

But in G. himself I at once felt something uncommon; and in the course of the evening this impression only strengthened. When I was taking leave of him the thought flashed into my mind that I must *at once, without delay*, arrange to meet him again, and that if I did not do so I might lose all connection with him. I asked him if I could not see him once more before my departure to Petersburg. He told me that he would be at the same café the following day, at the same time.

I came out with one of the young men. I felt myself very strange—a long reading which I very little understood, people who did not answer my questions, G. himself with his unusual manners and his influence on his people, which I all the time felt produced in me an unexpected desire to laugh, to shout, to sing, as though I had escaped from school or from some strange detention.

I wanted to tell my impressions to this young man, make some jokes about G., and about the rather tedious and pretentious story. I at once imagined myself telling all this to some of my friends. Happily I stopped myself in time. —"But he will go and telephone them at once. They are all friends."

So I tried to keep myself in hand, and quite silently we came to the tram and rode towards the center of Moscow. After rather a long journey we arrived at Okhotny Nad, near which place I stayed, and silently said good-by to one another, and parted.

I was at the same café where I had met G. the next day, and the day following, and every day afterwards. During the week I spent in Moscow I saw G. every day. It very soon became clear to me that he knew very much of what I wanted to know. Among other things he explained to me certain phenomena I had come across in India which no one had been able to explain to me either there, on the spot, or afterwards. In his explanations I felt the assurance of a specialist, a very fine analysis of facts, and a *system* which I could not grasp, but the presence of which I already felt because G.'s explanations made me think not only of the facts under discussion, but also of many other things I had observed or conjectured.

I did not meet G.'s group again. About himself G. spoke but little. Once or twice he mentioned his travels in the East. I was interested to know where he had been but this I was unable to make out exactly.

In regard to his work in Moscow G. said that he had two groups unconnected with one another and occupied in different work, "according to the state of their preparation and their powers," as he expressed it. Each member of these groups paid a thousand roubles a year, and was able to work with him while pursuing his ordinary activities in life.

I said that in my opinion a thousand roubles a year might be too large a payment for many people without private means.

G. replied that no other arrangement was possible, because, owing to the very nature of the work, he could not have many pupils. At the same time, he did not desire and *ought not*—he emphasized this—to spend his own money on the organization of the work. His work was not, and could not be, of a charitable nature and his pupils themselves ought to find the means for the hire of apartments where they could meet; for carrying out experiments; and so on. Besides this, he added that observation showed that people who were weak in life proved themselves weak in the work.

"There are several aspects of this idea," said G. "The work of each person may involve expenses, traveling, and so on. If his life is so badly organized that a thousand roubles embarrasses him it would be better for him not to undertake this work. Suppose that, in the course of the year, his work requires him to go to Cairo or some other place. He must have the means to do so. Through our demand we find out whether he is able to work with us or not.

"Besides," G. continued, "I have far too little spare time to be able to sacrifice it on others without being certain even that it will do them good. I value my time very much because I need it for my own work and because I cannot and, as I said before, do not want to spend it unproductively. There is also another side to this," said G. "People do not value a thing if they do not pay for it."

I listened to this with a strange feeling. On the one hand I was pleased with everything that G. said. I was attracted by the absence of any element of sentimentality, of conventional talk about "altruism," of words about "working for the good of humanity" and so forth. On the other hand I was surprised at G.'s apparent desire to *convince* me of something in connection with the question of money *when I needed no convincing.*

If there was anything I did not agree with it was simply that G. would be able to collect enough money in the way he described. I realized that none of those pupils whom I had seen would be able to pay a thousand roubles a year. If he had really found in the East visible and tangible traces of hidden knowledge and was continuing investigations in this direction, then it was clear that this work needed funds, like any other scientific enterprise, like an expedition into some unknown part of the world, the excavation of an ancient city, or an investigation requiring elaborate and numerous physical or chemical experiments. It was quite unnecessary to convince me of this. On the contrary, the thought was already in my mind that if G. gave me the possibility of a closer acquaintance with his activities, I should probably be able to find the funds necessary for him to place his work on a proper footing and also bring him more prepared people. But, of course, I still had only a very vague idea in what this work might consist.

Without saying it plainly, G. gave me to understand that he would accept me as one of his pupils if I expressed the wish. I told him that the chief obstacle on my side was that, at the moment, I could not stay in Moscow because I had made an arrangement with a publisher in Petersburg and was preparing several books for publication. G. told me that he sometimes went to Petersburg and he promised to come there soon and let me know of his arrival.

"But if I joined your group," I said to G., "I should be faced with a very difficult problem. I do not know whether you exact a promise from your pupils to keep secret what they learn from you, but I could give no such promise. There have been two occasions in my life when I had the possibility of joining groups engaged in work which appears to be similar to yours, at any rate by description, and which interested me very much at the time. But in both cases to join would have meant consenting or promising to keep secret everything that I might learn there. And I refused in both cases, because, before everything else, I am a writer, and I desire to be absolutely free and to decide for myself what I shall write and what I shall not write. If I promise to keep secret something I am told, it would be very difficult afterwards to separate what had been told me from what came to my own mind either in connection with it or even with no connection. For instance, I know very little about your ideas yet, but I do know that when we begin to talk we shall very soon come to questions of time and space, of higher dimensions, and so on. These are questions on which I have already been working for many years. I have no doubt whatever that they must occupy a large place in your system." G. nodded. "Well, you see, if we were now to talk under a pledge of secrecy, then, after the first conversation I should not know what I could write and what I could not write."

"But what are your own ideas on the subject?" said G. "One must not talk too much. There are things which are said only for disciples."

"I could accept such a condition only temporarily," I said. "Of course it would be ludicrous if I began at once to write about what I learn from you. But if, in principle, you do not wish to make a secret of your ideas and care only that they should not be transmitted in a distorted form, then I could accept such a condition and wait until I had a better understanding of your teaching. I once came across a group of people who were engaged in various scientific experiments on a very wide scale. They made no secret of their work. But they made it a condition that no one would have the right to speak of or describe any experiment unless he was able to carry it out himself. Until he was able to repeat the experiment himself he had to keep silent."

"There could be no better formulation," said G., "and if you will keep such a rule this question will never arise between us."

"Are there any conditions for joining your group?" I asked. "And is a man who joins it tied to it and to you? In other words, I want to know if he is free to go and leave your work, or does he take definite obligations upon himself? And how do you act towards him if he does not carry out his obligations?"

"There are no conditions of any kind," said G., "and there cannot be any. Our starting point is that man does not know himself, that he *is not*" (he emphasized these words), "that is, he is not what he can and what he should be. For this reason he cannot make any agreements or assume any obligations. He can decide nothing in regard to the future. Today he is one person and tomorrow another. He is in no way bound to us and if he likes he can at any time leave the work and go. There are no obligations of any kind either in our relationship to him or in his to us.

"If he likes he can study. He will have to study for a long time, and work a great deal on himself. When he has learned enough, then it is a different matter. He will see for himself whether he likes our work or not. If he wishes he can work with us; if not he may go away. Up to that moment he is free. If he stays after that he will be able to decide or make arrangements for the future.

"For instance, take one point. A situation may arise, not, of course, in the beginning but later on, when a man has to preserve secrecy, even if only for a time, about something he has learned. But can a man who does not know himself promise to keep a secret? Of course he can promise to do so, but can he keep his promise? For he is not one, there are many different people in him. *One in him* promises, and believes that he wants to keep the secret. But tomorrow *another in him* will tell it to his wife, or to a friend over a bottle of wine, or a clever man may question him in such a way that he himself will not notice that he is letting out everything. Finally, he may be hypnotized, or he may be shouted at unexpectedly and frightened, and he will do anything you like. What sort of obligations can he take upon himself? No, with such a man we will not talk seriously. To be able to keep a secret a man must *know himself* and he must *be.* And a man such as all men are is very far from this.

"Sometimes we make temporary conditions with people *as a test.* Usually they are broken very soon but we never give any serious secret to a man we don't trust so it does no matter much. I mean it matters nothing to us although it certainly breaks our connection with this man and he loses his chance to learn anything from us, if there is anything to learn from us. Also it may affect all his personal friends, although they may not expect it."

I remember that in one of my talks with G., during this first week of my acquaintance with him, I spoke of my intention of going again to the East.

"Is it worth thinking about it? And can I find what I want there?" I asked G.

"It is good to go for a rest, for a holiday," said G., "but it is not worth while going there for what you want. All that can be found here."

I understood that he was speaking of work with him.

"But do not schools which are on the spot, so to speak, in the midst of all the traditions, offer certain advantages?" I asked.

In answering this question G. told me several things which I did not understand till later.

"Even if you found schools you would find only 'philosophical' schools," he said. "In India there are only 'philosophical' schools. It was divided up in that way long ago; in India there was 'philosophy,' in Egypt 'theory,' and in present-day Persia, Mesopotamia, and Turkestan—'practice.' "

"And does it remain the same now?" I asked.

"In part even now," he said. "But you do not clearly understand what I mean by 'philosophy,' 'theory,' and 'practice.' These words must be understood in a different way, not in the way they are usually understood.

"But speaking of schools, there are only *special* schools; there are no general schools. Every teacher, or *guru,* is a specialist in some one thing. One is an astronomer, another a sculptor, a third a musician. And all the pupils of each teacher must first of all study the subject in which he has specialized, then, afterwards, another subject, and so on. It would take a thousand years to study everything."

"But how did you study?"

"I was not alone. There were all kinds of specialists among us. Everyone

studied on the lines of his particular subject. Afterwards, when we forgathered, we put together everything we had found."

"And where are your companions now?"

G. was silent for a time, and then said slowly, looking into the distance:
"Some have died, some are working, some have gone into seclusion."

This word from the monastic language, heard so unexpectedly, gave me
a strange and uncomfortable feeling.

At the same time I felt a certain "acting" on G.'s part, as though he
were deliberately trying from time to time to throw me a word that would
interest me and make me think in a definite direction.

When I tried to ask him more definitely where he had found what he
knew, what the source of his knowledge was, and how far this knowledge
went, he did not give me a direct answer.

"You know," G. said once, "when you went to India they wrote about
your journey and your aims in the papers. I gave my pupils the task of
reading your books, of determining by them *what you were*, and of establishing on this basis what you would be able to find. So we knew what
you would find while you were still on your way there."

With this the talk came to an end.

I once asked G. about the ballet which had been mentioned in the
papers and referred to in the story "Glimpses of Truth" and whether this
ballet would have the nature of a "mystery play."

"My ballet is not a 'mystery,'" said G. "The object I had in view was
to produce an interesting and beautiful spectacle. Of course there is a
certain meaning hidden beneath the outward form, but I have not pur-
sued the aim of exposing and emphasizing this meaning. An important
place in the ballet is occupied by certain dances. I will explain this to you
briefly. Imagine that in the study of the movements of the heavenly
bodies, let us say the planets of the solar system, a special mechanism is
constructed to give a visual representation of the laws of these movements and to remind us of them. In this mechanism each planet, which
is represented by a sphere of appropriate size, is placed at a certain distance from a central sphere representing the sun. The mechanism is set
in motion and all the spheres begin to rotate and to move along pre-
scribed paths, reproducing in a visual form the laws which govern the
movements of the planets. This mechanism reminds you of all you know
about the solar system. There is something like this in the rhythm of
certain dances. In the strictly defined movements and combinations of
the dancers, certain laws are visually reproduced which are intelligible to
those who know them. Such dances are called 'sacred dances.' In the
course of my travels in the East I have many times witnessed such dances
being performed during sacred services in various ancient temples. Some
of these dances are reproduced in 'The Struggle of the Magicians.' More-

over there are three ideas lying at the basis of 'The Struggle of the Magi-cians.' But if I produce the ballet on the ordinary stage the public will never understand these ideas."

I understood from what he said subsequently that this would not be a ballet in the strict meaning of the word, but a series of dramatic and mimic scenes held together by a common plot, accompanied by music and intermixed with songs and dances. The most appropriate name for these scenes would be "revue," but without any comic element. The "ballet" or "revue" was to be called "The Struggle of the Magicians." The important scenes represented the schools of a "Black Magician" and a "White Magician," with exercises by pupils of both schools and a struggle between the two schools. The action was to take place against the background of the life of an Eastern city, intermixed with sacred dances, Dervish dances, and various national Eastern dances, all this interwoven with a love story which itself would have an allegorical meaning.

I was particularly interested when G. said that *the same* performers would have to act and dance in the "White Magician" scene and in the "Black Magician" scene; and that they themselves and their movements had to be attractive and beautiful in the first scene and ugly and dis-cordant in the second.

"You understand that in this way they will see and study all sides of themselves; consequently the ballet will be of immense importance for self-study," said G.

I understood this far from clearly at the time, but I was struck by a certain discrepancy.

"In the notice I saw in the paper it was said that your 'ballet' would be staged in Moscow and that certain well-known ballet dancers would take part in it. How do you reconcile this with the idea of self-study?" I asked. "They will not play and dance in order to study themselves."

"All this is far from being decided," said G. "And the author of the notice you read was not fully informed. All this may be quite different. Although, on the other hand, those taking part in the ballet will see themselves whether they like it or not."

"And who is writing the music?" I asked.

"That also is not decided," said G. He did not say anything more, and I only came across the "ballet" again five years later.

Once I was talking with G. in Moscow. I was speaking about London, where I had been staying a short while before, about the terrifying mechanization that was being developed in the big European cities and without which it was probably impossible to live and work in those im-mense whirling "mechanical toys."

"People are turning into machines," I said. "And no doubt sometimes they become perfect machines. But I do not believe they can think. If they tried to think, they could not have been such fine machines."

"Yes," said G., "that is true, but only partly true. It depends first of all on the question *which* mind they use for their work. If they use the proper mind they will be able to think even better in the midst of all their work with machines. But, again, only if they think with the proper mind."

I did not understand what G. meant by "proper mind" and understood it only much later.

"And secondly," he continued, "the mechanization you speak of is not at all dangerous. A man may be a *man*" (he emphasized this word), "while working with machines. There is another kind of mechanization which is much more dangerous: being a machine oneself. Have you ever thought about the fact that all peoples *themselves* are machines?"

"Yes," I said, "from the strictly scientific point of view all people are machines governed by external influences. But the question is, can the scientific point of view be wholly accepted?"

"Scientific or not scientific is all the same to me," said G. "I want you to understand what I am saying. Look, all those people you see," he pointed along the street, "are simply machines—nothing more."

"I think I understand what you mean," I said. "And I have often thought how little there is in the world that can stand against this form of mechanization and choose its own path."

"This is just where you make your greatest mistake," said G. "You think there is something that chooses its own path, something that can stand against mechanization; you think that not everything is equally mechanical."

"Why, of course not!" I said. "Art, poetry, thought, are phenomena of quite a different order."

"Of exactly the same order," said G. "These activities are just as mechanical as everything else. Men are machines and nothing but mechanical actions can be expected of machines."

"Very well," I said. "But are there no people who are not machines?"

"It may be that there are," said G., "only not those people you see. And you do not know them. That is what I want you to understand."

I thought it rather strange that he should be so insistent on this point. What he said seemed to me obvious and incontestable. At the same time, I had never liked such short and all-embracing metaphors. They always omitted points of *difference*. I, on the other hand, had always maintained differences were the most important thing and that in order to understand things it was first necessary to see the points in which they differed. So I felt that it was odd that G. insisted on an idea which seemed to be obvious provided it were not made too absolute and exceptions were admitted.

"People are so unlike one another," I said. "I do not think it would be possible to bring them all under the same heading. There are savages, there are mechanized people, there are intellectual people, there are geniuses."

"Quite right," said G., "people are very unlike one another, but the real difference between people you do not know and cannot see. The difference of which you speak simply does not exist. This must be understood. All the people you see, all the people you know, all the people *you may get to know*, are machines, actual machines working solely under the power of external influences, as you yourself said. Machines they are born and machines they die. How do savages and intellectuals come into this? Even now, at this very moment, while we are talking, several millions of machines are trying to annihilate one another. What is the difference between them? Where are the savages and where are the intellectuals? They are all alike . . .

"But there is a possibility of ceasing to be a machine. It is of this we must think and not about the different kinds of machines that exist. Of course there are different machines; a motorcar is a machine, a gramophone is a machine, and a gun is a machine. But what of it? It is the same thing—they are all machines."

In connection with this conversation I remember another.

"What is your opinion of modern psychology?" I once asked G. with the intention of introducing the subject of psychoanalysis which I had mistrusted from the time when it had first appeared. But G. did not let me get as far as that.

"Before speaking of psychology we must be clear to whom it refers and to whom it does not refer," he said. "*Psychology* refers to people, to men, to human beings. What *psychology*" (he emphasized the word) "can there be in relation to machines? Mechanics, not psychology, is necessary for the study of machines. That is why we begin with mechanics. It is a very long way yet to psychology."

"Can one stop being a machine?" I asked.

"Ah! That is the question," said G. "If you had asked such questions more often we might, perhaps, have got somewhere in our talks. It is possible to stop being a machine, but for that it is necessary first of all *to know the machine*. A machine, a real machine, does not know itself and cannot know itself. When a machine knows itself it is then no longer a machine, at least, not such a machine as it was before. It already begins to be *responsible* for its actions."

"This means, according to you, that a man is not responsible for his actions?" I asked.

"A *man*" (he emphasized this word) "is responsible. A *machine* is not responsible."

In the course of one of our talks I asked G.:

"What, in your opinion, is the best preparation for the study of your method? For instance, is it useful to study what is called 'occult' or 'mystical' literature?"

In saying this I had in mind more particularly the "Tarot" and the literature on the "Tarot."

"Yes," said G. "A great deal can be found by reading. For instance, take yourself: you might already know a great deal if you *knew how to read*. I mean that, if you *understood* everything you have read in your life, you would already know what you are looking for now. If you understood everything you have written in your own book, what is it called?"—he made something altogether impossible out of the words "Tertium Organum"—"I should come and bow down to you and beg you to teach me. But *you do not understand* either what you read or what you write. You do not even understand what the word 'understand' means. Yet understanding is essential, and reading can be useful only if you understand what you read. But, of course, no book can give real preparation. So it is impossible to say which is better. What a man knows *well*" (he emphasized the word "well")—"that is his preparation. If a man knows how to make coffee well or how to make boots well, then it is already possible to talk to him. The trouble is that nobody knows anything well. Everything is known just anyhow, superficially."

This was another of those unexpected turns which G. gave to his explanations. G.'s words, in addition to their ordinary meaning, undoubtedly contained another, altogether different, meaning. I had already begun to realize that, in order to arrive at this hidden meaning in G.'s words, one had to begin with their usual and simple meaning. G.'s words were always significant in their ordinary sense, although this was not the whole of their significance. The wider or deeper significance remained hidden for a long time.

There is another talk which has remained in my memory.

I asked G. what a man had to do to assimilate this teaching.

"What *to do*?" asked G. as though surprised. "It is impossible *to do* anything. A man must first of all *understand* certain things. He has thousands of false ideas and false conceptions, chiefly about himself, and he must get rid of some of them before beginning to acquire anything new. Otherwise the new will be built on a wrong foundation and the result will be worse than before."

"How can one get rid of false ideas?" I asked. "We depend on the forms of our perception. False ideas are produced by the forms of our perception."

G. shook his head.

"Again you speak of something different," he said. "You speak of errors arising from perceptions but I am not speaking of these. Within the limits of given perceptions man can err more or err less. As I have said before, man's chief delusion is his conviction that he can *do*. All people think that they can do, all people want to do, and the first question all people ask is what they are to do. But actually nobody does anything and nobody can do anything. This is the first thing that must be understood. *Everything happens*. All that befalls a man, all that is done by him, all that comes from him—*all this happens*. And it happens in exactly the same way as rain falls as a result of a change in the temperature in the higher regions of the atmosphere or the surrounding clouds, as snow melts under the rays of the sun, as dust rises with the wind.

"Man is a machine. All his deeds, actions, words, thoughts, feelings, convictions, opinions, and habits are the results of external influences, external impressions. Out of himself a man cannot produce a single thought, a single action. Everything he says, does, thinks, feels—all this happens. Man cannot discover anything, invent anything. It all happens.

"To establish this fact for oneself, to understand it, to be convinced of its truth, means getting rid of a thousand illusions about man, about his being creative and consciously organizing his own life, and so on. There is nothing of this kind. Everything happens—popular movements, wars, revolutions, changes of government, all this happens. And it happens in exactly the same way as everything happens in the life of individual man. Man is born, lives, dies, builds houses, writes books, not as he wants to, but as it happens. Everything happens. Man does not love, hate, desire—all this happens.

"But no one will ever believe you if you tell him he can do nothing. This is the most offensive and the most unpleasant thing you can tell people. It is particularly unpleasant and offensive because it is the truth, and nobody wants to know the truth.

"When you understand this it will be easier for us to talk. But it is one thing to understand with the mind and another thing to feel it with one's 'whole mass,' to be really convinced that it is so and never forget it.

"With this question of *doing*" (G. emphasized the word), "yet another thing is connected. It always seems to people that others invariably do things wrongly, not in the way they should be done. Everybody always thinks he could do it better. They do not understand, and do not want to understand, that what is being done, and particularly what *has already been done* in one way, cannot be, and could not have been, done in another way. Have you noticed how everyone now is talking about the war? Everyone has his own plan, his own theory. Everyone finds that nothing is being done in the way it ought to be done. Actually everything is being done in the only way it can be done. If *one* thing could be different *everything* could be different. And then perhaps there would have been no war.

"Try to understand what I am saying: everything is dependent on everything else, everything is connected, nothing is separate. Therefore everything is going in the only way it can go. If people were different everything would be different. They are what they are, so everything is as it is."

This was very difficult to swallow.

"Is there nothing, absolutely nothing, that can be done?" I asked.

"Absolutely nothing."

"And can *nobody* do anything?"

"That is another question. In order *to do* it is necessary *to be*. And it is necessary first to understand what *to be* means. If we continue our talks you will see that we use a special language and that, in order to talk with us, it is necessary to learn this language. It is not worth while talking in ordinary language because, in that language, it is impossible to understand one another. This also, at the moment, seems strange to you. But it is true. In order to understand it is necessary to learn another language. In the language which people speak they cannot understand one another. You will see later on why this is so.

"Then one must learn to speak the truth. This also appears strange to you. You do not realize that one has to learn to speak the truth. It seems to you that it is enough to wish or to decide to do so. And I tell you that people comparatively rarely tell a deliberate lie. In most cases they think they speak the truth. And yet they lie all the time, both when they wish to lie and when they wish to speak the truth. They lie all the time, both to themselves and to others. Therefore nobody ever understands either himself or anyone else. Think—could there be such discord, such deep misunderstanding, and such hatred towards the views and opinions of others, if people were able to understand one another? But they cannot understand because they cannot help lying. To speak the truth is the most difficult thing in the world; and one must study a great deal and for a long time in order to be able to speak the truth. The wish alone is not enough. *To speak the truth one must know what the truth is and what a lie is, and first of all in oneself.* And this nobody wants to know."

Talks with G., and the unexpected turn he gave to every idea, interested me more and more every day. But I had to go to Petersburg.

I remember my last talk with him.

I had thanked him for the consideration he had given me and for his explanations which, I already saw, had changed many things for me.

"But all the same, you know, the most important thing is *facts*," I said. "If I could see genuine and real facts of a new and unknown character, only they would finally convince me that I am on the right way."

I was again thinking of "miracles."

"*There will be facts,*" said G. "I promise you. But many other things are necessary first."

I did not understand his last words then, I only understood them later when I really came up against "facts," for G. kept his word. But this was not until about a year and a half later, in August, 1916.

Of the last talks in Moscow there is still another which remains in my memory during which G. said several things which, again, became intelligible only subsequently.

He was talking about a man I had met while with him, and he spoke of his relations with certain people.

"He is a weak man," said G. "People take advantage of him, unconsciously of course. And all because he *considers* them. If he did not *consider* them, everything would be different, and they themselves would be different."

It seemed odd to me that a man should not consider others.

"What do you mean by the word 'consider'?" I asked. "I both understand you and do not understand you. This word has a great many different meanings."

"Precisely the contrary," said G. "There is only one meaning. Try to think about this."

Later on I understood what G. called "considering," and realized what an enormous place it occupies in life and how much it gives rise to. G. called "considering" that attitude which creates inner slavery, inner dependence. Afterwards we had occasion to speak a great deal about this.

I remember another talk about the war. We were sitting in the Phillipov's Café on the Tverskaya. It was very full of people and very noisy. War and profiteering had created an unpleasant, feverish atmosphere. I had even refused to go there. G. insisted and as always with him I gave way. I had already realized by then that he sometimes purposely created difficult conditions for conversation, as though demanding of me some sort of extra effort and a readiness to reconcile myself to unpleasant and uncomfortable surroundings *for the sake of talking with him.*

But this time the result was not particularly brilliant because, owing to the noise, the most interesting part of what he was saying failed to reach me. At first I understood what G. was saying. But the thread gradually began to slip away from me. After several attempts to follow his remarks, of which only isolated words reached me, I gave up listening and simply observed *how he spoke.*

The conversation began with my question: "Can war be stopped?" And G. answered: "Yes, it can." And yet I had been certain from previous talks that he would answer: "No, it cannot."

"But the whole thing is: how?" he said. "It is necessary to know a great deal in order to understand that. What is war? *It is the result of planetary influences.* Somewhere up there two or three planets have approached too near to each other; tension results. Have you noticed how, if a man passes quite close to you on a narrow pavement, you become all tense? The same tension takes place between planets. For them it lasts, perhaps, a second or two. But here, on the earth, people begin to slaughter one another, and they go on slaughtering maybe for several years. It seems to them at the time that they hate one another; or perhaps that they have to slaughter each other for some exalted purpose; or that they must defend somebody or something and that it is a very noble thing to do; or something else of the same kind. They fail to realize to what an extent they are mere pawns in the game. They think they signify something; they think they can move about as they like; they think they can decide to do this or that. But in reality all their movements, all their actions, are the result of planetary influences. And they themselves signify literally nothing. Then the moon plays a big part in this. But we will speak about the moon separately. Only it must be understood that neither Emperor Wilhelm, nor generals, nor ministers, nor parliaments, signify anything or can do anything. Everything that happens on a big scale is governed from outside, and governed either by accidental combinations of influences or by general cosmic laws."

This was all I heard. Only much later I understood what he wished to tell me—that is, how accidental influences could be diverted or transformed into something relatively harmless. It was really an interesting idea referring to the esoteric meaning of "sacrifices." But, in any case at the present time, this idea has only an historical and a psychological value. What was really important and what he said quite casually, so that I did not even notice it at once, and only remembered later in trying to reconstruct the conversation, was his words referring to the difference of time for planets and for man.

And even when I remembered it, for a long time I did not realize the full meaning of this idea. Later very much was based on it.

Somewhere about this time I was very much struck by a talk about the *sun*, the *planets*, and the *moon*. I do not remember how this talk began. But I remember that G. drew a small diagram and tried to explain what he called the "correlation of forces in different worlds." This was in connection with the previous talk, that is, in connection with the influences acting on humanity. The idea was roughly this: humanity, or more correctly, *organic life on earth*, is acted upon simultaneously by influences proceeding from various sources and different worlds: influences from the planets, influences from the moon, influences from the sun, influences from the stars. All these influences act simultaneously; one influence predominates at one moment and another influence at another moment. And for man there is a certain possibility of making a *choice of influences;* in other words, of passing from one influence to another.

"To explain *how,* would need a very long talk," said G. "So we will talk about this some other time. At this moment I want you to understand one thing: it is impossible to become free from one influence without becoming subject to another. The whole thing, all work on oneself, consists in choosing the influence to which you wish to subject yourself, and actually falling under this influence. And for this it is necessary to know beforehand which influence is the more profitable."

What interested me in this talk was that G. spoke of the planets and the moon as *living beings,* having definite ages, a definite period of life and possibilities of development and transition to other planes of being. From what he said it appeared that the moon was not a "dead planet," as is usually accepted, but, on the contrary, a "planet in birth"; a planet at the very initial stages of its development which had not yet reached "the degree of intelligence possessed by the earth," as he expressed it.

"But the moon is growing and developing," said G., "and some time, it will, possibly, attain the same level as the earth. Then, near it, a new moon will appear and the earth will become their sun. At one time the sun was like the earth and the earth like the moon. And earlier still the sun was like the moon."

This attracted my attention at once. Nothing had ever seemed to me more artificial, unreliable, and dogmatic than all the usual theories of the origin of planets **and** solar systems, beginning with the Kant-Laplace theory down to the very latest, with all their additions and variations. The "general public" considers these theories, or at any rate the last one known to it, to be scientific and proven. But in actual fact there is of course nothing less scientific and less proven than these theories. Therefore the fact that G.'s system accepted an altogether different theory, an *organic* theory having its origin in entirely new principles and showing a different universal order, appeared to me very interesting and important.

"In what relation does the intelligence of the earth stand to the intelligence of the sun?" I asked.

"The intelligence of the sun is divine," said G. "But the earth can become the same; only, of course, it is not guaranteed and the earth may die having attained nothing."

"Upon what does this depend?" I asked.

G.'s answer was very vague.

"There is a definite period," he said, "for a certain thing to be done. If, by a certain time, what ought to be done has not been done, the earth may perish without having attained what it could have attained."

"Is this period known?" I asked.

"It is known," said G. "But it would be no advantage whatever for people to know it. It would even be worse. Some would believe it, others would not believe it, yet others would demand proofs. Afterwards they would begin to break one another's heads. Everything ends this way with people."

In Moscow, at the same time, we also had several interesting talks about art. These were connected with the story which was read on the first evening that I saw G.

"At the moment it is not yet clear to you," G. once said, "that people living on the earth can belong to very different levels, although in appearance they look exactly the same. Just as there are very different levels of men, so there are different levels of art. Only you do not realize at present that the difference between these levels is far greater than you might suppose. You take different things on one level, far too near one another, and you think these different levels are accessible to you.

"I do not call art all that you call art, which is simply mechanical reproduction, imitation of nature or other people, or simply fantasy, or an attempt to be original. Real art is something quite different. Among works of art, especially works of ancient art, you meet with many things you cannot explain and which contain a certain something you do not feel in modern works of art. But as you do not realize what this difference is you very soon forget it and continue to take everything as one kind of art. And yet there is an enormous difference between your art and the art of which I speak. In your art everything is subjective—the artist's perception of this or that sensation; the forms in which he tries to express his sensations and the perception of these forms by other people. In one and the same phenomenon one artist may feel one thing and another artist quite a different thing. One and the same sunset may evoke a feeling of joy in one artist and sadness in another. Two artists may strive to express exactly the same perceptions by entirely different methods, in different forms; or entirely different perceptions in the same forms—according to how they were taught, or contrary to it. And the spectators, listeners, or readers will perceive, not what the artist wished to convey or what he felt, but what the forms in which he expresses his sensations will make them feel by association. Everything is subjective and everything is accidental, that is to say, based on accidental associations—the impression of the artist and his 'creation'" (he emphasized the word "creation"), "the perceptions of the spectators, listeners, or readers.

"In real art there is nothing accidental. It is mathematics. Everything in it can be calculated, everything can be known beforehand. The artist *knows* and *understands* what he wants to convey and his work cannot produce one impression on one man and another impression on another, presuming, of course, people on one level. It will always, and with mathematical certainty, produce one and the same impression.

"At the same time the same work of art will produce different impressions on people of different levels. And people of lower levels will never receive from it what people of higher levels receive. This is real, *objective* art. Imagine some scientific work—a book on astronomy or chemistry. It is impossible that one person should understand it in one way and another in another way. Everyone who is sufficiently prepared and who is able to read this book will understand what the author means, and precisely as the author means it. An objective work of art is just such a book, except that it affects the emotional and not only the intellectual side of man."

"Do such works of objective art exist at the present day?" I asked.

"Of course they exist," answered G. "The great Sphinx in Egypt is such a work of art, as well as some historically known works of architecture, certain statues of gods, and many other things. There are figures of gods and of various mythological beings that can be read like books, only not with the mind but with the emotions, provided they are sufficiently developed. In the course of our travels in Central Asia we found, in the desert at the foot of the Hindu Kush, a strange figure which we thought at first was some ancient god or devil. At first it produced upon us simply the impression of being a curiosity. But after a while we began to *feel* that this figure contained many things, a big, complete, and complex system of cosmology. And slowly, step by step, we began to decipher this system. It was in the body of the figure, in its legs, in its arms, in its head, in its eyes, in its ears; everywhere. In the whole statue there was nothing accidental, nothing without meaning. And gradually we understood the aim of the people who built this statue. We began to feel their thoughts, their feelings. Some of us thought that we saw their faces, heard their voices. At all events, we grasped the meaning of what they wanted to convey to us across thousands of years, and not only the meaning, but all the feelings and the emotions connected with it as well. That indeed was art!"

I was very interested in what G. said about art. His *principle* of the division of art into subjective and objective told me a great deal. I still did not understand everything he put into these words. I had always felt in art certain divisions and gradations which I could neither define nor formulate, and which nobody else had formulated. Nevertheless I knew that these divisions and gradations existed. So that all discussions about art without the recognition of these divisions and gradations seemed to me empty and useless, simply arguments about words. In what G. had said, in his indications of the different levels which we fail to see and understand, I felt an approach to the very gradations that I had felt but could not define.

In general, many things which G. said astonished me. There were ideas which I could not accept and which appeared to me fantastic and without foundation. Other things, on the contrary, coincided strangely with what I had thought myself and with what I had arrived at long ago. I was most of all interested in the *connectedness* of everything he said. I already felt that his ideas were not detached one from another, as all philosophical and scientific ideas are, but made one whole, of which, as yet, I saw only some of the pieces.

I thought about that in the night train, on the way from Moscow to Petersburg. I asked myself whether I had indeed found what I was looking for. Was it possible that G. actually *knew* what had to be known in order to proceed from words or ideas to deeds, to "facts"? I was still not certain of anything, nor could I formulate anything precisely. But I had an inner conviction that something had already changed for me and that now everything would go differently.

Chapter Two

IN PETERSBURG the summer passed with the usual literary work. I was preparing my books for new editions, reading proofs, and so on. This was the terrible summer of 1915 with its gradually lowering atmosphere, from which, in spite of all efforts, I could not free myself. The war was now being waged on Russian territory and was coming nearer to us. Everything was beginning to totter. The hidden suicidal activity which has determined so much in Russian life was becoming more and more apparent. A "trial of strength" was in progress. Printers were perpetually going on strike. My work was held up. And I was already beginning to think that the catastrophe would be upon us before I succeeded in doing what I intended. But my thoughts very often returned to the Moscow talks. Several times when things became particularly difficult I remember I said to myself, "I will give up everything and go to G. in Moscow." And at this thought I always felt easier.

Time passed. One day, it was already autumn, I was called to the telephone and heard G.'s voice. He had come to Petersburg for a few days. I went to see him at once and, in between conversations with other people who came to see him on various matters, he spoke to me just as he had in Moscow.

When he was leaving next day he told me he would soon be coming back again. And on this second visit, when I told him about a certain group I went to in Petersburg, where all possible subjects were discussed, from war to psychology, he said that acquaintance with similar groups might be useful, as he was thinking of starting the same kind of work in Petersburg as he was conducting in Moscow.

He went to Moscow and promised to return in a fortnight. I spoke of him to some of my friends and we began to await his arrival.

He returned again for a short time. I succeeded, however, in introducing some people to him. In regard to his plans and intentions, he said he wanted to organize his work on a larger scale, give public lectures, arrange a series of experiments and demonstrations, and attract to his work people with a wider and more varied preparation. All this reminded me of a part of what I had heard in Moscow. But I did not clearly understand what "experiments" and "demonstrations" he spoke of; this became clear only later.

I remember one talk—as usual with G.—in a small café on the Nevsky.

G. told me in some detail about the organization of groups for his work and about their role in that work. Once or twice he used the word "esoteric," which I had not heard from him before, and I was interested in what he meant by it. But when I tried to stop and ask what he meant by the word "esoteric" he avoided an answer.

"This is not important; well—call it what you like," he said. "That is not the point; the point is that a 'group' is the beginning of everything. One man can do nothing, can attain nothing. A group with a real leader can do more. A group of people can do what one man can never do.

"You do not realize your own situation. You are in prison. All you can wish for, if you are a sensible man, is to escape. But how escape? It is necessary to tunnel under a wall. One man can do nothing. But let us suppose there are ten or twenty men—if they work in turn and if one covers another they can complete the tunnel and escape.

"Furthermore, no one can escape from prison without the help of those *who have escaped before*. Only they can say in what way escape is possible or can send tools, files, or whatever may be necessary. But *one* prisoner alone cannot find these people or get into touch with them. An organization is necessary. Nothing can be achieved without an organization."

G. often returned afterwards to this example of "prison" and "escape from prison" in his talks. Sometimes he began with it, and then his favorite statement was that, if a man in prison was at any time to have a chance of escape, then he must first of all *realize that he is in prison.* So long as he fails to realize this, so long as he thinks he is free, he has no chance whatever. No one can help or liberate him by force, against his will, in opposition to his wishes. If liberation is possible, it is possible only as a result of great labor and great efforts, and, above all, of conscious efforts, towards a definite aim.

Gradually I introduced a greater and greater number of people to G. And every time he came to Petersburg I arranged talks and lectures, in which he took part, either at some private houses or with some already existing groups. Thirty or forty people used to come. After January, 1916, G. began to visit Petersburg regularly every fortnight, sometimes with some of his Moscow pupils.

I did not understand everything about the way these meetings were arranged. It seemed to me that G. was making much of it unnecessarily difficult. For instance, he seldom allowed me to fix a meeting beforehand. A former meeting usually ended with the announcement that G. was returning to Moscow the following day. On the following morning he would say that he had decided to stay till the evening. The whole day was passed in cafés where people came who wanted to see G. It was only in the evening, an hour or an hour and a half before we usually began our meetings, that he would say to me:

"Why not have a meeting tonight? Ring up those who wanted to come and tell them we shall be at such and such a place."

I used to rush to the telephone but, of course, at seven or half-past seven in the evening, everybody was already engaged and I could only collect a few people. And some who lived outside Petersburg, in Tsarskoye, etc., never succeeded in coming to our meetings.

A great deal I afterwards understood differently from the way I did then. And G.'s chief motives became clearer to me. He by no means wanted to make it *easy* for people to become acquainted with his ideas. On the contrary he considered that only by overcoming difficulties, however irrelevant and accidental, could people value his ideas.

"People do not value what is easily come by," he said. "And if a man has already felt something, believe me, he will sit waiting all day at the telephone in case he should be invited. Or he will himself ring up and ask and inquire. And whoever expects to be asked, and asked beforehand so that he can arrange his own affairs, let him go on expecting. Of course, for those who are not in Petersburg this is certainly difficult. But we cannot help it. Later on, perhaps, we shall have definite meetings on fixed days. At present it is impossible to do this. People must show themselves and their valuation of what they have heard."

All this and much else besides still remained for me at that time half-open to question.

But the lectures and, in general, all that G. said at that time, both at the meetings and outside them, interested me more and more.

On one occasion, at one of these meetings, someone asked about the possibility of reincarnation, and whether it was possible to believe in cases of communication with the dead.

"Many things are possible," said G. "But it is necessary to understand that man's being, both in life and after death, if it does exist after death, may be very different in quality. The 'man-machine' with whom everything depends upon external influences, with whom everything happens, who is now one, the next moment another, and the next moment a third, has no future of any kind; he is buried and that is all. *Dust returns to dust.* This applies to him. In order to be able to speak of any kind of future life there must be a certain crystallization, a certain fusion of man's inner qualities, a certain independence of external influences. If there is anything in a man able to resist external influences, then this very thing itself may also be able to resist the death of the physical body. But think for yourselves what there is to withstand physical death in a man who faints or forgets everything when he cuts his finger? If there is anything in a man, it may survive; if there is nothing, then there is nothing to survive. But even if something survives, its future can be very varied. In certain cases of fuller crystallization what people call 'reincarnation' may be possible after death, and, in other cases, what people call 'existence on the other side.' In both cases it is the continuation of life in the 'astral body,' or with the help of the 'astral body.' You know what the expression 'astral body' means. But the systems with which you are acquainted and which use this expression state that *all men* have an 'astral body.' This is quite wrong. What may be called the 'astral body' is obtained by means of fusion, that is, by means of terribly hard inner work and struggle. Man is not born with it. And only very few men acquire an 'astral body.' If it is formed it may continue to live after the death of the physical body, and it may be born again in another physical body. This is 'reincarnation.' If it is not re-born, then, in the course of time, it also dies; it is not immortal but it can live long after the death of the physical body.

"Fusion, inner unity, is obtained by means of 'friction,' by the struggle between 'yes' and 'no' in man. If a man lives without inner struggle, if everything happens in him without opposition, if he goes wherever he is drawn or wherever the wind blows, he will remain such as he is. But if a struggle begins in him, and particularly if there is a definite line in this struggle, then, gradually, permanent traits begin to form themselves, he begins to 'crystallize.' But crystallization is possible on a right foundation and it is possible on a wrong foundation. 'Friction,' the struggle between 'yes' and 'no,' can easily take place on a wrong foundation. For instance, a fanatical belief in some or other idea, or the 'fear of sin,' can evoke a terribly intense struggle between 'yes' and 'no,' and a man may crystallize on these foundations. But this would be a wrong, incomplete crystallization. Such a man will not possess the possibility of further development. In order to make further development possible he must be melted down again, and this can be accomplished only through terrible suffering.

"Crystallization is possible on any foundation. Take for example a brigand, a really good, genuine brigand. I knew such brigands in the Caucasus. He will stand with a rifle behind a stone by the roadside for eight hours without stirring. Could you do this? All the time, mind you, a struggle is going on in him. He is thirsty and hot, and flies are biting him; but he stands still. Another is a monk; he is afraid of the devil; all night long he beats his head on the floor and prays. Thus crystallization is achieved. In such ways people can generate in themselves an enormous inner strength; they can endure torture; they can get what they want. This means that there is now in them something solid, something permanent. Such people can become immortal. But what is the good of it? A man of this kind becomes an 'immortal thing,' although a certain amount of consciousness is sometimes preserved in him. But even this, it must be remembered, occurs very rarely."

I recollect that the talks which followed that evening struck me by the fact that many people heard something entirely different to what G. said; others only paid attention to G.'s secondary and nonessential remarks and remembered only these. The fundamental principles in what G. said escaped most of them. Only very few asked questions on the essential things he said. One of these questions has remained in my memory.

"In what way can one evoke the struggle between 'yes' and 'no' in oneself?" someone asked.

"Sacrifice is necessary," said G. "If nothing is sacrificed nothing is obtained. And it is necessary to sacrifice something precious at the moment, to sacrifice for a long time and to sacrifice a great deal. *But still, not forever.* This must be understood because often it is not understood. Sacrifice is necessary only while the process of crystallization is going on. When crystallization is achieved, renunciations, privations, and sacrifices are no longer necessary. Then a man may have everything he wants. There are no longer any laws for him, he is a law unto himself."

From among those who came to our lectures a small group of people was gradually formed who did not miss a single opportunity of listening to G. and who met together in his absence. This was the beginning of the first Petersburg group.

During that time I was a good deal with G. and began to understand him better. One was struck by a great inner simplicity and naturalness in him which made one completely forget that he was, for us, the representative of the world of the miraculous and the unknown. Furthermore, one felt very strongly in him the entire absence of any kind of affectation or desire to produce an impression. And together with this one felt an absence of personal interest in anything he was doing, a complete indifference to ease and comfort and a capacity for not sparing himself in work whatever that work might be. Sometimes he liked to be in gay and lively company; he liked to arrange big dinners, buying a quantity of wine and food of which however he often ate or drank practically nothing. Many people got the impression that he was a gourmand, a man fond of good living in general, and it seemed to us that he often *wanted* to create this impression, although all of us already saw that this was "acting."

Our feeling of this "acting" in G. was exceptionally strong. Among ourselves we often said we never saw him and never would. In any other man so much "acting" would have produced an impression of falsity. In him "acting" produced an impression of strength, although, as I have already mentioned, not always; sometimes there was too much of it.

I was particularly attracted by his sense of humor and the complete absence of any pretensions to "sanctity" or to the possession of "miraculous" powers, although, as we became convinced later, he possessed then the knowledge and ability of creating unusual phenomena of a psychological character. But he always laughed at people who expected miracles from him.

He was an extraordinarily versatile man; he knew everything and could do everything. He once told me he had brought back from his travels in the East a number of carpets among which were many duplicates and others having no particular value from an artistic point of view. During his visits he had found that the price of carpets in Petersburg was higher than in Moscow, and every time he came he brought a bale of carpets which he sold in Petersburg.

According to another version he simply bought the carpets in Moscow at the "Tolkutchka" and brought them to Petersburg to sell.

I did not altogether understand why he did this, but I felt it was connected with the idea of "acting."

The sale of these carpets was in itself remarkable. G. put an advertisement in the papers and all kinds of people came to buy carpets. On such occasions they took him, of course, for an ordinary Caucasian carpet-seller. I often sat for hours watching him as he talked to the people who came. I saw that he sometimes played on their weak side.

One day he was either in a hurry or had grown tired of acting the carpet-seller and he offered a lady, obviously rich but very grasping, who had selected a dozen fine carpets and was bargaining desperately, all the carpets in the room for about a quarter of the price of those she had chosen. At first she was surprised but then she began to bargain again. G. smiled and said he would think it over and give her his answer the next day. But next day he was no longer in Petersburg and the woman got nothing at all.

Something of this sort happened on nearly every occasion. With these carpets, in the role of traveling merchant, he again gave the impression of a man in disguise, a kind of Haroun-al-Raschid, or the man in the invisible cap of the fairy tale.

Once, when I was not there, an "occultist" of the charlatan type came to him, who played a certain part in some spiritualistic circles in Petersburg and who later became a "professor" under the bolsheviks. He began by saying he had heard a great deal about G. and his knowledge and wanted to make his acquaintance.

G., as he told me himself, played the part of a genuine carpet-seller. With the strongest Caucasian accent and in broken Russian he began to assure the "occultist" that he was mistaken and that he only sold carpets; and he immediately began to unroll and offer him some.

The "occultist" went away fully convinced he had been hoaxed by his friends.

"It was obvious that the rascal had not got a farthing," added G., "otherwise I would have screwed the price of a pair of carpets out of him."

A Persian used to come to him to mend carpets. One day I noticed that G. was very attentively watching how the Persian was doing his work.

"I want to understand how he does it and I don't understand yet," said G. "Do you see that hook he has? The whole thing is in that. I wanted to buy it from him but he won't sell it."

Next day I came earlier than usual. G. was sitting on the floor mending a carpet exactly as the Persian had done. Wools of various colors were strewn arorund him and in his hand was the same kind of hook I had seen with the Persian. It transpired that he had cut it with an ordinary file from the blade of a cheap penknife and, in the course of the morning, had fathomed all the mysteries of carpet mending.

He told me a great deal about carpets which, as he often said, represented one of the most ancient forms of art. He spoke of the ancient customs connected with carpet making in certain parts of Asia; of a whole village working together at one carpet; of winter evenings when all the villagers, young and old, gather together in one large building and, dividing into groups, sit or stand on the floor in an order previously known and determined by tradition. Each group then begins its own work. Some pick stones and splinters out of the wool. Others beat out the wool with sticks. A third group combs the wool. The fourth spins. The fifth dyes the wool. The sixth or maybe the twenty-sixth weaves the actual carpet. Men, women, and children, old men and old women, all have their own traditional work. And all the work is done to the accompaniment of music and singing. The women spinners with spindles in their hands dance a special dance as they work, and all the movements of all the people engaged in different work are like one movement in one and the same rhythm. Moreover each locality has its own special tune, its own special songs and dances, connected with carpet making from time immemorial.

And as he told me this the thought flashed across my mind that perhaps the design and coloring of the carpets are connected with the music, are its expression in line and color; that perhaps carpets are records of this music, the *notes* by which the tunes could be reproduced. There was nothing strange in this idea to me as I could often "see" music in the form of a complicated design.

From a few incidental talks with G. I obtained some idea of his previous life.

His childhood was passed on the frontier of Asia Minor in strange, very remote, almost biblical circumstances of life. Flocks of innumerable sheep. Wanderings from place to place. Coming into contact with various strange people. His imagination was particularly struck by the Yezidis, the "Devil Worshipers," who, from his earliest youth, had attracted his attention by their incomprehensible customs and strange dependence upon unknown laws. He told me, among other things, that when he was a child he had often observed how Yezidi boys were unable to step out of a circle traced round them on the ground.

He had passed his young years in an atmosphere of fairy tales, legends, and traditions. The "miraculous" around him was an actual fact. Predictions of the future which he heard, and which those around him fully believed, were fulfilled and made him believe in many other things.

All these things taken together had created in him at a very early age a leaning towards the mysterious, the incomprehensible, and the magical. He told me that when quite young he made several long journeys in the East. What was true in these stories I could never decide exactly. But, as he said, in the course of these journeys he again came across many phenomena telling him of the existence of a certain knowledge, of certain powers and possibilities exceeding the ordinary possibilities of man, and of people possessing clairvoyance and other miraculous powers. Gradually, he told me, his absences from home and his travels began to follow one definite aim. He went in search of knowledge and the people who possessed this knowledge. And, as he said, after great difficulties, he found the sources of this knowledge in company with several other people who were, like him, also seeking the miraculous.

In all these stories about himself a great deal was contradictory and hardly credible. But I had already realized that no ordinary demands could be made of him, nor could any ordinary standards be applied to him. One could be sure of nothing in regard to him. He might say one thing today and something altogether different tomorrow, and yet, somehow, he could never be accused of contradictions; one had to understand and connect everything together.

About schools and where he had found the knowledge he undoubtedly possessed he spoke very little and always superficially. He mentioned Tibetan monasteries, the Chitral, Mount Athos; Sufi schools in Persia, in Bokhara, and eastern Turkestan; he mentioned dervishes of various orders; but all of them in a very indefinite way.

During one conversation with G. in our group, which was beginning to become permanent, I asked: "Why, if ancient knowledge has been preserved and if, speaking in general, there exists a knowledge distinct from our science and philosophy or even surpassing it, is it so carefully concealed, why is it not made common property? Why are the men who possess this knowledge unwilling to let it pass into the general circulation of life for the sake of a better and more successful struggle against deceit, evil, and ignorance?"

This is, I think, a question which usually arises in everyone's mind on first acquaintance with the ideas of esotericism.

"There are two answers to that," said G. "In the first place, this knowledge is not concealed; and in the second place, it cannot, from its very nature, become common property. We will consider the second of these statements first. I will prove to you afterwards that *knowledge*" (he emphasized the word) "is far more accessible to those capable of assimilating it than is usually supposed; and that the whole trouble is that people either do not want it or cannot receive it.

"But first of all another thing must be understood, namely, that knowledge cannot belong to all, cannot even belong to many. Such is the law. You do not understand this because you do not understand that knowledge, like everything else in the world, is *material*. It is material, and this means that it possesses all the characteristics of materiality. One of the first characteristics of materiality is that matter is always limited, that is to say, the quantity of matter in a given place and under given conditions is limited. Even the sand of the desert and the water of the sea is a definite and unchangeable quantity. So that, if knowledge is material, then it means that there is a definite quantity of it in a given place at a given time. It may be said that, in the course of a certain period of time, say a century, humanity has a definite amount of knowledge at its disposal. But we know, even from an ordinary observation of life, that the *matter of knowledge* possesses entirely different qualities according to whether it is taken in small or large quantities. Taken in a large quantity in a given place, that is by one man, let us say, or by a small group of men, it produces very good results; taken in a small quantity (that is, by every one of a large number of people), it gives no results at all; or it may give even negative results, contrary to those expected. Thus if a certain definite quantity of knowledge is distributed among millions of people, each individual will receive very little, and this small amount of knowledge will change nothing either in his life or in his understanding of things. And however large the number of people who receive this small amount of knowledge, it will change nothing in their lives, except, perhaps, to make them still more difficult.

"But if, on the contrary, large quantities of knowledge are concentrated in a small number of people, then this knowledge will give very great results. From this point of view it is far more advantageous that knowledge should be preserved among a small number of people and not dispersed among the masses.

"If we take a certain quantity of gold and decide to gild a number of objects with it, we must know, or calculate, exactly what number of objects can be gilded with this quantity of gold. If we try to gild a greater number, they will be covered with gold unevenly, in patches, and will look much worse than if they had no gold at all; in fact we shall lose our gold.

"The distribution of knowledge is based upon exactly the same principle. If knowledge is given to all, nobody will get any. If it is preserved among a few, each will receive not only enough to keep, but to increase, what he receives.

"At the first glance this theory seems very unjust, since the position of those who are, so to speak, denied knowledge in order that others may receive a greater share appears to be very sad and undeservedly harder than it ought to be. Actually, however, this is not so at all; and in the distribution of knowledge there is not the slightest injustice.

"The fact is that the enormous majority of people do not want any knowledge whatever; they refuse their share of it and do not even take the ration allotted to them, in the general distribution, for the purposes of life. This is particularly evident in times of mass madness such as wars, revolutions, and so on, when men suddenly seem to lose even the small amount of common sense they had and turn into complete automatons, giving themselves over to wholesale destruction in vast numbers, in other words, even losing the instinct of self-preservation. Owing to this, enormous quantities of knowledge remain, so to speak, unclaimed and can be distributed among those who realize its value.

"There is nothing unjust in this, because those who receive knowledge take nothing that belongs to others, deprive others of nothing; they take only what others have rejected as useless and what would in any case be lost if they did not take it.

"The collecting of knowledge by some depends upon the rejection of knowledge by others.

"There are periods in the life of humanity, which generally coincide with the beginning of the fall of cultures and civilizations, when the masses irretrievably lose their reason and begin to destroy everything that has been created by centuries and millenniums of culture. Such periods of mass madness, often coinciding with geological cataclysms, climatic changes, and similar phenomena of a planetary character, release a very great quantity of the matter of knowledge. This, in its turn, necessitates the work of collecting this matter of knowledge which would otherwise be lost. Thus the work of collecting scattered matter of knowledge frequently coincides with the beginning of the destruction and fall of cultures and civilizations.

"This aspect of the question is clear. The crowd neither wants nor seeks knowledge, and the leaders of the crowd, in their own interests, try to strengthen its fear and dislike of everything new and unknown. The slavery in which mankind lives is based upon this fear. It is even difficult to imagine all the horror of this slavery. We do not understand *what* people are losing. But in order to understand the cause of this slavery it is enough to see how people live, what constitutes the aim of their existence, the object of their desires, passions, and aspirations, of what they think, of what they talk, what they serve and what they worship.

Consider what the cultured humanity of our time spends money on; even leaving the war out, what commands the highest price; where the biggest crowds are. If we think for a moment about these questions it becomes clear that humanity, as it is now, with the interests it lives by, cannot expect to have anything different from what it has. But, as I have already said, it cannot be otherwise. Imagine that for the whole of mankind half a pound of knowledge is allotted a year. If this knowledge is distributed among everyone, each will receive so little that he will remain the fool he was. But, thanks to the fact that very few want to have this knowledge, those who take it are able to get, let us say, a grain each, and acquire the possibility of becoming more intelligent. All cannot become intelligent even if they wish. And if they did become intelligent it would not help matters. There exists a general equilibrium which cannot be upset.

"That is one aspect. The other, as I have already said, consists in the fact that no one is concealing anything; there is no mystery whatever. But the acquisition or transmission of true knowledge demands great labor and great effort both of him who receives and of him who gives. And those who possess this knowledge are doing everything they can to transmit and communicate it to the greatest possible number of people, to facilitate people's approach to it and enable them to prepare themselves to receive the truth. But knowledge cannot be given by force to anyone and, as I have already said, an unprejudiced survey of the average man's life, of what fills his day and of the things he is interested in, will at once show whether it is possible to accuse men who possess knowledge of concealing it, of not wishing to give it to people, or of not wishing to teach people what they know themselves.

"He who wants knowledge must himself make the initial efforts to find the source of knowledge and to approach it, taking advantage of the help and indications which are given to all, but which people, as a rule, do not want to see or recognize. Knowledge cannot come to people without effort on their own part. They understand this very well in connection with ordinary knowledge, but in the case of *great knowledge*, when they admit the possibility of its existence, they find it possible to expect something different. Everyone knows very well that if, for instance, a man wants to learn Chinese, it will take several years of intense work; everyone knows that five years are needed to grasp the principles of medicine, and perhaps twice as many years for the study of painting or music. And yet there are theories which affirm that knowledge can come to people without any effort on their part, that they can acquire it *even in sleep*. The very existence of such theories constitutes an additional explanation of why knowledge cannot come to people. At the same time it is essential to understand that man's *independent* efforts to attain anything in this direction can also give no results. A man can only attain knowledge with the help of those who possess it. This must be understood from the very beginning. *One must learn from him who knows.*"

At one of the following meetings of the group G. continued, in reply to a question, to develop the ideas given by him before on reincarnation and the future life.

The talk began by one of those present asking:

"Can it be said that man possesses immortality?"

"Immortality is one of the qualities we ascribe to people without having a sufficient understanding of their meaning," said G. "Other qualities of this kind are 'individuality,' in the sense of an inner unity, a 'permanent and unchangeable I,' 'consciousness,' and 'will.' All these qualities *can* belong to man" (he emphasized the word "can"), "but this certainly does not mean that they *do belong* to him or belong to each and every one.

"In order to understand *what* man is at the present time, that is, at the present level of development, it is necessary to imagine to a certain extent what he can be, that is, what he can attain. Only by understanding the correct sequence of development possible will people cease to ascribe to themselves what, at present, they do not possess, and what, perhaps, they can only acquire after great effort and great labor.

"According to an ancient teaching, traces of which may be found in many systems, old and new, a man who has attained the full development possible for man, a man in the full sense of the word, *consists of four bodies*. These four bodies are composed of substances which gradually become finer and finer, mutually interpenetrate one another, and form four independent organisms, standing in a definite relationship to one another but capable of independent action.

"The reason why it is possible for four bodies to exist is that the human organism, that is, the physical body, has such a complex organization that, under certain conditions, a new independent organism can grow in it, affording a much more convenient and responsive instrument for the activity of consciousness than the physical body. The consciousness manifested in this new body is capable of governing it, and it has full power and full control over the physical body. In this second body, under certain conditions, a third body can grow, again having characteristics of its own. The consciousness manifested in this third body has full power and control over the first two bodies; and the third body possesses the possibility of acquiring knowledge inaccessible either to the first or to the second body. In the third body, under certain conditions, a fourth can grow, which differs as much from the third as the third differs from the second and the second from the first. The consciousness manifested in the fourth body has full control over the first three bodies and itself.

"These four bodies are defined in different teachings in various ways."

G. drew a diagram, reproduced in Figure 1, and said:

"The first is the physical body, in Christian terminology the 'carnal' body; the second, in Christian terminology, is the 'natural' body; the third is the 'spiritual' body; and the fourth, in the terminology of *esoteric Christianity*, is the 'divine' body. In theosophical terminology the first is the 'physical' body, the second is the 'astral,' the third is the 'mental,' and the fourth the 'causal.' [1]

"In the terminology of certain Eastern teachings the first body is the 'carriage' (body), the second body is the 'horse' (feelings, desires), the third the 'driver' (mind), and the fourth the 'master' (I, consciousness, will).

1st body	2nd body	3rd body	4th body
Carnal body	Natural body	Spiritual body	Divine body
"Carriage" (body)	"Horse" (feelings, desires)	"Driver" (mind)	"Master" (I, consciousness, will)
Physical body	Astral body	Mental body	Causal body

Fig. 1

"Such comparisons and parallels may be found in most systems and teachings which recognize something more in man than the physical body. But almost all these teachings, while repeating in a more or less familiar form the definitions and divisions of the ancient teaching, have forgotten or omitted its most important feature, which is: that man is not born with the finer bodies, and that they can only be artificially cultivated in him provided favorable conditions both internal and external are present.

"The 'astral body' is not an indispensable implement for man. It is a great luxury which only a few can afford. A man can live quite well without an 'astral body.' His physical body possesses all the functions necessary for life. A man without 'astral body' may even produce the impression of being a very intellectual or even *spiritual man*, and may deceive not only others but also himself.

"This applies still more, of course, to the 'mental body' and the fourth body. Ordinary man does not possess these bodies or their corresponding functions. But he often thinks, and makes others think, that he does. The reasons for this are, first, the fact that the physical body works with the same substances of which the higher bodies are composed, only these substances are not crystallized in him, do not belong to him; and secondly, it has all the functions analogous to those of the higher bodies, though of

[1] That is, the body which bears the *causes* of its actions within itself, is independent of external causes, and is the *body of will*.

course they differ from them considerably. The chief difference between the functions of a man possessing the physical body only and the functions of the *four bodies*, is that, in the first case, the functions of the *physical body* govern all the other functions, in other words, everything is governed by the body which, in its turn, is governed by external influences. In the second case, the command or control emanates from the higher body.

"The functions of the physical body may be represented as parallel to the functions of the four bodies."

G. drew another diagram (Fig. 2), representing the parallel functions of a man of physical body and a man of four bodies.

Automaton working by external influences.	Desires produced by automaton.	Thoughts proceeding from desires.	Different and contradictory "wills" created by desires.

Body obeying desires and emotions which are subject to intelligence.	Emotional powers and desires obeying thought and intelligence.	Thinking functions obeying consciousness and will.	Ego Consciousness Will

Fig. 2.

"In the first case," said G., "that is, in relation to the functions of a man of physical body only, the automaton depends upon external influences, and the next three functions depend upon the physical body and the external influences it receives. Desires or aversions—'I want,' 'I don't want,' 'I like,' 'I don't like'—that is, functions occupying the place of the second body, depend upon accidental shocks and influences. Thinking, which corresponds to the functions of the third body, is an entirely mechanical process. 'Will' is absent in ordinary mechanical man, he has desires only; and a greater or lesser *permanence* of desires and wishes is called a strong or a weak will.

"In the second case, that is, in relation to the functions of the four bodies, the automatism of the physical body depends upon the influences of the other bodies. Instead of the discordant and often contradictory activity of different desires, there is *one single I*, whole, indivisible, and permanent; there is *individuality*, dominating the physical body and its desires and able to overcome both its reluctance and its resistance. Instead of the mechanical process of thinking there is *consciousness*. And there is *will*, that is, a power, not merely composed of various often contradictory desires belonging to different "I's," but issuing from consciousness and governed by individuality or a single and permanent I. Only such a will can be called "free," for it is independent of accident and cannot be altered or directed from without.

"An Eastern teaching describes the functions of the four bodies, their gradual growth, and the conditions of this growth, in the following way:

"Let us imagine a vessel or a retort filled with various metallic powders. The powders are not in any way connected with each other and every accidental change in the position of the retort changes the relative position of the powders. If the retort be shaken or tapped with the finger, then the powder which was at the top may appear at the bottom or in the middle, while the one which was at the bottom may appear at the top. There is nothing permanent in the position of the powders and under such conditions there can be nothing permanent. This is an exact picture of our psychic life. Each succeeding moment, new influences may change the position of the powder which is on the top and put in its place another which is absolutely its opposite. Science calls this state of the powders the state of mechanical mixture. The essential characteristic of the interrelation of the powders to one another in this kind of mixture is the instability of these interrelations and their variability.

"It is impossible to stabilize the interrelation of powders in a state of mechanical mixture. But the powders may be fused; the nature of the powders makes this possible. To do this a special kind of fire must be lighted under the retort which, by heating and melting the powders, finally fuses them together. Fused in this way the powders will be in the state of a chemical compound. And now they can no longer be separated by those simple methods which separated and made them change places when they were in a state of mechanical mixture. The contents of the retort have become indivisible, 'individual.' This is a picture of the formation of the second body. The fire by means of which fusion is attained is produced by 'friction,' which in its turn is produced in man by the struggle between 'yes' and 'no.' If a man gives way to all his desires, or panders to them, there will be no inner struggle in him, no 'friction,' no fire. But if, for the sake of attaining a definite aim, he struggles with desires that hinder him, he will then create a fire which will gradually transform his inner world into a single whole.

"Let us return to our example. The chemical compound obtained by fusion possesses certain qualities, a certain specific gravity, a certain electrical conductivity, and so on. These qualities constitute the characteristics of the substance in question. But by means of work upon it of a certain kind the number of these characteristics may be increased, that is, the alloy may be given new properties which did not primarily belong to it. It may be possible to magnetize it, to make it radioactive, and so on.

"The process of imparting new properties to the alloy corresponds to the process of the formation of the third body and of the acquisition of new knowledge and powers with the help of the third body.

"When the third body has been formed and has acquired all the properties, powers, and knowledge possible for it, there remains the problem of fixing this knowledge and these powers, because, having been imparted to it by influences of a certain kind, they may be taken away by these same influences or by others. By means of a special kind of work for all three bodies the acquired properties may be made the permanent and inalienable possession of the third body.

"The process of fixing these acquired properties corresponds to the process of the formation of the fourth body.

"And only the man who possesses four fully developed bodies can be called a 'man' in the full sense of the word. This man possesses many properties which ordinary man does not possess. *One of these properties is immortality.* All religions and all ancient teachings contain the idea that, by acquiring the fourth body, man acquires immortality; and they all contain indications of the ways to acquire the fourth body, that is, immortality.

"In this connection certain teachings compare man to a house of four rooms. Man lives in one room, the smallest and poorest of all, and until he is told of it, he does not suspect the existence of the other rooms which are full of treasures. When he does learn of this he begins to seek the keys of these rooms and especially of the fourth, the most important, room. And when a man has found his way into this room he really becomes the master of his house, for only then does the house belong to him wholly and forever.

"The fourth room gives man immortality and all religious teachings strive to show the way to it. There are a great many ways, some shorter and some longer, some harder and some easier, but all, without exception, lead or strive to lead in one direction, that is, to immortality."

At the next meeting G. began where he had left off the time before.

"I said last time," he said, "that *immortality* is not a property with which man is born. But man can acquire immortality. All existing and generally known ways to immortality can be divided into three categories:

1. *The way of the fakir.*
2. *The way of the monk.*
3. *The way of the yogi.*

"The way of the fakir is the way of struggle with the physical body, the way of work on the first room. This is a long, difficult, and uncertain way. The fakir strives to develop physical will, power over the body. This is attained by means of terrible sufferings, by torturing the body. The whole way of the fakir consists of various incredibly difficult physical exercises. The fakir either stands motionless in the same position for hours, days, months, or years; or sits with outstretched arms on a bare stone in sun, rain, and snow; or tortures himself with fire, puts his legs into an ant-heap, and so on. If he does not fall ill and die before what may be called physical will is developed in him, then he attains the fourth room or the possibility of forming the fourth body. But his other functions— emotional, intellectual, and so forth—remain undeveloped. He has acquired will but he has nothing to which he can apply it, he cannot make use of it for gaining knowledge or for self-perfection. As a rule he is too old to begin new work.

"But where there are schools of fakirs there are also schools of yogis. Yogis generally keep an eye on fakirs. If a fakir attains what he has aspired to before he is too old, they take him into a yogi school, where first they heal him and restore his power of movement, and then begin to teach him. A fakir has to learn to walk and to speak like a baby. But he now possesses a will which has overcome incredible difficulties on his way and this will may help him to overcome the difficulties on the second part of the way, the difficulties, namely, of developing the intellectual and emotional functions.

"You cannot imagine what hardships fakirs undergo. I do not know whether you have seen real fakirs or not. I have seen many; for instance, I saw one in the inner court of a temple in India and I even slept near him. Day and night for twenty years he had been standing on the tips of his fingers and toes. He was no longer able to straighten himself. His pupils carried him from one place to another, took him to the river and washed him like some inanimate object. But this was not attained all at once. Think what he had to overcome, what tortures he must have suffered in order to get to that stage.

"And a man becomes a fakir not because he understands the possibilities and the results of this way, and not because of religious feeling. In all Eastern countries where fakirs exist there is a custom among the common people of promising to give to fakirs a child born after some happy event. Besides this, fakirs often adopt orphans, or simply buy little children from poor parents. These children become their pupils and imitate them, or are made to imitate them, some only outwardly, but some afterwards become fakirs themselves.

"In addition to these, other people become fakirs simply from being struck by some fakir they have seen. Near every fakir in the temples people can be seen who imitate him, who sit or stand in the same posture. Not for long of course, but still occasionally for several hours. And sometimes it happens that a man who went into the temple accidentally on a feast day, and began to imitate some fakir who particularly struck him, does not return home any more but joins the crowd of that fakir's disciples and later, in the course of time, becomes a fakir himself. You must understand that I take the word 'fakir' in quotation marks. In Persia *fakir* simply means a beggar; and in India a great many jugglers call themselves *fakirs*. And Europeans, particularly learned Europeans, very often give the name of fakir to *yogis,* as well as to *monks* of various wandering orders.

"But in reality the way of the fakir, the way of the monk, and the way of the yogi are entirely different. So far I have spoken of fakirs. This is the first way.

"The second way is the way of the monk. This is the way of faith, the way of religious feeling, religious sacrifice. Only a man with very strong religious emotions and a very strong religious imagination can become a 'monk' in the true sense of the word. The way of the monk also is very long and hard. A monk spends years and tens of years struggling with himself, but all his work is concentrated on the second room, on the second body, that is, on *feelings.* Subjecting all his other emotions to one emotion, that is, to faith, he develops *unity* in himself, will over the emotions, and in this way reaches the fourth room. But his physical body and his thinking capacities may remain undeveloped. In order to be able to make use of what he has attained, he must develop his body and his capacity to think. This can only be achieved by means of fresh sacrifices, fresh hardships, fresh renunciations. *A monk has to become a yogi and a fakir.* Very few get as far as this; even fewer overcome all difficulties. Most of them either die before this or become monks in outward appearance only.

"The third way is the way of the yogi. This is the way of knowledge, the way of mind. The way of the yogi consists in working on the third room and in striving to enter the fourth room by means of knowledge. The yogi reaches the fourth room by developing his mind, but his body and emotions remain undeveloped and, like the fakir and the monk, he is unable to make use of the results of his attainment. He knows everything but can do nothing. In order to begin to do he must gain the mastery over his body and emotions, that is, over the first and second rooms. To do this he must again set to work and again obtain results by means of prolonged efforts. In this case however he has the advantage of understanding his position, of knowing what he lacks, what he must do, and in what direction he must go. But, as on the way of the fakir or the monk, very few acquire this understanding on the way of the yogi, that is, that level in his work on which a man knows where he is going. A great many stop at one particular achievement and go no further.

"The ways also differ from each other by their relation to the teacher or leader.

"On the way of the fakir a man has no teacher in the true sense of the word. The teacher in this case does not teach but simply serves as an example. The pupil's work consists in imitating the teacher.

"On the way of the monk a man has a teacher, and a part of his duty, a part of his work, consists in having absolute faith in the teacher, in submitting to him absolutely, *in obedience*. But the chief thing on the way of the monk is faith in God, in the love of God, in constant efforts to obey and serve God, although, in his understanding of the idea of God and of serving God, there may be much that is subjective and contradictory.

"On the way of the yogi a man can do nothing, and must do nothing, without a teacher. In the beginning he must imitate his teacher like the fakir and believe in him like the monk. But, afterwards, a man on the way of the yogi gradually becomes his own teacher. He learns his teacher's methods and gradually learns to apply them to himself.

"But all the ways, the way of the fakir as well as the way of the monk and the way of the yogi, have one thing in common. They all begin with the most difficult thing, with a complete change of life, with a renunciation of all worldly things. A man must give up his home, his family if he has one, renounce all the pleasures, attachments, and duties of life, and go out into the desert, or into a monastery or a yogi school. From the very first day, from the very first step on his way, he must die to the world; only thus can he hope to attain anything on one of these ways.

"In order to grasp the essence of this teaching it is necessary clearly to understand the idea that the *ways* are the *only* possible methods for the development of man's hidden possibilities. This in turn shows how difficult and rare such development is. The development of these possibilities is not a law. The law for man is existence in the circle of mechanical influences, the state of 'man-machine.' The way of the development of hidden possibilities is a way *against nature, against God*. This explains the difficulties and the exclusiveness of the ways. The ways are narrow and strait. But at the same time only by them can anything be attained. In the general mass of everyday life, especially modern life, the ways are a small, quite imperceptible phenomenon which, from the point of view of life, need not exist at all. But this small phenomenon contains in itself *all* that man has for the development of his hidden possibilities. The ways are opposed to everyday life, based upon other principles and subject to other laws. In this consists their power and their significance. In everyday life, even in a life filled with scientific, philosophical, religious, or social interests, there is nothing, *and there can be nothing*, which could give the possibilities which are contained in the ways. The ways lead, or should lead, man to immortality. Everyday life, even at its best, leads man to death and can lead to nothing else. The idea of the ways cannot be understood if the possibility of man's evolution without their help is admitted.

"As a rule it is hard for man to reconcile himself to this thought; it seems to him exaggerated, unjust, and absurd. He has a poor understanding of the meaning of the word 'possibility.' He fancies that if he has any possibilities in himself they must be developed and that there must be means for their development in his environment. From a total refusal to acknowledge in himself any possibilities whatever, man generally proceeds forthwith to demand the imperative and inevitable development of these possibilities. It is difficult for him to accept the thought that his possibilities may remain altogether undeveloped and disappear, and that their development, on the other hand, requires of him tremendous effort and endurance. As a matter of fact, if we take all the people who are neither fakirs, monks, nor yogis, and of whom we may say with confidence that they never will be either fakirs, monks, or yogis, then we may say with undoubted certainty that their possibilities *cannot be developed and will not be developed*. This must be clearly understood in order to grasp all that follows.

"In the ordinary conditions of cultured life the position of a man, even of an intelligent man, who is seeking for knowledge is hopeless, because, in the circumstances surrounding him, there is nothing resembling either fakir or yogi schools, while the religions of the West have degenerated to such an extent that for a long time there has been nothing alive in them. Various occult and mystical societies and naïve experiments in the nature of spiritualism, and so on, can give no results whatever.

"And the position would indeed be hopeless if the possibility of yet a *fourth way* did not exist.

"The fourth way requires no retirement into the desert, does not require a man to give up and renounce everything by which he formerly lived. The fourth way begins much further on than the way of the yogi. This means that a man must be prepared for the fourth way and this preparation must be acquired in ordinary life and be a very serious one, embracing many different sides. Furthermore a man must be living in conditions favorable for work on the fourth way, or, in any case, in conditions which do not render it impossible. It must be understood that both in the inner and in the external life of a man there may be conditions which create insuperable barriers to the fourth way. Furthermore, the fourth way has no definite forms like the ways of the fakir, the monk, and the yogi. And, first of all, it has to *be found*. This is the first test. It is not as well known as the three traditional ways. There are many people who have never heard of the fourth way and there are others who deny its existence or possibility.

"At the same time the beginning of the fourth way is easier than the beginning of the ways of the fakir, the monk, and the yogi. On the fourth way it is possible to work and to follow this way while remaining in the usual conditions of life, continuing to do the usual work, preserving former relations with people, and without renouncing or giving up anything. On the contrary, the conditions of life in which a man is placed at the beginning of his work, in which, so to speak, the work finds him, are the *best possible* for him, at any rate at the beginning of the work. These conditions are natural for him. These conditions *are the man himself*, because a man's life and its conditions correspond to what he is. Any conditions different from those created by life would be artificial for a man and in such artificial conditions the work would not be able to touch every side of his being at once.

"Thanks to this, the fourth way affects simultaneously every side of man's being. It is work *on the three rooms at once*. The fakir works on the first room, the monk on the second, the yogi on the third. In reaching the fourth room the fakir, the monk, and the yogi leave behind them many things unfinished, and they cannot make use of what they have attained because they are not masters of all their functions. The fakir is master of his body but not of his emotions or his mind; the monk is master of his emotions but not of his body or his mind; the yogi is master of his mind but not of his body or his emotions.

"Then the fourth way differs from the other ways in that the principal demand made upon a man is the demand for understanding. A man must do nothing that he does not understand, except as an experiment under the supervision and direction of his teacher. The more a man understands what he is doing, the greater will be the results of his efforts. This is a fundamental principle of the fourth way. The results of work are in proportion to the consciousness of the work. No 'faith' is required on the fourth way; on the contrary, faith of any kind is opposed to the fourth way. On the fourth way a man must satisfy himself of the truth of what he is told. And until he is satisfied he must do nothing.

"The method of the fourth way consists in doing something in one room and simultaneously doing something corresponding to it in the two other rooms—that is to say, while working on the physical body to work simultaneously on the mind and the emotions; while working on the mind to work on the physical body and the emotions; while working on the emotions to work on the mind and the physical body. This can be achieved thanks to the fact that on the fourth way it is possible to make use of certain knowledge inaccessible to the ways of the fakir, the monk, and the yogi. This knowledge makes it possible to work in three directions simultaneously. A whole parallel series of physical, mental, and emotional exercises serves this purpose. In addition, on the fourth way it is possible to individualize the work of each separate person, that is to say, each person can do only what is necessary and not what is *useless for him*. This is due to the fact that the fourth way dispenses with a great deal of what is superfluous and preserved simply through tradition in the other ways.

"So that when a man attains will on the fourth way he can make use of it because he has acquired control of all his bodily, emotional, and intellectual functions. And besides, he has saved a great deal of time by working on the three sides of his being in parallel and simultaneously.

"The fourth way is sometimes called *the way of the sly man*. The 'sly man' knows some secret which the fakir, monk, and yogi do not know. How the 'sly man' learned this secret—it is not known. Perhaps he found it in some old books, perhaps he inherited it, perhaps he bought it, perhaps he stole it from someone. It makes no difference. The 'sly man' knows the secret and with its help outstrips the fakir, the monk, and the yogi.

"Of the four, the fakir acts in the crudest manner; he knows very little and understands very little. Let us suppose that by a whole month of intense torture he develops in himself a certain energy, a certain substance which produces certain changes in him. He does it absolutely blindly, with his eyes shut, knowing neither aim, methods, nor results, simply in imitation of others.

"The monk knows what he wants a little better; he is guided by religious feeling, by religious tradition, by a desire for achievement, for salvation; he trusts his teacher who tells him what to do, and he believes that his efforts and sacrifices are 'pleasing to God.' Let us suppose that a week of fasting, continual prayer, privations, and so on, enables him to attain what the fakir develops in himself by a month of self-torture.

"The yogi knows considerably more. He knows what he wants, he knows why he wants it, he knows how it can be acquired. He knows, for instance, that it is necessary for his purpose to produce a certain substance in himself. He knows that this substance can be produced in one day by a certain kind of mental exercises or concentration of consciousness. So he keeps his attention on these exercises for a whole day without allowing himself a single outside thought, and he obtains what he needs. In this way a yogi spends on the same thing only one day compared with a month spent by the fakir and a week spent by the monk.

"But on the fourth way knowledge is still more exact and perfect. A man who follows the fourth way knows quite definitely what substances he needs for his aims and he knows that these substances can be produced within the body by a month of physical suffering, by a week of emotional strain, or by a day of mental exercises—and also, *that they can be introduced into the organism from without if it is known how to do it.* And so, instead of spending a whole day in exercises like the yogi, a week in prayer like the monk, or a month in self-torture like the fakir, he simply prepares and swallows a little pill which contains all the substances he wants and, in this way, without loss of time, he obtains the required results.

"It must be noted further," said G., "that in addition to these proper and legitimate ways, there are also artificial ways which give temporary results only, and wrong ways which may even give permanent results, only wrong results. On these ways a man also seeks the key to the fourth room and sometimes finds it. But what he finds in the fourth room is not yet known.

"It also happens that the door to the fourth room is opened artificially with a skeleton key. And in both these cases the room may prove to be empty."

With this G. stopped.

At one of the following talks we again touched on the *ways*.

"For a man of Western culture," I said, "it is of course difficult to believe and to accept the idea that an ignorant fakir, a naïve monk, or a yogi who has retired from life may be on the way to evolution while an educated European, armed with 'exact knowledge' and all the latest methods of investigation, has no chance whatever and is moving in a circle from which there is no escape."

"Yes, that is because people believe in progress and culture," said G. *"There is no progress whatever.* Everything is just the same as it was thousands, and tens of thousands, of years ago. The outward form changes. The essence does not change. Man remains just the same. 'Civilized' and 'cultured' people live with exactly the same interests as the most ignorant savages. Modern civilization is based on violence and slavery and fine words. But all these fine words about 'progress' and 'civilization' are merely words."

This of course produced a particularly deep impression on us, because it was said in 1916, when the latest manifestation of "civilization," in the form of a war such as the world had not yet seen, was continuing to grow and develop, drawing more and more millions of people into its orbit.

I remembered that a few days before this talk I had seen two enormous lorries on the Liteiny loaded to the height of the first floor of the houses with new unpainted wooden *crutches*. For some reason I was particularly struck by these lorries. In these mountains of crutches *for legs which were not yet torn off* there was a particularly cynical mockery of all the things with which people deceive themselves. Involuntarily I imagined that similar lorries were sure to be going about in Berlin, Paris, London, Vienna, Rome, and Constantinople. And, as a result, all these cities, almost all of which I knew so well and liked just because they were so different and because they supplemented and gave contrast to one another, had now become hostile both to me and to each other and separated by new walls of hatred and crime.

I spoke to our people about these lorry-loads of crutches and of my thoughts about them at a meeting.

"What do you expect?" said G. "People are machines. Machines have to be blind and unconscious, they cannot be otherwise, and all their actions have to correspond to their nature. *Everything happens.* No one does anything. 'Progress' and 'civilization,' in the real meaning of these words, can appear only as the result of *conscious* efforts. They cannot appear as the result of unconscious mechanical actions. And what conscious effort can there be in machines? And if one machine is unconscious, then a hundred machines are unconscious, and so are a thousand machines, or a hundred thousand, or a million. And the unconscious activity of *a million machines* must necessarily result in destruction and extermination. It is precisely in unconscious involuntary manifestations that all evil lies. You do not yet understand and cannot imagine all the results of this evil. But the time will come when you will understand."

With this, so far as I remember, the talk ended.

Chapter Three

B Y THE beginning of November, 1915, I already had a grasp of
some of the fundamental points of G.'s system in relation to man.
The first point, on which he laid stress, was the *absence of unity
in man.*

"It is the greatest mistake," he said, "to think that man is always one
and the same. A man is never the same for long. He is continually changing. He seldom remains the same even for half an hour. We think that if
a man is called Ivan he is always Ivan. Nothing of the kind. Now he is
Ivan, in another minute he is Peter, and a minute later he is Nicholas,
Sergius, Matthew, Simon. And all of you think he is Ivan. You know
that Ivan cannot do a certain thing. He cannot tell a lie for instance.
Then you find he has told a lie and you are surprised he could have done
so. And, indeed, Ivan cannot lie; it is Nicholas who lied. And when the
opportunity presents itself Nicholas *cannot help lying.* You will be astonished when you realize what a multitude of these Ivans and Nicholases
live in one man. If you learn to observe them there is no need to go to
a cinema."

"Has this anything to do with the consciousnesses of separate parts and
organs of the body?" I asked him on this occasion. "I understand this idea
and have often felt the reality of these consciousnesses. I know that not
only separate organs, but every part of the body having a separate function has a separate consciousness. The right hand has one consciousness
and the left hand another. Is that what you mean?"

"Not altogether," said G. "These consciousnesses also exist but they
are comparatively harmless. Each of them knows its own place and its
own business. The hands know they must work; the feet know they must
walk. But these Ivans, Peters, and Nicholases are different. They all call
themselves 'I.' That is, they consider themselves masters and none wants
to recognize another. Each of them is caliph for an hour, does what he
likes regardless of everything, and, later on, the others have to pay for it.
And there is no order among them whatever. Whoever gets the upper
hand is master. He whips everyone on all sides and takes heed of nothing.
But the next moment another seizes the whip and beats him. And so it
goes on all one's life. Imagine a country where everyone can be king for

five minutes and do during these five minutes just what he likes with the whole kingdom. That is our life."

During one of the talks G. again returned to the idea of the different bodies of man.

"That man can have several bodies," he said, "must be understood as an idea, as a principle. But it does not apply to us. We know we have the one physical body and we know nothing else. It is the physical body that we must study. Only, we must remember that the question is not limited to the physical body and that there are people who may have two, three, or more bodies. But it makes no difference to us personally either one way or another. Someone like Rockefeller in America may have a great many millions, but his millions do not help me if I have nothing to eat. It is the same thing in this connection. Everyone must think of himself; it is useless and senseless to rely on others or to console oneself with thoughts of what others possess."

"How is one to know if a man has an 'astral body'?" I asked.

"There are definite ways of knowing that," answered G. "Under certain conditions the 'astral body' can be seen; it can be separated from the physical body and even photographed at the side of the physical body. The existence of the 'astral body' can be still more easily and simply established *by its functions*. The 'astral body' has definite functions which the physical body cannot have. The presence of these functions indicates the presence of the 'astral body.' The absence of these functions shows the absence of the 'astral body.' But it is too early to speak of this now. All our attention must be concentrated on the study of the physical body. It is necessary to understand the structure of the human machine. Our principal error is that we think we have *one mind*. We call the functions of this mind 'conscious'; everything that does not enter this mind we call 'unconscious' or 'subconscious.' This is our chief error. Of the conscious and the unconscious we will speak later. At this moment I want to explain to you that the activity of the human machine, that is, of the physical body, is controlled, not by one, but by several *minds*, entirely independent of each other, having separate functions and separate spheres in which they manifest themselves. This must be understood first of all, because unless this is understood nothing else can be understood."

After this G. went on to explain man's various functions and centers controlling these functions in the way they are set out in the psychological lectures.

These explanations, and all the talks connected with them, took a fairly long time, while at almost every talk we returned to the fundamental ideas of man's mechanicalness, of the absence of unity in man, of man's having no choice, of his being unable *to do*, and so on. There is no possibility of giving all these talks in the way they actually took place. For this reason I collected all the psychological and all the cosmological material in two separate series of lectures.

In this connection it must be noted that the ideas were not given us in the form in which they are set out in my lectures. G. gave the ideas little by little, as though defending or protecting them from us. When touching on new themes for the first time he gave only general principles, often holding back the most essential. Sometimes he himself pointed out apparent discrepancies in the theories given, which were, in fact, precisely due to these reservations and suppressions. The next time, in approaching the same subject, whenever possible from a different angle, he gave more. The third time he gave still more. On the question of functions and centers for instance. On the first occasion he spoke of *three centers*, the intellectual, the emotional, and the moving, and tried to make us distinguish these functions, find examples, and so on. Afterwards the instinctive center was added, as an independent and self-supporting machine. Afterwards the sex center. I remember that some of his remarks arrested my attention. For instance, when speaking of the sex center he said it practically never worked independently because it was always dependent on other centers, the intellectual, the emotional, the instinctive, and the moving. Then in speaking of the energy of centers he often returned to what he called wrong work of centers and to the role of the sex center in this work. He spoke a great deal about how all centers rob the sex center of its energy and produce with this energy quite wrong work full of useless excitement and, in return, give to the sex center useless energy with which it was unable to work.

I remember his words.

"It is a very big thing when the sex center works with its own energy, but it happens very seldom."

I recollect another remark which afterwards proved a ground for much wrong reasoning and many wrong conclusions. This was that the three centers of the lower story: the instinctive, the moving, and the sex centers, work, in relation to each other, in the order of *three forces*—and that the sex center, in normal cases, acts as neutralizing force in relation to the instinctive and moving centers acting as active and passive forces.

The method of exposition of which I am speaking, and G.'s suppressions in his first talks, resulted in the creation of such misunderstanding, more particularly in later groups not connected with my work.

Many people found contradictions between the first exposition of a given idea and subsequent explanations and sometimes, in trying to hold as closely as possible to the first, they created fantastic theories having no relation to what G. actually said. Thus the idea of *three centers* was retained by certain groups (which, I repeat, were not connected with me). And this idea was, in some way, linked up with the idea of *three forces*, with which in reality it had no connection, first of all because there are not three centers but five in the ordinary man.

This uniting of two ideas of an entirely different order, scale, and significance gave rise to many further misunderstandings and completely distorted the whole system for those who thought in this manner.

It is possible that the idea of the three centers (intellectual, emotional, and moving) being the expression of the three forces arose from G.'s wrongly repeated and wrongly received remarks on the relationship to each other of the three centers of the lower story.

During the first and subsequent talks on centers G. added something new at almost every talk. As I said in the beginning he spoke first of three centers, then of four, then of five, and afterwards of seven centers.

Parts of centers hardly came into these talks. G. said that centers were divided into positive and negative parts, but he did not point out that this division was *not identical* for all the different centers. Then he said that each center was divided into three parts or *three stories* which, in their turn, were also divided into three; but he gave no examples, nor did he point out that observation of attention made it possible to distinguish the work of parts of centers. All this and much else besides was established later. For instance, although he undoubtedly gave the fundamental basis for the study of the role and the significance of negative emotions, as well as methods of struggling against them, referring to non-identification, non-considering, and not expressing negative emotions, he did not complete these theories or did not explain that negative emotions were entirely *unnecessary* and that no normal center for them existed.

I shall, further on, reproduce the talks and lectures of the St. Petersburg and later groups in the way I remember them while endeavoring to avoid what has already been given in the first and second series of lectures. But it is impossible to avoid repetition in certain cases and the original exposition of the ideas of the system in the way G. gave them is, in my opinion, of great interest.

Somebody asked at a meeting:

"How should evolution be understood?"

"The evolution of man," G. replied, "can be taken as the development in him of those powers and possibilities which never develop by themselves, that is, mechanically. Only this kind of development, only this kind of growth, marks the real evolution of man. There is, and there can be, no other kind of evolution whatever.

"We have before us man at the present moment of his development. Nature has made him such as he is, and, in large masses, so far as we can see, such he will remain. Changes likely to violate the general requirements of nature can only take place in separate units.

"In order to understand the law of man's evolution it is necessary to grasp that, beyond a certain point, this evolution is not at all necessary, that is to say, it is not necessary for nature at a given moment in its own development. To speak more precisely: the evolution of mankind corresponds to the evolution of the planets, but the evolution of the planets proceeds, for us, in infinitely prolonged cycles of time. Throughout the stretch of time that human thought can embrace, no essential changes can take place in the life of the planets, and, consequently, no essential changes can take place in the life of mankind.

"Humanity neither progresses nor evolves. What seems to us to be progress or evolution is a partial modification which can be immediately counterbalanced by a corresponding modification in an opposite direction.

"Humanity, like the rest of organic life, exists on earth for the needs and purposes of the earth. And it is exactly as it should be for the earth's requirements at the present time.

"Only thought as theoretical and as far removed from fact as modern European thought could have conceived the evolution of man to be possible *apart from surrounding nature,* or have regarded the evolution of man as a gradual *conquest of nature.* This is quite impossible. In living, in dying, in evolving, in degenerating, man equally serves the purposes of nature—or, rather, nature makes equal use, though perhaps for different purposes, of the products of both evolution and degeneration. And, at the same time, humanity as a whole can never escape from nature, for, even in struggling against nature man acts in conformity with her purposes. The evolution of large masses of humanity is opposed to nature's purposes. The evolution of a certain small percentage may be in accord with nature's purposes. Man contains within him the possibility of evolution. But the evolution of humanity as a whole, that is, the development of these possibilities in all men, or in most of them, or even in a large number of them, is not necessary for the purposes of the earth or of the planetary world in general, and it might, in fact, be injurious or fatal. There exist, therefore, special forces (of a planetary character) which oppose the evolution of large masses of humanity and keep it at the level it ought to be.

"For instance, the evolution of humanity beyond a certain point, or, to speak more correctly, above a certain percentage, would be fatal for the *moon.* The moon at present *feeds* on organic life, on humanity. Humanity is a part of organic life; this means that humanity is *food* for the moon. If all men were to become too intelligent they would not want to be eaten by the moon.

"But, at the same time, possibilities of evolution exist, and they may be developed in *separate* individuals with the help of appropriate knowledge and methods. Such development can take place only in the interests of the man himself against, so to speak, the interests and forces of the

planetary world. The man must understand this: his evolution is necessary only to himself. No one else is interested in it. And no one is
obliged or intends to help him. On the contrary, the forces which oppose
the evolution of large masses of humanity also oppose the evolution of
individual men. A man must outwit them. And *one* man can outwit them,
humanity *cannot*. You will understand later on that all these obstacles
are very useful to a man; if they did not exist they would have to be
created intentionally, because it is by overcoming obstacles that man
develops those qualities he needs.

"This is the basis of the correct view of human evolution. There is no
compulsory, mechanical evolution. Evolution is the result of conscious
struggle. Nature does not need this evolution; it does not want it and
struggles against it. Evolution can be necessary only to man himself
when he realizes his position, realizes the possibility of changing this
position, realizes that he has powers that he does not use, riches that
he does not see. And, in the sense of gaining possession of these powers
and riches, evolution is possible. But if *all men*, or most of them, realized
this and desired to obtain what belongs to them by right of birth, evolution would again become impossible. What is possible for individual
man is impossible for the masses.

"The advantage of the separate individual is that he is very small and
that, in the economy of nature, it makes no difference whether there is
one mechanical man more or less. We can easily understand this correlation of magnitudes if we imagine the correlation between a microscopic
cell and our own body. The presence or absence of one cell will change
nothing in the life of the body. We cannot be conscious of it, and it
can have no influence on the life and functions of the organism. In
exactly the same way a separate individual is too small to influence the
life of the cosmic organism to which he stands in the same relation (with
regard to size) as a cell stands to our own organism. And this is precisely
what makes his 'evolution' possible; on this are based his 'possibilities.'

"In speaking of evolution it is necessary to understand from the outset
that no mechanical evolution is possible. The evolution of man is the
evolution of his consciousness. And 'consciousness' cannot evolve unconsciously. The evolution of man is the evolution of his will, and 'will' cannot evolve involuntarily. The evolution of man is the evolution of his
power of doing, and 'doing' cannot be the result of things which 'happen.'

"People do not know what man is. They have to do with a very complex machine, far more complex than a railway engine, a motorcar, or an
aeroplane—but they know nothing, or almost nothing, about the construction, working, or possibilities of this machine; they do not even
understand its simplest functions, because they do not know the purpose
of these functions. They vaguely imagine that a man should learn to
control his machine, just as he has to learn to control a railway engine, a

motorcar, or an aeroplane, and that incompetent handling of the human
machine is just as dangerous as incompetent handling of any other complex machine. Everybody understands this in relation to an aeroplane, a
motorcar, or a railway engine. But it is very rarely that anyone takes this
into account in relation to man in general or to himself in particular.
It is considered right and legitimate to think that nature has given men
the necessary knowledge of their machine. And yet men understand that
an instinctive knowledge of the machine is by no means enough. Why
do they study medicine and make use of its services? Because, of course,
they realize they do not know their machine. But they do not suspect
that it can be known much better than science knows it; they do not
suspect that then it would be possible to get quite different work out
of it."

Very often, almost at every talk, G. returned to the absence of unity
in man.

"One of man's important mistakes," he said, "one which must be remembered, is his illusion in regard to his I.

"Man such as we know him, the 'man-machine,' the man who cannot
'do,' and with whom and through whom everything 'happens,' cannot
have a permanent and single I. His I changes as quickly as his thoughts,
feelings, and moods, and he makes a profound mistake in considering himself always one and the same person; in reality he is *always a different
person*, not the one he was a moment ago.

"*Man has no permanent and unchangeable I.* Every thought, every
mood, every desire, every sensation, says 'I.' And in each case it seems to
be taken for granted that this I belongs to the Whole, to the whole man,
and that a thought, a desire, or an aversion is expressed by this Whole.
In actual fact there is no foundation whatever for this assumption. Man's
every thought and desire appears and lives quite separately and independently of the Whole. And the Whole never expresses itself, for the
simple reason that it exists, as such, only physically as a thing, and in the
abstract as a concept. Man has no individual I. But there are, instead,
hundreds and thousands of separate small I's, very often entirely unknown
to one another, never coming into contact, or, on the contrary, hostile to
each other, mutually exclusive and incompatible. Each minute, each moment, man is saying or thinking 'I.' And each time his I is different. Just
now it was a thought, now it is a desire, now a sensation, now another
thought, and so on, endlessly. *Man is a plurality.* Man's name is legion.

"The alternation of I's, their continual obvious struggle for supremacy,
is controlled by accidental external influences. Warmth, sunshine, fine
weather, immediately call up a whole group of I's. Cold, fog, rain, call
up another group of I's, other associations, other feelings, other actions.
There is nothing in man able to control this change of I's, chiefly because

man does not notice, or know of it; he lives always in the last I. Some I's, of course, are stronger than others. But it is not their own conscious strength; they have been created by the strength of accidents or mechanical external stimuli. Education, imitation, reading, the hypnotism of religion, caste, and traditions, or the glamour of new slogans, create very strong I's in man's personality, which dominate whole series of other, weaker, I's. But their strength is the strength of the 'rolls' in the centers. And all I's making up a man's personality have the same origin as these 'rolls'; they are the results of external influences; and both are set in motion and controlled by fresh external influences.

"Man has no individuality. He has no single, big I. Man is divided into a multiplicity of small I's.

"And each separate small I is able to call itself by the name of the Whole, to act in the name of the Whole, to agree or disagree, to give promises, to make decisions, with which another I or the Whole will have to deal. This explains why people so often make decisions and so seldom carry them out. A man decides to get up early beginning from the following day. One I, or a group of I's, decide this. But getting up is the business of another I who entirely disagrees with the decision and may even know absolutely nothing about it. Of course the man will again go on sleeping in the morning and in the evening he will again decide to get up early. In some cases this may assume very unpleasant consequences for a man. A small accidental I may promise something, not to itself, but to someone else at a certain moment simply out of vanity or for amusement. Then it disappears, but the man, that is, the whole combination of other I's who are quite innocent of this, may have to pay for it all his life. It is the tragedy of the human being that any small I has the right to sign checks and promissory notes and the man, that is, the Whole, has to meet them. People's whole lives often consist in paying off the promissory notes of small accidental I's.

"Eastern teachings contain various allegorical pictures which endeavor to portray the nature of man's being from this point of view.

"Thus, in one teaching, man is compared to a house in which there is a multitude of servants but no master and no steward. The servants have all forgotten their duties; no one wants to do what he ought; everyone tries to be master, if only for a moment; and, in this kind of disorder, the house is threatened with grave danger. The only chance of salvation is for a group of the more sensible servants to meet together and elect a *temporary* steward, that is, a *deputy steward*. This *deputy steward* can then put the other servants in their places, and make each do his own work: the cook in the kitchen, the coachman in the stables, the gardener in the garden, and so on. In this way the 'house' can be got ready for the arrival of the real steward who will, in his turn, prepare it for the arrival of the master.

"The comparison of a man to a house awaiting the arrival of the master is frequently met with in Eastern teachings which have preserved traces of ancient knowledge, and, as we know, the subject appears under various forms in many of the parables in the Gospels.

"But even the clearest understanding of his possibilities will not bring man any nearer to their realization. In order to realize these possibilities he must have a very strong desire for liberation and be willing to sacrifice everything, to risk everything, for the sake of this liberation."

To this period, that is, to the beginning of the St. Petersburg lectures, are related two interesting talks.

On one occasion I showed G. a photograph I had taken in Benares of a "fakir on nails."

This fakir was not merely a clever juggler like those I saw in Ceylon, although he was undoubtedly a "professional." I had been told that, in the court of the Aurangzeb Mosque on the bank of the Ganges, there was a fakir lying on a bed studded with iron nails. This sounded very mysterious and terrifying. But when I arrived the bed with iron nails alone was there, without the fakir; the fakir, I was told, had gone to fetch the cow. The second time I went the fakir was there. He was not lying on his bed and, so far as I could understand, he only got on it when spectators came. But for a rupee he showed me all his skill. He really did lie almost entirely naked on the bed which was covered with long rather sharp iron nails. And, although he evidently took care not to make any quick movements, he turned round on the nails, lay upon them on his back, his sides, his stomach, and obviously they neither pricked nor scratched him. I took two photographs of him but I could give myself no explanation of the meaning of this phenomenon. The fakir did not produce the impression of being either an intelligent or a religious man. His face wore a dull, bored, and indifferent expression, and there was nothing in him that spoke of aspirations toward self-sacrifice or self-torture.

I told all this to G., showing him the photograph, and I asked him what he thought of it.

"It is difficult to explain in two words," answered G. "First of all the man is not, of course, a 'fakir' in the sense in which I have been using the word. At the same time you are right in thinking it is not altogether a trick. *But he does not know himself how he does it.* If you bribed him and made him tell you what he knows he would probably tell you that he knows *a certain word* which he has to say to himself, after which he is able to lie down on the nails. He might even consent to tell you this word. But it would not help you in the least, because it would be a perfectly ordinary word which would have no effect whatever on you. This man has come from a school, only he was not a disciple. *He was an experiment.* They simply experimented with him and on him. He had evidently been hypnotized many times and under hypnosis his skin had been rendered first insensitive to pricks and afterwards able to resist them. In a small way this is quite possible even for ordinary European hypnotism. Then afterwards both the insensitiveness and impenetrability of the skin were made permanent in him by means of post-hypnotic suggestion. You know what post-hypnotic suggestion is. A man is put to sleep and told that five hours after he wakes up he must do a certain thing; or he is told to pronounce a certain word and that as soon as he does so he will feel thirsty, or think himself dead, or something like that. Then he is awakened. When the time comes he feels an irresistible desire to do what he was told to do; or, if he remembers the word that was given to him, on pronouncing it he immediately falls into a trance. This is just what was done to your 'fakir.' They accustomed him to lie on nails under hypnosis; then they began to wake him and tell him that if he pronounced a certain word he would again be able to lie down on the nails. This word puts him into a hypnotic state. This is perhaps why he had such a sleepy, apathetic look. This often happens in such cases. They worked on him, perhaps, for many years and then simply let him go, to live as he could. So he put up that iron bed for himself and probably earns a few rupees a week. There are many such men in India. Schools take them for experiment, generally buying them when they are children from parents who gladly sell them because they afterwards profit from it. But of course the man himself does not know or understand what he is doing or how it is done."

This explanation interested me very much because I had never before heard or read an explanation quite like this. In all the attempts to explain "fakirs' miracles" that I had come across, whether the "miracles" were explained as tricks or otherwise, it was always assumed that the performer knew what he was doing and how he did it, and that, if he did not speak of it, it was because he did not want to or was afraid. In the present instance the position was quite different. G.'s explanation seemed to me not only probable but, I dare say, the only one possible. The fakir himself did not know how he worked his "miracle," and, of course, could not have explained it.

On another occasion we were talking of Buddhism in Ceylon. I expressed the opinion that Buddhists *must have magic*, the existence of which they do not acknowledge, and the possibility of which is denied in official Buddhism. Entirely without connection with this remark, and while, I think, I was showing my photographs to G., I spoke about a small shrine in a private house in Colombo in which there was, as usual, a statue of Buddha, and at the foot of the Buddha a small, bell-shaped ivory dagoba, that is, a small carved replica of a dagoba, hollow inside. They opened this in my presence and showed me something inside it that was regarded as a relic—a small round ball the size of a large shot, carved, as I thought, out of ivory or mother-of-pearl.

G. listened to me attentively.

"Did they not explain to you what this ball meant?" he asked.

"They told me it was a piece of bone of one of Buddha's disciples; that it was of very great antiquity and holiness."

"It is so and it is not so," said G. "The man who showed it to you either did not know or did not want to say. It was not a piece of bone but a particular bone formation which some people get round the neck in the form of a necklace as a result of special exercises. Have you heard the expression 'Buddha's necklace'?"

"Yes," I said, "but this means something quite different. The chain of Buddha's reincarnation is called 'Buddha's necklace.' "

"Yes," said G., "that is one meaning of the expression, but I am speaking of another meaning. This necklace of bones which encircles the neck beneath the skin is directly connected with what is called the 'astral body.' The 'astral body' is, so to speak, attached to it, or, to be more accurate, this 'necklace' connects the physical body to the astral. Now if the 'astral body' continues to live after the death of the physical body, the person possessing a bone of this 'necklace' can always communicate with the 'astral body' of the dead man. This is magic. But they never speak of it openly. You are right about their having magic and this is an instance of it. It does not follow, of course, that the bone you saw was a real one. You will find these bones in almost every house; but I am telling you of the belief which lies at the bottom of this custom."

And again I had to admit that I had never before met with such an explanation.

G. drew a small sketch for me showing the position of the small bones under the skin; they went in a semicircle round the back of the neck, beginning a little in front of the ears.

This sketch at once reminded me of an ordinary diagrammatic representation of the lymphatic glands in the neck, such as can be seen in anatomical charts. But I could learn nothing else about it.

Chapter Four

G'S LECTURES led to many talks in our groups.
There was still a good deal that was not clear to me, but
many things had become connected and one thing often quite
unexpectedly explained another which seemed to have no connection
with it whatever. Certain parts of the system had already begun vaguely
to take shape, like figures or a landscape which gradually appears in the
developing of a photographic plate, but many places still remained blank
and incomplete. At the same time many things were contrary to what I
expected. Only I tried not to come to conclusions but wait. Often one new
word that I had not heard before altered the whole picture and I was
obliged to rebuild for myself everything I had built up before. I realized
very clearly that a great deal of time must pass before I could tell myself
that I could outline the whole system correctly. And it was very strange
for me to hear how people, after having come to us for one lecture, at
once *understood* what we were talking about, explained it to others, and
had completely settled and definite opinions about us. I must confess that,
at such times, I often recalled my own first meeting with G. and the
evening with the Moscow group. I also, at that time, had been very near
passing a ready judgment on G. and his pupils. But something had stopped
me then. And now, when I had begun to realize what a tremendous value
these ideas had, I became almost terrified at the thought of how easily
I could have passed them by, how easily I could have known nothing
whatever of G.'s existence, or how easily I could have again lost sight of
him if I had not asked then whether I could see him again.

In almost every one of his lectures G. reverted to a theme which he
evidently considered to be of the utmost importance but which was very
difficult for many of us to assimilate.

"There are," he said, "two lines along which man's development proceeds, the line of *knowledge* and the line of *being*. In right evolution the
line of knowledge and the line of being develop simultaneously, parallel
to, and helping one another. But if the line of knowledge gets too far
ahead of the line of being, or if the line of being gets ahead of the
line of knowledge, man's development goes wrong, and sooner or later it
must come to a standstill.

"People understand what 'knowledge' means. And they understand the possibility of different levels of knowledge. They understand that knowledge may be lesser or greater, that is to say, of one quality or of another quality. But they do not understand this in relation to 'being.' 'Being,' for them, means simply 'existence' to which is opposed just 'non-existence.' They do not understand that being or existence may be of very different levels and categories. Take for instance the being of a mineral and of a plant. It is a different being. The being of a plant and of an animal is again a different being. The being of an animal and of a man is a different being. But the being of two people can differ from one another more than the being of a mineral and of an animal. This is exactly what people do not understand. And they do not understand that *knowledge* depends on *being*. Not only do they not understand this latter but they definitely do not wish to understand it. And especially in Western culture it is considered that a man may possess great knowledge, for example he may be an able scientist, make discoveries, advance science, and at the same time he may be, and has the right to be, a petty, egoistic, caviling, mean, envious, vain, naïve, and absent-minded man. It seems to be considered here that a professor must always forget his umbrella everywhere.

"And yet it is his being. And people think that his knowledge does not depend on his being. People of Western culture put great value on the level of a man's knowledge but they do not value the level of a man's being and are not ashamed of the low level of their own being. They do not even understand what it means. And they do not understand that a man's knowledge depends on the level of his being.

"If knowledge gets far ahead of being, it becomes theoretical and abstract and inapplicable to life, or actually harmful, because instead of serving life and helping people the better to struggle with the difficulties they meet, it begins to complicate man's life, brings new difficulties into it, new troubles and calamities which were not there before.

"The reason for this is that knowledge which is not in accordance with being cannot be large enough for, or sufficiently suited to, man's real needs. It will always be a knowledge of *one thing* together with ignorance of *another thing*; a knowledge of the *detail* without a knowledge of the *whole*; a knowledge of the *form* without a knowledge of the *essence*.

"Such preponderance of knowledge over being is observed in present-day culture. The idea of the value and importance of the level of being is completely forgotten. And it is forgotten that the level of knowledge is determined by the level of being. Actually at a given level of being the possibilities of knowledge are limited and finite. Within the limits of a given being the *quality* of knowledge cannot be changed, and the accumulation of information of one and the same nature, within already known limits, alone is possible. A change in the nature of knowledge is possible only with a change in the nature of being.

"Taken in itself, a man's being has many different sides. The most characteristic feature of a modern man is the *absence of unity in him* and, further, the absence in him of even traces of those properties which he most likes to ascribe to himself, that is, 'lucid consciousness,' 'free will,' a 'permanent ego or I,' and the 'ability to do.' It may surprise you if I say that the chief feature of a modern man's being which explains *everything else that is lacking in him* is *sleep.*

"A modern man lives in sleep, in sleep he is born and in sleep he dies. About sleep, its significance and its role in life, we will speak later. But at present just think of one thing, what *knowledge* can a sleeping man have? And if you think about it and at the same time remember that *sleep* is the chief feature of our being, it will at once become clear to you that if a man really wants knowledge, he must first of all think about how to wake, that is, about how to change his *being.*

"Exteriorly man's being has many different sides: activity or passivity; truthfulness or a tendency to lie; sincerity or insincerity; courage, cowardice; self-control, profligacy; irritability, egoism, readiness for self-sacrifice, pride, vanity, conceit, industry, laziness, morality, depravity; all these and much more besides make up the being of man.

"But all this is entirely *mechanical* in man. If he lies it means that he cannot help lying. If he tells the truth it means that he cannot help telling the truth, and so it is with everything. Everything happens, a man can do nothing either in himself or outside himself.

"But of course there are limits and bounds. Generally speaking, the being of a modern man is of very inferior quality. But it can be of such bad quality that no change is possible. This must always be remembered. People whose being can still be changed are very lucky. But there are people who are definitely diseased, broken machines with whom nothing can be done. And such people are in the majority. If you think of this you will understand why only few can receive real knowledge. Their being prevents it.

"Generally speaking, the *balance* between knowledge and being is even more important than a separate development of either one or the other. And a separate development of knowledge or of being is not desirable in any way. Although it is precisely this *one-sided* development that often seems particularly attractive to people.

"If knowledge outweighs being a man *knows but has no power to do.* It is useless knowledge. On the other hand if being outweighs knowledge a man *has the power to do,* but does not know, that is, he can do something but does not know what to do. The being he has acquired becomes aimless and efforts made to attain it prove to be useless.

"In the history of humanity there are known many examples when entire civilizations have perished because knowledge outweighed being or being outweighed knowledge."

"What are the results of the development of the line of knowledge without being, or the development of the line of being without knowledge?" someone asked during a talk upon this subject.

"The development of the line of knowledge without the line of being gives a *weak yogi*," said G., "that is to say, a man who knows a great deal but can do nothing, a man who *does not understand*" (he emphasized these words) "what he knows, a man without *appreciation*, that is, a man for whom there is no difference between one kind of knowledge and another. And the development of the line of being without knowledge gives a *stupid saint*, that is, a man who can do a great deal but who does not know what to do or with what object; and if he does anything he acts in obedience to his subjective feelings which may lead him greatly astray and cause him to commit grave mistakes, that is, actually to do the opposite of what he wants. In either case both the *weak yogi* and the *stupid saint* are brought to a standstill. Neither the one nor the other can develop further.

"In order to understand this and, in general, the nature of knowledge and the nature of being, as well as their interrelation, it is necessary to understand the relation of knowledge and being to 'understanding.'

"*Knowledge is one thing, understanding is another thing.*

"People often confuse these concepts and do not clearly grasp what is the difference between them.

"Knowledge by itself does not give understanding. Nor is understanding increased by an increase of knowledge alone. Understanding depends upon the relation of knowledge to being. Understanding is the resultant of knowledge and being. And knowledge and being must not diverge too far, otherwise understanding will prove to be far removed from either. At the same time the relation of knowledge to being does not change with a mere growth of knowledge. It changes only when being grows simultaneously with knowledge. In other words, understanding grows only with the growth of being.

"In ordinary thinking, people do not distinguish understanding from knowledge. They think that greater understanding depends on greater knowledge. Therefore they accumulate knowledge, or that which they call knowledge, but they do not know how to accumulate understanding and do not bother about it.

"And yet a person accustomed to self-observation knows for certain that at different periods of his life he has understood one and the same idea, one and the same thought, in totally different ways. It often seems strange to him that he could have understood so wrongly that which, in his opinion, he now understands rightly. And he realizes, at the same time, that his knowledge has not changed, and that he knew as much about the given subject before as he knows now. What, then, has changed? His being has changed. And once being has changed understanding must change also.

"The difference between knowledge and understanding becomes clear when we realize that *knowledge* may be the function of one center. Understanding, however, is the function of three centers. Thus the thinking apparatus may *know* something. But *understanding* appears only when a man *feels* and *senses* what is connected with it.

"We have spoken earlier about mechanicalness. A man cannot say that he understands the idea of mechanicalness if he only *knows* about it with his mind. He must *feel* it with his whole mass, with his whole being; then he will understand it.

"In the sphere of practical activity people know very well the difference between mere knowledge and understanding. They realize that to know and *to know how to do* are two different things, and that *knowing how to do* is not created by knowledge alone. But outside the sphere of practical activity people do not clearly understand what 'understanding' means.

"As a rule, when people realize that they do not understand a thing they try *to find a name* for what they do not 'understand,' and when they find a name they say they 'understand.' But to 'find a name' does not mean to 'understand.' Unfortunately, people are usually satisfied with names. A man who knows a great many names, that is, a great many words, is deemed to understand a great deal—again excepting, of course, any sphere of practical activity wherein his ignorance very soon becomes evident.

"One of the reasons for the divergence between the line of knowledge and the line of being in life, and the lack of understanding which is partly the cause and partly the effect of this divergence, is to be found in the language which people speak. This language is full of wrong concepts, wrong classifications, wrong associations. And the chief thing is that, owing to the essential characteristics of ordinary thinking, that is to say, to its vagueness and inaccuracy, every word can have thousands of different meanings according to the material the speaker has at his disposal and the complex of associations at work in him at the moment. People do not clearly realize to what a degree their language is subjective, that is, what different things each of them says while using the same words. They are not aware that each one of them speaks in a language of his own, understanding other people's language either vaguely or not at all, and having no idea that each one of them speaks in a language unknown to him. People have a very firm conviction, or belief, that they speak the same language, that they understand one another.

Actually this conviction has no foundation whatever. The language in which they speak is adapted to practical life only. People can communicate to one another information of a practical character, but as soon as they pass to a slightly more complex sphere they are immediately lost, and they cease to understand one another, although they are unconscious of it. People imagine that they often, if not always, understand one another, or that they can, at any rate, understand one another if they try or want to; they imagine that they understand the authors of the books they read and that other people understand them. This also is one of the illusions which people create for themselves and in the midst of which they live. As a matter of fact, no one understands anyone else. Two men can say the same thing with profound conviction but call it by different names, or argue endlessly together without suspecting that they are thinking exactly the same. Or, vice versa, two men can say the same words and imagine that they agree with, and understand, one another, whereas they are actually saying absolutely different things and do not understand one another in the least.

"If we take the simplest words that occur constantly in speech and endeavor to analyze the meaning given to them, we shall see at once that, at every moment of his life, every man puts into each word a special meaning which another man can never put into it or suspect.

"Let us take the word 'man' and imagine a conversation among a group of people in which the word 'man' is often heard. Without any exaggeration it can be said that the word 'man' will have as many meanings as there are people taking part in the conversation, and that these meanings will have nothing in common.

"In pronouncing the word 'man' everyone will involuntarily connect with this word the point of view from which he is generally accustomed to regard man, or from which, for some reason or other, he regards him at the moment. One man at the moment may be occupied with the question of the relation between the sexes. Then the word 'man' will have no general meaning for him and on hearing this word he will first of all ask himself—Which? man or woman? Another man may be religious and his first question will be—A Christian or not a Christian? The third man may be a doctor and the concept 'man' will mean for him a 'sick man' or a 'healthy man,' and, of course from the point of view of his speciality. A spiritualist will think of 'man' from the point of view of his 'astral body,' of 'life on the other side,' and so on, and he may say, if he is asked, that men are divided into mediums and non-mediums. A naturalist speaking of man will place the center of gravity of his thoughts in the idea of man as a zoological type, that is to say, in speaking of man he will think of the structure of his teeth, his fingers, his facial angle, the distance between the eyes. A lawyer will see in 'man' a statistical unit, or a subject for the application of laws, or a potential criminal, or a possible client.

A moralist pronouncing the word 'man' will invariably introduce into it the idea of good and evil, and so on, and so on.

"People do not notice all these contradictions, do not notice that they never understand one another, that they always speak about different things. It is quite clear that, for proper study, for an exact exchange of thoughts, an exact language is necessary, which would make it possible to establish what a man actually means, would include an indication of the point of view from which a given concept is taken and determine the center of gravity of this concept. The idea is perfectly clear and every branch of science endeavors to elaborate and to establish an exact language for itself. But there is no universal language. People continually confuse the languages of different sciences and can never establish their exact correlation. And even in each separate branch of science new terminologies, new nomenclatures, are constantly appearing. And the further it goes the worse it becomes. Misunderstanding grows and increases instead of diminishing and there is every reason to think that it will continue to increase in the same way. And people will understand one another ever less and less.

"For exact understanding exact language is necessary. And the study of systems of ancient knowledge begins with the study of a language which will make it possible to establish at once exactly what is being said, from what point of view, and in what connection. This new language contains hardly any new terms or new nomenclature, but *it bases the construction of speech upon a new principle, namely, the principle of relativity;* that is to say, it introduces relativity into all concepts and thus makes possible an accurate determination of the angle of thought—for what precisely ordinary language lacks are expressions of relativity.

"When a man has mastered this language, then, with its help, there can be transmitted and communicated to him a great deal of knowledge and information which cannot be transmitted in ordinary language even by using all possible scientific and philosophical terms.

"The fundamental property of the new language is that *all* ideas in it are concentrated round *one* idea, that is, they are taken in their mutual relationship from the point of view of one idea. This idea is the idea of *evolution*. Of course, not evolution in the sense of *mechanical* evolution, because such an evolution does not exist, but in the sense of a conscious and volitional evolution, which alone is possible.

"Everything in the world, from solar systems to man, and from man to atom, either rises or descends, either evolves or degenerates, either develops or decays. *But nothing evolves mechanically.* Only degeneration and destruction proceed mechanically. That which cannot evolve consciously—degenerates. Help from outside is possible only in so far as it is valued and accepted, even if it is only by feeling in the beginning.

"The language in which understanding is possible is constructed upon the indication of the relation of the object under examination to the evolution possible for it; upon the indication of its *place* in the evolutionary ladder.

"For this purpose many of our usual ideas are *divided* according to the steps of this evolution.

"Once again let us take the idea. *man.* In the language of which I speak, instead of the word 'man,' *seven words* are used, namely: man number one, man number two, man number three, man number four, man number five, man number six, and man number seven. With these seven ideas people are already able to understand one another when speaking of man.

"Man number seven means a man who has reached the full development possible to man and who possesses everything a man can possess, that is, will, consciousness, permanent and unchangeable I, individuality, immortality, and many other properties which, in our blindness and ignorance, we ascribe to ourselves. It is only when to a certain extent we understand man number seven and his properties that we can understand the gradual stages through which we can approach him, that is, understand the process of development possible for us.

"Man number six stands very close to man number seven. He differs from man number seven only by the fact that some of his properties have not as yet become *permanent*.

"Man number five is also for us an unattainable standard of man, for it is a man who has reached *unity*.

"Man number four is an intermediate stage. I shall speak of him later.

"Man number one, number two, and number three, these are people who constitute mechanical humanity on the same level on which they are born.

"*Man number one* means man in whom the center of gravity of his psychic life lies in the moving center. This is the man of the physical body, the man with whom the moving and the instinctive functions constantly outweigh the emotional and the thinking functions.

"*Man number two* means man on the same level of development, but man in whom the center of gravity of his psychic life lies in the emotional center, that is, man with whom the *emotional* functions outweigh all others; the man of feeling, the emotional man.

"*Man number three* means man on the same level of development but man in whom the center of gravity of his psychic life lies in the intellectual center, that is, man with whom the thinking functions gain the upper hand over the moving, instinctive, and emotional functions; the man of reason, who goes into everything from theories, from mental considerations.

"Every man is born number one, number two, or number three.

"*Man number four* is not born ready-made. He is born one, two, or three, and becomes four only as a result of efforts of a definite character. Man number four is always the *product of school work*. He can neither be born, nor develop accidentally or as the result of ordinary influences of bringing up, education, and so on. Man number four already stands on a different level to man number one, two, and three; he has a *permanent center of gravity* which consists in his ideas, in his valuation of the work, and in his relation to the school. In addition his psychic centers have already begun to be balanced; one center in him cannot have such a preponderance over others as is the case with people of the first three categories. He already begins to know himself and begins to know whither he is going.

"*Man number five* has already been crystallized; he cannot change as man number one, two, and three change. But it must be noted that man number five can be the result of right work and he can be the result of wrong work. He can become number five from number four and he can become number five *without having been four*. And in this case he cannot develop further, cannot become number six and seven. In order to become number six he must again melt his crystallized essence, must intentionally lose his being of man number five. And this can be achieved only through terrible sufferings. Fortunately these cases of wrong development occur very rarely.

"The division of man into seven categories, or seven numbers, explains thousands of things which otherwise cannot be understood. This division gives the first conception of *relativity* as applied to man. Things may be one thing or another thing according to the kind of man from whose point of view, or in relation to whom, they are taken.

"In accordance with this, all the inner and all the outer manifestations of man, all that belongs to man, and all that is created by him, is also divided into seven categories.

"It can now be said that there exists a knowledge number one, based upon imitation or upon instincts, or learned by heart, crammed or drilled into a man. Number one, if he is man number one in the full sense of the term, learns everything like a parrot or a monkey.

"The knowledge of man number two is merely the knowledge of what he likes; what he does not like he does not know. Always and in everything he wants something pleasant. Or, if he is a sick man, he will, on the contrary, know only what he dislikes, what repels him and what evokes in him fear, horror, and loathing.

"The knowledge of man number three is knowledge based upon subjectively logical thinking, upon words, upon literal understanding. It is the knowledge of bookworms, of scholastics. Men number three, for example, have counted how many times each letter of the Arabic alphabet is repeated in the Koran of Mohammed, and upon this have based a whole system of interpretation of the Koran.

"The knowledge of man number four is a very different kind of knowledge. It is knowledge which comes from man number five, who in turn receives it from man number six, who has received it from man number seven. But, of course, man number four assimilates of this knowledge only what is possible according to his powers. But, in comparison with man number one, man number two, and man number three, man number four has begun to get free from the subjective elements in his knowledge and to move along the path towards objective knowledge.

"The knowledge of man number five is whole, indivisible knowledge. He has now one indivisible I and *all* his knowledge belongs to this I. He cannot have one I that knows something which another does not know. What he knows, the whole of him knows. His knowledge is nearer to objective knowledge than the knowledge of man number four.

"The knowledge of man number six is the complete knowledge possible to man; but it can still be lost.

"The knowledge of man number seven is his own knowledge, which cannot be taken away from him; it is the *objective* and completely *practical* knowledge of *All.*

"It is exactly the same with being. There is the being of man number one, that is, the being of a man living by his instincts and his sensations; the being of man number two, that is to say, the being of the sentimental, the emotional man; the being of man number three, that is, the being of the rational, the theoretical man, and so on. It is quite clear why knowledge cannot be far away from being. Man number one, two, or three cannot, by reason of his being, possess the knowledge of man number four, man number five, and higher. Whatever you may give him, he may interpret it in his own way, he will reduce every idea to the level on which he is himself.

"The same order of division into seven categories must be applied to everything relating to man. There is art number one, that is the art of man number one, imitative, copying art, or crudely primitive and sensuous art such as the dances and music of savage peoples. There is art number two, sentimental art; art number three, intellectual, invented art; and there must be art number four, number five, and so on.

"In exactly the same way there exists the religion of man number one, that is to say, a religion consisting of rites, of external forms, of sacrifices and ceremonies of imposing splendor and brilliance, or, on the contrary, of a gloomy, cruel, and savage character, and so on. There is the religion of man number two; the religion of faith, love, adoration, impulse, enthusiasm, which soon becomes transformed into the religion of persecution, oppression, and extermination of 'heretics' and 'heathens.' There is the religion of man number three; the intellectual, theoretical religion of proofs and arguments, based upon logical deductions, considerations, and interpretations. Religions number one, number two, and number three are really the only ones we know; all known and existing religions and denominations in the world belong to one of these three categories. What the religion of man number four or the religion of man number five and so on is, we do not know, and we cannot know so long as we remain what we are.

"If instead of religion in general we take Christianity, then again there exists a Christianity number one, that is to say, paganism in the guise of Christianity. Christianity number two is an emotional religion, sometimes very pure but without force, sometimes full of bloodshed and horror leading to the Inquisition, to religious wars. Christianity number three, instances of which are afforded by various forms of Protestantism, is based upon dialectic, argument, theories, and so forth. Then there is Christianity number four, of which men number one, number two, and number three have no conception whatever.

"In actual fact Christianity number one, number two, and number three is simply external imitation. Only man number four strives to be a Christian and only man number five can actually be a Christian. For to be a Christian means to have the being of a Christian, that is, to live in accordance with Christ's precepts.

"Man number one, number two, and number three cannot live in accordance with Christ's precepts because with them everything 'happens.' Today it is one thing and tomorrow it is quite another thing. Today they are ready to give away their last shirt and tomorrow to tear a man to pieces becauses he refuses to give up his shirt to them. They are swayed by every chance event. They are not masters of themselves and therefore they cannot decide to be Christians and really be Christians.

"Science, philosophy, and all manifestations of man's life and activity can be divided in exactly the same way into seven categories. But the ordinary language in which people speak is very far from any such divisions, and this is why it is so difficult for people to understand one another.

"In analyzing the various subjective meanings of the word 'man' we have seen how varied and contradictory, and, above all, how concealed and unnoticeable even to the speaker himself are the meanings and the shades of meaning created by habitual associations that can be put into a word.

"Let us take some other word, for example, the term 'world.' Each man understands it in his own way, and each man in an entirely different way. Everyone when he hears or pronounces the word 'world' has associations entirely foreign and incomprehensible to another. Every 'conception of the world,' every habitual form of thinking, carries with it its own associations, its own ideas.

"In a man with a religious conception of the world, a Christian, the word 'world' will call up a whole series of religious ideas, will necessarily become connected with the idea of God, with the idea of the creation of the world or the end of the world, or of the 'sinful' world, and so on.

"For a follower of the Vedantic philosophy the world before anything else will be illusion, 'Maya.'

"A theosophist will think of the different 'planes,' the physical, the astral, the mental, and so on.

"A spiritualist will think of the world 'beyond,' the world of spirits.

"A physicist will look upon the world from the point of view of the structure of matter; it will be a world of molecules or atoms, or electrons.

"For the astronomer the world will be a world of stars and nebulae.

"And so on and so on. The phenomenal and the noumenal world, the world of the fourth and other dimensions, the world of good and the world of evil, the material world and the immaterial world, the proportion of power in the different nations of the world, can man be 'saved' in the world, and so on, and so on.

"People have thousands of different ideas about the world but not one general idea which would enable them to understand one another and to determine at once from what point of view they desire to regard the world.

"It is impossible to study a system of the universe without studying man. At the same time it is impossible to study man without studying the universe. Man is an image of the world. He was created by the same laws which created the whole of the world. By knowing and understanding himself he will know and understand the whole world, all the laws that create and govern the world. And at the same time by studying the world and the laws that govern the world he will learn and understand the laws that govern him. In this connection some laws are understood and assimilated more easily by studying the objective world, while man can only understand other laws by studying himself. The study of the world and the study of man must therefore run parallel, one helping the other.

"In relation to the term 'world' it is necessary to understand from the very outset that there are many worlds, and that we live not in one world, but in several worlds. This is not readily understood because in ordinary language the term 'world' is generally used in the singular. And if the plural 'worlds' is used it is merely to emphasize, as it were, the same idea, or to express the idea of various worlds existing parallel to one another. Our language does not have the idea of worlds contained one within another. And yet the idea that we live in different worlds precisely implies worlds contained one within another to which we stand in different relations.

"If we desire an answer to the question what is the world or worlds in which we live, we must first of all ask ourselves what it is that we may call 'world' in the most intimate and immediate relation to us.

"To this we may answer that we often give the name of 'world' to the world of people, to humanity, in which we live, of which we form part. But humanity forms an inseparable part of organic life on earth, therefore it would be right to say that the world nearest to us is *organic life on earth*, the world of plants, animals, and men.

"But organic life is also in the world. What then is 'world' for organic life?

"To this we can answer that for organic life our planet the earth is 'world.'

"But the earth is also in the world. What then is 'world' for the earth?

" 'World' for the earth is the planetary world of the solar system, of which it forms a part.

"What is 'world' for all the planets taken together? The sun, or the sphere of the sun's influence, or the solar system, of which the planets form a part.

"For the sun, in its turn, 'world' is our world of stars, or the Milky Way, an accumulation of a vast number of solar systems.

"Furthermore, from an astronomical point of view, it is quite possible to presume a multitude of worlds existing at enormous distances from one another in the space of 'all worlds.' These worlds taken together will be 'world' for the Milky Way.

"Further, passing to philosophical conclusions, we may say that 'all worlds' must form some, for us, incomprehensible and unknown *Whole* or *One* (as an apple is one). This Whole, or One, or *All*, which may be called the 'Absolute,' or the 'Independent' because, including everything within itself, it is not dependent upon anything, is 'world' for 'all worlds.' Logically it is quite possible to think of a state of things where All forms one single Whole. Such a whole will certainly be the Absolute, which means the Independent, because it, that is, the All, is infinite and indivisible.

"The Absolute, that is, the state of things when the All constitutes one Whole, is, as it were, the primordial state of things, out of which, by division and differentiation, arises the diversity of the phenomena observed by us.

"Man lives in all these worlds but in different ways.

"This means that he is first of all influenced by the *nearest* world, the one immediate to him, of which he forms a part. Worlds further away also influence man, directly as well as through other intermediate worlds, but their action is diminished in proportion to their remoteness or to the increase in the difference between them and man. As will be seen later, the *direct* influence of the Absolute does not reach man. But the influence of the next world and the influence of the star world are already perfectly clear in the life of man, although they are certainly unknown to science."

With this G. ended the lecture.

On the next occasion we had very many questions chiefly about the influences of the various worlds and why the influence of the Absolute does not reach us.

"Before examining these influences," began G., "and the laws of transformation of Unity into Plurality, we must examine the *fundamental law* that creates all phenomena in all the diversity or unity of all universes.

"This is the 'Law of Three' or the law of the *three principles* or the *three forces*. It consists of the fact that every phenomenon, on whatever scale and in whatever world it may take place, from molecular to cosmic phenomena, is the result of the combination or the meeting of three different and opposing forces. Contemporary thought realizes the existence of two forces and the necessity of these two forces for the production of a phenomenon: force and resistance, positive and negative magnetism, positive and negative electricity, male and female cells, and so on. But it does not observe even these two forces always and everywhere. No question has ever been raised as to the third, or if it has been raised it has scarcely been heard.

"According to real, exact knowledge, one force, or two forces, can never produce a phenomenon. The presence of a third force is necessary, for it is only with the help of a third force that the first two can produce what may be called a phenomenon, no matter in what sphere.

"The teaching of the three forces is at the root of all ancient systems. The first force may be called active or positive; the second, passive or negative; the third, neutralizing. But these are *merely names*, for in reality all three forces are equally active and appear as active, passive, and neutralizing, only at their meeting points, that is to say, *only in relation to one another at a given moment*. The first two forces are more or less comprehensible to man and the third may sometimes be discovered either at the point of application of the forces, or in the 'medium,' or in the 'result.' But, speaking in general, the third force is not easily accessible to direct observation and understanding. The reason for this is to be found in the functional limitations of man's ordinary psychological activity and in the fundamental categories of our perception of the phenomenal world, that is, in our sensation of space and time resulting from these limitations. People cannot perceive and observe the third force directly any more than they can spatially perceive the 'fourth dimension.'

"But by studying himself, the manifestations of his thought, consciousness, activity—his habits, his desires, and so on—man may learn to observe and to see in himself the action of the three forces. Let us suppose, for instance, that a man wants to work on himself in order to change certain of his characteristics, to attain a higher level of being. His desire, his initiative, is the active force. The inertia of all his habitual psychological life which shows opposition to his initiative will be the passive or the negative force. The two forces will either counterbalance one another, or one will completely conquer the other, but, at the same time, it will become too weak for any further action. Thus the two forces will, as it were, revolve one around the other, one absorbing the other and producing no result whatever. This may continue for a lifetime. A man may feel desire and initiative. But all this initiative may be absorbed in overcoming the habitual inertia of life, leaving nothing for the purpose towards which the initiative ought to be directed. And so it may go on until the third force makes its appearance, in the form, for instance, of *new knowledge,* showing at once the advantage or the necessity of work on oneself and, in this way, supporting and strengthening the initiative. Then the initiative, with the support of this third force, may conquer inertia and the man becomes active in the desired direction.

"Examples of the action of the three forces, and the moments of entry of the third force, may be discovered in all manifestations of our psychic life, in all phenomena of the life of human communities and of humanity as a whole, and in all the phenomena of nature around us.

"But at the beginning it is enough to understand the general principle: every phenomenon, of whatever magnitude it may be, is inevitably the manifestation of three forces; one or two forces cannot produce a phenomenon, and if we observe a stoppage in anything, or an endless hesitation at the same place, we can say that, at the given place, the third force is lacking. In trying to understand this it must be remembered at the same time that people cannot observe phenomena as manifestations of three forces because we cannot observe the objective world in our subjective states of consciousness. And in the subjectively observed phenomenal world we see in phenomena only the manifestation of one or two forces. If we could see the manifestation of three forces in every action, we should then see the world as it is (things in themselves). Only it must here be remembered that a phenomenon which appears to be simple may actually be very complicated, that is, it may be a very complex combination of trinities. But we know that we cannot observe the world as it is and this should help us to understand why we cannot see the third force. The third force is a property of the real world. The subjective or phenomenal world of our observation is only relatively real, at any rate it is not complete.

"Returning to the world in which we live we may now say that in the Absolute, as well as in everything else, three forces are active: the active, the passive, and the neutralizing. But since by its very nature everything in the Absolute constitutes one whole the three forces also constitute one whole. Moreover in forming one independent whole the three forces possess a full and independent will, full consciousness, full understanding of themselves and of everything they do.

"The idea of the unity of the three forces in the Absolute forms the basis of many ancient teachings—consubstantial and indivisible Trinity, Trimurti—Brahma, Vishnu, and Siva, and so on.

"The three forces of the Absolute, constituting one whole, separate and unite by their own will and by their own decision, and at the points of junction they create phenomena, or 'worlds.' These worlds, created by the will of the Absolute, depend entirely upon this will in everything that concerns their own existence. In each of these worlds the three forces again act. Since, however, each of these worlds is now not the whole, but only a part, then the three forces in them do not form a single whole. It is now a case of three wills, three consciousnesses, three unities. Each of the three forces contains within it the possibility of all three forces, but at the meeting point of the three forces each of them manifests only one principle—the active, the passive, or the neutralizing. The three forces together form a trinity which produces new phenomena. But this trinity is different, it is not that which was in the Absolute, where the three forces formed an indivisible whole and possessed one single will and one single consciousness. In the worlds of the second order the three forces are now divided and their meeting points are now of a different nature. In the Absolute the moment and the point of their meeting is determined by their single will. In the worlds of the second order, where there is no longer a single will but three wills, the points of issue are each determined by a separate will, independent of the others, and therefore the meeting point becomes accidental or mechanical. The will of the Absolute creates the worlds of the second order and governs them, but it does not govern their creative work, in which a mechanical element makes its appearance.

"Let us imagine the Absolute as a circle and in it a number of other circles, worlds of the second order. Let us take one of these circles. The Absolute is designated by the number 1, because the three forces constitute one whole in the Absolute, and the small circles we will designate by the number 3, because in a world of the second order the three forces are already divided.

"The three divided forces in the worlds of the second order, meeting together in each of these worlds, create new worlds of the third order. Let us take one of these worlds. The worlds of the third order, created by the three forces which act semi-mechanically, no longer depend upon the single will of the Absolute but upon three mechanical laws. These worlds are created by the three forces. And having been created they manifest three new forces of their own. Thus the number of forces acting in the worlds of the third order will be six. In the diagram the circle of the third order is designated by the number 6 (3 plus 3). In these worlds are created worlds of a new order, the fourth order. In the worlds of the fourth order there act three forces of the world of the second order, six forces of the world of the third order, and three of their own, twelve forces altogether. Let us take one of these worlds and designate it by the number 12 (3 plus 6 plus 3). Being subject to a greater number of laws these worlds stand still further away from the single will of the Absolute and are still more mechanical. The worlds created within these worlds will be governed by twenty-four forces (3 plus 6 plus 12 plus 3). The worlds created within these worlds will be governed by forty-eight forces, the number 48 being made up as follows: three forces of the world immediately following the Absolute, six of the next one, twelve of the next, twenty-four of the one after, and three of its own (3 plus 6 plus 12 plus 24 plus 3), forty-eight in all. Worlds created within worlds 48 will be governed by ninety-six forces (3 plus 6 plus 12 plus 24 plus 48 plus 3). The worlds of the next order, if there are any, will be governed by 192 forces, and so on.

"If we take one of the many worlds created in the Absolute, that is, world 3, it will be the world representing the total number of starry worlds similar to our Milky Way. If we take world 6, it will be one of the worlds created within this world, namely the accumulation of stars which we call the Milky Way. World 12 will be one of the suns that compose the Milky Way, our sun. World 24 will be the planetary world, that is to say, all the planets of the solar system. World 48 will be the earth. World 96 will be the moon. If the moon had a satellite it would be world 192, and so on.

"The chain of worlds, the links of which are the Absolute, all worlds, all suns, our sun, the planets, the earth, and the moon, forms the 'ray of creation' in which we find ourselves. The ray of creation is for us the 'world' in the widest sense of the term. Of course, the ray of creation does not include the 'world' in the full sense of the term, since the Absolute gives birth to a number, perhaps to an infinite number, of different worlds, each of which begins a new and separate ray of creation. Furthermore, each of these worlds contains a number of worlds representing a further breaking up of the ray and again of these worlds we select only one—our Milky Way; the Milky Way consists of a number of suns, but of this number we select one sun which is nearest to us, upon which we immediately depend, and in which we live and move and have our being. Each of the other suns means a new breaking up of the ray, but we cannot study these rays in the same way as our ray, that is, the ray in which we are situated. Further, within the solar system the planetary world is nearer to us than the sun itself, and within the planetary world the nearest of all to us is the earth, the planet on which we live. We have no need to study other planets in the same way as we study the earth, it is sufficient for us to take them all together, that is to say, on a considerably smaller scale than we take the earth.

"The number of forces in each world, 1, 3, 6, 12, and so on, indicates the number of laws to which the given world is subject.

"The fewer laws there are in a given world, the nearer it is to the will of the Absolute; the more laws there are in a given world, the greater the mechanicalness, the further it is from the will of the Absolute. We live in a world subject to forty-eight orders of laws, that is to say, very far from the will of the Absolute and in a very remote and dark corner of the universe.

"In this way the ray of creation helps us to determine and to realize our place in the world. But, as you see, we have not yet come to questions about influences. In order to understand the difference between the influences of various worlds we must better understand the law of three and then, further, still another fundamental law—the Law of Seven, or the *law of octaves*."

Chapter Five

"WE TAKE the three-dimensional universe and consider the world as a world of *matter* and *force* in the simplest and most elementary meaning of these terms. Higher dimensions and new theories of matter, space, and time, as well as other categories of knowledge of the world which are unknown to science, we will discuss later. At present it is necessary to represent the universe in the diagrammatic form of the 'ray of creation,' from the Absolute to the moon.

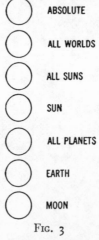

ABSOLUTE

ALL WORLDS

ALL SUNS

SUN

ALL PLANETS

EARTH

MOON

Fig. 3

"The 'ray of creation' seems at the first glance to be a very elementary plan of the universe, but actually, as one studies it further, it becomes clear that with the help of this simple plan it is possible to bring into accord, and to make into a single whole, a multitude of various and conflicting philosophical as well as religious and scientific views of the world. The idea of the ray of creation belongs to ancient knowledge and many of the naïve geocentric systems of the universe known to us are actually either incompetent expositions of the idea of the ray of creation or distortions of this idea due to literal understanding.

"It must be observed that the idea of the ray of creation and its growth from the Absolute contradicts some of the modern views, although not really scientific views. Take, for instance, the stage—sun, earth, moon. According to the usual understanding the moon is a cold, dead celestial body which was once like the earth, that is to say, it possessed internal heat and at a still earlier period was a molten mass like the sun. The earth, according to the usual views, was once like the sun, and is also gradually cooling down and, sooner or later, will become a frozen mass like the moon. It is usually supposed that the sun is also cooling down and that it will become, in time, similar to the earth and later on, to the moon.

"First of all, of course, it must be remarked that this view cannot be called 'scientific' in the strict sense of the term, because in science, that is, in astronomy, or rather, in astrophysics, there are many different and contradictory hypotheses and theories on the subject, none of which has any serious foundation. But this view is the one most widely spread and one which has become the view of the average man of modern times in regard to the world in which we live.

"The idea of the ray of creation and its growth from the Absolute contradicts these general views of our day.

"According to this idea the moon is still an unborn planet, one that is, so to speak, being born. It is becoming warm gradually and in time (given a favorable development of the ray of creation) it will become like the earth and have a satellite of its own, a new moon. A new link will have been added to the ray of creation. The earth, too, is not getting colder, it is getting warmer, and may in time become like the sun. We observe such a process for instance in the system of Jupiter, which is a sun for its satellites.

"Summing up all that has been said before about the ray of creation, from world 1 down to world 96, it must be added that the figures by which worlds are designated indicate the number of forces, or orders of laws, which govern the worlds in question. In the Absolute there is only one force and only one law—the single and independent will of the Absolute. In the next world there are three forces or three orders of laws. In the next there are six orders of laws; in the following one, twelve; and so on. In our world, that is, the earth, forty-eight orders of laws are operating to which we are subject and by which our whole life is governed. If we lived on the moon we should be subject to ninety-six orders of laws, that is, our life and activity would be still more mechanical and we should not have the possibilities of escape from mechanicalness that we now have.

"As has been said already, the will of the Absolute is only manifested in the immediate world created by it within itself, that is, in world 3; the immediate will of the Absolute does not reach world 6 and is manifested in it only in the form of mechanical laws. Further on, in worlds 12, 24, 48, and 96, the will of the Absolute has less and less possibility of manifesting itself. This means that in world 3 the Absolute creates, as it were, a general plan of all the rest of the universe, which is then further developed mechanically. The will of the Absolute cannot manifest itself in subsequent worlds apart from this plan, and, in manifesting itself in accordance with this plan, it takes the form of mechanical laws. This means that if the Absolute wanted to manifest its will, say, in our world, in opposition to the mechanical laws in operation there, it would then have to destroy all the worlds intermediate between itself and our world.

"The idea of a miracle in the sense of a violation of laws by the will which made them is not only contrary to common sense but to the very idea of will itself. A 'miracle' can only be a manifestation of laws which are unknown to men or rarely met with. A 'miracle' is the manifestation in this world of the laws of another world.

"On the earth we are very far removed from the will of the Absolute; we are separated from it by forty-eight orders of mechanical laws. If we could free ourselves from one half of these laws, we should find ourselves subject to only twenty-four orders of laws, that is, to the laws of the planetary world, and then we should be one stage nearer to the Absolute and its will. If we could then free ourselves from one half of these laws, we should be subject to the laws of the sun (twelve laws) and consequently one stage nearer still to the Absolute. If, again, we could free ourselves from half of these laws, we should be subject to the laws of the starry world and separated by only one stage from the immediate will of the Absolute.

"And the possibility for man thus gradually to free himself from mechanical laws exists.

"The study of the forty-eight orders of laws to which man is subject cannot be abstract like the study of astronomy; they can be studied only by observing them in oneself and by *getting free from them*. At the beginning a man must simply understand that he is quite needlessly subject to a thousand petty but irksome laws which have been created for him by other people and by himself. When he attempts to get free from them he will see that he cannot. Long and persistent attempts to gain freedom from them will convince him of his slavery. The laws to which man is subject can only be studied by struggling with them, by trying to get free from them. But a great deal of knowledge is needed in order to become free from one law without creating for oneself another in its place.

"The orders of laws and their forms vary according to the point of view from which we consider the ray of creation.

"In our system the end of the ray of creation, the growing end, so to speak, of the branch, is the moon. The energy for the growth, that is, for the development of the moon and for the formation of new shoots, goes to the moon from the earth, where it is created by the joint action of the sun, of all the other planets of the solar system, and of the earth itself. This energy is collected and preserved in a huge accumulator situated on the earth's surface. This accumulator is organic life on earth. Organic life on earth feeds the moon. Everything living on the earth, people, animals, plants, is food for the moon. The moon is a huge living being feeding upon all that lives and grows on the earth. The moon could not exist without organic life on earth, any more than organic life on earth could exist without the moon. Moreover, in relation to organic life the moon is a huge electromagnet. If the action of the electromagnet were suddenly to stop, organic life would crumble to nothing.

"The process of the growth and the warming of the moon is connected with life and death on the earth. Everything living sets free at its death a certain amount of the energy that has 'animated' it; this energy, or the 'souls' of everything living—plants, animals, people—is attracted to the moon as though by a huge electromagnet, and brings to it the warmth and the life upon which its growth depends, that is, the growth of the ray of creation. In the economy of the universe nothing is lost, and a certain energy having finished its work on one plane goes to another.

"The souls that go to the moon, possessing perhaps even a certain amount of consciousness and memory, find themselves there under ninety-six laws, in the conditions of mineral life, or to put it differently, in conditions from which there is no escape apart from a general evolution in immeasurably long planetary cycles. The moon is 'at the extremity,' at the end of the world; it is the 'outer darkness' of the Christian doctrine 'where there will be weeping and gnashing of teeth.'

"The influence of the moon upon everything living manifests itself in all that happens on the earth. The moon is the chief, or rather, the nearest, the immediate, motive force of all that takes place in organic life on the earth. All movements, actions, and manifestations of people, animals, and plants depend upon the moon and are controlled by the moon. The sensitive film of organic life which covers the earthly globe is entirely dependent upon the influence of the huge electromagnet that is sucking out its vitality. Man, like every other living being, cannot, in the ordinary conditions of life, tear himself free from the moon. All his movements and consequently all his actions are controlled by the moon. If he kills another man, the moon does it; if he sacrifices himself for others, the moon does that also. All evil deeds, all crimes, all self-sacrificing actions, all heroic exploits, as well as all the actions of ordinary everyday life, are controlled by the moon.

"The liberation which comes with the growth of mental powers and faculties is liberation from the moon. The mechanical part of our life depends upon the moon, is subject to the moon. If we develop in ourselves consciousness and will, and subject our mechanical life and all our mechanical manifestations to them, we shall escape from the power of the moon.

"The next idea which it is necessary to master is the materiality of the universe which is taken in the form of the ray of creation. Everything in this universe can be weighed and measured. The Absolute is as material, as weighable and measurable, as the moon, or as man. If the Absolute is God it means that God can be weighed and measured, resolved into component elements, 'calculated,' and expressed in the form of a definite formula.

"But the concept 'materiality' is as relative as everything else. If we recall how the concept 'man' and all that refers to him—good, evil, truth, falsehood, and so on—is divided into different categories ('man number one,' 'man number two,' and so on), it will be easy for us to understand that the concept 'world,' and everything that refers to the world, is also divided into different categories. The ray of creation establishes seven planes in the world, seven worlds one within another. Everything that refers to the world is also divided into seven categories, one category within another. The materiality of the Absolute is a materiality of an order different from that of 'all worlds.' The materiality of 'all worlds' is of an order different from the materiality of 'all suns.' The materiality of 'all suns' is of an order different from the materiality of our sun. The materiality of our sun is of an order different from the materiality of 'all planets.' The materiality of 'all planets' is of an order different from the materiality of the earth, and the materiality of the earth is of an order different from the materiality of the moon. This idea is at first difficult to grasp. People are accustomed to think that *matter* is everywhere the same. The whole of physics, of astrophysics, of chemistry, such methods as spectroanalysis, and so on, are based upon this assumption. And it is true that matter is the same, but materiality is different. And different degrees of materiality depend directly upon the qualities and properties of the energy manifested at a given point.

"Matter or substance necessarily presupposes the existence of force or energy. This does not mean that a dualistic conception of the world is necessary. The concepts of matter and force are as relative as everything else. In the Absolute, where all is one, matter and force are also one. But in this connection matter and force are not taken as real principles of the world in itself, but as properties or characteristics of the phenomenal world observed by us. To begin the study of the universe it is sufficient to have an elementary idea of matter and energy, such as we get by immediate observation through our organs of sense. The 'constant' is taken as material, as matter, and 'changes' in the state of the 'constant,' or of matter, are called manifestations of force or energy. All these changes can be regarded as the result of vibrations or undulatory motions which begin in the center, that is, in the Absolute, and go in all directions, crossing one another, colliding, and merging together, until they stop altogether at the end of the ray of creation.

"From this point of view, then, the world consists of vibrations and matter, or of matter in a state of vibration, of vibrating matter. The rate of vibration is in inverse ratio to the density of matter.

"In the Absolute vibrations are the most rapid and matter is the least dense. In the next world vibrations are slower and matter denser; and further on matter is still more dense and vibrations correspondingly slower.

"'Matter' may be regarded as consisting of 'atoms.' Atoms in this connection are taken also as the result of the final division of matter. In every order of matter they are simply certain small *particles* of the given matter which are indivisible only on the given plane. The atoms of the Absolute alone are really indivisible, the atom of the next plane, that is, of world 3, consists of three atoms of the Absolute or, in other words, it is three times bigger and three times heavier, and its movements are correspondingly slower. The atom of world 6 consists of six atoms of the Absolute merged together, as it were, and forming one atom. Its movements are correspondingly slower. The atom of the next world consists of twelve primordial particles, and of the next worlds, of twenty-four, forty-eight, and ninety-six. The atom of world 96 is of an enormous size compared with the atom of world 1; its movements are correspondingly slower, and the matter which is made up of such atoms is correspondingly denser.

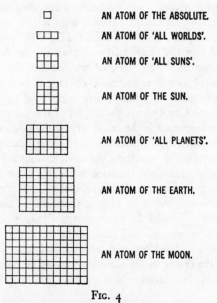

□ AN ATOM OF THE ABSOLUTE.

AN ATOM OF 'ALL WORLDS'.

AN ATOM OF 'ALL SUNS'.

AN ATOM OF THE SUN.

AN ATOM OF 'ALL PLANETS'.

AN ATOM OF THE EARTH.

AN ATOM OF THE MOON.

FIG. 4

"The seven worlds of the ray of creation represent seven orders of materiality. The materiality of the moon is different from the materiality of the earth; the materiality of the earth is different from the materiality of the planetary world; the materiality of the planetary world is different from the materiality of the sun, and so on.

"Thus instead of one concept of matter we have seven kinds of matter, but our ordinary conception of materiality only with difficulty embraces the materiality of worlds 96 and 48. The matter of world 24 is much too rarefied to be regarded as matter from the scientific point of view of our physics and chemistry; such matter is practically hypothetical. The still finer matter of world 12 has, for ordinary investigation, no characteristics of materiality at all. All these matters belonging to the various orders of the universe are not separated into layers but are intermixed, or, rather, they interpenetrate one another. We can get an idea of similar interpenetration of matters of different densities from the penetration of one matter by another matter of different densities known to us. A piece of wood may be saturated with water, water may in its turn be filled with gas. Exactly the same relation between different kinds of matter may be observed in the whole of the universe: the finer matters permeate the coarser ones.

"Matter that possesses characteristics of materiality comprehensible to us is divided for us into several states according to its density: solid, liquid, gaseous; further gradations of matter are: radiant energy, that is, electricity, light, magnetism; and so on. But on every plane, that is to say, in every order of materiality, similar relations and divisions of the various states of a given matter may be found; but, as has been already said, matter of a higher plane is not material at all for the lower planes.

"All the matter of the world that surrounds us, the food that we eat, the water that we drink, the air that we breathe, the stones that our houses are built of, our own bodies—everything is permeated by all the matters that exist in the universe. There is no need to study or investigate the sun in order to discover the matter of the solar world: this matter exists in ourselves and is the result of the division of our atoms. In the same way we have in us the matter of all other worlds. Man is, in the full sense of the term, a 'miniature universe'; in him are all the matters of which the universe consists; the same forces, the same laws that govern the life of the universe, operate in him; therefore in studying man we can study the whole world, just as in studying the world we can study man.

"But a complete parallel between man and the world can only be drawn if we take 'man' in the full sense of the word, that is, a man whose inherent powers are developed. An undeveloped man, a man who has not completed the course of his evolution, cannot be taken as a complete picture or plan of the universe—he is an unfinished world.

"As has been said already, the study of oneself must go side by side with the study of the fundamental laws of the universe. The laws are the same everywhere and on all planes. But the very same laws manifesting themselves in different worlds, that is, under different conditions, produce different phenomena. The study of the relation of laws to the planes upon which they are manifested brings us to the study of *relativity*.

"The idea of relativity occupies a very important place in this teaching, and, later on, we shall return to it. But before anything else it is necessary to understand the relativity of each thing and of each manifestation *according to the place* it occupies in the cosmic order.

"We are on the earth and we depend entirely upon the laws that are operating on the earth. The earth is a very bad place from the cosmic point of view—it is like the most remote part of northern Siberia, very far from everywhere, it is cold, life is very hard. Everything that in another place either comes by itself or is easily obtained, is here acquired only by hard labor; everything must be fought for both in life and in the work. In life it still happens sometimes that a man gets a legacy and afterwards lives without doing anything. But such a thing does not happen in the work. All are equal and all are equally beggars.

"Returning to the law of three, one must learn to find the manifestations of this law in everything we do and in everything we study. The application of this law in any sphere at once reveals much that is new, much that we did not see before. Take chemistry, for instance. Ordinary science does not know of the law of three and it studies matter without taking into consideration its cosmic properties. But besides ordinary chemistry there exists another, a special chemistry, or alchemy if you like, which studies matter taking into consideration its cosmic properties. As has been said before, the cosmic properties of each substance are determined first *by its place*, and secondly by the force which is acting through it at the given moment. Even in the same place the nature of a given substance undergoes a great change dependent upon the force which is being manifested through it. Each substance can be the conductor of any one of the three forces and, in accordance with this, it can be *active, passive,* or *neutralizing*. And it can be neither the first, nor the second, nor the third, if no force is manifesting through it at the given moment or if it is taken without relation to the manifestation of forces. In this way every substance appears, as it were, in four different aspects or states. In this connection it must be noted that when we speak of matter we do not speak of chemical elements. The special chemistry of which I speak looks upon every substance having a separate function, even the most complex, as an element. In this way only is it possible to study the cosmic properties of matter, because all complex compounds have their own cosmic purpose and significance. From this point of view an atom of a given substance is the smallest amount of the given substance which retains all its chemical, physical, and *cosmic* properties. Consequently the size of the 'atom' of different substances is not the same. And in some cases an 'atom' may be a particle even visible to the naked eye.

"The four aspects or states of every substance have definite names.

"When a substance is the conductor of the first or the active force, it is called 'carbon,' and, like the carbon of chemistry, it is designated by the letter C.

"When a substance is the conductor of the second or the passive force, it is called 'oxygen,' and, like the oxygen of chemistry, it is designated by the letter O.

"When a substance is the conductor of the third or neutralizing force, it is called 'nitrogen,' and, like the nitrogen of chemistry, it is designated by the letter N.

"When a substance is taken without relation to the force manifesting itself through it, it is called 'hydrogen,' and, like the hydrogen of chemistry, it is designated by the letter H.

"The active, the passive, and the neutralizing forces are designated by the figures 1, 2, 3, and the substances by the letters C, O, N, and H. These designations must be understood."

"Do these four elements correspond to the old four alchemical elements, fire, air, water, earth?" asked one of us.

"Yes, they do correspond," said G., "but we will use these. You will understand why afterwards."

What I heard interested me very much for it connected G.'s system with the system of the Tarot, which had seemed to me at one time to be a possible key to hidden knowledge. Moreover it showed me a relation of *three* to *four* which was new to me and which I had not been able to understand from the Tarot. The Tarot is definitely constructed upon the *law of four principles*. Until now G. had spoken only of the *law of three principles*. But now I saw how *three* passed into *four* and understood the necessity for this division so long as the division of *force* and *matter* exists for our immediate observation. "Three" referred to force and "four" referred to matter. Of course, the further meaning of this was still obscure for me, but even the little that G. said promised a great deal for the future.

In addition I was very interested in the names of the elements: "carbon," "oxygen," "nitrogen," and "hydrogen." I must here remark that although G. had definitely promised to explain precisely why these names were taken and not others, he never did so. Later on I shall return once again to these names. Attempts to establish the origin of these names explained to me a great deal concerning the whole of G.'s system as well as its history.

✦

At one of the meetings, to which a fairly large number of new people had been invited who had not heard G. before, he was asked the question: "Is man immortal or not?"

"I shall try to answer this question," said G., "but I warn you that this cannot be done fully enough with the material to be found in ordinary knowledge and in ordinary language.

"You ask whether man is immortal or not.

"I shall answer, Both yes and no.

"This question has many different sides to it. First of all what does *immortal* mean? Are you speaking of absolute immortality or do you admit different degrees? If for instance after the death of the body something remains which lives for some time preserving its consciousness, can this be called immortality or not? Or let us put it this way: how long a period of such existence is necessary for it to be called immortality? Then does this question include the possibility of a different 'immortality' for different people? And there are still many other different questions. I am saying this only in order to show how vague they are and how easily such words as 'immortality' can lead to illusion. In actual fact nothing is immortal, even God is mortal. But there is a great difference between man and God, and, of course, God is mortal in a different way to man. It would be much better if for the word 'immortality' we substitute the words '*existence after death.*' Then I will answer that man has the possibility of existence after death. But *possibility* is one thing and the realization of the possibility is quite a different thing.

"Let us now try to see what this possibility depends upon and what its realization means."

Then G. repeated briefly all that had been said before about the structure of man and the world. He drew the diagram of the ray of creation and the diagram of the four bodies of man [see Figs. 1, 3]. But in relation to the bodies of man he introduced a detail which we had not had before.

He again used the Eastern comparison of man with a carriage, horse, driver, and master, and drew the diagram with one addition that was not there before.

"Man is a complex organization," he said, "consisting of four parts which may be connected or unconnected, or badly connected. The carriage is connected with the horse by shafts, the horse is connected with the driver by reins, and the driver is connected with the master by the master's voice. But the driver must hear and understand the master's voice. He must know how to drive and the horse must be trained to obey the reins. As to the relation between the horse and the carriage, the horse must be properly harnessed. Thus there are three connections between the four sections of this complex organization [see Fig. 5b]. If something is lacking in one of the connections, the organization cannot act as a single whole. The connections are therefore no less important than the actual 'bodies.' Working on himself man works simultaneously on the 'bodies' and on the 'connections.' But it is different work.

"Work on oneself must begin with the driver. The driver is the mind. In order to be able to hear the master's voice, the driver, first of all, must *not be asleep*, that is, he must wake up. Then it may prove that the master speaks a language that the driver does not understand. The driver must learn this language. When he has learned it, he will understand the master. But concurrently with this he must learn to drive the horse, to harness it to the carriage, to feed and groom it, and to keep the carriage in order—because what would be the use of his understanding the master if he is not in a position to do anything? The master tells him to go yonder. But he is unable to move, because the horse has not been fed, it is not harnessed, and he does not know where the reins are. The horse is our emotions. The carriage is the body. The mind must learn to control the emotions. The emotions always pull the body after them. This is the order in which work on oneself must proceed. But observe again that work on the 'bodies,' that is, on the driver, the horse, and the carriage, is one thing. And work on the 'connections'—that is, on the 'driver's understanding,' which unites him to the master; on the 'reins,' which connect him with the horse; and on the 'shafts' and the 'harness,' which connect the horse with the carriage—is quite another thing.

"It sometimes happens that the bodies are quite good and in order, but that the 'connections' are not working. What then is the use of the whole organization? Just as in the case of undeveloped bodies, the whole organization is inevitably controlled from *below*, that is, not by the will of the master, but by accident.

"In a man with two bodies the second body is active in relation to the physical body; this means that the consciousness in the 'astral body' may have power over the physical body."

G. put a plus over the 'astral body' and a minus over the physical. [See Fig. 5c.]

"In a man with three bodies, the third or 'mental body' is active in relation to the 'astral body' and to the physical body; this means that the consciousness in the 'mental body' has complete power over the 'astral body' and over the physical body."

G. put a plus over the 'mental body' and a minus over the 'astral' and the physical bodies, bracketed together.

"In a man with four bodies the active body is the fourth. This means that the consciousness in the fourth body has complete power over the 'mental,' the 'astral,' and the physical bodies."

G. put a plus over the fourth body and a minus over the other three bracketed together.

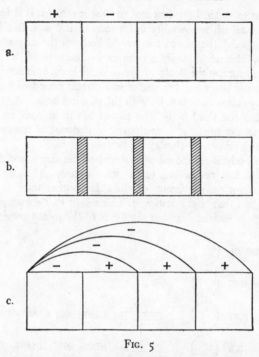

FIG. 5

"As you see," he said, "there exist four quite different situations. In one case all the functions are controlled by the physical body. It is active; in relation to it everything else is passive. [See Fig. 5a.] In another case the second body has power over the physical. In the third case the 'mental' body has power over the 'astral' and the physical. And in the last case the fourth body has power over the first three. We have seen before that in man of physical body only, exactly the same order of relationship is possible between his various functions. The physical functions may control feeling, thought, and consciousness. Feeling may control the physical functions. Thought may control the physical functions and feeling. And *consciousness* may control the physical functions, feeling, and thought.

"In man of two, three, and four bodies, the most active body also lives the longest, that is, it is 'immortal' in relation to a lower body."

He again drew the diagram of the ray of creation and by the side of earth he placed the physical body of man.

"This is ordinary man," he said, "man number one, two, three, and four. He has only the physical body. The physical body dies and nothing is left of it. The physical body is composed of earthly material and at death it returns to earth. *It is dust and to dust it returns.* It is impossible to talk of any kind of 'immortality' for a man of this sort. But if a man has the second body" (he placed the second body on the diagram parallel to the planets), "this second body is composed of material of the planetary world and it can survive the death of the physical body. It is not immortal in the full sense of the word, because after a certain period of time it also dies. But at any rate it does not die with the physical body.

"If a man has the third body" (he placed the third body on the diagram parallel to the sun), "it is composed of material of the sun and it can exist after the death of the 'astral' body.

"The fourth body is composed of material of the *starry world*, that is, of material that does not belong to the solar system, and therefore, if it has crystallized within the limits of the solar system there is nothing within this system that could destroy it. *This means that a man possessing the fourth body is immortal within the limits of the solar system.* [Fig. 6.]

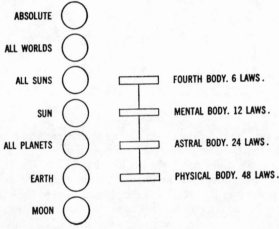

ABSOLUTE	◯		
ALL WORLDS	◯		
ALL SUNS	◯	▭	FOURTH BODY. 6 LAWS.
SUN	◯	▭	MENTAL BODY. 12 LAWS.
ALL PLANETS	◯	▭	ASTRAL BODY. 24 LAWS.
EARTH	◯	▭	PHYSICAL BODY. 48 LAWS.
MOON	◯		

Fig. 6

"You see, therefore, why it is impossible to answer at once the question: Is man immortal or not? One man is immortal, another is not, a third tries to become immortal, a fourth considers himself immortal and is, therefore, simply a lump of flesh."

When G. went to Moscow our permanent group met without him.

There remain in my memory several talks in our group which were connected with what we had recently heard from G.

We had many talks about the idea of miracles, and about the fact that the Absolute cannot manifest its will in our world and that this will manifests itself only in the form of mechanical laws and cannot manifest itself by violating these laws.

I do not remember which of us was first to remember a well-known, though not very respectful school story, in which we at once saw an illustration of this law.

The story is about an over-aged student of a seminary who, at a final examination, does not understand the idea of God's omnipotence.

"Well, give me an example of something that the Lord cannot do," said the examining bishop.

"It won't take long to do that, your Eminence," answered the seminarist. "Everyone knows that even the Lord himself cannot beat the ace of trumps with the ordinary deuce."

Nothing could be more clear.

There was more sense in this silly story than in a thousand theological treatises. The laws of a game make the essence of the game. A violation of these laws would destroy the entire game. The Absolute can as little interfere in our life and substitute other results in the place of the natural results of causes created by us, or created accidentally, as he can beat the ace of trumps with the deuce. Turgenev wrote somewhere that all ordinary prayers can be reduced to one: "Lord, make it so that twice two be not four." This is the same thing as the ace of trumps of the seminarist.

Another talk was about the moon and its relation to organic life on earth. And again one of our group found a very good example showing the relation of the moon to organic life.

The moon is the weight on a clock. Organic life is the mechanism of the clock brought into motion by the weight. The gravity of the weight, the pull of the chain on the cogwheel, set in motion the wheels and the hands of the clock. If the weight is removed all movements in the mechanism of the clock will at once stop. The moon is a colossal weight hanging on to organic life and thus setting it in motion. Whatever we may be doing, whether it is good or bad, clever or stupid, all the movements of the wheels and the hands of our organism depend upon this weight, which is continually exerting its pressure upon us.

Personally I was very interested in the question of relativity in connection with *place*, that is, with place in the world. I had long since come to the idea of a relativity dependent upon the interrelation of sizes and velocities. But the idea of *place*, in the cosmic order, was entirely new both to me and to all the others. How strange it was for me when, some time later, I became convinced that it was the same thing, in other words, that size and velocity determined the *place* and the *place* determined size and velocity.

I remember yet another talk that took place during the same period. Someone asked him about the possibility of a *universal language*—in what connection I do not remember.

"A universal language is possible," said G., "only people will never invent it."

"Why not?" asked one of us.

"First because it was invented a long time ago," answered G., "and second because to understand this language and to express ideas in it depends not only upon the knowledge of this language, but also on *being*. I will say even more. There exists not one, but three universal languages. The first of them can be spoken and written while remaining within the limits of one's own language. The only difference is that when people speak in their ordinary language they do not understand one another, but in this other language they do understand. In the second language, written language is the same for all peoples, like, say, figures or mathematical formulae; but people still speak their own language, yet each of them understands the other even though the other speaks in an unknown language. The third language is the same for all, both the written and the spoken. The difference of language disappears altogether on this level."

"Is not this the same thing which is described in the Acts as the descent of the Holy Ghost upon the Apostles, when they began to understand divers languages?" asked someone.

I noticed that such questions always irritated G.

"I don't know, I wasn't there," he said.

But on other occasions some opportune question led to new and unexpected explanations.

Someone asked him on one occasion during a talk whether there was anything real and leading to some end in the teachings and rites of existing religions.

"Yes and no," said G. "Imagine that we are sitting here talking of religions and that the maid Masha hears our conversation. She, of course, understands it in her own way and she repeats what she has understood to the porter Ivan. The porter Ivan again understands it in his own way and he repeats what he has understood to the coachman Peter next door. The coachman Peter goes to the country and recounts in the village what the gentry talk about in town. Do you think that what he recounts will at all resemble what we said? This is precisely the relation between existing religions and that which was their basis. You get teachings, traditions, prayers, rites, not at fifth but at twenty-fifth hand, and, of course, almost everything has been distorted beyond recognition and everything essential forgotten long ago.

"For instance, in all the denominations of Christianity a great part is played by the tradition of the Last Supper of Christ and his disciples. Liturgies and a whole series of dogmas, rites, and sacraments are based upon it. This has been a ground for schism, for the separation of churches, for the formation of sects; how many people have perished because they would not accept this or that interpretation of it. But, as a matter of fact, nobody understands what this was precisely, or what was done by Christ and his disciples that evening. There exists no explanation that even approximately resembles the truth, because what is written in the Gospels has been, in the first place, much distorted in being copied and translated; and secondly, it was written *for those who know*. To those who do not know it can explain nothing, but the more they try to understand it, the deeper they are led into error.

"To understand what took place at the Last Supper it is first of all necessary to know certain laws.

"You remember what I said about the 'astral body'? Let us go over it briefly. People who have an 'astral body' can communicate with one another at a distance without having recourse to ordinary physical means. But for such communication to be possible they must establish some 'connection' between them. For this purpose when going to different places or different countries people sometimes take with them something belonging to another, especially things that have been in contact with his body and are permeated with his emanations, and so on. In the same way, in order to maintain a connection with a dead person, his friends used to keep objects which had belonged to him. These things leave, as it were, a *trace* behind them, something like invisible wires or threads which remain stretched out through space. These threads connect a given object with the person, living or in certain cases dead, to whom the object belonged. Men have known this from the remotest antiquity and have made various uses of this knowledge.

"Traces of it may be found among the customs of many peoples. You know, for instance, that several nations have the custom of *blood-brotherhood*. Two men, or several men, mix their blood together in the same cup and then drink from this cup. After that they are regarded as *brothers by blood*. But the origin of this custom lies deeper. In its origin it was a magical ceremony for establishing a connection between 'astral bodies.' Blood has special qualities. And certain peoples, for instance the Jews, ascribed a special significance of magical properties to blood. Now, you see, if a connection between 'astral bodies' had been established, then again according to the beliefs of certain nations it is not broken by death.

"Christ knew that he must die. It had been decided thus beforehand. He knew it and his disciples knew it. And each one knew what part he had to play. But at the same time they wanted to establish a permanent link with Christ. And for this purpose he gave them his blood to drink and his flesh to eat. It was not bread and wine at all, but real flesh and real blood.

"The Last Supper was a *magical ceremony* similar to 'blood-brotherhood' for establishing a connection between 'astral bodies.' But who is there who knows about this in existing religions and who understands what it means? All this has been long forgotten and everything has been given quite a different meaning. The words have remained but their meaning has long been lost."

This lecture and particularly its ending provoked a great deal of talk in our groups. Many were repelled by what G. said about Christ and the Last Supper; others, on the contrary, felt in this a *truth* which they never could have reached by themselves.

Chapter Six

ONE of the next lectures began with a question asked by one of those present: *What was the aim of his teaching?*

"I certainly have an aim of my own," said G. "But you must permit me to keep silent about it. At the present moment my aim cannot have any meaning for you, because it is important that you should define your own aim. *The teaching by itself cannot pursue any definite aim.* It can only show the best way for men to attain whatever aims they may have. The question of aim is a very important question. Until a man has defined his own aim for himself he will not be able even to begin 'to do' anything. How is it possible 'to do' anything without having an aim? Before anything else 'doing' presupposes an aim."

"But the question of the aim of existence is one of the most difficult of philosophical questions," said one of those present. "You want us to begin by solving this question. But perhaps we have come here because we are seeking an answer to this question. You expect us to have known it beforehand. If a man knows this, he really knows everything."

"You misunderstood me," said G. "I was not speaking of the philosophical significance of the aim of existence. Man does not know it and he cannot know it so long as he remains what he is, first of all, because there is not one but many aims of existence. On the contrary, attempts to answer this question using ordinary methods are utterly hopeless and useless. I was asking about an entirely different thing. I was asking about your *personal* aim, about what *you* want to attain, and not about the reason for your existence. Everyone must have his own aim: one man wants riches, another health, a third wants the kingdom of heaven, the fourth wants to be a general, and so on. It is about aims of this sort that I am asking. If you tell me what your aim is, I shall be able to tell you whether we are going along the same road or not.

"Think of how you formulated your own aim to yourselves before you came here."

"I formulated my own aim quite clearly several years ago," I said. "I said to myself then that I want *to know the future.* Through a theoretical study of the question I came to the conclusion that the future *can* be known, and several times I was even successful in experiments in knowing the exact future. I concluded from this that we ought, and that we have a right, to know the future, and that until we do know it we shall not be able to organize our lives. A great deal was connected for me with this question. I considered, for instance, that a man can know, and has a right to know, exactly how much time is left to him, how much time he has at his disposal, or, in other words, he can and has a right to know the day and hour of his death. I always thought it humiliating for a man to live without knowing this and I decided at one time not to begin doing anything in any sense whatever until I did know it. For what is the good of beginning any kind of work when one doesn't know whether one will have time to finish it or not?"

"Very well," said G., "to know the future is the first aim. Who else can formulate his aim?"

"I should like to be convinced that I shall go on existing after the death of the physical body, or, if this depends upon me, I should like to work in order to exist after death," said one of the company.

"I don't care whether I know the future or not, or whether I am certain or not certain of life after death," said another, "if I remain what I am now. What I feel most strongly is that I am not master of myself, and if I were to formulate my aim, I should say that I want to be *master of myself*."

"I should like to understand the teaching of Christ, and to be a Christian in the true sense of the term," said the next.

"I should like to be able to *help people*," said another.

"I should like to know how to stop wars," said another.

"Well, that's enough," said G., "we have now sufficient material to go on with. The best formulation of those that have been put forward is the wish to be one's own master. Without this nothing else is possible and without this nothing else will have any value. But let us begin with the first question, or the first aim.

"In order to know the future it is necessary first to know the present in all its details, as well as to know the past. Today is what it is because yesterday was what it was. And if today is like yesterday, tomorrow will be like today. If you want tomorrow to be different, you must make today different. If today is simply a consequence of yesterday, tomorrow will be a consequence of today in exactly the same way. And if one has studied thoroughly what happened yesterday, the day before yesterday, a week ago, a year, ten years ago, one can say unmistakably what will and what will not happen tomorrow. But at present we have not sufficient material at our disposal to discuss this question seriously. What happens or may happen to us may depend upon three causes: upon accident, upon fate, or upon our own will. Such as we are, we are almost wholly dependent upon accident. We can have no fate in the real sense of the word any more than we can have will. If we had will, then through this alone we should know the future, because we should then make our future, and make it such as we want it to be. If we had fate, we could also know the future, because fate corresponds to type. If the type is known, then its fate can be known, that is, both the past and the future. But accidents cannot be foreseen. Today a man is one, tomorrow he is different: today one thing happens to him, tomorrow another."

"But are you not able to foresee what is going to happen to each of us," somebody asked, "that is to say, foretell what result each of us will reach in work on himself and whether it is worth his while to begin work?"

"It is impossible to say," said G. "One can only foretell the future for *men*. It is impossible to foretell the future for *mad machines*. Their direction changes every moment. At one moment a machine of this kind is going in one direction and you can calculate where it can get to, but five minutes later it is already going in quite a different direction and all your calculations prove to be wrong. Therefore, before talking about knowing the future, one must know whose future is meant. If a man wants to know his own future he must first of all know himself. Then he will see whether it is worth his while to know the future. Sometimes, maybe, it is better not to know it.

"It sounds paradoxical but we have every right to say that we know our future. It will be exactly the same as our past has been. Nothing can change of itself.

"And in practice, in order to study the future one must learn to notice and to remember the moments when we really know the future and when we act in accordance with this knowledge. Then judging by results, it will be possible to demonstrate that we really do know the future. This happens in a simple way in business, for instance. Every good commercial businessman knows the future. If he does not know the future his business goes smash. In work on oneself one must be a good businessman, a good merchant. And knowing the future is worth while only when a man can be his own master.

"There was a question here about the future life, about how to create it, how to avoid final death, how not to die.

"For this it is necessary 'to be.' If a man is changing every minute, if there is nothing in him that can withstand external influences, it means that there is nothing in him that can withstand death. But if he becomes independent of external influences, if there appears in him something that can live *by itself*, this something may not die. In ordinary circumstances we die every moment. External influences change and we change with them, that is, many of our I's die. If a man develops in himself a permanent I that can survive a change in external conditions, it can survive the death of the physical body. The whole secret is that one cannot work for a future life without working for this one. In working for life a man works for death, or rather, for immortality. Therefore work for immortality, if one may so call it, cannot be separated from general work. In attaining the one, a man attains the other. A man may strive *to be* simply for the sake of his own life's interests. Through this alone he may become immortal. We do not speak specially of a future life and we do not study whether it exists or not, because the laws are everywhere the same. In studying his own life as he knows it, and the lives of other men, from birth to death, a man is studying all the laws which govern life and death and immortality. If he becomes the master of his life, he may become the master of his death.

"Another question was *how to become a Christian*.

"First of all it is necessary to understand that a Christian is not a man who calls himself a Christian or whom others call a Christian. A Christian is one who lives in accordance with Christ's precepts. Such as we are we cannot be Christians. In order to be Christians we must be able 'to do.' We cannot do; with us everything 'happens.' Christ says: 'Love your enemies,' but how can we love our enemies when we cannot even love our friends? Sometimes 'it loves' and sometimes 'it does not love.' Such as we are we cannot even really desire to be Christians because, again, sometimes 'it desires' and sometimes 'it does not desire.' And one and the same thing cannot be desired for long, because suddenly, instead of desiring to be a Christian, a man remembers a very good but very expensive carpet that he has seen in a shop. And instead of wishing to be a Christian he begins to think how he can manage to buy this carpet, forgetting all about Christianity. Or if somebody else does not believe what a wonderful Christian he is, he will be ready to eat him alive or to roast him on hot coals. In order to be a good Christian one must *be*. To be means to be master of oneself. If a man is not his own master he has nothing and can have nothing. And he cannot be a Christian. He is simply a machine, an automaton. A machine cannot be a Christian. Think for yourselves, is it possible for a motorcar or a typewriter or a gramophone to be Christian? They are simply things which are controlled by chance. They are not responsible. They are machines. To be a Christian means to be responsible. Responsibility comes later when a man even partially ceases to be a machine, and begins in fact, and not only in words, to desire to be a Christian."

"What is the relation of the teaching you are expounding to Christianity as we know it?" asked somebody present.

"I do not know what you know about *Christianity*," answered G., emphasizing this word. "It would be necessary to talk a great deal and to talk for a long time in order to make clear what you understand by this term. But for the benefit of those who know already, I will say that, if you like, *this is esoteric Christianity*. We will talk in due course about the meaning of these words. At present we will continue to discuss our questions.

"Of the desires expressed the one which is most right is the desire to be *master of oneself*, because without this nothing else is possible. And in comparison with this desire all other desires are simply childish dreams, desires of which a man could make no use even if they were granted to him.

"It was said, for instance, that somebody wanted to help people. In order to be able to *help people* one must first learn to help oneself. A great number of people become absorbed in thoughts and feelings about helping others simply out of laziness. They are too lazy to work on themselves; and at the same time it is very pleasant for them to think that they are able to help others. This is being false and insincere with oneself. If a man looks at himself as he really is, he will not begin to think of helping other people: he will be ashamed to think about it. Love of mankind, altruism, are all very fine words, but they only have meaning when a man is able, of his own choice and of his own decision, to love or not to love, to be an altruist or an egoist. Then his choice has a value. But if there is no choice at all, if he cannot be different, if he is only such as chance has made or is making him, an altruist today, an egoist tomorrow, again an altruist the day after tomorrow, then there is no value in it whatever. In order to help others one must first learn to be an egoist, a conscious egoist. Only a conscious egoist can help people. Such as we are we can do nothing. A man decides to be an egoist but gives away his last shirt instead. He decides to give away his last shirt, but instead, he strips of his last shirt the man to whom he meant to give his own. Or he decides to give away his own shirt but gives away somebody else's and is offended if somebody refuses to give him his shirt so that he may give it to another. This is what happens most often. And so it goes on.

"And above all, in order to do what is difficult, one must first learn to do what is easy. One cannot begin with the most difficult.

"There was a question about *war. How to stop wars?* Wars cannot be stopped. War is the result of the slavery in which men live. Strictly speaking men are not to blame for war. War is due to cosmic forces, to planetary influences. But in men there is no resistance whatever against these influences, and there cannot be any, because men are slaves. If they were *men* and were capable of 'doing,' they would be able to resist these influences and refrain from killing one another."

"But surely those who realize this can do something?" said the man who had asked the question about war. "If a sufficient number of men came to a definite conclusion that there should be no war, could they not influence others?"

"Those who dislike war have been trying to do so almost since the creation of the world," said G. "And yet there has never been such a war as the present. Wars are not decreasing, they are increasing and war cannot be stopped by ordinary means. All these theories about universal peace, about peace conferences, and so on, are again simply laziness and hypocrisy. Men do not want to think about themselves, do not want to work on themselves, but think of how to make other people do what they want. If a sufficient number of people who wanted to stop war really did gather together they would first of all begin by making war upon those who disagreed with them. And it is still more certain that they would make war on people who also want to stop wars but in another way. And so they would fight. Men are what they are and they cannot be different. War has many causes that are unknown to us. Some causes are in men themselves, others are outside them. One must begin with the causes that are in man himself. How can he be independent of the external influences of great cosmic forces when he is the slave of everything that surrounds him? He is controlled by everything around him. If he becomes free from things, he may then become free from planetary influences.

"Freedom, liberation, this must be the aim of man. To become free, to be liberated from slavery: this is what a man ought to strive for when he becomes even a little conscious of his position. There is nothing else for him, and nothing else is possible so long as he remains a slave both inwardly and outwardly. But he cannot cease to be a slave outwardly while he remains a slave inwardly. Therefore in order to become free, man must gain inner freedom.

"The first reason for man's inner slavery is his ignorance, and above all, his ignorance of himself. Without self-knowledge, without understanding the working and functions of his machine, man cannot be free, he cannot govern himself and he will always remain a slave, and the plaything of the forces acting upon him.

"This is why in all ancient teachings the first demand at the beginning of the way to liberation was: 'Know thyself.'

"We shall speak of these words now."

The next lecture began precisely with the words: "*Know thyself*."

"These words," said G., "which are generally ascribed to Socrates, actually lie at the basis of many systems and schools far more ancient than the Socratic. But although modern thought is aware of the existence of this principle it has only a very vague idea of its meaning and significance. The ordinary man of our times, even a man with philosophic or scientific interests, does not realize that the principle 'know thyself' speaks of the necessity of knowing one's machine, the 'human machine.' Machines are made more or less the same way in all men; therefore, before anything else man must study the structure, the functions, and the laws of his organism. In the human machine everything is so interconnected, one thing is so dependent upon another, that it is quite impossible to study any one function without studying all the others. In order to know one thing, one must know everything. To know *everything* in man is possible, but it requires much time and labor, and above all, the application of the right method and, what is equally necessary, right guidance.

"The principle 'know thyself' embraces a very rich content. It demands, in the first place, that a man who wants to know himself should understand what this means, with what it is connected, what it necessarily depends upon.

"Knowledge of oneself is a very big, but a very vague and distant, aim. Man in his present state is very far from self-knowledge. Therefore, strictly speaking, his aim cannot even be defined as self-knowledge. Self-study must be his big aim. It is quite enough if a man understands that he must study himself. It must be man's aim to begin to study himself, *to know himself*, in the right way.

"Self-study is the work or the way which leads to self-knowledge.

"But in order to study oneself one must first learn *how to study*, where to begin, what methods to use. A man must learn how to study himself, and he must study the methods of self-study.

"The chief method of self-study is self-observation. Without properly applied self-observation a man will never understand the connection and the correlation between the various functions of his machine, will never understand how and why on each separate occasion everything in him 'happens.'

"But to learn the methods of self-observation and of right self-study requires a certain understanding of the functions and the characteristics of the human machine. Thus in observing the functions of the human machine it is necessary to understand the correct divisions of the functions observed and to be able to define them exactly and at once; and the definition must not be a verbal but an inner definition; by taste, by sensation, in the same way as we define all inner experiences.

"There are two methods of self-observation: *analysis*, or attempts at analysis, that is, attempts to find the answers to the questions: upon what does a certain thing depend, and why does it happen; and the second method is registering, simply '*recording*' in one's mind what is observed at the moment.

"Self-observation, especially in the beginning, must on no account become analysis or attempts at analysis. Analysis will only become possible much later when a man knows all the functions of his machine and all the laws which govern it.

"In trying to analyze some phenomenon that he comes across within him, a man generally asks: 'What is this? Why does it happen in this way and not in some other way?' And he begins to seek an answer to these questions, forgetting all about further observations. Becoming more and more engrossed in these questions he completely loses the thread of self-observation and even forgets about it. Observation stops. It is clear from this that only one thing can go on: either observation or attempts at analysis.

"But even apart from this, attempts to analyze separate phenomena without a knowledge of general laws are a completely useless waste of time. Before it is possible to analyze even the most elementary phenomena, a man must accumulate a sufficient quantity of material by means of 'recording.' 'Recording,' that is, the result of a direct observation of what is taking place at a given moment, is the most important material in the work of self-study. When a certain number of 'records' have been accumulated and when, at the same time, laws to a certain extent have been studied and understood, analysis becomes possible.

"From the very beginning, observation, or 'recording,' must be based upon the understanding of the fundamental principles of the activity of the human machine. Self-observation cannot be properly applied without knowing these principles, without constantly bearing them in mind. Therefore ordinary self-observation, in which all people are engaged all their lives, is entirely useless and leads nowhere.

"Observation must begin with the division of functions. All the activity of the human machine is divided into four sharply defined groups, each of which is controlled by its own special mind or 'center.' In observing himself a man must differentiate between the four basic functions of his machine: the thinking, the emotional, the moving, and the instinctive. Every phenomenon that a man observes in himself is related to one or the other of these functions. Therefore, before beginning to observe, a man must understand how the functions differ; what intellectual activity means, what emotional activity means, what moving activity means, and what instinctive activity means.

"Observation must begin from the beginning. All previous experience, the results of all previous self-observation, must be laid aside. They may contain much valuable material. But all this material is based upon wrong divisions of the functions observed and is itself wrongly divided. It cannot therefore be utilized, at any rate it cannot be utilized at the beginning of the work of self-study. What is of value in it will, at the proper time, be taken up and made use of. But it is necessary to begin from the beginning. A man must begin observing himself as though he did not know himself at all, as though he had never observed himself.

"When he begins to observe himself, he must try to determine at once to what group, to which center, belong the phenomena he is observing at the moment.

"Some people find it difficult to understand the difference between thought and feeling, others have difficulty in understanding the difference between feeling and sensation, between a thought and a moving impulse.

"Speaking on very broad lines, one may say that the thinking function always works by means of comparison. Intellectual conclusions are always the result of the comparison of two or more impressions.

"Sensation and emotion do not reason, do not compare, they simply define a given impression by its aspect, by its being pleasant or unpleasant in one sense or another, by its color, taste, or smell. Moreover, *sensations* can be indifferent—neither warm nor cold, neither pleasant nor unpleasant: 'white paper,' 'red pencil.' In the sensation of white or red there is nothing either pleasant or unpleasant. At any rate there need not necessarily be anything pleasant or unpleasant connected with this or that color. These sensations, the so-called 'five senses,' and others, like the feeling of warmth, cold, and so on, are instinctive. Feeling functions or emotions are always pleasant or unpleasant; indifferent emotions do not exist.

"The difficulty of distinguishing between the functions is increased by the fact that people differ very much in the way they feel their functions. This is what we do not generally understand. We take people to be much more alike than they really are. In reality, however, there exist between them great differences in the forms and methods of their perception. Some perceive chiefly through their mind, others through their feeling, and others through sensation. It is very difficult, almost impossible for men of different categories and of different modes of perception to understand one another, because they call one and the same thing by different names, and they call different things by the same name. Besides this, various other combinations are possible. One man perceives by thoughts and sensations, another by thoughts and feelings, and so on. One or another mode of perception is immediately connected with one or another kind of reaction to external events. The result of this difference in perception and reaction to external events is expressed in the first place by the fact that people do not understand one another and in the second by the fact that they do not understand themselves. Very often a man calls his thoughts or his intellectual perceptions his feelings, calls his feelings his thoughts, and his sensations his feelings. This last is the most common. If two people perceive the same thing differently, let us say that one perceives it through feeling and another through sensation—they may argue all their lives and never understand in what consists the difference of their attitude to a given object. Actually, one sees one aspect of it, and the other a different aspect.

"In order to find a way of discriminating we must understand that every normal psychic function is a means or an instrument of knowledge. With the help of the mind we see one aspect of things and events, with the help of emotions another aspect, with the help of sensations a third aspect. The most complete knowledge of a given subject possible for us can only be obtained if we examine it simultaneously with our mind, feelings, and sensations. Every man who is striving after right knowledge must aim at the possibility of attaining such perception. In ordinary conditions man sees the world through a crooked, uneven window. And even if he realizes this, he cannot alter anything. This or that mode of perception depends upon the work of his organism as a whole. All functions are interconnected and counterbalance one another, all functions strive to keep one another in the state in which they are. Therefore when a man begins to study himself he must understand that if he discovers in himself something that he dislikes he will not be able to change it. To study is one thing, and to change is another. But study is the first step towards the possibility of change in the future. And in the beginning, to study himself he must understand that for a long time all his work will consist in study only.

"Change under ordinary conditions is impossible, because, in wanting to change something a man wants to change this one thing only. But everything in the machine is interconnected and every function is inevitably counterbalanced by some other function or by a whole series of other functions, although we are not aware of this interconnection of the various functions within ourselves. The machine is balanced in all its details at every moment of its activity. If a man observes in himself something that he dislikes and begins making efforts to alter it, he may succeed in obtaining a certain result. But together with this result he will inevitably obtain another result, which he did not in the least expect or desire and which he could not have suspected. By striving to destroy and annihilate everything that he dislikes, by making efforts to this end, he upsets the balance of the machine. The machine strives to re-establish the balance and re-establishes it by creating a new function which the man could not have foreseen. For instance, a man may observe that he is very absent-minded, that he forgets everything, loses everything, and so on. He begins to struggle with this habit and, if he is sufficiently methodical and determined, he succeeds, after a time, in attaining the desired result: he ceases to forget and to lose things. This he notices, but there is something else he does not notice, which other people notice, namely, that he has grown irritable, pedantic, fault-finding, disagreeable. Irritability has appeared as the result of his having lost his absent-mindedness. Why? It is impossible to say. Only detailed analysis of a particular man's mental qualities can show why the loss of one quality has caused the appearance of another. This does not mean that loss of absent-mindedness must necessarily give rise to irritability. It is just as easy for some other characteristic to appear that has no relation to absent-mindedness at all, for instance stinginess or envy or something else.

"So that if one is working on oneself properly, one must consider the possible supplementary changes, and take them into account beforehand. Only in this way is it possible to avoid undesirable changes, or the appearance of qualities which are utterly opposed to the aim and the direction of the work.

"But in the general plan of the work and functions of the human machine there are certain points in which a change may be brought about without giving rise to any supplementary results.

"It is necessary to know what these points are and it is necessary to know how to approach them, for if one does not begin *with them* one will either get no result at all or wrong and undesirable results.

"Having fixed in his own mind the difference between the intellectual, the emotional, and the moving functions, a man must, as he observes himself, immediately refer his impressions to this or that category. And at first he must take mental note of only such observations as regards which he has no doubt whatever, that is, those where he sees at once to what category they belong. He must reject all vague or doubtful cases and remember only those which are unquestionable. If the work is carried on properly, the number of unquestionable observations will rapidly increase. And that which seemed doubtful before will be clearly seen to belong to the first, the second, the third center. Each center has its own memory, its own associations, its own thinking. As a matter of fact each center consists of three parts: the thinking, the emotional, and the moving. But we know very little about this side of our nature. In each center we know only one part. Self-observation, however, will very quickly show us that our mental life is much richer than we think, or in any case that it contains more possibilities than we think.

"At the same time as we watch the work of the centers we shall observe, side by side with their right working, their wrong working, that is, the working of one center for another: the attempts of the thinking center to feel or to pretend that it feels, the attempts of the emotional center to think, the attempts of the moving center to think and feel. As has been said already, one center working for another is useful in certain cases, for it preserves the continuity of mental activity. But in becoming habitual it becomes at the same time harmful, since it begins to interfere with right working by enabling each center to shirk its own direct duties and to do, not what it ought to be doing, but what it likes best at the moment. In a normal healthy man each center does its own work, that is, the work for which it was specially destined and which it can best perform. There are situations in life which the thinking center alone can deal with and can find a way out of. If at this moment the emotional center begins to work instead, it will make a muddle of everything and the result of its interference will be most unsatisfactory. In an unbalanced kind of man the substitution of one center for another goes on almost continually and this is precisely what 'being unbalanced' or 'neurotic' means. Each center strives, as it were, to pass its work on to another and, at the same time, it strives to do the work of another center for which it is not fitted. The emotional center working for the thinking center brings unnecessary nervousness, feverishness, and hurry into situations where, on the contrary, calm judgment and deliberation are essential. The thinking center working for the emotional center brings deliberation into situations which require quick decisions and makes a man incapable of distinguishing the peculiarities and the fine points of the position. Thought is too slow. It works out a certain plan of action and continues to follow it even though the circumstances have changed and quite a different course of action is necessary. Besides, in some cases the interference of the thinking center gives rise to entirely wrong reactions, because the thinking center is simply incapable of understanding the shades and distinctions of many events. Events that are quite different for the moving center and for the emotional center appear to be alike to it. Its decisions are much too general and do not correspond to the decisions which the emotional center would have made. This becomes perfectly clear if we imagine the interference of thought, that is, of the theoretical mind, in the domain of feeling, or of sensation, or of movement; in all three cases the interference of the mind leads to wholly undesirable results. The mind cannot understand shades of feeling. We shall see this clearly if we imagine one man reasoning about the emotions of another. He is not feeling anything himself so the feelings of another do not exist for him. A *full man does not understand a hungry one.* But for the other *they have a very definite existence.* And the decisions of the first, that is of the mind, can never satisfy him. In exactly the same way the mind cannot appreciate sensations. For it they are dead. Nor is it capable of controlling movement. Instances of this kind are the easiest to find. Whatever work a man may be doing, it is enough for him to try to do each action deliberately, with his mind, following every movement, and he will see that the quality of his work will change immediately. If he is typing, his fingers, controlled by his moving center, find the necessary letters themselves, but if he tries to ask himself before every letter: 'Where is "k"?' 'Where is the comma?' 'How is this word spelled?' he at once begins to make mistakes or to write very slowly. If one drives a car with the help of one's mind, one can go only in the lowest gear. The mind cannot keep pace with all the movements necessary for developing a greater speed. To drive at full speed, especially in the streets of a large town, while steering with the help of one's mind is absolutely impossible for an ordinary man.

"Moving center working for thinking center produces, for example, mechanical reading or mechanical listening, as when a man reads or listens to nothing but words and is utterly unconscious of what he is reading or hearing. This generally happens when attention, that is, the direction of the thinking center's activity, is occupied with something else and when the moving center is trying to replace the absent thinking center; but this very easily becomes a habit, because the thinking center is generally distracted not by useful work, by thought, or by contemplation, but simply by daydreaming or by imagination.

" 'Imagination' is one of the principal sources of the wrong work of centers. Each center has its own form of imagination and daydreaming, but as a rule both the moving and the emotional centers make use of the thinking center which very readily places itself at their disposal for this purpose, because daydreaming corresponds to its own inclinations. Daydreaming is absolutely the opposite of 'useful' mental activity. 'Useful' in this case means activity directed towards a definite aim and undertaken for the sake of obtaining a definite result. Daydreaming does not pursue any aim, does not strive after any result. The motive for daydreaming always lies in the emotional or in the moving center. The actual process is carried on by the thinking center. The inclination to daydream is due partly to the laziness of the thinking center, that is, its attempts to avoid the efforts connected with work directed towards a definite aim and going in a definite direction, and partly to the tendency of the emotional and the moving centers to repeat to themselves, to keep alive or to recreate experiences, both pleasant and unpleasant, that have been previously lived through or 'imagined.' Daydreaming of disagreeable, morbid things is very characteristic of the unbalanced state of the human machine. After all, one can understand daydreaming of a pleasant kind and find logical justification for it. Daydreaming of an unpleasant character is an utter absurdity. And yet many people spend nine tenths of their lives in just such painful daydreams about misfortunes which may overtake them or their family, about illnesses they may contract or sufferings they will have to endure. Imagination and daydreaming are instances of the wrong work of the thinking center.

"Observation of the activity of imagination and daydreaming forms a very important part of self-study.

"The next object of self-observation must be habits in general. Every grown-up man consists wholly of habits, although he is often unaware of it and even denies having any habits at all. This can never be the case. All three centers are filled with habits and a man can never know himself until he has studied all his habits. The observation and the study of habits is particularly difficult because, in order to see and 'record' them, one must escape from them, free oneself from them, if only for a moment. So long as a man is governed by a particular habit, he does not observe it, but at the very first attempt, however feeble, to struggle against it, he feels it and notices it. Therefore in order to observe and study habits one must try to struggle against them. This opens up a practical method of self-observation. It has been said before that a man cannot change anything in himself, that he can only observe and 'record.' This is true. But it is also true that a man cannot observe and 'record' anything if he does not try to struggle with himself, that is, with his habits. This struggle cannot yield direct results, that is to say, it cannot lead to any change, especially to any permanent and lasting change. But it shows what is

there. Without a struggle a man cannot see what he consists of. The struggle with small habits is very difficult and boring, but without it self-
observation is impossible.

"Even at the first attempt to study the elementary activity of the moving
center a man comes up against habits. For instance, a man may want to
study his movements, may want to observe how he walks. But he will
never succeed in doing so for more than a moment if he continues to
walk in the usual way. But if he understands that his usual way of walking consists of a number of habits, for instance, of taking steps of a
certain length, walking at a certain speed, and so on, and he tries to alter
them, that is, to walk faster or slower, to take bigger or smaller steps, he
will be able to observe himself and to study his movements as he walks.
If a man wants to observe himself when he is writing, he must take note
of how he holds his pen and try to hold it in a different way from usual;
observation will then become possible. In order to observe himself a man
must try to walk not in his habitual way, he must sit in unaccustomed
attitudes, he must stand when he is accustomed to sit, he must sit when
he is accustomed to stand, and he must make with his left hand the
movements he is accustomed to make with his right hand and vice versa.
All this will enable him to observe himself and study the habits and
associations of the moving center.

"In the sphere of the emotions it is very useful to try to struggle with
the habit of giving immediate expression to all one's unpleasant emotions.
Many people find it very difficult to refrain from expressing their feelings
about bad weather. It is still more difficult for people not to express unpleasant emotions when they feel that something or someone is violating
what they may conceive to be order or justice.

"Besides being a very good method for self-observation, the struggle
against expressing unpleasant emotions has at the same time another
significance. It is one of the few directions in which a man can change
himself or his habits without creating other undesirable habits. Therefore
self-observation and self-study must, from the first, be accompanied by
the struggle against the *expression of unpleasant emotions.*

"If he carries out all these rules while he observes himself, a man will
record a whole series of very important aspects of his being. To begin
with he will record with unmistakable clearness the fact that his actions,
thoughts, feelings, and words are the result of external influences and
that nothing comes from himself. He will understand and see that he is
in fact an automaton acting under the influences of external stimuli. He
will feel his complete mechanicalness. Everything 'happens,' he cannot
'do' anything. He is a machine controlled by accidental shocks from outside. Each shock calls to the surface one of his I's. A new shock and that
I disappears and a different one takes its place. Another small change in
the environment and again there is a new I. A man will begin to under-

stand that he has no control of himself whatever, that he does not know what he may say or do the next moment, he will begin to understand that he cannot answer for himself even for the shortest length of time. He will understand that if he remains the same and does nothing unexpected, it is simply because no unexpected outside changes are taking place. He will understand that his actions are entirely controlled by external conditions and he will be convinced that there is nothing permanent in him from which control could come, not a single permanent function, not a single permanent state."

There were several points in G.'s psychological theories that particularly aroused my interest. The first thing was the possibility of self-change, that is, the fact that in beginning to observe himself *in the right way* a man immediately begins to change himself, and that he can never find himself to be *right*.

The second thing was the demand "not to express unpleasant emotions." I at once felt something big behind this. And the future showed that I was right, for the study of emotions and the work on emotions became the basis of the subsequent development of the whole system. But this was much later.

The third thing, which at once attracted my attention and of which I began to think the very first time I heard of it, was the idea of the *moving center*. The chief thing that interested me here was the question of the relation in which G. placed moving functions to instinctive functions. Were they the same thing or were they different? And further, in what relation did the divisions made by G. stand to the divisions customary in ordinary psychology? With certain reservations and additions I had considered it possible to accept the old divisions, that is, to divide man's actions into "conscious" actions, "automatic" actions (which must at first be conscious), "instinctive" actions (expedient, but without consciousness of purpose), and "reflexes," simple and complex, which are never conscious and which can, in certain cases, be inexpedient. In addition there were actions performed under the influence of hidden emotional dispositions or inner unknown impulses.

G. turned all this structure upside down.

First of all he completely rejected "conscious" actions because, as it appeared from what he said, there was nothing that was conscious. The term "subconscious" which plays such a big part in the theories of some authors became quite useless and even misleading, because phenomena of quite different categories were classified under the category of "subconscious."

The division of actions according to the centers controlling them did away with all uncertainty and all possible doubts as to the correctness of these divisions.

What was particularly important in G.'s system was the indication that the same actions could originate in different centers. An example is the recruit and the old soldier at rifle drill. One has to perform the drill with his thinking center, the other does it with the moving center, which does it *much better*.

But G. did not call actions governed by the moving center "automatic." He used the name "automatic" only for the actions which a man performs *imperceptibly for himself*. If the same actions are *observed* by a man, they cannot be called "automatic." He allotted a big place to automatism, but regarded the moving functions as distinct from the automatic functions, and, what is most important, he found automatic actions *in all centers*; he spoke, for instance, of "automatic thoughts" and of "automatic feelings." When I asked him about reflexes he called them "instinctive actions." And as I understood from what followed, among external movements he considered only reflexes to be *instinctive* actions.

I was very interested in the interrelation of moving and instinctive functions in his description and I often returned to this subject in my talks with him.

First of all G. drew attention to the constant misuse of the words "instinct" and "instinctive." It transpired from what he said that these words could be applied, by rights, only to the *inner* functions of the organism. The beating of the heart, breathing, the circulation of blood, digestion—these were *instinctive functions*. The only external functions that belong to this category are *reflexes*. The difference between instinctive and moving functions was as follows: the moving functions of man, as well as of animals, of a bird, of a dog, *must be learned*; but instinctive functions are inborn. A man has very few inborn external movements; an animal has more, though they vary, some have more, others have less; but that which is usually explained as "instinct" is very often a series of complex moving functions which young animals learn from older ones. One of the chief properties of the moving center is its ability to imitate. The moving center imitates what it sees without reasoning. This is the origin of the legends that exist about the wonderful "intelligence" of animals or the "instinct" that takes the place of intelligence and makes them perform a whole series of very complex and expedient actions.

The idea of an independent moving center, which, on the one hand, does not depend upon the mind, does not require the mind, and which is a mind in itself, and which, on the other hand, does not depend upon instinct and has first of all to learn, placed very many problems on entirely new ground. The existence of a moving center working by means of imitation explained the preservation of the "existing order" in beehives, termitaries, and ant-hills. Directed by imitation, one generation has had to shape itself absolutely upon the model of another. There could be no changes, no departure whatever from the model. But "imitation" did not explain how such an order was arrived at in the first place. I often wanted very much to speak to G. about this as well as about many other things connected with it. But G. eluded such conversations by leading them up to man and to real problems of self-study.

Then a great deal was elucidated for me by the idea that each center was not only a motive force but also a "receiving apparatus," working as receiver for different and sometimes very distant influences. When I thought of what had been said about wars, revolutions, migrations of peoples, and so on; when I pictured how masses of humanity could move under the control of planetary influences, I began to understand our fundamental mistake in determining the actions of an individual. We regard the actions of an individual as originating in himself. We do not imagine that the "masses" may consist of automatons obeying external stimuli and may move, not under the influence of the will, consciousness, or inclination of individuals, but under the influence of external stimuli coming possibly from very far away.

"Can the instinctive and the moving functions be controlled by two distinct centers?" I asked G. once.

"They can," said G., "and to them must be added the sex center. These are the three centers of the lower story. The sex center is the neutralizing center in relation to the instinctive and the moving centers. The lower story can exist by itself, because the three centers in it are the conductors of the three forces. The thinking and the emotional centers are not indispensable for life."

"Which of them is active and which is passive in the lower story?"

"It changes," said G., "one moment the moving center is active and the instinctive is passive. Another moment the instinctive is active and the moving is passive. You must find examples of both states in yourself. But besides different states there are also different types. In some people the moving center is more active, in others the instinctive center. But for the sake of convenience in reasoning and particularly in the beginning, when it is important only to explain the principles, we take them as one center with different functions which are on the same level. If you take the thinking, the emotional, and the moving centers, then they work on different levels. The moving and the instinctive—on one level. Later on you will understand what these levels mean and upon what they depend."

Chapter Seven

O N ONE occasion while talking with G. I asked him whether he considered it possible to attain "cosmic consciousness," not for a brief moment only but for a longer period. I understood the expression "cosmic consciousness" in the sense of a higher consciousness possible for man in the sense in which I had previously written about it in my book *Tertium Organum.*

"I do not know what you call 'cosmic consciousness,'" said G., "it is a vague and indefinite term; anyone can call anything he likes by it. In most cases what is called 'cosmic consciousness' is simply fantasy, associative daydreaming connected with intensified work of the emotional center. Sometimes it comes near to ecstasy but most often it is merely a subjective emotional experience on the level of dreams. But even apart from all this before we can speak of 'cosmic consciousness' we must define in general *what consciousness is.*

"How do you define consciousness?"

"*Consciousness* is considered to be indefinable," I said, "and indeed, how can it be defined if it is an inner quality? With the ordinary means at our disposal it is impossible to prove the presence of consciousness in another man. We know it only in ourselves."

"All this is rubbish," said G., "the usual scientific sophistry. It is time you got rid of it. Only one thing is true in what you have said: that you *can know* consciousness only in yourself. Observe that I say you *can know*, for you can know it only when you have it. And when you have not got it, you can know that you have not got it, not at that very moment, but afterwards. I mean that when it comes again you can see that it has been absent a long time, and you can find or remember the moment when it disappeared and when it reappeared. You can also define the moments when you are nearer to consciousness and further away from consciousness. But by observing in yourself the appearance and the disappearance of consciousness you will inevitably see one fact which you neither see nor acknowledge now, and that is that moments of consciousness are very short and are separated by long intervals of completely unconscious, mechanical working of the machine. You will then see that you can think, feel, act. speak, work, *without being conscious of it.* And if you learn to see in yourselves the moments of consciousness and the long periods of mechanicalness, you will as infallibly see in other people when they are conscious of what they are doing and when they are not.

"Your principal mistake consists in thinking that you *always have consciousness*, and in general, either that consciousness is *always present* or that it is *never present*. In reality consciousness is a property which is continually changing. Now it is present, now it is not present. And there are different degrees and different levels of consciousness. Both consciousness and the different degrees of consciousness must be understood in oneself by sensation, by taste. No definitions can help you in this case and no definitions are possible so long as you do not understand *what* you have to define. And science and philosophy cannot define consciousness because they want to define it where it does not exist. It is necessary to distinguish *consciousness* from the *possibility of consciousness*. We have only the possibility of consciousness and rare flashes of it. Therefore we cannot define what consciousness is."

I cannot say that what was said about consciousness became clear to me at once. But one of the subsequent talks explained to me the principles on which these arguments were based.

On one occasion at the beginning of a meeting G. put a question to which all those present had to answer in turn. The question was: "What is the most important thing that we notice during self-observation?"

Some of those present said that during attempts at self-observation, what they had felt particularly strongly was an incessant flow of thoughts which they had found impossible to stop. Others spoke of the difficulty of distinguishing the work of one center from the work of another. I had evidently not altogether understood the question, or I answered my own thoughts, because I said that what struck me most was the connectedness of one thing with another in the system, the wholeness of the system, as if it were an "organism," and the entirely new significance of the word *to know* which included not only the idea of knowing this thing or that, but the connection between this thing and everything else.

G. was obviously dissatisfied with our replies. I had already begun to understand him in such circumstances and I saw that he expected from us indications of something definite that we had either missed or failed to understand.

"Not one of you has noticed the most important thing that I have pointed out to you," he said. "That is to say, not one of you has noticed that *you do not remember yourselves.*" (He gave particular emphasis to these words.) "You do not feel *yourselves*; you are not conscious of *yourselves*. With you, 'it observes' just as 'it speaks,' 'it thinks,' 'it laughs.' You do not feel: *I* observe, *I* notice, *I* see. Everything still 'is noticed,' 'is seen.' . . . In order really to observe oneself one must first of all *remem-*

ber oneself." (He again emphasized these words.) "Try to *remember yourselves* when you observe yourselves and later on tell me the results. Only those results will have any value that are accompanied by self-remembering. Otherwise you yourselves do not exist in your observations. In which case what are all your observations worth?"

These words of G.'s made me think a great deal. It seemed to me at once that they were the key to what he had said before about conscious-ness. But I decided to draw no conclusions whatever, but to try to *remember myself* while observing myself.

The very first attempts showed me how difficult it was. Attempts at *self-remembering* failed to give any results except to show me that in actual fact we never remember ourselves.

"What else do you want?" said G. "This is a very important realization. People who *know this*" (he emphasized these words) "already know a great deal. The whole trouble is that nobody knows it. If you ask a man whether he can remember himself, he will of course answer that he can. If you tell him that he cannot remember himself, he will either be angry with you, or he will think you an utter fool. The whole of life is based on this, the whole of human existence, the whole of human blindness. If a man really knows that he cannot remember himself, he is already near to the understanding of his being."

All that G. said, all that I myself thought, and especially all that my attempts at self-remembering had shown me, very soon convinced me that I was faced with an *entirely new problem which science and philosophy had not, so far, come across.*

But before making deductions, I will try to describe my attempts to remember myself.

The first impression was that attempts to remember myself or to be conscious of myself, to say to myself, *I* am walking, *I* am doing, and con-tinually to feel this *I, stopped thought.* When I was feeling *I,* I could neither think nor speak; even sensations became dimmed. Also, one could only remember oneself in this way for a very short time.

I had previously made certain experiments in stopping thought which are mentioned in books on Yoga practices. For example there is such a description in Edward Carpenter's book *From Adam's Peak to Elephanta,* although it is a very general one. And my first attempts to self-remember reminded me exactly of these, my first experiments. Actually it was almost the same thing with the one difference that in stopping thoughts atten-tion is wholly directed towards the effort of not admitting thoughts, while in self-remembering attention becomes divided, one part of it is directed towards the same effort, and the other part to the feeling of self.

This last realization enabled me to come to a certain, possibly a very incomplete, definition of "self-remembering," which nevertheless proved to be very useful in practice.

I am speaking of the division of attention which is the characteristic feature of self-remembering.

I represented it to myself in the following way:

When I observe something, my attention is directed towards what I observe—a line with one arrowhead:

I ————————————————→ the observed phenomenon.

When at the same time, I try to remember myself, my attention is directed both towards the object observed and towards myself. A second arrowhead appears on the line:

I ←———————————————→ the observed phenomenon.

Having defined this I saw that the problem consisted in directing attention on oneself without weakening or obliterating the attention directed on something else. Moreover this "something else" could as well be within me as outside me.

The very first attempts at such a division of attention showed me its possibility. At the same time I saw two things clearly.

In the first place I saw that self-remembering resulting from this method had nothing in common with "self-feeling," or "self-analysis." It was a new and very interesting state with a strangely familiar flavor.

And secondly I realized that moments of self-remembering do occur in life, although rarely. Only the deliberate production of these moments created the sensation of novelty. Actually I had been familiar with them from early childhood. They came either in new and unexpected surroundings, in a new place, among new people while traveling, for instance, when suddenly one looks about one and says: *How strange! I and in this place*; or in very emotional moments, in moments of danger, in moments when it is necessary to keep one's head, when one hears one's own voice and sees and observes oneself from the outside.

I saw quite clearly that my first recollections of life, in my own case very early ones, were moments of *self-remembering*. This last realization revealed much else to me. That is, I saw that I really only remember those moments of the past in which I *remembered myself*. Of the others *I know only that they took place*. I am not able wholly to revive them, to experience them again. But the moments when I had remembered myself were alive and were in no way different from the present. I was still afraid to come to conclusions. But I already saw that I stood upon the threshold of a very great discovery. I had always been astonished at the weakness and the insufficiency of our memory. So many things disappear. For some reason or other the chief absurdity of life for me consisted in this. Why experience so much in order to forget it afterwards? Besides there was something degrading in this. A man feels something which seems to him very big, he thinks he will never forget it; one or two years pass by—and nothing remains of it. It now became clear to me why this was so and why it could not be otherwise. If our memory really keeps alive only moments of self-remembering, it is clear why our memory is so poor.

All these were the realizations of the first days. Later, when I began to learn to divide attention, I saw that self-remembering gave wonderful sensations which, in a natural way, that is, by themselves, come to us only very seldom and in exceptional conditions. Thus, for instance, at that time I used very much to like to wander through St. Petersburg at night and to "sense" the houses and the streets. St. Petersburg is full of these strange sensations. Houses, especially old houses, were quite alive, I all but spoke to them. There was no "imagination" in it. I did not think of anything, I simply walked along while trying to remember myself and looked about; the sensations came by themselves.

Later on I was to discover many unexpected things in the same way. But I will speak of this further on.

Sometimes self-remembering was not successful; at other times it was accompanied by curious observations.

I was once walking along the Liteiny towards the Nevsky, and in spite of all my efforts I was unable to keep my attention on self-remembering. The noise, movement, everything distracted me. Every minute I lost the thread of attention, found it again, and then lost it again. At last I felt a kind of ridiculous irritation with myself and I turned into the street on the left having firmly decided to keep my attention on the fact that *I would remember myself* at least for some time, at any rate until I reached the following street. I reached the Nadejdinskaya without losing the thread of attention except, perhaps, for short moments. Then I again turned towards the Nevsky realizing that, in quiet streets, it was easier for me not to lose the line of thought and wishing therefore to test myself in more noisy streets. I reached the Nevsky still remembering myself, and was already beginning to experience the strange emotional state of inner peace and confidence which comes after great efforts of this kind. Just round the corner on the Nevsky was a tobacconist's shop where they made my cigarettes. Still remembering myself I thought I would call there and order some cigarettes.

Two hours later I *woke up* in the Tavricheskaya, that is, far away. I was going by *izvostchik* to the printers. The sensation of awakening was extraordinarily vivid. I can almost say that I *came to*. I remembered everything at once. How I had been walking along the Nadejdinskaya, how I had been remembering myself, how I had thought about cigarettes, and how at this thought I seemed all at once to fall and disappear into a deep sleep.

At the same time, while immersed in this sleep, I had continued to perform consistent and expedient actions. I left the tobacconist, called at my flat in the Liteiny, telephoned to the printers. I wrote two letters.

Then again I went out of the house. I walked on the left side of the Nevsky up to the Gostinoy Dvor intending to go to the Offitzerskaya. Then I had changed my mind as it was getting late. I had taken an *izvostchik* and was driving to the Kavalergardskaya to my printers. And on the way while driving along the Tavricheskaya I began to feel a strange uneasiness, as though I had forgotten something.—*And suddenly I remembered that I had forgotten to remember myself.*

I spoke of my observations and deductions to the people in our group as well as to my various literary friends and others.

I told them that this was the center of gravity of the whole system and of all work on oneself; that now work on oneself was not only empty words but a real fact full of significance thanks to which psychology becomes an exact and at the same time a practical science.

I said that European and Western psychology in general had overlooked a fact of tremendous importance, namely, that *we do not remember ourselves;* that we live and act and reason in deep sleep, not metaphorically but in absolute reality. And also that, at the same time, we *can* remember ourselves if we make sufficient efforts, that we *can awaken.*

I was struck by the difference between the understanding of the people who belonged to our groups and that of people outside them. The people who belonged to our groups understood, though not all at once, that we had come into contact with a "miracle," and that it was something "new," something that had never existed anywhere before.

The other people did not understand this; they took it all too lightly and sometimes they even began to prove to me that such theories had existed before.

A. L. Volinsky, whom I had often met and with whom I had talked a great deal since 1909 and whose opinions I valued very much, did not find in the idea of "self-remembering" anything that he had not known before.

"This is an *apperception.*" He said to me, "Have you read Wundt's *Logic?* You will find there his latest definition of apperception. It is exactly the same thing you speak of. 'Simple observation' is perception. 'Observation with self-remembering,' as you call it, is apperception. Of course Wundt knew of it."

I did not want to argue with Volinsky. I had read Wundt. And of course what Wundt had written was not at all what I had said to Volinsky. Wundt had come close to this idea, but others had come just as close and had afterwards gone off in a different direction. He had not seen the magnitude of the idea which was hidden behind his thoughts about different forms of *perception.* And not having seen the magnitude of the idea he of course could not see the central position which the idea of the absence of consciousness and the idea of the possibility of the voluntary creation of this consciousness ought to occupy in our thinking. Only it seemed strange to me that Volinsky could not see this even *when I pointed it out to him.*

I subsequently became convinced that this idea was hidden by an impenetrable veil for many otherwise very intelligent people—and still later on I saw *why* this was so.

The next time G. came from Moscow he found us immersed in experiments in self-remembering and in discussions about these experiments. But at his first lecture he spoke of something else.

"In right knowledge the study of man must proceed on parallel lines with the study of the world, and the study of the world must run parallel with the study of man. Laws are everywhere the same, in the world as well as in man. Having mastered the principles of any one law we must look for its manifestation in the world and in man simultaneously. Moreover, some laws are more easily observed in the world, others are more easily observed in man. Therefore in certain cases it is better to begin with the world and then to pass on to man, and in other cases it is better to begin with man and then to pass on to the world.

"This parallel study of the world and of man shows the student the fundamental unity of everything and helps him to find analogies in phenomena of different orders.

"The number of fundamental laws which govern all processes both in the world and in man is very small. Different numerical combinations of a few elementary forces create all the seeming variety of phenomena.

"In order to understand the mechanics of the universe it is necessary to resolve complex phenomena into these elementary forces.

"The first fundamental law of the universe is the law of three forces, or three principles, or, as it is often called, *the law of three.* According to this law every action, every phenomenon in all worlds without exception, is the result of a simultaneous action of three forces—the positive, the negative, and the neutralizing. Of this we have already spoken, and in future we will return to this law with every new line of study.

"The next fundamental law of the universe is the *law of seven* or the *law of octaves.*

"In order to understand the meaning of this law it is necessary to regard the universe as *consisting of vibrations.* These vibrations proceed in all kinds, aspects, and densities of the matter which constitutes the universe, from the finest to the coarsest; they issue from various sources and proceed in various directions, crossing one another, colliding, strengthening, weakening, arresting one another, and so on.

"In this connection according to the usual views accepted in the West, vibrations are continuous. This means that vibrations are usually regarded as proceeding uninterruptedly, ascending or descending so long as there continues to act the force of the original impulse which caused the vibration and which overcomes the resistance of the medium in which the vibrations proceed. When the force of the impulse becomes exhausted and the resistance of the medium gains the upper hand the vibrations naturally die down and stop. But until this moment is reached, that is, until the beginning of the natural weakening, the vibrations develop uniformly and gradually, and, in the absence of resistance, can even be endless. So that one of the fundamental propositions of our physics is the *continuity of vibrations*, although this has never been precisely formulated because it has never been opposed. In certain of the newest theories this proposition is beginning to be shaken. Nevertheless physics is still very far from a correct view on the nature of vibrations, or what corresponds to our conception of vibrations, in the real world.

"In this instance the view of ancient knowledge is opposed to that of contemporary science because at the base of the understanding of vibrations ancient knowledge places the principle of the *discontinuity of vibrations*.

"The principle of the *discontinuity of vibration* means the definite and necessary characteristic of all vibrations in nature, whether ascending or descending, to develop *not uniformly* but with periodical accelerations and retardations. This principle can be formulated still more precisely if we say that the force of the original impulse in vibrations does not act uniformly but, as it were, becomes alternately stronger and weaker. The force of the impulse acts without changing its nature and vibrations develop in a regular way only for a certain time which is determined by the nature of the impulse, the medium, the conditions, and so forth. But at a certain moment a kind of change takes place in it and the vibrations, so to speak, cease to obey it and for a short time they slow down and to a certain extent change their nature or direction; for example, ascending vibrations at a certain moment begin to ascend more slowly, and descending vibrations begin to descend more slowly. After this temporary retardation, both in ascending and descending, the vibrations again enter the former channel and for a certain time ascend or descend uniformly up to a certain moment when a check in their development again takes place. In this connection it is significant that the periods of uniform action of the momentum are not equal and that the moments of retardation of the vibrations are not symmetrical. One period is shorter, the other is longer.

"In order to determine these moments of retardation, or rather, the checks in the ascent and descent of vibrations, the lines of development of vibrations are divided into periods corresponding to the *doubling* or the *halving* of the number of vibrations in a given space of time.

"Let us imagine a line of increasing vibrations. Let us take them at the moment when they are vibrating at the rate of one thousand a second. After a certain time the number of vibrations is doubled, that is, reaches two thousand.

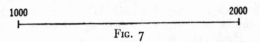

1000   2000

Fig. 7

"It has been found and established that in this interval of vibrations, between the given number of vibrations and a number twice as large, there are two places where a *retardation in the increase of vibrations* takes place. One is near the beginning but not at the beginning itself. The other occurs almost at the end.

"Approximately:

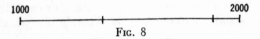

1000   2000

Fig. 8

"The laws which govern the retardation or the deflection of vibrations from their primary direction were known to ancient science. These laws were duly incorporated into a particular formula or diagram which has been preserved up to our times. In this formula the period in which vibrations are doubled was divided into *eight* unequal steps corresponding to the rate of increase in the vibrations. The eighth step repeats the first step with double the number of vibrations. This period of the doubling of the vibrations, or the line of the development of vibrations, between a given number of vibrations and double that number, is called an *octave*, that is to say, *composed of eight*.

"The principle of dividing into eight unequal parts the period, in which the vibrations are doubled, is based upon the observation of the non-uniform increase of vibrations in the entire octave, and separate 'steps' of the octave show acceleration and retardation at different moments of its development.

"In the guise of this formula ideas of the octave have been handed down from teacher to pupil, from one school to another. In very remote times one of these schools found that it was possible to apply this formula to music. In this way was obtained the seven-tone musical scale which was known in the most distant antiquity, then forgotten, and then discovered or 'found' again.

"The seven-tone scale is the formula of a cosmic law which was worked out by ancient schools and applied to music. At the same time, however, if we study the manifestations of the law of octaves in vibrations of other kinds we shall see that the laws are everywhere the same, and that light, heat, chemical, magnetic, and other vibrations are subject to the same laws as sound vibrations. For instance, the light scale is known to physics; in chemistry the periodic system of the elements is without doubt closely connected with the principle of octaves although this connection is still not fully clear to science.

"A study of the structure of the seven-tone musical scale gives a very good foundation for understanding the cosmic law of octaves.

"Let us again take the ascending octave, that is, the octave in which the frequency of vibrations increases. Let us suppose that this octave begins with one thousand vibrations a second. Let us designate these thousand vibrations by the note do. Vibrations are growing, that is, their frequency is increasing. At the point where they reach two thousand vibrations a second there will be a second do, that is, the do of the next octave.

do ———————————————————————————————— do

FIG. 9

"The period between one do and the next, that is, an octave, is divided into seven *unequal* parts because the frequency of vibrations does not increase uniformly.

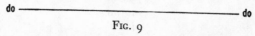
FIG. 10

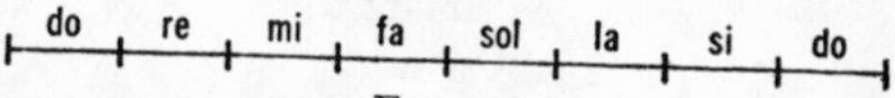

"The ratio of the pitch of the notes, or of the frequency of vibrations will be as follows:

"If we take do as 1 then re will be $9/8$, mi $5/4$, fa $4/3$, sol $3/2$, la $5/3$, si $15/8$, and do 2.

1	9/8	5/4	4/3	3/2	5/3	15/8	2
do	re	mi	fa	sol	la	si	do

FIG. 11

"The differences in the acceleration or increase in the notes or the difference in tone will be as follows:

$$\text{between do and re} \quad 9/8 : 1 = 9/8$$
$$\text{between re and mi} \quad 5/4 : 9/8 = 10/9$$
$$\text{between mi and fa} \quad 4/3 : 5/4 = 16/15 \quad \text{increase retarded}$$
$$\text{between fa and sol} \quad 3/2 : 4/3 = 9/8$$
$$\text{between sol and la} \quad 5/3 : 3/2 = 10/9$$
$$\text{between la and si} \quad 15/8 : 5/3 = 9/8$$
$$\text{between si and do} \quad 2 : 15/8 = 16/15 \quad \text{increase again retarded}$$

"The differences in the notes or the differences in the pitch of the notes are called *intervals*. We see that there are three kinds of intervals in the octave: $\frac{9}{8}$, $\frac{10}{9}$, and $\frac{16}{15}$, which in whole numbers correspond to 405, 400, and 384. The smallest interval $\frac{16}{15}$ occurs between mi and fa and between si and do. These are precisely the places of retardation in the octave.

"In relation to the musical (seven-tone) scale it is generally considered (theoretically) that there are two semitones between each two notes, with the exception of the intervals mi–fa and si–do, which have only one semitone and in which one semitone is regarded as being left out.

"In this manner *twenty* notes are obtained, eight of which are fundamental:

do, re, mi, fa, sol, la, si, do

and twelve intermediate: two between each of the following two notes:

do–re
re–mi
fa–sol
sol–la
la–si

and one between each of the following two notes :

mi–fa
si–do

"But in practice, that is, in music, instead of twelve intermediate semitones only five are taken, that is one semitone between:

do–re
re–mi
fa–sol
sol–la
la–si

"Between mi and fa and between si and do the semitone is not taken at all.

"In this way the structure of the musical seven-tone scale gives a scheme of the cosmic law of 'intervals,' or absent semitones. In this respect when octaves are spoken of in a 'cosmic' or a 'mechanical' sense, only those intervals between mi–fa and si–do are called '*intervals*.'

"If we grasp its full meaning the law of octaves gives us an entirely new explanation of the whole of life, of the progress and development of phenomena on all planes of the universe observed by us. This law explains why there are no straight lines in nature and also why we can neither think nor do, why everything with us *is thought*, why everything *happens* with us and happens usually in a way opposed to what we want or expect. All this is the clear and direct effect of the 'intervals,' or retardations in the development of vibrations.

"What precisely does happen at the moment of the retardation of vibrations? A deviation from the original direction takes place. The octave begins in the direction shown by the arrow:

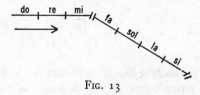

FIG. 12

"But a deviation takes place between mi and fa; the line begun at do changes its direction

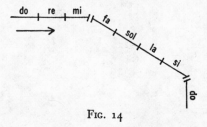

FIG. 13

and through fa, sol, la, and si it descends at an angle to its original direction, shown by the first three notes. Between si and do the second 'interval' occurs—a fresh deviation, a further change of direction.

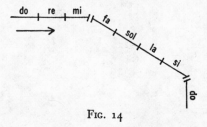

FIG. 14

"The next octave gives an even more marked deviation, the one following that a deviation that is more marked still, so that the line of octaves may at last turn completely round and proceed in a direction opposite to the original direction.

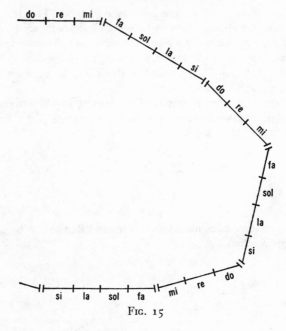

FIG. 15

"In developing further, the line of octaves or the line of development of vibrations may return to the original direction, in other words, make a complete circle.

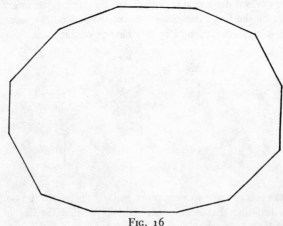

FIG. 16

"This law shows why straight lines never occur in our activities, why, having begun to do one thing, we in fact constantly do something entirely different, often the opposite of the first, although we do not notice this and continue to think that we are doing the same thing that we began to do.

"All this and many other things can only be explained with the help of the law of octaves together with an understanding of the role and significance of 'intervals' which cause the line of the development of force constantly to change, to go in a broken line, to turn round, to become its 'own opposite' and so on.

"Such a course of things, that is, a change of direction, we can observe in everything. After a certain period of energetic activity or strong emotion or a right understanding a reaction comes, work becomes tedious and tiring; moments of fatigue and indifference enter into feeling; instead of right thinking a search for compromises begins; suppression, evasion of difficult problems. But the line continues to develop though now not in the same direction as at the beginning. Work becomes mechanical, feeling becomes weaker and weaker, descends to the level of the common events of the day; thought becomes dogmatic, literal. Everything proceeds in this way for a certain time, then again there is reaction, again a stop, again a deviation. The development of the force may continue but the work which was begun with great zeal and enthusiasm has become an obligatory and useless formality; a number of entirely foreign elements have entered into feeling—considering, vexation, irritation, hostility; thought goes round in a circle, repeating what was known before, and the way out which had been found becomes more and more lost.

"The same thing happens in all spheres of human activity. In literature, science, art, philosophy, religion, in individual and above all in social and political life, we can observe how the line of the development of forces deviates from its original direction and goes, after a certain time, in a diametrically opposite direction, *still preserving its former name.* A study of history from this point of view shows the most astonishing facts which mechanical humanity is far from desiring to notice. Perhaps the most interesting examples of such change of direction in the line of the development of forces can be found in the history of religion, particularly in the history of Christianity if it is studied dispassionately. Think how many turns the line of development of forces must have taken to come from the Gospel preaching of love to the Inquisition; or to go from the ascetics of the early centuries studying *esoteric* Christianity to the scholastics who calculated how many angels could be placed on the point of a needle.

"The law of octaves explains many phenomena in our lives which are incomprehensible.

"First is the principle of the deviation of forces.

"Second is the fact that nothing in the world stays in the same place, or remains what it was, everything moves, everything is going somewhere, is changing, and *inevitably either develops or goes down,* weakens or degenerates, that is to say, it moves along either an ascending or a descending line of octaves.

"And third, that in the actual development itself of both ascending and descending octaves, fluctuations, rises and falls are constantly taking place.

"We have spoken so far chiefly *about the discontinuity of vibrations and about the deviation of forces.* We must now clearly grasp two other principles: the inevitability of either ascent or descent in every line of development of forces, and also the periodic fluctuations, that is, rises and falls, in every line whether ascending or descending.

"Nothing can develop by staying on one level. Ascent or descent is the inevitable cosmic condition of any action. We neither understand nor see what is going on around and within us, either because we do not allow for the inevitability of descent when there is no ascent, or because we take descent to be ascent. These are two of the fundamental causes of our self-deception. We do not see the first one because we continually think that things can remain for a long time at the same level; and we do not see the second because *ascents* where we see them are in fact impossible, as impossible as it is to increase consciousness by mechanical means.

"Having learned to distinguish ascending and descending octaves in life we must learn to distinguish ascent and descent within the octaves themselves. Whatever sphere of our life we take we can see that nothing can ever remain level and constant; everywhere and in everything proceeds the swinging of the pendulum, everywhere and in everything the waves rise and fall. Our energy in one or another direction which suddenly increases and afterwards just as suddenly weakens; our moods which 'become better' or 'become worse' without any visible reason; our feelings, our desires, our intentions, our decisions—all from time to time pass through periods of ascent or descent, become stronger or weaker.

"And there are perhaps a hundred pendulums moving here and there in man. These ascents and descents, these wave-like fluctuations of moods, thought, feelings, energy, determination, are periods of the development of forces between 'intervals' in the octaves as well as the 'intervals' themselves.

"Upon the law of octaves in its three principal manifestations depend many phenomena both of a psychic nature as well as those immediately connected with our life. Upon the law of octaves depends the imperfection and the incompleteness of our knowledge in all spheres without exception, chiefly because we always begin in one direction and afterwards without noticing it proceed in another.

"As has been said already, the law of octaves in all its manifestations was known to ancient knowledge.

"Even our division of time, that is, the days of the week into work days and Sundays, is connected with the same properties and inner conditions of our activity which depend upon the general law. The Biblical myth of the creation of the world in six days and of the seventh day in which God rested from his labors is also an expression of the law of octaves or an indication of it, though an incomplete one.

"Observations based on an understanding of the law of octaves show that 'vibrations' may develop in different ways. In interrupted octaves they merely begin and fall, are drowned or swallowed up by other, stronger, vibrations which intersect them or which go in an opposite direction. In octaves which deviate from the original direction the vibrations change their nature and give results opposite to those which might have been expected at the beginning.

"And it is only in octaves of a cosmic order, both descending and ascending, that vibrations develop in a consecutive and orderly way, following the same direction in which they started.

"Further observations show that a right and consistent development of octaves, although rare, can be observed in all the occasions of life and in the activity of nature and even in human activity.

"The right development of these octaves is based on what looks an *accident*. It sometimes happens that octaves going parallel to the given octave, intersecting or meeting it, in some way or another *fill up its 'intervals'* and make it possible for the vibrations of the given octave to develop in freedom and without checks. Observation of such rightly developing octaves establishes the fact that if at the necessary moment, that is, at the moment when the given octave passes through an 'interval,' there enters into it an 'additional shock' which corresponds in force and character, it will develop further without hindrance along the original direction, neither losing anything nor changing its nature.

"In such cases there is an essential difference between ascending and descending octaves.

"In an ascending octave the first 'interval' comes between mi and fa. If corresponding additional energy enters at this point the octave will develop without hindrance to si, but between si and do it needs a *much stronger 'additional shock'* for its right development than between mi and fa, because the vibrations of the octave at this point are of a considerably higher pitch and to overcome a check in the development of the octave a greater intensity is needed.

"In a descending octave, on the other hand, the greatest 'interval' occurs at the very beginning of the octave, immediately after the first do and the material for filling it is very often found either in do itself or in the lateral vibrations evoked *by do*. For this reason a descending octave develops much more easily than an ascending octave and in passing beyond si it reaches fa without hindrance; here an 'additional shock' is necessary, though *considerably less strong* than the first 'shock' between do and si.

"In the big cosmic octave, which reaches us in the form of the *ray of creation*, we can see the first complete example of the law of octaves. The ray of creation begins with the Absolute. The Absolute is *the All. The All*, possessing full unity, full will, and full consciousness, creates worlds within itself, in this way beginning the *descending* world octave. The Absolute is the do of this octave. The worlds which the Absolute creates in itself are si. The 'interval' between do and si in this case is filled by the *will of the Absolute*. The process of creation is developed further by the force of the original impulse and an 'additional shock.' Si passes into la which for us is our star world, the *Milky Way*. La passes into sol—our *sun*, the solar system. Sol passes into fa—the planetary world. And here between the planetary world as a whole and our earth occurs an '*interval*.' This means that the planetary radiations carrying various influences to the earth are not able to reach it, or, to speak more correctly, they are not received, the earth reflects them. In order to fill the 'interval' at this point of the ray of creation a special apparatus is created for receiving and transmitting the influences coming from the planets. This apparatus is *organic life on earth*. Organic life transmits to the earth all the influences intended for it and makes possible the further development and growth of the earth, mi of the cosmic octave, and then of the moon or re, after which follows another do—*Nothing*. Between *All* and *Nothing* passes the ray of creation.

"You know the prayer 'Holy God, Holy the Firm, Holy the Immortal'? This prayer comes from ancient knowledge. *Holy God* means the Absolute or All. *Holy the Firm* also means the Absolute or Nothing. *Holy the Immortal* signifies that which is between them, that is, the six notes of the ray of creation, with organic life. All three taken together make one. This is the coexistent and indivisible Trinity.

"We must now dwell on the idea of the 'additional shocks' which make it possible for the lines of forces to reach a projected aim. As I said before, shocks may occur accidentally. Accident is of course a very uncertain thing. But those lines of development of forces which are straightened out by accident, and which man can sometimes see, or suppose, or expect, create in him more than anything else the illusion of *straight lines*. That is to say, he thinks that straight lines are the rule and broken and interrupted lines the exception. This in its turn creates in him the illusion that it is possible *to do*; possible to attain a projected aim. In reality a man can do nothing. If by accident his activity gives a result, even though it resembles only in appearance or in name the original aim, a man assures himself and others that he has attained the aim which he set before himself and that anyone else would also be able to attain his aim, and others believe him. In reality this is illusion. A man *can* win at roulette. But this would be accident. Attaining an aim which one has set before oneself in life or in any particular sphere of human activity is just the same kind of accident. The only difference is that in regard to roulette a man at least knows for certain whether he has lost or won on each separate occasion, that is, on each separate stake. But in the activities of his life, particularly with activities of the kind that many people are concerned in and when years pass between the beginning of something and its result, a man can very easily deceive himself and take the result 'obtained' as the result desired, that is, believe that he has won when on the whole he has lost.

"The greatest insult for a 'man-machine' is to tell him that he can do nothing, can attain nothing, that he can never move towards any aim whatever and that in striving towards one he will inevitably create another. Actually of course it cannot be otherwise. The 'man-machine' is in the power of accident. His activities may fall by accident into some sort of channel which has been created by cosmic or mechanical forces and they may by accident move along this channel for a certain time, giving the illusion that aims of some kind are being attained. Such accidental correspondence of results with the aims we have set before us or the attainment of aims in small things *which can have no consequences* creates in mechanical man the conviction that he is able to attain any aim, 'is able to conquer nature' as it is called, is able to 'arrange the whole of his life,' and so on.

"As a matter of fact he is of course unable to do anything of the kind because not only has he no control over things outside himself but he has no control even over things within himself. This last must be very clearly understood and assimilated; at the same time it must be understood that control over things begins with control over things in ourselves, *with control over ourselves*. A man who cannot control himself, or the course of things within himself, can control nothing.

"In what way can control be attained?

"The technical part of this is explained by the law of octaves. Octaves can develop consecutively and continuously in the desired direction if 'additional shocks' enter them at the moments necessary, that is, at the moments when vibrations slow down. If 'additional shocks' do not enter at the necessary moments octaves change their direction. To entertain hopes of accidental 'shocks' coming from somewhere by themselves at the moments necessary is of course out of the question. There remains for a man the choice either of finding a direction for his activities which corresponds to the mechanical line of events of a given moment, in other words of 'going where the wind blows' or 'swimming with the stream,' even if this contradicts his inner inclinations, convictions, and sympathies, or of reconciling himself to the failure of everything he starts out to do; or he can learn to recognize the moments of the 'intervals' in all lines of his activity and learn to *create* the 'additional shocks,' in other words, learn to apply to his own activities the method which cosmic forces make use of in *creating 'additional shocks'* at the moments necessary.

"The possibility of artificial, that is, specially created, 'additional shocks' gives a practical meaning to the study of the law of octaves and makes this study obligatory and necessary if a man desires to step out of the role of passive spectator of that which is happening to him and around him.

"The 'man-machine' can do nothing. To him and around him everything *happens*. In order *to do* it is necessary to know the law of octaves, to know the moments of the 'intervals' and be able to create necessary 'additional shocks.'

"It is only possible to learn this in a *school*, that is to say, in a rightly organized school which follows all esoteric traditions. Without the help of a school a man by himself can never understand the law of octaves, the points of the 'intervals,' and the order of creating 'shocks.' He cannot understand because certain conditions are necessary for this purpose, and these conditions can only be created in a school *which is itself created upon these principles.*

"How a school is created on the principles of the law of octaves will be explained in due course. And this in its turn will explain to you one aspect of the union of the *law of seven* with the *law of three*. In the meantime it can be said only that in school teaching, a man is given examples of both descending (creative) and ascending (or evolutionary) cosmic octaves. Western thought, knowing neither about octaves nor about the law of three, confuses the ascending and the descending lines and does not understand that the line of evolution is opposed to the line of creation, that is to say, it goes against it as though against the stream.

"In the study of the law of octaves it must be remembered that octaves in their relation to each other are divided into *fundamental* and *subordinate*. The fundamental octave can be likened to the trunk of a tree giving off branches of lateral octaves. The seven fundamental notes of the octave and the two 'intervals,' *the bearers of new directions*, give altogether nine links of a chain, three groups of three links each.

"The fundamental octaves are connected with the secondary or subordinate octaves in a certain definite way. Out of the subordinate octaves of the first order come the subordinate octaves of the second order, and so on. The construction of octaves can be compared with the construction of a tree. From the straight basic trunk there come out boughs on all sides which divide in their turn and pass into branches, becoming smaller and smaller, and finally are covered with leaves. The same process goes on in the construction of the leaves, in the formation of the veins, the serrations, and so on.

"Like everything in nature the human body which represents a certain whole bears both within and without the same correlations. According to the number of the notes of the octave and its 'intervals,' the human body has nine basic measurements expressed by the numbers of a definite measure. In individuals these numbers of course differ widely but within certain definite limits. These nine basic measurements, giving a full octave of the first order, by combining in a certain definite way pass into measurements of subordinate octaves, which give rise in their turn to other subordinate octaves, and so on. In this way it is possible to obtain the measurements of any member or any part of the human body as they are all in a definite relationship one to another."

The law of octaves naturally gave rise to a great many talks in our group and to much perplexity. G. warned us all the time against too much theorizing.

"You must understand and feel this law in yourselves," he said. "Only then will you see it outside yourselves."

This of course is true. But the difficulty was not only in this. Merely a "technical" understanding of the law of octaves requires a lot of time. And we returned to it continually, sometimes making unexpected discoveries, sometimes again losing what had seemed to us already established.

It is now difficult to convey how at different periods now one and now another idea became the center of gravity in our work, attracted the greatest attention, gave rise to most talks. The idea of the law of octaves became in its way a permanent center of gravity. We returned to it on every occasion; we spoke of it and discussed its various aspects at every meeting until we began gradually to think of everything from the point of view of this idea.

In his first talk G. gave only a general outline of the idea and he constantly returned to it himself, pointing out to us its different aspects and meanings.

At one of the following meetings he gave us a very interesting picture of another meaning of the law of octaves which went deeply into things.

"In order better to understand the significance of the law of octaves it is necessary to have a clear idea of another property of vibrations, namely the so-called 'inner vibrations.' This means that within vibrations other vibrations proceed, and that every octave can be resolved into a great number of inner octaves.

"Each note of any octave can be regarded as an octave on another plane.

"Each note of these inner octaves again contains a whole octave and so on, for some considerable way, *but not ad infinitum*, because there is a definite limit to the development of inner octaves.

FIG. 17

"These inner vibrations proceed simultaneously in 'media' of different density, interpenetrating one another; they are reflected in one another, give rise to one another; stop, impel, or change one another.

"Let us imagine vibrations in a substance or a medium of a certain definite density. Let us suppose this substance or medium to consist of the comparatively coarse atoms of world 48, each of which is, so to speak, an agglomeration of forty-eight primordial atoms. The vibrations which proceed in this medium are divisible into octaves and the octaves are divisible into notes. Let us imagine that we have taken one octave of these vibrations for the purpose of some kind of investigation. We must realize that within the limits of this octave proceed the vibrations of a still finer substance. The substance of world 48 is saturated with substance of world 24; the vibrations in the substance of world 24 stand in a definite relation to the vibrations in the substance of world 48; namely, each note of the vibrations in the substance of world 48 contains a whole octave of vibrations in the substance of world 24.

"These are the *inner* octaves.

"The substance of world 24 is, in its turn, permeated with the substance of world 12. In this substance also there are vibrations and each note of the vibrations of world 24 contains a whole octave of the vibrations of world 12. The substance of world 12 is permeated with the substance of world 6. The substance of world 6 is permeated with the substance of world 3. World 3 is permeated with the substance of world 1. Corresponding vibrations exist in each of these worlds and the order remains always the same, namely, each note of the vibrations of a coarser substance contains a whole octave of the vibrations of a finer substance.

"If we begin with vibrations of world 48, we can say that one note of the vibrations in this world contains an octave or seven notes of the vibrations of the planetary world. Each note of the vibrations of the planetary world contains seven notes of the vibrations of the world of the sun. Each vibration of the world of the sun will contain seven notes of the vibrations of the starry world and so on.

"The study of inner octaves, the study of their relation to outer octaves and the possible influence of the former upon the latter, constitute a very important part of the study of the world and of man."

At the next meeting G. again spoke of the ray of creation, partly repeating and partly supplementing and developing what he had already said.

"The ray of creation like every other process which is complete at a given moment can be regarded as an octave. This would be a descending octave in which do passes into si, si into la and so on.

"The Absolute or *All* (world 1) will be do; all worlds (world 3)—si; all suns (world 6)—la; our sun (world 12)—sol; all planets (world 24)—fa; the earth (world 48)—mi; the moon (world 96)—re. The ray of creation begins with the Absolute. The Absolute is *All*. It is—do.

"The ray of creation ends in the moon. Beyond the moon there is *nothing*. This also is the Absolute—do.

"In examining the ray of creation or cosmic octave we see that 'intervals' should come in the development of this octave: the first between do and si, that is between world 1 and world 3, between the Absolute and 'all worlds,' and the second between fa and mi, that is, between world 24 and world 48, between 'all planets' and the earth. But the first 'interval' is filled by the will of the Absolute. One of the manifestations of the will of the Absolute consists precisely in the filling of this 'interval' by means of a conscious manifestation of neutralizing force which fills up the 'interval' between the active and the passive forces. With the second 'interval' the situation is more complicated. Something is missing between the planets and the earth. Planetary influences cannot pass to the earth consecutively and fully. An 'additional shock' is indispensable; the creation of some new conditions to insure a proper passage of forces is indispensable.

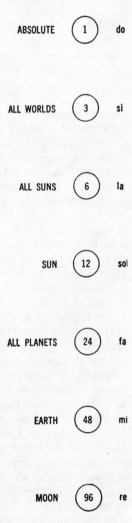

ABSOLUTE	1	do
ALL WORLDS	3	si
ALL SUNS	6	la
SUN	12	sol
ALL PLANETS	24	fa
EARTH	48	mi
MOON	96	re
ABSOLUTE		do

Fig. 18

"The conditions to insure the passage of forces are created by the arrangement of a special mechanical contrivance between the planets and the earth. This mechanical contrivance, this 'transmitting station of forces' is *organic life on earth*. Organic life on earth was created to fill the interval between the planets and the earth.

"Organic life represents so to speak the *earth's organ of perception*. Organic life forms something like a sensitive film which covers the whole of the earth's globe and takes in those influences coming from the planetary sphere which otherwise would not be able to reach the earth. The vegetable, animal, and human kingdoms are equally important for the earth in this respect. A field merely covered with grass takes in planetary influences of a definite kind and transmits them to the earth. The same field with a crowd of people on it will take in and transmit other influences. The population of Europe takes in one kind of planetary influences and transmits them to the earth. The population of Africa takes in planetary influences of another kind, and so on.

"All great events in the life of the human masses are caused by planetary influences. They are the result of the taking in of planetary influences. Human society is a highly sensitive mass for the reception of planetary influences. And any accidental small tension in planetary spheres can be reflected for years in an increased animation in one or another sphere of human activity. Something accidental and very transient takes place in planetary space. This is immediately received by the human masses, and people begin to hate and to kill one another, justifying their actions by some theory of brotherhood, or equality, or love, or justice.

"Organic life is the organ of perception of the earth and it is at the same time an organ of radiation. With the help of organic life each portion of the earth's surface occupying a given area sends every moment certain kinds of rays in the direction of the sun, the planets, and the moon. In connection with this the sun needs one kind of radiations, the planets another kind, and the moon another. Everything that happens on earth creates radiations of this kind. And many things often *happen* just because certain kinds of radiation are required from a certain place on the earth's surface."

In saying this G. drew our attention in particular to the nonconformity of time, that is, of the duration of events in the planetary world and in human life. The significance of his insistence on this point became clear to me only later.

At the same time he constantly emphasized the fact that no matter what took place in the thin film of organic life it always served the interests of the earth, the sun, the planets, and the moon; nothing unnecessary and nothing independent could happen in it because it was created for a definite purpose and was merely subordinate.

And once dwelling on this theme he gave us a diagram of the structure of the octave in which one of the links was "organic life on earth."

"This additional or lateral octave in the ray of creation begins in the sun," he said.

"The sun, sol of the cosmic octave, begins at a certain moment to sound as do, *sol–do.*

"It is necessary to realize that every note of any octave, in the present instance every note of the cosmic octave, may represent do of some other lateral octave issuing from it. Or it would be still more exact to say that any note of any octave may at the same time be any note of any other octave passing through it.

"In the present instance sol begins to sound as do. Descending to the level of the planets this new octave passes into si; descending still lower it produces three notes, la, sol, fa, which create and constitute organic life on earth in the form that we know it; mi of this octave blends with mi of the cosmic octave, that is, with *the earth,* and re with the re of the cosmic octave, that is, with *the moon.*"

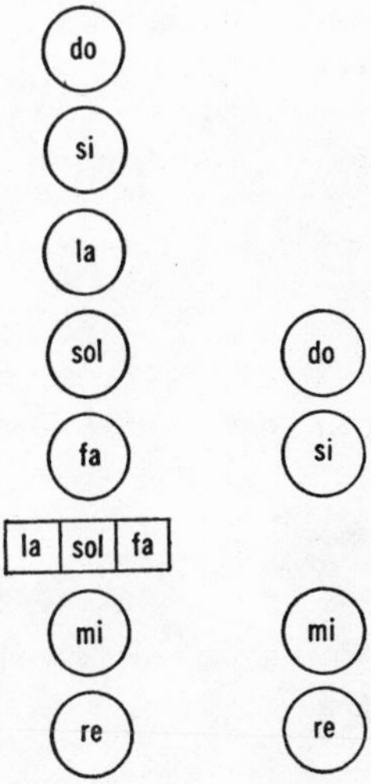

We at once felt that there was a great deal of meaning in this lateral octave. First of all it showed that organic life, represented in the diagram by three notes, had two higher notes, one on the level of the planets and one on the level of the sun, and that it *began in the sun.* This last was the most important point because once more, as with many other things in G.'s system, it contradicted the usual modern idea of life having originated so to speak from *below.* In his explanations life came from above.

Then much talk arose about the notes mi, re, of the lateral octave. We could not, of course, define what re was. But it was clearly connected with the idea of food for the moon. Some product of the disintegration of organic life went to the moon; this must be re. In regard to mi it was possible to speak quite definitely. Organic life undoubtedly disappeared in the earth. The role of organic life in the structure of the earth's surface was indisputable. There was the growth of coral islands and limestone mountains, the formation of coal seams and accumulations of petroleum; the alteration of the soil under the influence of vegetation, the growth of vegetation in lakes, the "formation of rich arable lands by worms," change of climate due to the draining of swamps and the destruction of forests, and many other things that we know of and do not know of.

FIG. 19

But in addition to this the lateral octave showed with particular clarity how easily and correctly things were classified in the system we were studying. Everything anomalous, unexpected, and accidental disappeared, and an immense and strictly thought-out plan of the universe began to make its appearance.

Chapter Eight

A T ONE of the following lectures G. returned to the question of consciousness.

"Neither the psychical nor the physical functions of man can be understood," he said, "unless the fact has been grasped that they can both work in different states of consciousness.

"In all there are four states of consciousness possible for *man*" (he emphasized the word "man"). "But ordinary man, that is, man number one, number two, and number three, lives in the two lowest states of consciousness only. The two higher states of consciousness are inaccessible to him, and although he may have flashes of these states, he is unable to understand them and he judges them from the point of view of those states in which it is usual for him to be.

"The two usual, that is, the lowest, states of consciousness are first, *sleep*, in other words a passive state in which man spends a third and very often a half of his life. And second, the state in which men spend the other part of their lives, in which they walk the streets, write books, talk on lofty subjects, take part in politics, kill one another, which they regard as active and call 'clear consciousness' or the 'waking state of consciousness.' The term 'clear consciousness' or 'waking state of consciousness' seems to have been given in jest, especially when you realize what *clear consciousness* ought in reality to be and what the state in which man lives and acts really is.

"The third state of consciousness is *self-remembering* or self-consciousness or consciousness of one's being. It is usual to consider that we have this state of consciousness or that we can have it if we want it. Our science and philosophy have overlooked the fact that *we do not possess* this state of consciousness and that we cannot create it in ourselves by desire or decision alone.

"The fourth state of consciousness is called the *objective state of consciousness*. In this state a man can see things *as they are*. Flashes of this state of consciousness also occur in man. In the religions of all nations there are indications of the possibility of a state of consciousness of this kind which is called 'enlightenment' and various other names but which cannot be described in words. But the only right way to objective con-

sciousness is through the development of self-consciousness. If an ordinary man is artificially brought into a state of objective consciousness
and afterwards brought back to his usual state he will remember nothing
and he will think that for a time he had lost consciousness. But in the
state of self-consciousness a man can have flashes of objective consciousness and remember them.

"The fourth state of consciousness in man means an altogether different state of being; it is the result of inner growth and of long and
difficult work on oneself.

"But the third state of consciousness constitutes the natural right of
man *as he is,* and if man does not possess it, it is only because of the
wrong conditions of his life. It can be said without any exaggeration that
at the present time the third state of consciousness occurs in man only
in the form of very rare flashes and that it can be made more or less
permanent in him only by means of special training.

"For most people, even for educated and thinking people, the chief
obstacle in the way of acquiring self-consciousness consists in the fact
that they think *they possess it,* that is, that they possess self-consciousness
and everything connected with it; individuality in the sense of a permanent
and unchangeable I, will, ability *to do,* and so on. It is evident that a man
will not be interested if you tell him that he can acquire by long and
difficult work something which, in his opinion, he already has. On the
contrary he will think either that you are mad or that you want to deceive
him with a view to personal gain.

"The two higher states of consciousness—'self-consciousness' and 'objective consciousness'—are connected with the functioning of the *higher
centers* in man.

"In addition to those centers of which we have so far spoken there are
two other centers in man, the 'higher emotional' and the 'higher thinking.' These centers are in us; they are fully developed and are working all
the time, but their work fails to reach our ordinary consciousness. The
cause of this lies in the special properties of our so-called 'clear consciousness.'

"In order to understand what the difference between states of consciousness is, let us return to the first state of consciousness which is
sleep. This is an entirely subjective state of consciousness. A man is immersed in dreams, whether he remembers them or not does not matter.
Even if some real impressions reach him, such as sounds, voices, warmth,
cold, the sensation of his own body, they arouse in him only fantastic
subjective images. Then a man wakes up. At first glance this is a quite
different state of consciousness. He can move, he can talk with other
people, he can make calculations ahead, he can see danger and avoid
it, and so on. It stands to reason that he is in a better position than
when he was asleep. But if we go a little more deeply into things, if we

take a look into his inner world, into his thoughts, into the causes of his actions, we shall see that he is in almost the same state as when he is asleep. And it is even worse, because in sleep he is passive, that is, he cannot do anything. In the waking state, however, he can do something all the time and the results of all his actions will be reflected upon him or upon those around him. *And yet he does not remember himself*. He is a machine, everything with him *happens*. He cannot stop the flow of his thoughts, he cannot control his imagination, his emotions, his attention. He lives in a subjective world of 'I love,' 'I do not love,' 'I like,' 'I do not like,' 'I want,' 'I do not want,' that is, of what he thinks he likes, of what he thinks he does not like, of what he thinks he wants, of what he thinks he does not want. He does not see the real world. The real world is hidden from him by the wall of imagination. *He lives in sleep*. He is asleep. What is called 'clear consciousness' is sleep and a far more dangerous sleep than sleep at night in bed.

"Let us take some event in the life of humanity. For instance, war. There is a war going on at the present moment. What does it signify? It signifies that several millions of sleeping people are trying to destroy several millions of other sleeping people. They would not do this, of course, if they were to wake up. Everything that takes place is owing to this sleep.

"Both states of consciousness, sleep and the waking state, are equally subjective. Only by beginning to *remember himself* does a man really awaken. And then all surrounding life acquires for him a different aspect and a different meaning. He sees that it is *the life of sleeping people*, a life in sleep. All that men say, all that they do, they say and do in sleep. All this can have no value whatever. Only awakening and what leads to awakening has a value in reality.

"How many times have I been asked here whether wars can be stopped? Certainly they can. For this it is only necessary that people should awaken. It seems a small thing. It is, however, the most difficult thing there can be because this sleep is induced and maintained by the whole of surrounding life, by all surrounding conditions.

"How can one awaken? How can one escape this sleep? These questions are the most important, the most vital that can ever confront a man. But before this it is necessary to be convinced of the very fact of sleep. But it is possible to be convinced of this only by trying to awaken. When a man understands that he does not remember himself and that to remember himself means to awaken to some extent, and when at the same time he sees by experience how difficult it is to remember himself, he will understand that he cannot awaken simply by having the desire to do so. It can be said still more precisely that a man cannot awaken *by himself*. But if, let us say, twenty people make an agreement that whoever of them awakens first shall wake the rest, they already have some chance. Even this, however, is insufficient because all the twenty can go to sleep at the same time and dream that they are waking up. Therefore more still is necessary. They must be looked after by a man who is not asleep or who does not fall asleep as easily as they do, or who goes to sleep consciously when this is possible, when it will do no harm either to himself or to others. They must find such a man *and hire him* to wake them and not allow them to fall asleep again. Without this it is impossible to awaken. This is what must be understood.

"It is possible to think for a thousand years; it is possible to write whole libraries of books, to create theories by the million, and all this in sleep, without any possibility of awakening. On the contrary, these books and these theories, written and created in sleep, will merely send other people to sleep, and so on.

"There is nothing new in the idea of sleep. People have been told almost since the creation of the world that they are asleep and that they must awaken. How many times is this said in the Gospels, for instance? 'Awake,' 'watch,' 'sleep not.' Christ's disciples even slept when he was praying in the Garden of Gethsemane for the last time. It is all there. But do men understand it? Men take it simply as a form of speech, as an expression, as a metaphor. They completely fail to understand that it must be taken literally. And again it is easy to understand why. In order to understand this literally it is necessary to awaken a little, or at least to try to awaken. I tell you seriously that I have been asked several times why nothing is said about sleep in the Gospels. Although it is there spoken of almost on every page. This simply shows that people read the Gospels in sleep. So long as a man sleeps profoundly and is wholly immersed in dreams he cannot even think about the fact that he is asleep. If he were to think that he was asleep, he would wake up. So everything goes on. And men have not the slightest idea what they are losing because of this sleep. As I have already said, as he is organized, that is, being such as nature has created him, man can be a self-conscious being. Such he is created and such he is born. But he is born among sleeping people, and, of course, he falls asleep among them just at the very time when he should have begun to be conscious of himself. Everything has a hand in this: the involuntary imitation of older people on the part of the child, voluntary and involuntary suggestion, and what is called 'education.' Every attempt to awaken on the child's part is instantly stopped. This is inevitable. And a great many efforts and a great deal of help are necessary in order to awaken later when thousands of sleep-compelling habits have been accumulated. And this very seldom happens. In most cases, a man when still a child already loses the possibility of awakening; he lives in sleep all his life and he dies in sleep. Furthermore, many people die long before their physical death. But of such cases we will speak later on.

"Now turn your attention to what I have pointed out to you before. A fully developed man, which I call 'man in the full sense of the word,' should possess four states of consciousness. Ordinary man, that is, man number one, number two, and number three, lives in two states of consciousness only. He knows, or at least he can know, of the existence of the fourth state of consciousness. All these 'mystical states' and so on are wrong definitions but when they are not deceptions or imitations they are flashes of what we call an objective state of consciousness.

"But man does not know of the third state of consciousness or even suspect it. Nor can he suspect it because if you were to explain to him what the third state of consciousness is, that is to say, in what it consists, he would say that it was his usual state. He considers himself to be a conscious being governing his own life. Facts that contradict that, he considers to be accidental or temporary, which will change by themselves. By considering that he possesses self-consciousness, as it were by nature, a man will not of course try to approach or obtain it. And yet without self-consciousness, or the third state, the fourth, except in rare flashes, is impossible. Knowledge, however, the real *objective* knowledge towards which man, as he asserts, is struggling, is possible only in the fourth state of consciousness, that is, it is conditional upon the full possession of the fourth state of consciousness. Knowledge which is acquired in the ordinary state of consciousness is intermixed with dreams. There you have a complete picture of the being of man number one, two, and three."

G. began the next talk as follows:

"Man's possibilities are very great. You cannot conceive even a shadow of what man is capable of attaining. But nothing can be attained in sleep. In the consciousness of a sleeping man his illusions, his 'dreams' are mixed with reality. He lives in a subjective world and he can never escape from it. And this is the reason why he can never make use of all the powers he possesses and why he always lives in only a small part of himself.

"It has been said before that self-study and self-observation, if rightly conducted, bring man to the realization of the fact that something is wrong with his machine and with his functions in their ordinary state. A man realizes that it is precisely because he is asleep that he lives and works in a small part of himself. It is precisely for this reason that the vast majority of his possibilities remain unrealized, the vast majority of his powers are left unused. A man feels that he does not get out of life all that it can give him, that he fails to do so owing to definite functional defects in his machine, in his receiving apparatus. The idea of self-study acquires in his eyes a new meaning. He feels that possibly it may not even be worth while studying himself as he is now. He sees every function as it is now and as it could be or ought to be. Self-observation brings man to the realization of the necessity for self-change. And in observing himself a man notices that self-observation itself brings about certain changes in his inner processes. He begins to understand that self-observation is an instrument of self-change, a means of awakening. By observing himself he throws, as it were, a ray of light onto his inner processes which have hitherto worked in complete darkness. And under the influence of this light the processes themselves begin to change. There are a great many chemical processes that can take place only in the absence of light. Exactly in the same way many psychic processes can take place only in the dark. Even a feeble light of consciousness is enough to change completely the character of a process, while it makes many of them altogether impossible. Our inner psychic processes (our inner alchemy) have much in common with those chemical processes in which light changes the character of the process and they are subject to analogous laws.

"When a man comes to realize the necessity not only for self-study and self-observation but also for work on himself with the object of changing himself, the character of his self-observation must change. He has so far studied the details of the work of the centers, trying only to register this or that phenomenon, to be an impartial witness. He has studied the work of the machine. Now he must begin to see himself, that is to say, to see, not separate details, not the work of small wheels and levers, but to see everything taken together as a whole—the whole of himself such as others see him.

"For this purpose a man must learn to take, so to speak, 'mental photographs' of himself at different moments of his life and in different emotional states: and not photographs of details, but photographs of the whole as he saw it. In other words these photographs must contain simultaneously everything that a man can see in himself at a given moment. Emotions, moods, thoughts, sensations, postures, movements, tones of voice, facial expressions, and so on. If a man succeeds in seizing interesting moments for these photographs he will very soon collect a whole album of pictures of himself which, taken together, will show him quite clearly what he is. But it is not so easy to learn how to take these photographs at the most interesting and characteristic moments, how to catch characteristic postures, characteristic facial expressions, characteristic emotions, and characteristic thoughts. If the photographs are taken successfully and if there is a sufficient number of them, a man will see that his usual conception of himself, with which he has lived from year to year, is very far from reality.

"Instead of the man he had supposed himself to be he will see quite another man. This 'other' man is himself and at the same time not himself. It is he as other people know him, as he imagines himself and as he appears in his actions, words, and so on; but not altogether such as he actually is. For a man himself knows that there is a great deal that is unreal, invented, and artificial in this other man whom other people know and whom he knows himself. You must learn to divide the real from the invented. And to begin self-observation and self-study it is necessary to divide oneself. A man must realize that he indeed consists of two men.

"One is the man he calls 'I' and whom others call 'Ouspensky,' 'Zakharov,' or 'Petrov.' The other is the real *he*, the real *I*, which appears in his life only for very short moments and which can become firm and permanent only after a very lengthy period of work.

"So long as a man takes himself as *one person* he will never move from where he is. His work on himself starts from the moment when he begins to feel *two men* in himself. One is passive and the most it can do is to register or observe what is happening to it. The other, which calls itself 'I,' is active, and speaks of itself in the first person, is in reality only 'Ouspensky,' 'Petrov,' or 'Zakharov.'

"This is the first realization that a man can have. Having begun to think correctly he very soon sees that he is completely in the power of his 'Ouspensky,' 'Petrov,' or 'Zakharov.' No matter what he plans or what he intends to do or say, it is not 'he,' not 'I,' that will carry it out, do or say it, but his 'Ouspensky,' 'Petrov,' or 'Zakharov,' and of course they will do or say it, not in the way 'I' would have done or said it, but in their own way with their own shade of meaning, and often this shade of meaning completely changes what 'I' wanted to do.

"From this point of view there is a very definite danger arising from the very first moment of self-observation. It is 'I' who begins self-observation, but it is immediately taken up and continued by 'Ouspensky,' 'Zakharov,' or 'Petrov.' But 'Ouspensky,' 'Zakharov,' or 'Petrov' from the very first steps introduces a slight alteration into this self-observation, an alteration which seems to be quite unimportant but which in reality fundamentally alters the whole thing.

"Let us suppose, for example, that a man called Ivanov hears the description of this method of self-observation. He is told that a man must divide himself, 'he' or 'I' on one side and 'Ouspensky,' 'Petrov,' or 'Zakharov' on the other side. And he divides himself *literally as he hears it*. 'This is I,' he says, 'and that is "Ouspensky," "Petrov," or "Zakharov." ' He will never say 'Ivanov.' He finds that unpleasant, so he will inevitably use somebody else's surname or Christian name. Moreover he calls 'I' what he likes in himself or at any rate what he considers to be strong, while he calls 'Ouspensky,' 'Petrov,' or 'Zakharov' what he does not like or what he considers to be weak. On this basis he begins to reason in many ways about himself, quite wrongly of course from the very beginning, since he has already deceived himself in the most important point and has taken not his real self, that is, he has taken, not Ivanov, but the imaginary 'Ouspensky,' 'Petrov,' or 'Zakharov.'

"It is difficult even to imagine how often a man dislikes to use his own name in speaking of himself in the third person. He tries to avoid it in every possible way. He calls himself by another name, as in the instance just mentioned; he devises an artificial name for himself, a name by which nobody ever has or ever will call him, or he calls himself simply 'he,' and so on. In this connection people who are accustomed in their mental conversations to call themselves by their Christian name or surname or by pet names are no exception. When it comes to self-observation they prefer to call themselves 'Ouspensky' or to say 'Ouspensky in me,' as though there could be an 'Ouspensky' in them. There is quite enough of 'Ouspensky' for Ouspensky himself.

"But when a man understands his helplessness in the face of 'Ouspensky,' his attitude towards himself and towards 'Ouspensky' in him ceases to be either indifferent or unconcerned.

"Self-observation becomes observation of 'Ouspensky.' A man understands that he is not 'Ouspensky,' that 'Ouspensky' is nothing but the mask he wears, the part that he unconsciously plays and which unfortunately he cannot stop playing, a part which rules him and makes him do and say thousands of stupid things, thousands of things which he would never do or say himself.

"If he is sincere with himself he feels that he is in the power of 'Ouspensky' and at the same time he feels that he is not 'Ouspensky.'

"He begins to be afraid of 'Ouspensky,' begins to feel that he is his 'enemy.' No matter what he would like to do, everything is intercepted and altered by 'Ouspensky.' 'Ouspensky' is his 'enemy.' 'Ouspensky's' desires, tastes, sympathies, antipathies, thoughts, opinions, are either opposed to his own views, feelings, and moods, or they have nothing in common with them. And, at the same time, 'Ouspensky' is his master. He is the slave. He has no will of his own. He has no means of expressing his desires because whatever he would like to do or say would be done for him by 'Ouspensky.'

"On this level of self-observation a man must understand that his whole aim is to free himself from 'Ouspensky.' And since he cannot in fact free himself from 'Ouspensky,' because he is himself, he must therefore master 'Ouspensky' and make him do, not what the 'Ouspensky' of the given moment wants, but what he himself wants to do. From being the master, 'Ouspensky' must become the servant.

"The first stage of work on oneself consists in separating oneself from 'Ouspensky' mentally, in being separated from him in actual fact, in keeping apart from him. But the fact must be borne in mind that the whole attention must be concentrated upon 'Ouspensky' for a man is unable to explain *what he himself really is.* But he can explain 'Ouspensky' to himself and with this he must begin, remembering at the same time that he is not 'Ouspensky.'

"The most dangerous thing in this case is to rely on one's own judgment. If a man is lucky he may at this time have someone near him who can tell him where he is and where 'Ouspensky' is. But he must moreover trust this person, because he will undoubtedly think that he understands everything himself and that he knows where he is and where 'Ouspensky' is. And not only in relation to himself but in relation also to other people will he think that he knows and sees their 'Ouspenskys.' All this is of course self-deception. At this stage a man can see nothing either in relation to himself or to others. The more convinced he is that he can, the more he is mistaken. But if he can be even to a slight extent sincere with himself and really wants to know the truth, then he can find an exact and infallible basis for judging rightly first about himself and then about other people. But the whole point lies in being sincere with oneself. And this is by no means easy. People do not understand that sincerity must be learned. They imagine that to be sincere or not to be sincere depends upon their desire or decision. But how can a man be sincere with himself when in actual fact he *sincerely* does not see what he ought to see in himself? Someone has to show it to him. And his attitude towards the person who shows him must be a right one, that is, such as will help him to see what is shown him and not, as often happens, hinder him if he begins to think that he already knows better.

"This is a very serious moment in the work. A man who loses his direction at this moment will never find it again afterwards. It must be remembered that man such as he is does not possess the means of distinguishing 'I' and 'Ouspensky' in himself. Even if he tries to, he will lie to himself and invent things, and he will never see himself as he really is. It must be understood that without outside help a man can never see himself.

"In order to know why this is so you must remember a great deal of what has been said earlier. As was said earlier, self-observation brings a man to the realization of the fact that he does not remember himself. Man's inability to remember himself is one of the chief and most characteristic features of his being and the cause of everything else in him. The inability to remember oneself finds expression in many ways. A man does not remember his decisions, he does not remember the promises he has made to himself, does not remember what he said or felt a month, a week, a day, or even an hour ago. He begins work of some kind and after a certain lapse of time he does not remember *why* he began it. It is especially in connection with work on oneself that this happens particularly often. A man can remember a promise given to another person only with the help of artificial associations, associations which have been *educated* into him, and they, in their turn, are connected with conceptions which are also artificially created of 'honor,' 'honesty,' 'duty,' and so on. But speaking in general one can say truthfully that if a man remembers one thing he forgets ten other things which are much more important for him to remember. And a man particularly easily forgets what relates to himself, those 'mental photographs' of himself which perhaps he has previously taken.

"And this deprives man's views and opinions of any stability and precision. A man does not remember what he has thought or what he has said; and he does not remember *how* he thought or *how* he spoke.

"This in its turn is connected with one of the fundamental characteristics of man's attitude towards himself and to all his surroundings. Namely, his constant 'identification' with what at a given moment has attracted his attention, his thoughts or his desires, and his imagination.

" 'Identification' is so common a quality that for purposes of observation it is difficult to separate it from everything else. Man is always in a state of identification, only the object of identification changes.

"A man identifies with a small problem which confronts him and he completely forgets the great aims with which he began his work. He identifies with one thought and forgets other thoughts; he is identified with one feeling, with one mood, and forgets his own wider thoughts, emotions, and moods. In work on themselves people are so much identified with separate aims that they fail to see the wood for the trees. Two or three trees nearest to them represent for them the whole wood.

" 'Identifying' is one of our most terrible foes because it penetrates everywhere and deceives a man at the moment when it seems to him that he is struggling with it. It is especially difficult to free oneself from identifying because a man naturally becomes more easily identified with the things that interest him most, to which he gives his time, his work, and his attention. In order to free himself from identifying a man must be constantly on guard and be merciless with himself, that is, he must not be afraid of seeing all the subtle and hidden forms which identifying takes.

"It is necessary to see and to study identifying to its very roots in oneself. The difficulty of struggling with identifying is still further increased by the fact that when people observe it in themselves they consider it a very good trait and call it 'enthusiasm,' 'zeal,' 'passion,' 'spontaneity,' 'inspiration,' and names of that kind, and they consider that only in a state of identifying can a man really produce good work, no matter in what sphere. In reality of course this is illusion. Man cannot do anything sensible when he is in a state of identifying. If people could see what the state of identifying means they would alter their opinion. A man becomes a thing, a piece of flesh; he loses even the small semblance of a human being that he has. In the East where people smoke hashish and other drugs it often happens that a man becomes so identified with his pipe that he begins to consider he is a pipe himself. This is not a joke but a fact. He actually becomes a pipe. This is identifying. And for this, hashish or opium are entirely unnecessary. Look at people in shops, in theaters, in restaurants;

or see how they identify with words when they argue about something or try to prove something, particularly something they do not know themselves. They become greediness, desires, or *words*; of themselves nothing remains.

"Identifying is the chief obstacle to self-remembering. A man who identifies with anything is unable to remember himself. In order to remember oneself it is necessary first of all *not to identify*. But in order to learn not to identify man must first of all *not be identified with himself*, must not call himself 'I' always and on all occasions. He must remember that there are two in him, that there is *himself*, that is 'I' in him, and there is *another* with whom he must struggle and whom he must conquer if he wishes at any time to attain anything. So long as a man identifies or can be identified, he is the slave of everything that can happen to him. Freedom is first of all freedom from identification.

"After general forms of identification attention must be given to a particular form of identifying, namely identifying with people, which takes the form of 'considering' them.

"There are several different kinds of 'considering.'

"On the most prevalent occasions a man is identified with what others think about him, how they treat him, what attitude they show towards him. He always thinks that people do not value him enough, are not sufficiently polite and courteous. All this torments him, makes him think and suspect and lose an immense amount of energy on guesswork, on suppositions, develops in him a distrustful and hostile attitude towards people. How somebody looked at him, what somebody thought of him, what somebody said of him—all this acquires for him an immense significance.

"And he 'considers' not only separate persons but society and historically constituted conditions. Everything that displeases such a man seems to him to be unjust, illegal, wrong, and illogical. And the point of departure for his judgment is always that these things can and should be changed. 'Injustice' is one of the words in which very often considering hides itself. When a man has convinced himself that he is indignant with some injustice, then for him to stop considering would mean 'reconciling himself to injustice.'

"There are people who are able to consider not only injustice or the failure of others to value them enough but who are able to consider for example the weather. This seems ridiculous but it is a fact. People are able to consider climate, heat, cold, snow, rain; they can be irritated by the weather, be indignant and angry with it. A man can take everything in such a personal way as though everything in the world had been specially arranged in order to give him pleasure or on the contrary to cause him inconvenience or unpleasantness.

"All this and much else besides is merely a form of identification. Such considering is wholly based upon 'requirements.' A man inwardly 're-quires' that everyone should see what a remarkable man he is and that they should constantly give expression to their respect, esteem, and ad-miration for him, for his intellect, his beauty, his cleverness, his wit, his presence of mind, his originality, and all his other qualities. Requirements in their turn are based on a completely fantastic notion about themselves such as very often occurs with people of very modest appearance. Various writers, actors, musicians, artists, and politicians, for instance, are almost without exception sick people. And what are they suffering from? First of all from an extraordinary opinion of themselves, then from requirements, and then from considering, that is, being ready and prepared beforehand to take offense at lack of understanding and lack of appreciation.

"There is still another form of considering which can take a great deal of energy from a man. This form starts with a man beginning to think that he is *not considering another person enough*, that this other person is offended with him for not considering him sufficiently. And he begins to think himself that perhaps he does not think enough about this other, does not pay him enough attention, does not give way to him enough. All this is simply weakness. People are afraid of one another. But this can lead very far. I have seen many such cases. In this way a man can finally lose his balance, if at any time he had any, and begin to perform entirely senseless actions. He gets angry with himself and feels that it is stupid, and he cannot stop, whereas in such cases the whole point is precisely 'not to consider.'

"It is the same case, only perhaps worse, when a man considers that in his opinion he 'ought' to do something when as a matter of fact he ought not to do so at all. 'Ought' and 'ought not' is also a difficult subject, that is, difficult to understand when a man really 'ought' and when he 'ought not.' This can be approached only from the point of view of 'aim.' When a man has an aim he 'ought' to do only what leads towards his aim and he 'ought not' to do anything that hinders him from going towards his aim.

"As I have already said, people very often think that if they begin to struggle with considering within themselves it will make them 'insincere' and they are afraid of this because they think that in this event they will be losing something, losing a part of themselves. In this case the same thing takes place as in attempts to struggle against the outward expression of unpleasant emotions. The sole difference is that in one case a man struggles with the outward expression of emotions and in the other case with an inner manifestation of perhaps the same emotions.

"This fear of losing sincerity is of course self-deception, one of those formulas of lying upon which human weaknesses are based. Man cannot help identifying and considering inwardly and he cannot help expressing his unpleasant emotions, simply because he is weak. Identifying, considering, the expressing of unpleasant emotions, are manifestations of his weakness, his impotence, his inability to control himself. But not wishing to acknowledge this weakness to himself, he calls it 'sincerity' or 'honesty' and he tells himself that he does not want to struggle against sincerity, whereas in fact he is unable to struggle against his weaknesses.

"Sincerity and honesty are in reality something quite different. What a man calls 'sincerity' in this case is in reality simply being unwilling to restrain himself. And deep down inside him a man is aware of this. But he lies to himself when he says that he does not want to lose sincerity.

"So far I have spoken of internal considering. It would be possible to bring forward many more examples. But you must do this yourselves, that is, you must seek these examples in your observations of yourselves and of others.

"The opposite of internal considering and what is in part a means of fighting against it is external considering. External considering is based upon an entirely different relationship towards people than internal considering. It is adaptation towards people, to their understanding, to their requirements. By considering externally a man does that which makes life easy for other people and for himself. External considering requires a knowledge of men, an understanding of their tastes, habits, and prejudices. At the same time external considering requires a great power over oneself, a great control over oneself. Very often a man desires *sincerely* to express or somehow or other show to another man what he really thinks of him or feels about him. And if he is a weak man he will of course give way to this desire and afterwards justify himself and say that he did not want to lie, did not want to pretend, he wanted to be sincere. Then he convinces himself that it was the other man's fault. He really wanted to consider him, even to give way to him, not to quarrel, and so on. But *the other man* did not at all want to consider him so that nothing could be done with him. It very often happens that a man begins with a blessing and ends with a curse. He begins by deciding not to consider and afterwards blames other people for not considering him. This is an example of how external considering passes into internal considering. But if a man really remembers himself he understands that another man is a machine just as he is himself. And then he will *enter into his position*, he will put himself in his place, and he will be really able to understand and feel what another man thinks and feels. If he can do this his work becomes easier for him. But if he approaches a man with his own requirements nothing except new internal considering can ever be obtained from it.

"Right external considering is very important in the work. It often happens that people who understand very well the necessity of external considering in life do not understand the necessity of external considering in the work; they decide that just because they are in the work they have the right not to consider. Whereas in reality, in the work, that is, for a man's own successful work, ten times more external considering is necessary than in life, because *only* external considering on his part shows his valuation of the work and his understanding of the work; and success in the work is always proportional to the valuation and understanding of it. Remember that work cannot begin and cannot proceed on a level lower than that of the *obyvatel*,[1] that is, on a level lower than ordinary life. This is a very important principle which, for some reason or other, is very easily forgotten. But we will speak about this separately afterwards."

G. began one of the following talks with the fact that we forget about the difficulties of our position.

"You often think in a very naïve way," he said. "You already think you can *do*. To get rid of this conviction is more difficult than anything else for a man. You do not understand all the complexity of your organization and you do not realize that every effort, in addition to the results desired, even if it gives these, gives thousands of unexpected and often undesirable results, and the chief thing that you forget is that you are not beginning from the beginning with a nice clean, new machine. There stand behind you many years of a wrong and stupid life, of indulgence in every kind of weakness, of shutting your eyes to your own errors, of striving to avoid all unpleasant truths, of constant lying to yourselves, of self-justification, of blaming others, and so on, and so on. All this cannot help affecting the machine. The machine is dirty, in places it is rusty, and in some places artificial appliances have been formed, the necessity for which has been created by its own wrong way of working.

"These artificial appliances will now interfere very much with all your good intentions.

"They are called 'buffers.'

"'Buffer' is a term which requires special explanation. We know what buffers on railway carriages are. They are the contrivances which lessen the shock when carriages or trucks strike one another. If there were no buffers the shock of one carriage against another would be very unpleasant and dangerous. Buffers soften the results of these shocks and render them unnoticeable and imperceptible.

"Exactly the same appliances are to be found within man. They are created, not by nature but by man himself, although involuntarily. The cause of their appearance is the existence in man of many contradictions; contradictions of opinions, feelings, sympathies, words, and actions. If a man throughout the whole of his life were to feel all the contradictions that are within him he could not live and act as calmly as he lives and

---

[1] For the definition of *obyvatel*, see page 362 et seq.

acts now. He would have constant friction, constant unrest. We fail to see how contradictory and hostile the different I's of our personality are to one another. If a man were to feel all these contradictions he would feel what *he really is.* He would feel that he is mad. It is not pleasant to anyone to feel that he is mad. Moreover, a thought such as this deprives a man of self-confidence, weakens his energy, deprives him of 'self-respect.' Somehow or other he must master this thought or banish it. He must either destroy contradictions or cease to see and to feel them. A man cannot destroy contradictions. But if 'buffers' are created in him he can cease to feel them and he will not feel the impact from the clash of contradictory views, contradictory emotions, contradictory words.

" 'Buffers' are created slowly and gradually. Very many 'buffers' are created artificially through 'education.' Others are created under the hypnotic influence of all surrounding life. A man is surrounded by people who live, speak, think, and feel by means of 'buffers.' Imitating them in their opinions, actions, and words, a man involuntarily creates similar 'buffers' in himself. 'Buffers' make a man's life more easy. It is very hard to live without 'buffers.' But they keep man from the possibility of inner development because 'buffers' are made to lessen shocks and it is only shocks that can lead a man out of the state in which he lives, that is, waken him. 'Buffers' lull a man to sleep, give him the agreeable and peaceful sensation that all will be well, that no contradictions exist and that he can sleep in peace. *'Buffers' are appliances by means of which a man can always be in the right.* 'Buffers' help a man not to feel his conscience.

" 'Conscience' is again a term that needs explanation.

"In ordinary life the concept 'conscience' is taken too simply. As if we had a conscience. Actually the concept 'conscience' in the sphere of the emotions is equivalent to the concept 'consciousness' in the sphere of the intellect. And as we have no consciousness we have no conscience.

"*Consciousness* is a state in which a man *knows all at once* everything that he in general knows and in which he can see how little he does know and how many contradictions there are in what he knows.

"*Conscience* is a state in which a man *feels all at once* everything that he in general feels, or can feel. And as everyone has within him thousands of contradictory feelings which vary from a deeply hidden realization of his own nothingness and fears of all kinds to the most stupid kind of self-conceit, self-confidence, self-satisfaction, and self-praise, to feel all this *together* would not only be painful but literally unbearable.

"If a man whose entire inner world is composed of contradictions were suddenly to feel all these contradictions simultaneously within himself, if he were to feel all at once that he loves everything he hates and hates everything he loves; that he lies when he tells the truth and that he tells the truth when he lies; and if he could feel the shame and horror of it all, this would be the state which is called 'conscience.' A man cannot live in this state; he must either destroy contradictions or destroy conscience. He cannot destroy conscience, but if he cannot destroy it he can put it to sleep, that is, he can separate by impenetrable barriers one feeling of self from another, never see them together, never feel their incompatibility, the absurdity of one existing alongside another.

"But fortunately for man, that is, for his peace and for his sleep, this state of conscience is very rare. From early childhood 'buffers' begin to grow and strengthen in him, taking from him the possibility of seeing his inner contradictions and therefore, for him, there is no danger whatever of a sudden awakening. Awakening is possible only for those who seek it and want it, for those who are ready to struggle with themselves and work on themselves for a very long time and very persistently in order to attain it. For this it is necessary to destroy 'buffers,' that is, to go out to meet all those inner sufferings which are connected with the sensations of contradictions. Moreover the destruction of 'buffers' in itself requires very long work and a man must agree to this work realizing that the result of his work will be every possible discomfort and suffering from the awakening of his conscience.

"But conscience is the fire which alone can fuse all the powders in the glass retort which was mentioned before and create the unity which a man lacks in that state in which he begins to study himself.

"The concept 'conscience' has nothing in common with the concept 'morality.'

"Conscience is a general and a *permanent* phenomenon. Conscience is the same for all men and conscience is possible only in the absence of 'buffers.' From the point of view of understanding the different categories of man we may say that there exists the conscience of a man in whom there are no contradictions. This conscience is not suffering; on the contrary it is joy of a totally new character which we are unable to understand. But even a momentary awakening of conscience in a man who has thousands of different I's is bound to involve suffering. And if these moments of conscience become longer and if a man does not fear them but on the contrary co-operates with them and tries to keep and prolong them, an element of very subtle joy, a foretaste of the future 'clear consciousness' will gradually enter into these moments.

"There is nothing general in the concept of 'morality.' Morality consists of buffers. There is no general morality. What is moral in China is immoral in Europe and what is moral in Europe is immoral in China. What is moral in Petersburg is immoral in the Caucasus. And what is moral in the Caucasus is immoral in Petersburg. What is moral in one class of society is immoral in another and vice versa. Morality is always and everywhere an artificial phenomenon. It consists of various 'taboos,' that is, restrictions, and various demands, sometimes sensible in their basis and sometimes having lost all meaning or never even having had any meaning, and having been created on a false basis, on a soil of superstition and false fears.

"Morality consists of 'buffers.' And since 'buffers' are of various kinds, and as the conditions of life in different countries and in different ages or among different classes of society vary considerably, so the morality created by them is also very dissimilar and contradictory. A morality common to all does not exist. It is even impossible to say that there exists any general idea of morality, for instance, in Europe. It is said sometimes that the general morality for Europe is 'Christian morality.' But first of all the idea of 'Christian morality' itself admits of very many different interpretations and many different crimes have been justified by 'Christian morality.' And in the second place modern Europe has very little in common with 'Christian morality,' no matter how we understand this morality.

"In any case, if 'Christian morality' brought Europe to the war which is now going on, then it would be as well to be as far as possible from such morality."

"Many people say that they do not understand the moral side of your teaching," said one of us. "And others say that your teaching has no morality at all."

"Of course not," said G. "People are very fond of talking about morality. But morality is merely self-suggestion. *What is necessary is conscience.* We do not teach morality. We teach how to find conscience. People are not pleased when we say this. They say that we have no *love.* Simply because we do not encourage weakness and hypocrisy but, on the contrary, take off all masks. He who desires the truth will not speak of love or of Christianity because he knows how far he is from these. Christian teaching is for Christians. And Christians are those who live, that is, who do everything, according to Christ's precepts. Can they who talk of love and morality live according to Christ's precepts? Of course they cannot; but there will always be talk of this kind, there will always be people to whom words are more precious than anything else. But this is a true sign! He who speaks like this is an empty man; it is not worth while wasting time on him.

"Morality and conscience are quite different things. One conscience can never contradict another conscience. One morality can always very easily contradict and completely deny another. A man with 'buffers' may be very moral. And 'buffers' can be very different, that is, two very moral men may consider each other very immoral. As a rule it is almost inevitably so. The more 'moral' a man is, the more 'immoral' does he think other moral people.

"The idea of morality is connected with the idea of good and evil conduct. But the idea of good and evil is always different for different people, always subjective in man number one, number two, and number three, and is connected only with a given moment or a given situation. A subjective man can have no general concept of good and evil. For a subjective man evil is everything that is opposed to his desires or interests or to his conception of good.

"One may say that evil does not exist for subjective man at all, that there exist only different conceptions of good. *Nobody ever does anything deliberately in the interests of evil, for the sake of evil.* Everybody acts in the interests of good, *as he understands it.* But everybody understands it in a different way. Consequently men drown, slay, and kill one another *in the interests of good.* The reason is again just the same, men's ignorance and the deep sleep in which they live.

"This is so obvious that it even seems strange that people have never thought of it before. However, the fact remains that they fail to understand this and everyone considers *his good* as the only good and all the rest as evil. It is naïve and useless to hope that men will ever understand this and that they will evolve a general and identical idea of good."

"But do not good and evil exist in themselves apart from man?" asked someone present.

"They do," said G., "only this is very far away from us and it is not worth your while even to try to understand this at present. Simply remember one thing. The only possible permanent idea of good and evil for man is connected with the idea of evolution; not with mechanical evolution, of course, but with the idea of man's development through conscious efforts, the change of his being, the creation of unity in him, and the formation of a permanent I.

"A permanent idea of good and evil can be formed in man only in connection with a permanent aim and a permanent understanding. If a man understands that he is asleep and if he wishes to awake, then everything that helps him to awake will be *good* and everything that hinders him, everything that prolongs his sleep, will be *evil.* Exactly in the same way will he understand what is good and evil for other people. What helps them to awake is good, what hinders them is evil. But this is so only for those who want to awake, that is, for those who understand that they are asleep. Those who do not understand that they are asleep and those who can have no wish to awake, cannot have understanding of good and evil. And as the overwhelming majority of people do not realize and will never realize that they are asleep, neither good nor evil can actually exist for them.

"This contradicts generally accepted ideas. People are accustomed to think that good and evil must be the same for everyone, and above all, that good and evil exist for everyone. In reality, however, good and evil exist only for a few, for those who have an aim and who pursue that aim. Then what hinders the pursuit of that aim is evil and what helps is good.

"But of course most sleeping people will say that they have an aim and that they are going somewhere. The realization of the fact that he has no aim and that he is not going anywhere is the first sign of the approaching awakening of a man or of awakening becoming really possible for him. Awakening begins when a man realizes that he is going nowhere and does not know where to go.

"As has been explained before, there are many qualities which men attribute to themselves, which in reality can belong only to people of a higher degree of development and of a higher degree of evolution than man number one, number two, and number three. Individuality, a single and permanent I, consciousness, will, the *ability to do,* a state of inner freedom, all these are qualities which ordinary man does not possess. To the same category belongs the idea of good and evil, the very existence of which is connected with a *permanent* aim, with a *permanent* direction and a *permanent* center of gravity.

"The idea of good and evil is sometimes connected with the idea of truth and falsehood. But just as good and evil do not exist for ordinary man, neither do truth and falsehood exist.

"Permanent truth and permanent falsehood can exist only for a permanent man. If a man himself continually changes, then for him truth and falsehood will also continually change. And if people are all in different states at every given moment, their conceptions of truth must be as varied as their conceptions of good. A man never notices how he begins to regard as true what yesterday he considered as false and vice versa. He does not notice these transitions just as he does not notice the transitions of his own I's one into another.

"In the life of an ordinary man truth and falsehood have no moral value of any kind because a man can never keep to one single truth. His truth changes. If for a certain time it does not change, it is simply because it is kept by 'buffers.' And a man can never *tell the truth.* Sometimes *'it tells' the truth,* sometimes *'it tells'* a lie. Consequently his truth and his falsehood have no value; neither of them depends upon him, both of them depend upon accident. And this is equally true when applied to a man's words, to his thoughts, his feelings, and to his conceptions of truth and falsehood.

"In order to understand the interrelation of truth and falsehood in life a man must understand falsehood in himself, the constant incessant lies he tells himself.

"These lies are created by 'buffers.' In order to destroy the lies in oneself as well as lies told unconsciously to others, 'buffers' must be destroyed. But then a man cannot live without 'buffers.' 'Buffers' automatically control a man's actions, words, thoughts, and feelings. If 'buffers' were to be destroyed all control would disappear. A man cannot exist without control even though it is only automatic control. Only a man who possesses will, that is, conscious control, can live without 'buffers.' Consequently, if a man begins to destroy 'buffers' within himself he must at the same time develop a will. And as will cannot be created to order in a short space of time a man may be left with 'buffers' demolished and with a will that is not as yet sufficiently strengthened. The only chance he has during this period is to be controlled by another will which has already been strengthened.

"This is why in school work, which includes the destruction of 'buffers,' a man must be ready to obey another man's will so long as his own will is not yet fully developed. Usually this subordination to another man's will is studied before anything else. I use the word 'studied' because a man must understand why such obedience is necessary and he must learn to obey. The latter is not at all easy. A man beginning the work of self-study with the object of attaining control over himself is accustomed to believe in his own decisions. Even the fact that he has seen the necessity for changing himself shows him that his decisions are correct and strengthens his belief in them. But when he begins to work on himself a man must give up his own decisions, 'sacrifice his own decisions,' because otherwise the will of the man who directs his work will not be able to control his actions.

"In schools of the religious way 'obedience' is demanded before anything else, that is, full and unquestioning submission although without understanding. Schools of the fourth way demand understanding before anything else. Results of efforts are always proportional to understanding.

"Renunciation of his own decisions, subordination to the will of another, may present insuperable difficulties to a man if he had failed to realize beforehand that actually he neither sacrifices nor changes anything in his life, that all his life he has been subject to some extraneous will and has never had any decisions of his own. But a man is not conscious of this. He considers that he has the right of free choice. It is hard for him to renounce the illusion that he directs and organizes his life himself. But no work on himself is possible until a man is free from this illusion.

"He must realize that *he does not exist*; he must realize that he can lose nothing because he has nothing to lose; he must realize his 'nothingness' in the full sense of the term.

"This *consciousness of one's nothingness* alone can conquer the fear of subordination to the will of another. However strange it may seem, this fear is actually one of the most serious obstacles on a man's path. A man is afraid that he will be made to do things that are opposed to his principles, views, and ideas. Moreover, this fear immediately creates in him the illusion that he really has principles, views, and convictions which in reality he never has had and never could have. A man who has never in his life thought of morality suddenly begins to fear that he will be made to do something immoral. A man who has never thought of his health and who has done everything possible to ruin it begins to fear that he will be made to do something which will injure it. A man who has lied to everyone, everywhere, all his life in the most barefaced manner begins suddenly to fear that he will be made to tell lies, and so on without end. I knew a drunkard who was afraid more than anything else that he would be made to drink.

"The fear of being subordinated to another man's will very often proves stronger than anything else. A man does not realize that a subordination to which he consciously agrees is the only way to acquire a will of his own."

Next time G. began again with the question of will.

"The question of will, of one's own will and of another man's will, is much more complicated than it seems at the first glance. A man has not sufficient will *to do*, that is, to control himself and all his actions, but he has sufficient will to obey another person. And only in this way can he escape from the *law of accident*. There is no other way.

"I mentioned before about *fate* and *accident* in man's life. We will now take the meaning of these words in more detail. Fate also exists but not for everyone. Most people are separated from their fate and live under the law of accident only. Fate is the result of planetary influences which correspond to a man's type. We will speak about types later. In the meantime you must grasp one thing. A man can have the fate which corresponds to his type but he practically never does have it. This arises because fate has relation to only one part of man, namely to his *essence*.

"It must be understood that man consists of two parts: *essence* and *personality*. Essence in man is what is *his own*. Personality in man is what is 'not his own.' 'Not his own' means what has come from outside, what he has learned, or reflects, all traces of exterior impressions left in the memory and in the sensations, all words and movements that have been learned, all feelings created by imitation—all this is 'not his own,' all this is personality.

"From the point of view of ordinary psychology the division of man into personality and essence is hardly comprehensible. It is more exact to say that such a division does not exist in psychology at all.

"A small child has no personality as yet. He is what he really is. He is essence. His desires, tastes, likes, dislikes, express his being such as it is.

"But as soon as so-called 'education' begins personality begins to grow. Personality is created partly by the intentional influences of other people, that is, by 'education,' and partly by involuntary imitation of them by the child itself. In the creation of personality a great part is also played by 'resistance' to people around him and by attempts to conceal from them something that is 'his own' or 'real.'

"Essence is the truth in man; personality is the false. But in proportion as personality grows, essence manifests itself more and more rarely and more and more feebly and it very often happens that essence stops in its growth at a very early age and grows no further. It happens very often that the essence of a grown-up man, even that of a very intellectual and, in the accepted meaning of the word, highly 'educated' man, stops on the level of a child of five or six. This means that everything we see in this man is in reality 'not his own.' What is his own in man, that is, his essence, is usually only manifested in his instincts and in his simplest emotions. There are cases, however, when a man's essence grows in parallel with his personality. Such cases represent very rare exceptions especially in the circumstances of cultured life. Essence has more chances of development in men who live nearer to nature in difficult conditions of constant struggle and danger.

"But as a rule the personality of such people is very little developed. They have more of what is their own, but very little of what is 'not their own,' that is to say, they lack education and instruction, they lack culture. Culture creates personality and is at the same time the product and the result of personality. We do not realize that the whole of our life, all we call civilization, all we call science, philosophy, art, and politics, is created by people's personality, that is, by what is 'not their own' in them.

"The element that is 'not his own' differs from what is man's 'own' by the fact that it can be lost, altered, or taken away by artificial means.

"There exists a possibility of experimental verification of the relation of personality to essence. In Eastern schools ways and means are known by the help of which it is possible to separate man's personality from his essence. For this purpose they sometimes use hypnosis, sometimes special narcotics, sometimes certain kinds of exercises. If personality and essence are for a time separated in a man by one or another of these means, two beings, as it were, are formed in him, who speak in different voices, have completely different tastes, aims, and interests, and one of these two beings often proves to be on the level of a small child. Continuing the experiment further it is possible to put one of these beings to sleep, or the experiment may begin by putting to sleep either personality or essence. Certain narcotics have the property of putting personality to sleep without affecting essence. And for a certain time after taking this narcotic a man's personality disappears, as it were, and only his essence remains. And it happens that a man full of the most varied and exalted ideas, full of sympathies and antipathies, love, hatred, attachments, patriotism, habits, tastes, desires, convictions, suddenly proves quite empty, without thoughts, without feelings, without convictions, without views. Everything that has agitated him before now leaves him completely indifferent. Sometimes he sees the artificiality and the imaginary character of his usual moods or his high-sounding words, sometimes he simply forgets them as though they had never existed. Things for which he was ready to sacrifice his life now appear to him ridiculous and meaningless and unworthy of his attention. All that he can find in himself is a small number of instinctive inclinations and tastes. He is fond of sweets, he likes warmth, he dislikes cold, he dislikes the thought of work, or on the contrary he likes the idea of physical movement. And that is all.

"Sometimes, though very seldom, and sometimes when it is least expected, essence proves fully grown and fully developed in a man, even in cases of undeveloped personality, and in this case essence unites together everything that is serious and real in a man.

"But this happens very seldom. As a rule a man's essence is either primitive, savage, and childish, or else simply stupid. The development of essence depends on work on oneself.

"A very important moment in the work on oneself is when a man begins to distinguish between his personality and his essence. A man's real I, his individuality, can grow only from his essence. It can be said that a man's individuality is his essence, grown up, mature. But in order to enable essence to grow up, it is first of all necessary to weaken the constant pressure of personality upon it, because the obstacles to the growth of essence are contained in personality.

"If we take an average cultured man, we shall see that in the vast majority of cases his personality is the active element in him while his essence is the passive element. The inner growth of a man cannot begin so long as this order of things remains unchanged. Personality must become passive and essence must become active. This can happen only if 'buffers' are removed or weakened, because 'buffers' are the chief weapon by the help of which personality holds essence in subjection.

"As has been said earlier, in the case of less cultured people essence is often more highly developed than it is in cultured man. It would seem that they ought to be nearer the possibility of growth, but in reality it is not so because their personality proves to be insufficiently developed. For inner growth, for work on oneself, a certain development of personality as well as a certain strength of essence are necessary. Personality consists of 'rolls,' and of 'buffers' resulting from a certain work of the centers. An insufficiently developed personality means a lack of 'rolls,' that is, a lack of knowledge, a lack of information, a lack of the material upon which work on oneself must be based. Without some store of knowledge, without a certain amount of material 'not his own,' a man cannot begin to work on himself, he cannot begin to study himself, he cannot begin to struggle with his mechanical habits, simply because there will be no reason or motive for undertaking such work.

"It does not mean that all the ways are closed to him. The way of the fakir and the way of the monk, which do not require any intellectual development, remain open to him. But the methods and the means which are possible for a man of a developed intellect are impossible for him. Thus evolution is equally difficult for a cultured or an uncultured man. A cultured man lives far from nature, far from natural conditions of existence, in artificial conditions of life, developing his personality at the expense of his essence. A less cultured man, living in more normal and more natural conditions, develops his essence at the expense of his personality. A successful beginning of work on oneself requires the happy occurrence of an equal development of personality and essence. Such an occurrence will give the greatest assurance of success. If essence is very little developed, a long preparatory period of work is required and this work will be quite fruitless if a man's essence is rotten inside or if it develops some irreparable defects. Conditions of this kind occur fairly often. An abnormal development of personality very often arrests the development of essence at such an early stage that the essence becomes a small deformed thing. From a small deformed thing nothing else can be got.

"Moreover, it happens fairly often that essence dies in a man while his personality and his body are still alive. A considerable percentage of the people we meet in the streets of a great town are people who are empty inside, that is, they are actually *already dead*.

"It is fortunate for us that we do not see and do not know it. If we knew what a number of people are actually dead and what a number of these dead people govern our lives, we should go mad with horror. And indeed people often do go mad because they find out something of this nature without the proper preparation, that is, they see something they are not supposed to see. In order to see without danger one must be on the way. If a man who can do nothing sees the truth he will certainly go mad. Only this rarely happens. Usually everything is so arranged that a man can see nothing prematurely. Personality sees only what it likes to see and what does not interfere with its life. It never sees what it does not like. This is both good and bad at the same time. It is good if a man wants to sleep, bad if he wants to awaken."

"If essence is subject to the influence of fate, does it mean that compared with accident fate is always favorable to a man?" asked somebody present. "And can fate bring a man to the work?"

"No, it does not mean this at all," G. answered him. "Fate is better than accident only in the sense that it is possible to take it into account, it is possible to know it beforehand; it is possible to prepare for what is ahead. In regard to accident one can know nothing. But fate can be also unpleasant or difficult. In this event, however, there are means for isolating oneself from one's fate. The first step towards this consists in getting away from *general laws*. Just as there is individual accident, so is there general or collective accident. And in the same way as there is individual fate, there is a general or collective fate. Collective accident and collective fate are governed by *general laws*. If a man wishes to create individuality of his own he must first free himself from *general laws*. General laws are by no means all obligatory for man; he can free himself from many of them if he frees himself from 'buffers' and from imagination. All this is connected with liberation from personality. Personality feeds on imagination and falsehood. If the falsehood in which man lives is decreased and imagination is decreased, personality very soon weakens and a man begins to be controlled either by fate or by a *line of work* which is in its turn controlled by another man's will; this will lead him until a will of his own has been formed, capable of withstanding both accident and, when necessary, fate."

The talks given embrace a period of a few months. It stands to reason that it is not possible to re-establish the talks in their exact order because very often G. touched upon twenty different subjects in an evening. Much was repeated, much depended upon the questions asked by those present, many ideas were so closely connected that they could only be separated artificially.

At this time certain definite types of people had already begun to show a negative attitude towards our work. Besides the absence of "love" many people were very indignant at the demand for payment, for money. In this connection it was very characteristic that those who were indignant were not those who could pay only with difficulty, but people of means for whom the sum demanded was a mere trifle.

Those who could not pay or who could pay very little always understood that they could not count upon getting something for nothing, and that G.'s work, his journeys to Petersburg, and the time that he and others gave to the work cost money. Only those who had money did not understand and did not want to understand this.

"Does this mean that we must pay to enter the Kingdom of Heaven?" they said. "People do not pay nor is money asked for such things. Christ said to his disciples: 'Take neither purse nor scrip,' and you want a thousand roubles. A very good business could be made of it. Suppose that you had a hundred members. This would already make a hundred thousand, and if there were two hundred, three hundred? Three hundred thousand a year is very good money."

G. always smiled when I told him about talks like this.

"Take neither purse nor scrip! And need not a railway ticket be taken either? The hotel paid? You see how much falsehood and hypocrisy there is here. No, even if we needed no money at all it would still be necessary to keep this payment. It rids us at once of many useless people. Nothing shows up people so much as their attitude towards money. They are ready to waste as much as you like on their own personal fantasies but they have no valuation whatever of another person's labor. I must work for them and give them gratis everything that they vouchsafe to take from me. 'How is it possible to *trade in knowledge? This* ought to be free.' It is precisely for this reason that the demand for this payment is necessary. Some people will never pass this barrier. And if they do not pass this one, it means that they will never pass another. Besides, there are other considerations. Afterwards you will see."

The other considerations were very simple ones. Many people indeed could not pay. And although in principle G. put the question very strictly, in practice he never refused anybody on the grounds that they had no money. And it was found out later that he even supported many of his pupils. The people who paid a thousand roubles paid not only for themselves but for others.

Chapter Nine

A T ONE lecture G. began to draw the diagram of the universe in an entirely new way.

"So far we have spoken of the forces that create worlds," he said, "of the process of creation proceeding from the Absolute. We will now speak of the processes which take place in the already created and existing world. But you must remember that the process of creation never stops, although, on a planetary scale, growth proceeds so slowly that if we reckon it in our time planetary conditions can be regarded as permanent for us.

"Therefore, let us take the 'ray of creation' after the universe has already been created.

"The action of the Absolute upon the world, or upon the worlds created by it or within it, continues. The action of each of these worlds upon subsequent worlds continues in exactly the same way. 'All suns' of the Milky Way influence our sun. The sun influences the planets. 'All planets' influence our earth and the earth influences the moon. These influences are transmitted by means of radiations passing through starry and interplanetary space.

"In order to study these radiations let us take the 'ray of creation' in an abridged form: Absolute–sun–earth–moon, or in other words let us imagine the 'ray of creation' in the form of *three octaves of radiations*: the first octave between the Absolute and the sun, the second octave between the sun and the earth, and the third octave between the earth and the moon; and let us examine the passage of radiations between these four fundamental points of the universe.

"We have to find our place and understand our functions in this universe, which is taken in the form of *three octaves of radiations* between four points.

"In the first octave the Absolute will include two notes, do and si, with the 'interval' between them.

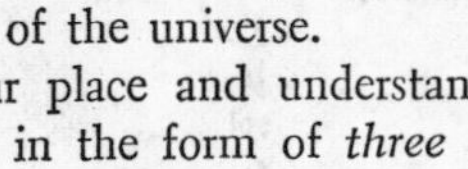

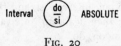

Interval   do/si   ABSOLUTE

Fig. 20

"Then will follow notes la, sol, fa: that is,

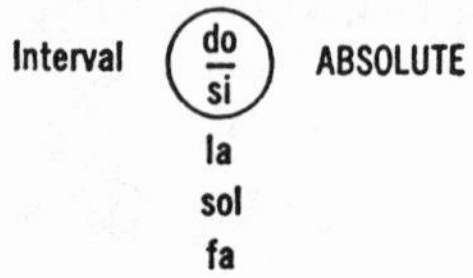

Interval ⟮ do / si ⟯ ABSOLUTE
la
sol
fa

FIG. 21

"Then an interval, and the 'shock' filling it, unknown to us but nevertheless inevitably existing, then mi, re.

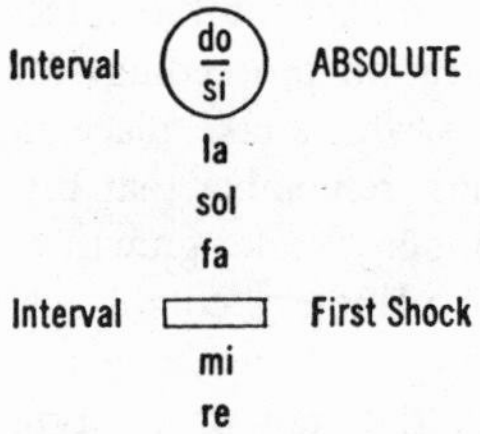

Interval ⟮ do / si ⟯ ABSOLUTE
la
sol
fa
Interval ☐ First Shock
mi
re

FIG. 22

"The radiations reach the sun. Two notes are included in the sun itself, do, an 'interval,' and si, then follow la, sol, fa—radiations going towards the earth.

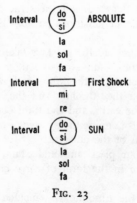

Interval ⟮ do / si ⟯ ABSOLUTE
la
sol
fa
Interval ☐ First Shock
mi
re
Interval ⟮ do / si ⟯ SUN
la
sol
fa

FIG. 23

"Then an 'interval' and the 'shock' of organic life which fills it, then mi and re. The earth: do, an 'interval,' si, and then la, sol, fa—radiations going towards the moon; then again an 'interval,' a 'shock' unknown to us, then mi, re, and the moon, do.

"These three octaves of radiations, in which form we shall now imagine the universe, will enable us to explain the relation of matters and forces of different planes of the world to our own life.

"It must be observed that, although there are six 'intervals' in these three octaves, only three of them actually require to be supplemented from outside. The first 'interval' between do and si is filled by the will of the Absolute. The second 'interval' do–si is filled by the influence of the sun's mass upon radiations passing through it. And the third 'interval' do–si is filled by the action of the earth's mass upon radiations passing through it. Only the 'intervals' between fa and mi have to be filled by 'additional shocks.' These 'additional shocks' can come either from other octaves which pass across the given point or from parallel octaves which start from higher points. We know nothing about the nature of the 'shock' between mi–fa in the first octave Absolute–Sun. But the 'shock' in the octave Sun–Earth is *organic life on earth,* that is, the three notes *la, sol, fa* of the octave which starts in the sun. The nature of the 'shock' between mi and fa in the octave Earth–Moon is unknown to us.

"It must be noted that the term 'a point of the universe' which I have used, has

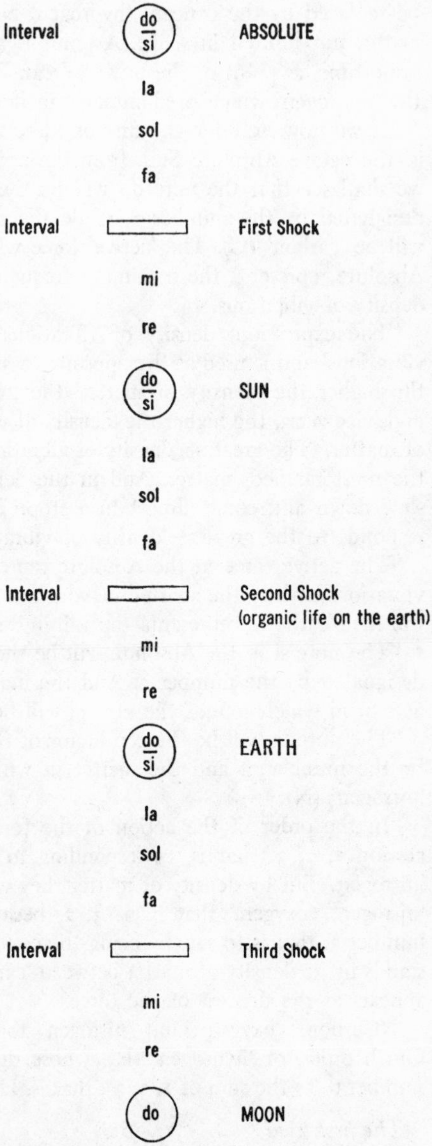

Interval	(do / si)	ABSOLUTE
	la	
	sol	
	fa	
Interval	[First Shock]	First Shock
	mi	
	re	
	(do / si)	SUN
	la	
	sol	
	fa	
Interval	[Second Shock]	Second Shock (organic life on the earth)
	mi	
	re	
	(do / si)	EARTH
	la	
	sol	
	fa	
Interval	[Third Shock]	Third Shock
	mi	
	re	
	(do)	MOON

FIG. 24

a quite definite meaning, namely, a 'point" represents a certain combination of hydrogens which is organized in a definite place and fulfills a definite function in one or another system. The concept 'point' cannot be replaced by the concept 'hydrogen' because 'hydrogen' means simply matter not limited in space. A point is always limited in space. At the same time, a 'point of the universe' can be designated by the *number* of the 'hydrogen' which predominates in it or is central in it.

"If we now examine the first of these three octaves of radiations, that is, the octave Absolute–Sun, from the point of view of the law of three, we shall see that the note do will be the conductor of the active force, designated by the number 1, while the matter in which this force acts will be 'carbon' (C). The 'active' force which creates the note do in the Absolute represents the maximum frequency of vibrations or the greatest density of vibrations.

"The expression 'density of vibrations' corresponds to 'frequency of vibrations' and is used as the opposite to 'density of matter,' that is to say, the higher the 'density of matter' the lower the 'density of vibrations,' and, vice versa, the higher the 'density of vibrations' the lower the 'density of matter.' The greatest 'density of vibrations' is to be found in the finest, the most rarefied, matter. And in the densest matter possible vibrations slow down and come almost to a stop. Therefore the finest matter corresponds to the greatest 'density of vibrations.'

"The active force in the Absolute represents the maximum 'density of vibrations,' while the matter in which these vibrations proceed, that is, the first 'carbon,' represents the minimum density of matter.

"The note si in the Absolute will be the conductor of the passive force designated by the number 2. And the matter in which this passive force acts or in which sounds the note si will be 'oxygen' (O).

"The note la will be the conductor of the neutralizing force designated by the number 3, and the matter in which sounds the note la will be 'nitrogen' (N).

"In the order of the action of the forces they will stand in the succession 1, 2, 3, that is, corresponding to the matters 'carbon,' 'oxygen,' 'nitrogen.' But by density of matter they will stand in the order: 'carbon,' 'nitrogen,' 'oxygen,' that is, 1, 3, 2, because 'nitrogen' by retaining the number 3, that is to say, by being the conductor of the neutralizing force, stands by its density of matter between 'carbon' and 'oxygen,' and 'oxygen' appears as the densest of the three.

"'Carbon,' 'oxygen,' and 'nitrogen' together will give matter of the fourth order, or 'hydrogen' (H), whose density we will designate by the number 6 (as the sum of 1, 2, 3), that is, H6:

The first triad

do	C	1	1	1	
si	O	2	3	2	H6
la	N	3	2	3	

"C, O, N retain their numbers 1, 2, 3. 'Carbon' is always 1, 'oxygen' is always 2, and 'nitrogen' is always 3.

"But being more active than 'oxygen,' 'nitrogen' enters as the active principle in the next triad and enters with the density of 2. In other words 'nitrogen' has a density of 2 and 'oxygen' a density of 3.

"So that the note la of the first triad is the conductor of the active force in the next triad which it enters with the density of 2. If 'carbon' enters with the density of 2, then 'oxygen' and 'nitrogen' must correspond to it in densities, repeating the ratio of densities of the first triad. In the first triad the ratio of densities was 1, 2, 3; in the second triad it should be 2, 4, 6, that is, 'carbon' of the second triad will possess the density of 2, 'nitrogen' a density of 4, 'oxygen' a density of 6. Taken together they will give 'hydrogen' 12 (H12):

The second triad

la	C	2	2	2	
sol	O	4	6	4	H12
fa	N	6	4	6	

"According to the same plan and order the following triad will be constructed: fa, 'shock,' mi. 'Carbon' which was 'nitrogen' in the second triad enters with a density of 4; the 'nitrogen' and 'oxygen' corresponding to it must have a density of 8 and 12; together they will give 'hydrogen' 24 (H24):

The third triad

fa	C	4	4	4	
—	O	8	12	8	H24
mi	N	12	8	12	

"The next triad mi, re, do, by the same plan and order will give 'hydrogen' 48 (H48):

The fourth triad

mi	C	8	8	8	
re	O	16	24	16	H48
do	N	24	16	24	

"The triad do, si, la will give 'hydrogen' 96 (H96):

The fifth triad

do	C	16	16	16	
si	O	32	48	32	H96
la	N	48	32	48	

the triad la, sol, fa—'hydrogen' 192 (H192):

The sixth triad

la	C	32	32	32	
sol	O	64	96	64	H192
fa	N	96	64	96	

fa, 'shock,' mi—'hydrogen' 384 (H384):

The seventh triad

fa	C	64	64	64
—	O	128	192	128
mi	N	192	128	192

} H384

mi, re, do—'hydrogen' 768 (H768):

The eighth triad

mi	C	128	128	128
re	O	256	384	256
do	N	384	256	384

} H768

do, si, la—'hydrogen' 1536 (H1536):

The ninth triad

do	C	256	256	256
si	O	512	768	512
la	N	768	512	768

} H1536

la, sol, fa—'hydrogen' 3072 (H3072):

The tenth triad

la	C	512	512	512
sol	O	1024	1536	1024
fa	N	1536	1024	1536

} H3072

fa, 'shock,' mi—'hydrogen' 6144 (H6144):

The eleventh triad

fa	C	1024	1024	1024
—	O	2048	3072	2048
mi	N	3072	2048	3072

} H6144

mi, re, do—'hydrogen' 12288 (H12288):

The twelfth triad

mi	C	2048	2048	2048
re	O	4096	6144	4096
do	N	6144	4096	6144

} H12288

"Twelve 'hydrogens' are obtained with densities ranging from 6 to 12288. (See Table 1.)

"These twelve 'hydrogens' represent twelve categories of matter contained in the universe from the Absolute to the moon, and if it were possible to establish exactly which of these matters constitute man's organism and act in it, this alone would determine what place man occupies in the world.

					H					H		H
do	C	1	1	1	H6						do	
si	O	2	3	2							si	H6
la	N	3	2	3		C	2	2	2		la	
sol						O	4	6	4	H12	sol	H12
fa	C	4	4	4		N	6	4	6		fa	
—	O	8	12	8	H24						—	H24
mi	N	12	8	12		C	8	8	8		mi	
re						O	16	24	16	H48	re	H48
do	C	16	16	16		N	24	16	24		do	
si	O	32	48	32	H96						si	H96
la	N	48	32	48		C	32	32	32		la	
sol						O	64	96	64	H192	sol	H192
fa	C	64	64	64		N	96	64	96		fa	
—	O	128	192	128	H384						—	H384
mi	N	192	128	192		C	128	128	128		mi	
re						O	256	384	256	H768	re	H768
do	C	256	256	256		N	384	256	384		do	
si	O	512	768	512	H1536						si	H1536
la	N	768	512	768		C	512	512	512		la	
sol						O	1024	1536	1024	H3072	sol	H3072
fa	C	1024	1024	1024		N	1536	1024	1536		fa	
—	O	2048	3072	2048	H6144						—	H6144
mi	N	3072	2048	3072		C	2048	2048	2048		mi	
re						O	4096	6144	4096	H12288	re	H12288
do						N	6144	4096	6144		do	

TABLE 1

"But at the place where we are situated, within the limits of our ordinary powers and capacities 'hydrogen' 6 is irresolvable; we can take it therefore as 'hydrogen' 1; the next 'hydrogen' 12 as 'hydrogen' 6. Reducing all the hydrogens that follow by 2 we obtain a scale from 'hydrogen' 1 to 'hydrogen' 6144. (See Table 2.)

"But 'hydrogen' 6 is nevertheless still irresolvable for us. Therefore we can also take it as 'hydrogen' 1, take the next 'hydrogen' after it as 'hydrogen' 6 and reduce all the following again by two.

TABLE 2

do		
si, la	H6	H1
sol, fa	H12	H6
—, mi	H24	H12
re, do	H48	H24
si, la	H96	H48
sol, fa	H192	H96
—, mi	H384	H192
re, do	H768	H384
si, la	H1536	H768
sol, fa	H3072	H1536
—, mi	H6144	H3072
re, do	H12288	H6144

TABLE 3

do			
si, la	H6	H1	
sol, fa	H12	H6	H1
—, mi	H24	H12	H6
re, do	H48	H24	H12
si, la	H96	H48	H24
sol, fa	H192	H96	H48
—, mi	H384	H192	H96
re, do	H768	H384	H192
si, la	H1536	H768	H384
sol, fa	H3072	H1536	H768
—, mi	H6144	H3072	H1536
re, do	H12288	H6144	H3072

"The scale obtained in this way from 1 to 3072 can serve us for the study of man. (See Table 3.)

"All matters from 'hydrogen' 6 to 'hydrogen' 3072 are to be found and play a part in the human organism. Each of these 'hydrogens' includes a very large group of chemical substances known to us, linked together by some function in connection with our organism. In other words, it must not be forgotten that the term 'hydrogen' has a very wide meaning. Any simple element is a 'hydrogen' of a certain density, but any combination of elements which possesses a definite function, either in the world or in the human organism, is also a 'hydrogen.'

"This kind of definition of matters enables us to classify them in the order of their relation to life and to the functions of our organism.

"Let us begin with 'hydrogen' 768. This 'hydrogen' is defined as *food*, in other words, 'hydrogen' 768 includes all substances which can serve as 'food' for man. Substances which cannot serve as 'food,' such as a piece of wood, refer to 'hydrogen' 1536; a piece of iron to 'hydrogen' 3072. On the other hand, a 'thin' matter, with poor nutritive properties, will be nearer to 'hydrogen' 384.

" 'Hydrogen' 384 will be defined as *water*.

" 'Hydrogen' 192 is the air of our atmosphere which we breathe.

" 'Hydrogen' 96 is represented by rarefied gases which man cannot breathe, but which play a very important part in his life; and further, this is the matter of animal magnetism, of emanations from the human body, of 'n-rays,' hormones, vitamins, and so on; in other words, with 'hydrogen' 96 ends what is called matter or what is regarded as matter by our physics and chemistry. 'Hydrogen' 96 also includes matters that are almost imperceptible to our chemistry or perceptible only by their traces or results, often merely presumed by some and denied by others.

" 'Hydrogens' 48, 24, 12, and 6 are matters unknown to physics and chemistry, matters of our psychic and spiritual life on different levels.

"Altogether in examining the 'table of hydrogens,' it must always be remembered that each 'hydrogen' of this table includes an enormous number of different substances connected together by one and the same function in our organism and representing a definite 'cosmic group.'

" 'Hydrogen' 12 corresponds to the 'hydrogen' of chemistry (atomic weight 1). 'Carbon,' 'nitrogen,' and 'oxygen' (of chemistry) have the atomic weights: 12, 14, and 16.

"In addition it is possible to point out in the table of atomic weights elements which correspond to certain hydrogens, that is, elements whose atomic weights stand almost in the correct *octave* ratio to one another. Thus 'hydrogen' 24 corresponds to fluorine, Fl., atomic weight 19; 'hydrogen' 48 corresponds to Chlorine, Cl., atomic weight 35.5; 'hydrogen' 96 corresponds to Bromine, Br., atomic weight 80; and 'hydrogen' 192 corresponds to Iodine, I., atomic weight 127. The atomic weights of these elements stand almost in the ratio of an octave to one another, in other words, the atomic weight of one of them is almost twice as much as the atomic weight of another. The slight inexactitude, that is, the incomplete octave relationship, is brought about by the fact that ordinary chemistry does not take into consideration all the properties of a substance, namely, it does not take into consideration 'cosmic properties.' The chemistry of which we speak here studies matter on a different basis from ordinary chemistry and takes into consideration not only the chemical and physical, but also the psychic and cosmic properties of matter.

"This chemistry or alchemy regards matter first of all from the point of view of its functions which determine its place in the universe and its relations to other matters and then from the point of view of its relation to man and to man's functions. By an atom of a substance is meant a certain small quantity of the given substance that retains all its chemical, cosmic, and psychic properties, because, in addition to its cosmic properties, every substance also possesses psychic properties, that is, a certain degree of intelligence. The concept 'atom' may therefore refer not only to elements, but also to all compound matters possessing definite functions in the universe or in the life of man. There can be an atom of water, an atom of air (that is, atmospheric air suitable for man's breathing), an atom of bread, an atom of meat, and so on. An atom of water will in this case be one-tenth of one-tenth of a cubic millimeter of water taken at a certain temperature by a special thermometer. This will be a tiny drop of water which under certain conditions can be seen with the naked eye.

"This atom is the smallest quantity of water that retains *all the properties of water*. On further division some of these properties disappear, that is to say, it will not be water but something approaching the gaseous state of water, steam, which does not differ chemically in any way from water in a liquid state but possesses different functions and therefore different cosmic and psychic properties.

"The 'table of hydrogens' makes it possible to examine all substances making up man's organism from the point of view of their relation to different planes of the universe. And as every function of man is a result of the action of definite substances, and as each substance is connected with a definite plane in the universe, this fact enables us to establish the relation between man's functions and the planes of the universe."

I ought to say at this point that the "three octaves of radiations" and the "table of hydrogens" derived from them were a stumbling block to us for a long time. The fundamental and the most essential principle of the transition of the triads and the structure of matter I understood only later, and I will speak of it in its proper place.

In my exposition of G.'s lectures in general, I am trying to observe a chronological order, although this is not always possible as some things were repeated very many times and entered, in one form or another, into almost all lectures.

Upon me personally the "table of hydrogens" produced a very strong impression which, later on, was to become still stronger. I felt in this "ladder reaching from earth to heaven" something very like the sensations of the world which came to me several years before during my strange experiments when I felt so strongly the connectedness, the wholeness, and the "mathematicalness" of everything in the world.[1] This lecture, with different variations, was repeated many times, that is, either in connection with the explanation of the "ray of creation" or in connection with the explanation of the law of octaves. But in spite of the strange sensation it gave to me I was far from giving it its proper value the first times I heard it. And above all, I did not understand at once that these ideas are much more difficult to assimilate and are much deeper in their content than they appeared from their simple exposition.

I have preserved in my memory one episode. It happened at one of the repetitions of this lecture on the structure of matter in connection with the mechanics of the universe. The lecture was read by P., a young engineer belonging to G.'s Moscow pupils, whom I have mentioned.

I arrived when the lecture had already begun. Hearing familiar words I decided that I had already heard this lecture and therefore, sitting down in a corner of the large drawing room, I smoked and thought of something else. G. was there too.

"Why did you not listen to the lecture?" he asked me after it was over.

"But I have already heard it," I said. G. shook his head reproachfully. And quite honestly I did not understand what he expected from me, why I ought to listen for a second time to the same lecture.

I understood only much later, when lectures were over and when I tried to sum up mentally all I had heard. Often, in thinking a question over, I remembered quite distinctly that it had been spoken of at one of the lectures. But what precisely had been said I could unfortunately by no means always remember and I would have given a great deal to hear it once more.

Nearly two years later, in November, 1917, a small party of us consisting of six people, among whom was G., was living on the Black Sea shore twenty-five miles north of Tuapse, in a small country house more than a mile from the nearest habitation. One evening we sat and talked. It was already late and the weather was very bad, a northeast wind was blowing which brought now rain, now snow, in squalls.

I was thinking just of certain deductions from the 'table of hydrogens,' chiefly about one inconsistency in this diagram as compared with another of which we heard later. My question referred to hydrogens below the normal level. Later on I will explain exactly what it was I asked and what, long afterwards, G. answered.

[1] *A New Model of the Universe*, ch. 8, "Experimental Mysticism."

This time he did not give me a direct answer.

"You ought to know that," he said, "it was spoken of in the lectures in St. Petersburg. You could not have listened. Do you remember a lecture that you did not want to hear, saying you knew it already? But what was said then is precisely what you ask about now." After a short silence he said: "Well, if you now heard that somebody was giving the same lecture at Tuapse, would you go there on foot?"

"I would," I said.

And indeed, though I felt very strongly how long, difficult, and cold the road could be, at the same time I knew that this would not stop me.

G. laughed.

"Would you really go?" he asked. "Think—twenty-five miles, darkness, snow, rain, wind."

"What is there to think about?" I said. "You know I have walked the whole way more than once, when there were no horses or when there was no room for me in the cart, and for no reward, simply because there was nothing else to be done. Of course I would go without a word if somebody were going to give a lecture on these things at Tuapse."

"Yes," said G., "if only people really reasoned in this way. But in reality they reason in exactly the opposite way. Without any particular necessity they would face any difficulties you like. But on a matter of importance that can really bring them something they will not move a finger. Such is human nature. Man never on any account wants to pay for anything; and above all he does not want to pay for what is most important for him. You now know that everything must be paid for and that it must be paid for in proportion to what is received. But usually a man thinks to the contrary. For trifles, for things that are perfectly useless to him, he will pay anything. But for something important, never. This must come to him of itself.

"And as to the lecture, what you ask was actually spoken of in St. Petersburg. If you had listened then, you would now understand that there is no contradiction whatever between the diagrams and that there cannot be any."

But to return to St. Petersburg.

In looking back now I cannot help being astonished at the speed with which G. transmitted to us the principal ideas of his system. Of course a great deal depended upon his manner of exposition, upon his astonishing capacity for bringing into prominence all principal and essential points and for not going into unnecessary details until the principal points had been understood.

After the 'hydrogens' G. at once went further.

"We want to 'do,' but" (he began the next lecture) "in everything we do we are tied and limited by the amount of energy produced by our organism. Every function, every state, every action, every thought, every emotion, requires a certain definite energy, a certain definite substance.

"We come to the conclusion that we must 'remember ourselves.' But we can 'remember ourselves' only if we have in us the energy for 'self-remembering.' We can study something, understand or feel something, only if we have the energy for understanding, feeling, or studying.

"What then is a man to do when he begins to realize that he has not enough energy to attain the aims he has set before himself?

"The answer to this is that every normal man has quite enough energy to *begin* work on himself. It is only necessary to learn how to save the greater part of the energy we possess for useful work instead of wasting it unproductively.

"Energy is spent chiefly on unnecessary and unpleasant emotions, on the expectation of unpleasant things, possible and impossible, on bad moods, on unnecessary haste, nervousness, irritability, imagination, day-dreaming, and so on. Energy is wasted on the wrong work of centers; on unnecessary tension of the muscles out of all proportion to the work produced; on perpetual chatter which absorbs an enormous amount of energy; on the 'interest' continually taken in things happening around us or to other people and having in fact no interest whatever; on the constant waste of the force of 'attention'; and so on, and so on.

"In beginning to struggle with all these habitual sides of his life a man saves an enormous amount of energy, and with the help of this energy he can easily begin the work of self-study and self-perfection.

"Further on, however, the problem becomes more difficult. Having to a certain extent balanced his machine and ascertained for himself that it produces much more energy than he expected, a man nevertheless comes to the conclusion that this energy is not enough and that, if he wishes to continue his work, he must increase the amount of energy produced.

"The study of the working of the human organism shows this to be quite possible.

"The human organism represents a chemical factory planned for the possibility of a very large output. But in the ordinary conditions of life the output of this factory never reaches the full production possible to it, because only a small part of the machinery is used which produces only that quantity of material necessary to maintain its own existence. Factory work of this kind is obviously uneconomic in the highest degree. The factory actually produces nothing—all its machinery, all its elaborate equipment, actually serve no purpose at all, in that it maintains only with difficulty its own existence.

"The work of the factory consists in transforming one kind of matter into another, namely, the coarser matters, in the cosmic sense, into finer ones. The factory receives, as raw material from the outer world, a number of coarse 'hydrogens' and transforms them into finer hydrogens by means of a whole series of complicated *alchemical* processes. But in the ordinary conditions of life the production by the human factory of the finer 'hydrogens,' in which, from the point of view of the possibility of higher states of consciousness and the work of higher centers, we are particularly interested, is insufficient and they are all wasted on the existence of the factory itself. If we could succeed in bringing the production up to its possible maximum we should then begin to save the fine 'hydrogens.' Then the whole of the body, all the tissues, all the cells, would become saturated with these fine 'hydrogens' which would gradually settle in them, crystallizing in a special way. This crystallization of the fine 'hydrogens' would gradually bring the whole organism onto a higher level, onto a higher plane of being.

"This, however, cannot happen in the ordinary conditions of life, because the 'factory' expends all that it produces.

" 'Learn to separate the fine from the coarse'—this principle from the 'Emerald Tablets of Hermes Trismegistus' refers to the work of the human factory, and if a man learns to 'separate the fine from the coarse,' that is, if he brings the production of the fine 'hydrogens' to its possible maximum, he will by this very fact create for himself the possibility of an inner growth which can be brought about by no other means. Inner growth, the growth of the inner bodies of man, the astral, the mental, and so on, is a material process completely analogous to the growth of the physical body. In order to grow, a child must have good food, his organism must be in a healthy condition to prepare from this food the material necessary for the growth of the tissues. The same thing is necessary for the growth of the 'astral body'; out of the various kinds of food entering it, the organism must produce the substances necessary for the growth of the 'astral body.' Moreover, the 'astral body' requires for its growth the same substances as those necessary to maintain the physical body, only in much greater quantities. If the physical organism begins to produce a sufficient quantity of these fine substances and the 'astral body' within it becomes formed, this astral organism will require for its maintenance less of these substances than it required during its growth. The surplus from these substances can then be used for the formation and growth of the 'mental body' which will grow with the help of the same substances that feed the 'astral body,' but of course the growth of the 'mental body' will require more of these substances than the growth and feeding of the 'astral body.' The surplus of the substances left over from the feeding of the 'mental body' will go to the growth of the fourth body. But in all cases the surplus will have to be very large. All the fine substances necessary for the growth and feeding of the higher bodies must be produced within the physical organism, and the physical organism is able to produce them provided the human factory is working properly and economically.

"All the substances necessary for the maintenance of the life of the organism, for psychic work, for the higher functions of consciousness and the growth of the higher bodies, are produced by the organism from the food which enters it from outside.

"The human organism receives three kinds of food:

1. The ordinary food we eat
2. The air we breathe
3. Our impressions.

"It is not difficult to agree that air is a kind of food for the organism. But in what way impressions can be food may appear at first difficult to understand. We must however remember that, with every external impression, whether it takes the form of sound, or vision, or smell, we receive from outside a certain amount of energy, a certain number of vibrations; this energy which enters the organism from outside is food. Moreover, as has been said before, energy cannot be transmitted without matter. If an external impression brings external energy with it into the organism it means that external matter also enters which feeds the organism in the full meaning of the term.

"For its normal existence the organism must receive all three kinds of food, that is, physical food, air, and impressions. The organism cannot exist on one or even on two kinds of food, all three are required. But the relation of these foods to one another and their significance for the organism is not the same. The organism can exist for a comparatively long time without a supply of fresh physical food. Cases of starvation are known lasting for over sixty days, when the organism lost none of its vitality and recovered very quickly as soon as it began to take food. Of course starvation of this kind cannot be considered as complete, since in all cases of such artificial starvation people have taken water. Nevertheless, even without water a man can live without food for several days. Without air he can exist only for a few minutes, not more than two or three; as a rule a man dies after being four minutes without air. Without impressions a man cannot live a single moment. If the flow of impressions were to be stopped in some way or if the organism were deprived of its capacity for receiving impressions, it would immediately die. The flow of impressions coming to us from outside is like a driving belt communicating motion to us. The principal motor for us is nature, the surrounding world. Nature transmits to us through our impressions the energy by which we live and move and have our being. If the inflow of this energy is arrested, our machine will immediately stop working. Thus, of the three kinds of food the most important for us is impressions, although it stands to reason that a man cannot exist for long on impressions alone. Impressions and air enable a man to exist a little longer. Impressions, air, and physical food enable the organism to live to the end of its normal term of life and to produce the substances necessary not only for the maintenance of life, but also for the creation and growth of higher bodies.

"The process of transforming the substances which enter the organism into finer ones is governed by the law of *octaves*.

"Let us take the human organism in the form of a three-story factory. The upper floor of this factory consists of a man's head; the middle floor, of the chest; and the lower, of the stomach, back, and the lower part of the body.

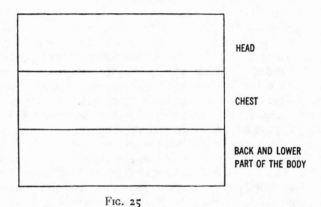

FIG. 25

"Physical food is H768, or la, sol, fa of the third cosmic octave of radiations. This 'hydrogen' enters the lower story of the organism as 'oxygen,' do 768.

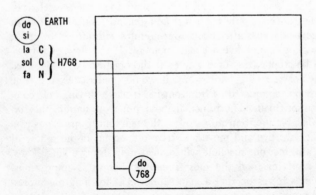

The entrance of food (H768) into the organism.

FIG. 26

" 'Oxygen' 768 meets with 'carbon' 192 which is present in the organism. From the union of O768 and C192 is obtained N384. N384 is the next note re.

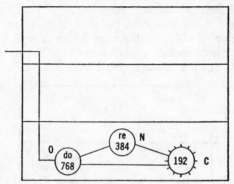

The beginning of the digestion of food (H768) in the organism.

Note: "Carbons" which are present in the organism are marked

Fɪɢ. 27

"Re 384 which becomes 'oxygen' in the next triad meets with 'carbon' 96 in the organism and together with it produces a new 'nitrogen' 192 which is the note mi 192.

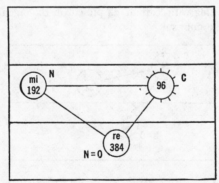

Continuation of the digestion of food (H768) in the organism.

Fɪɢ. 28

"As it is known from the law of octaves mi cannot pass independently into fa in an ascending octave; an 'additional shock' is necessary. If an 'additional shock' is not received the substance mi 192 cannot by itself pass into the full note fa.

"At the given place in the organism where mi 192 ought, apparently, to come to a stop there enters the 'second food'—air, in the form of do 192, that is, mi, re, do of the second cosmic octave of radiations. The note do possesses all the necessary semitones, that is, all the energy necessary for the transition to the next note, and it gives as it were a part of its energy to the note mi which has the same density as itself. The energy of do gives mi 192 force enough, while uniting with 'carbon' 48 already in the organism, to pass into 'nitrogen' 96. 'Nitrogen' 96 will be the note fa.

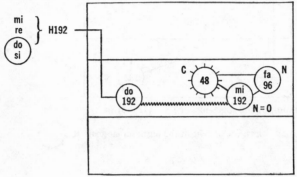

The entrance of air (H192) into the organism and the "shock" which air gives in the interval mi–fa of the food octave.

FIG. 29

"Fa 96 by uniting with 'carbon' 24 present in the organism passes into 'nitrogen' 48—the note sol.

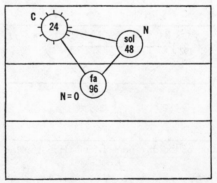

Continuation of the food octave, transition of products of nutrition into sol 48.

FIG. 30

"The note sol 48 by uniting with 'carbon' 12 present in the organism passes into 'nitrogen' 24—la 24.

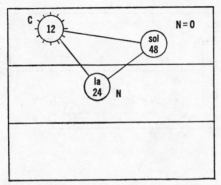

Continuation of the food octave, transition of products of nutrition into la 24.

FIG. 31

"La 24 unites with 'carbon' 6 present in the organism and is transformed into 'nitrogen' 12, or si 12. Si 12 is the highest substance produced in the organism from physical food with the help of the 'additional shock' obtained from the air.

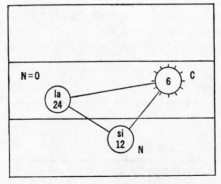

Continuation of the food octave, transition of the products of nutrition into si 12.

FIG. 32

"Do 192 (air) entering the middle story of the factory in the character of 'oxygen' and giving part of its energy to mi 192 unites in its turn at a certain place with 'carbon' 48 present in the organism and passes into re 96.

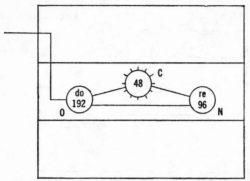

The beginning of the digestion of air in the organism.

Fig. 33

"Re 96 passes into mi 48 with the help of 'carbon' 24 and with this the development of the second octave comes to a stop. For the transition of mi into fa, an 'additional shock' is necessary, but at this point nature has not prepared any 'additional shock' and the second octave, that is, the air octave, cannot develop further and in the ordinary conditions of life it does not develop further.

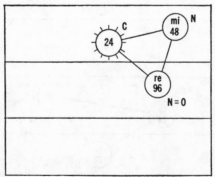

Continuation of the air octave in the organism.

Fig. 34

"The third octave begins with do 48.

"Impressions enter the organism in the form of 'oxygen' 48, that is, la, sol, fa of the second cosmic octave Sun–Earth.

"Do 48 has sufficient energy to pass into the following note but at that place in the organism where do 48 enters, the 'carbon' 12 necessary for this is not present. At the same time do 48 does not come into contact with mi 48 so that it can neither itself pass into the next note nor give part of its energy to mi 48.

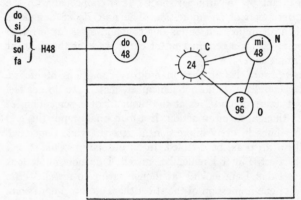

Entry of impressions into the organism.

FIG. 35

"Under normal conditions, that is, the conditions of normal existence, the production of the fine matters by the factory at this point comes to a stop and the third octave sounds as do only. The highest substance produced by the factory is si 12 and for all its higher functions the factory is able to use only this higher matter.

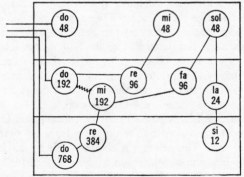

The three kinds of food and the digestion of H768 and H192 in the organism with the help of one *mechanical* "shock." The normal state of the organism and the normal production of finer substances from the products of nutrition.

FIG. 36

"There is, however, a possibility of increasing the output, that is, of enabling the air octave and the impression octave to develop further. For this purpose it is necessary to create a special kind of 'artificial shock' at the point where the beginning of the third octave is arrested. This means that the 'artificial shock' must be applied to the *note do 48*.

"But what is meant by an 'artificial shock'? It is connected with the moment of the reception of an impression. The note do 48 designates the moment when an impression enters our consciousness. An 'artificial shock' at this point means a certain kind of effort made at the moment of receiving an impression.

"It has been explained before that in ordinary conditions of life we do not *remember ourselves*; we do not remember, that is, we do not feel ourselves, are not aware of ourselves at the moment of a perception, of an emotion, of a thought or of an action. If a man understands this and tries to remember himself, every impression he receives while remembering himself will, so to speak, be doubled. In an ordinary psychic state I simply look at a street. But if I remember myself, I do not simply look at the street; I feel that I am looking, as though saying to myself: 'I am looking.' Instead of one impression of the street there are two impressions, one of the street and another of myself looking at it. This second impression, produced by the fact of my remembering myself, is the 'additional shock.' Moreover, it very often happens that the additional sensation connected with self-remembering brings with it an element of emotion, that is, the work of the machine attracts a certain amount of 'carbon' 12 to the place in question. Efforts to remember oneself, observation of oneself at the moment of receiving an impression, observation of one's impressions at the moment of receiving them, registering, so to speak, the reception of impressions and the simultaneous defining of the impressions received, all this taken together doubles the intensity of the impressions and carries do 48 to re 24. At the same time the effort connected with the transition of one note to another and the passage of 48 itself to 24 enables do 48 of the third octave to come into contact with mi 48 of the second octave and to give this note the requisite amount of energy necessary for the transition of mi to fa. In this way the 'shock' given to do 48 extends also to mi 48 and enables the second octave to develop.

"Mi 48 passes to fa 24; fa 24 passes to sol 12; sol 12 passes to la 6. La 6 is the highest matter produced by the organism from air, that is, from the second kind of food. *This however is obtained only by making a conscious effort at the moment an impression is received.* (See Fig. 37.)

"It is necessary to understand what this means. We all breathe the same air. Apart from the elements known to our science the air contains a great number of substances unknown to science, indefinable for it and inaccessible to its observation. But exact analysis is possible both of the air inhaled and of the air exhaled. This exact analysis shows that although

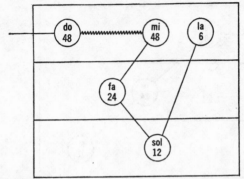

The development of the air octave after the first *conscious* "shock."

FIG. 37

the air inhaled by different people is exactly the same, the air exhaled is quite different. Let us suppose that the air we breathe is composed of twenty different elements unknown to our science. A certain number of these elements are absorbed by every man when he breathes. Let us suppose that five of these elements are always absorbed. Consequently the air exhaled by every man is composed of fifteen elements; five of them have gone to feeding the organism. But some people exhale not fifteen but only ten elements, that is to say, they absorb five elements more. These five elements are higher 'hydrogens.' These higher 'hydrogens' are present in every small particle of air we inhale. By inhaling air we introduce these higher 'hydrogens' into ourselves, but if our organism does not know how to extract them out of the particles of air, and retain them, they are exhaled back into the air. If the organism is able to extract and retain them, they remain in it. In this way we all breathe the same air but we extract different substances from it. Some extract more, others less.

"In order to extract more, it is necessary to have in our organism a certain quantity of corresponding fine substances. Then the fine substances contained in the organism act *like a magnet* on the fine substances contained in the inhaled air. We come again to the old alchemical law: 'In order to make gold, it is first of all necessary to have a certain quantity of real gold.' 'If no gold whatever is possessed, there is no means whatever of making it.'

"The whole of alchemy is nothing but an allegorical description of the human factory and its work of transforming base metals (coarse substances) into precious ones (fine substances).

"We have followed the development of two octaves. The third octave, that is, the octave of impressions, begins through a *conscious* effort. Do 48 passes to re 24; re 24 passes to mi 12. At this point the development of the octave comes to a stop. (See Fig. 38.)

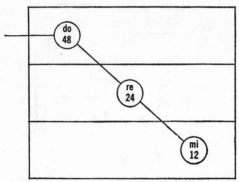

Development of the octave of impressions after the first *conscious* "shock."

FIG. 38

"Now if we examine the result of the development of these three octaves, we shall see that the first octave has reached si 12, the second la 6, and the third mi 12. Thus the first and third octaves stop at notes which are unable to pass to the following notes.

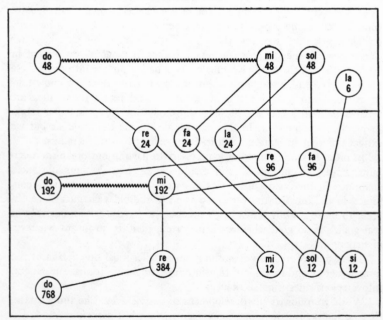

The complete picture of the intensive work of the organism and of the intensive production of substances from the products of nutrition after the first *conscious* "shock."

FIG. 39

"For the two octaves to develop further, a second *conscious* shock is needed at a certain point in the machine, a new conscious effort is necessary which will enable the two octaves to continue their development. The nature of this effort demands special study. From the point of view of the general work of the machine it can be said in general that this effort is connected with the emotional life, that it is a special kind of influence over one's emotions. But what this kind of influence really is, and how it has to be produced, can be explained only in connection with a general description of the work of the human factory or the human machine.

"The practice of not expressing unpleasant emotions, of not 'identifying,' of not 'considering inwardly,' is the preparation for the *second* effort.

"If we now take the work of the human factory as a whole, we shall be able to see at the moments when the production of fine substances is arrested by what means we can increase the productivity of the factory. We see that, under ordinary conditions and working with one mechanical 'shock,' the factory produces a very small quantity of the fine substances, in fact only si 12. Working with one mechanical and one conscious 'shock' the factory now produces a much greater quantity of the fine substances. Working with two conscious 'shocks' the factory will produce a quantity of the fine substances such as, in the course of time, will completely change the character of the factory itself.

"The three-story factory represents the universe in miniature and is constructed according to the same laws and on the same plan as the whole universe.

"In order to understand the analogy between man, the human organism, and the universe, let us take the world as we did before in the form of three octaves from the Absolute to the sun, from the sun to the earth, and from the earth to the moon. Each of these three octaves lacks a semitone between fa and mi and in each octave the place of this missing semitone is taken by a certain kind of 'shock' which is created artificially at the given point. If we now begin to look for an analogy between the three-story factory and the three octaves of the universe, we ought to realize that the three 'additional shocks' in the three octaves of the universe correspond to the three kinds of food entering the human organism. The 'shock' in the lower octave corresponds to physical food; this 'shock' is do 768 of the cosmic three-story factory. The 'shock' in the middle octave corresponds to air. It is do 192 of the cosmic factory. The 'shock' in the upper octave corresponds to impressions; it is do 48 of the cosmic factory. In the inner work of this cosmic three-story factory all three kinds of food undergo the same transformation as in the human factory, on the same plan and in accordance with the same laws. A further study of the analogy between man and the universe is possible only after an exact study of the human machine and after the respective 'places' of each of the 'hydrogens' in our organism has been established exactly. This means that to proceed with any further study we must find the exact purpose of each 'hydrogen,' that is to say, each 'hydrogen' must be defined chemically, psychologically, physiologically, and anatomically, in other words, its functions, its place in the human organism, and, if possible, the peculiar sensations connected with it must be defined.

"The study of the work of the human organism as a chemical factory shows us three stages in the evolution of the human machine.

"The first stage refers to the work of the human organism as it has been created by nature, that is to say, to the life and functions of man number one, number two, and number three. The first octave, that is, the octave of food, develops in a normal way to mi 192. At this point it automatically receives a 'shock' from the beginning of the second octave, and its development goes on consecutively to si 12. The second octave, that is, the air octave, begins with do 192 and develops to mi 48 where it stops. The third octave, that is, the octave of impressions, begins with do 48 and stops there. Thus seven notes of the first octave, three notes of the second, and one note of the third octave represent a complete picture of the work of the 'human factory' in its first or natural stage. Nature has provided only one 'shock,' that is, the 'shock' received from the entrance of the second octave which helps mi of the first octave to pass to fa. But nature did not foresee and did not provide for the second 'shock,' that is, the 'shock' that would help the development of the third octave and thereby enable mi of the second octave to pass to fa. A man must create this 'shock' by his own personal efforts if he desires to increase the output of the fine hydrogens in his organism.

"The second stage refers to the work of the human organism when a man creates a conscious volitional 'shock' at the point do 48. In the first place this volitional 'shock' is transmitted to the second octave which develops as far as sol 12, or even further up to la 6 and so on, if the work of the organism is sufficiently intense. The same 'shock' also enables the third octave to develop, that is, the octave of impressions which in this event reaches mi 12. Thus in the second stage of the work of the human organism, we see the full development of the second octave and three notes of the third octave. The first octave has stopped at the note si 12, the third at the note mi 12. Neither of these octaves can proceed any further without a fresh 'shock.' The nature of this second 'shock' cannot be so easily described as the nature of the first volitional 'shock' at do 48. In order to understand the nature of this 'shock' it is necessary to understand the meaning of si 12 and mi 12.

"The effort which creates this 'shock' must consist in work on the emotions, in the transformation and transmutation of the emotions. This transmutation of the emotions will then help the transmutation of si 12 in the human organism. No serious growth, that is, no growth of higher bodies within the organism, is possible without this transmutation. The idea of this transmutation was known to many ancient teachings as well as to some comparatively recent ones, such as the alchemy of the Middle Ages. But the alchemists spoke of this transmutation in the allegorical forms of the transformation of base metals into precious ones. In reality, however, they meant the transformation of coarse 'hydrogens' into finer ones in the human organism, chiefly of the transformation of mi 12. If this transformation is attained, a man can be said to have achieved what he was striving for, and it can also be said that, until this transformation is attained, all results attained by a man can be lost because they are not fixed in him in any way; moreover, they are attained only in the spheres of thought and emotion. Real, objective results can be obtained only after the transmutation of mi 12 has begun.

"Alchemists who spoke of this transmutation began directly with it. They knew nothing, or at least they said nothing, about the nature of the first volitional 'shock.' It is upon this, however, that the whole thing depends. The second volitional 'shock' and transmutation become physically possible only after long practice on the first volitional 'shock,' which consists in self-remembering, and in observing the impressions received. On the way of the monk and on the way of the fakir work on the second 'shock' begins before work on the first 'shock,' but as mi 12 is created only as a result of the first 'shock,' work, in the absence of other material, has of necessity to be concentrated on si 12, and it very often gives quite wrong results. Right development on the fourth way must begin with the first volitional 'shock' and then pass on to the second 'shock' at mi 12.

"The third stage in the work of the human organism begins when man creates in himself a conscious second volitional 'shock' at the point mi 12, when the transformation or transmutation of these 'hydrogens' into higher 'hydrogens' begins in him. The second stage and the beginning of the third stage refer to the life and functions of man number four. A fairly considerable period of transmutation and crystallization is needed for the transition of man number four to the level of man number five.

"When the 'table of hydrogens' has been sufficiently understood, it shows immediately many new features in the work of the human machine, establishing clearly before anything else the reasons for the differences between the centers and their respective functions.

"The centers of the human machine work with different 'hydrogens.' This constitutes their chief difference. The center working with a coarser, heavier, denser 'hydrogen' works the slower. The center working with light, more mobile 'hydrogen' works the quicker.

'The thinking or intellectual center is the slowest of all the three centers we have examined up to now. It works with 'hydrogen' 48 (according to the third scale of the 'table of hydrogens').

"The moving center works with 'hydrogen' 24. 'Hydrogen' 24 is many times quicker and more mobile than 'hydrogen' 48. The intellectual center is never able to follow the work of the moving center. We are unable to follow either our own movements or other people's movements unless they are artificially slowed down. Still less are we able to follow the work of the inner, the instinctive functions of our organism, the work of the instinctive mind which constitutes, as it were, one side of the moving center.

"The emotional center can work with 'hydrogen' 12. In reality, however, it very seldom works with this fine 'hydrogen.' And in the majority of cases its work differs little in intensity and speed from the work of the moving center or the instinctive center.

"In order to understand the work of the human machine and its possibilities, one must know that, apart from these three centers and those connected with them, we have two more centers, fully developed and properly functioning, but they are not connected with our usual life nor with the three centers in which we are aware of ourselves.

"The existence of these higher centers in us is a greater riddle than the hidden treasure which men who believe in the existence of the mysterious and the miraculous have sought since the remotest times.

"All mystical and occult systems recognize the existence of higher forces and capacities in man although, in many cases, they admit the existence of these forces and capacities only in the form of possibilities, and speak of the necessity for *developing* the hidden forces in man. This present teaching differs from many others by the fact that it affirms that the higher centers exist in man and are fully developed.

"*It is the lower centers that are undeveloped.* And it is precisely this lack of development, or the incomplete functioning, of the lower centers that prevents us from making use of the work of the higher centers.

"As has been said earlier, there are two higher centers:

"The higher emotional center, working with hydrogen 12, and

"The higher thinking center, working with hydrogen 6.

"If we consider the work of the human machine from the point of view of the 'hydrogens' which work the centers, we shall see why the higher centers cannot be connected with the lower ones.

"The intellectual center works with hydrogen 48; the moving center with hydrogen 24.

"If the emotional center were to work with hydrogen 12, its work would be connected with the work of the higher emotional center. In those cases where the work of the emotional center reaches the intensity and speed of existence which is given by hydrogen 12, a temporary connection with the higher emotional center takes place and man experiences new emotions, new impressions hitherto entirely unknown to him, for the description of which he has neither words nor expressions. But in ordinary conditions the difference between the speed of our usual emotions and the speed of the higher emotional center is so great that no connection can take place and we fail to hear within us the voices which are speaking and *calling to us* from the higher emotional center.

"The higher thinking center, working with hydrogen 6, is still further removed from us, still less accessible. Connection with it is possible only through the higher emotional center. It is only from descriptions of mystical experiences, ecstatic states, and so on, that we know cases of such connections. These states can occur on the basis of religious emotions, or, for short moments, through particular narcotics; or in certain pathological states such as epileptic fits or accidental traumatic injuries to the brain, in which cases it is difficult to say which is the cause and which is the effect, that is, whether the pathological state results from this connection or is its cause.

"If we could connect the centers of our ordinary consciousness with the higher thinking center deliberately and at will, it would be of no use to us whatever in our present general state. In most cases where accidental contact with the higher thinking center takes place a man becomes unconscious. The mind refuses to take in the flood of thoughts, emotions, images, and ideas which suddenly burst into it. And instead of a vivid thought, or a vivid emotion, there results, on the contrary, a complete blank, a state of unconsciousness. The memory retains only the first moment when the flood rushed in on the mind and the last moment when the flood was receding and consciousness returned. But even these moments are so full of unusual shades and colors that there is nothing with which to compare them among the ordinary sensations of life. This is usually all that remains from so-called 'mystical' and 'ecstatic' experiences, which represent a temporary connection with a higher center. Only very seldom does it happen that a mind which has been better prepared succeeds in grasping and remembering something of what was felt and understood at the moment of ecstasy. But even in these cases the thinking, the moving, and the emotional centers remember and transmit everything in their own way, translate absolutely new and never previously experienced sensations into the language of usual everyday sensations, transmit in worldly three-dimensional forms things which pass completely beyond the limits of worldly measurements; in this way, of course, they entirely distort every trace of what remains in the memory of these unusual experiences. Our ordinary centers, in transmitting the impressions of the higher centers, may be compared to a blind man speaking of colors, or to a deaf man speaking of music.

"In order to obtain a correct and permanent connection between the lower and the higher centers, it is necessary to regulate and quicken the work of the lower centers.

"Moreover, as has been already said, lower centers work in a wrong way, for very often, instead of their own proper functions, one or another of them takes upon itself the work of other centers. This considerably reduces the speed of the general work of the machine and makes acceleration of the work of the centers very difficult. Thus in order to regulate and accelerate the work of the lower centers, the primary object must consist in freeing each center from work foreign and unnatural to it, and in bringing it back to its own work which it can do better than any other center.

"A great deal of energy is also spent on work which is completely unnecessary and harmful in every respect, such as on the activity of unpleasant emotions, on the expression of unpleasant sensations, on worry, on restlessness, on haste, and on a whole series of automatic actions which are completely useless. As many examples as you like can be found of such unnecessary activity. First of all there is the constantly moving flow of thoughts in our mind, which we can neither stop nor control, and which takes up an enormous amount of our energy. Secondly there is the quite unnecessary constant tension of the *muscles* of our organism. The muscles are tense even when we are doing nothing. As soon as we start to do even a small and insignificant piece of work, a whole system of muscles necessary for the hardest and most strenuous work is immediately set in motion. We pick up a needle from the floor and we spend on this action as much energy as is needed to lift up a man of our own weight. We write a short letter and use as much muscular energy upon it as would suffice to write a bulky volume. But the chief point is that we spend muscular energy continually and at all times, even when we are doing nothing. When we walk the muscles of our shoulders and arms are tensed unnecessarily; when we sit the muscles of our legs, neck, back, and stomach are tensed in an unnecessary way. We even sleep with the muscles of our arms, of our legs, of our face, of the whole of our body tensed, and we do not realize that we spend much more energy on this continual readiness for work we shall never do than on all the real, useful work we do during our life.

"Still further we can point to the habit of continually talking with anybody and about anything, or if there is no one else, with ourselves; the habit of indulging in fantasies, in daydreaming; the continual change of mood, feelings, and emotions, and an enormous number of quite useless things which a man considers himself obliged to feel, think, do, or say.

"In order to regulate and balance the work of the three centers whose functions constitute our life, it is necessary to learn to economize the energy produced by our organism, not to waste this energy on unnecessary functions, and to save it for that activity which will gradually connect the lower centers with the higher.

"All that has been said before about work on oneself, about the formation of inner unity and of the transition from the level of man number

one, number two, and number three to the level of man number four and
further, pursues one and the same aim. What is called according to one
terminology the 'astral body,' is called in another terminology the 'higher
emotional center,' although the difference here does not lie in the terminology alone. These are, to speak more correctly, different aspects of the
next stage of man's evolution. It can be said that the 'astral body' is necessary for the complete and proper functioning of the 'higher emotional
center' in unison with the lower. Or it can be said that the 'higher emotional center' is necessary for the work of the 'astral body.'

"The 'mental body' corresponds to the 'higher thinking center.' It
would be wrong to say that they are one and the same thing. But one
requires the other, one cannot exist without the other, one is the expression of certain sides and functions of the other.

"The fourth body requires the complete and harmonious working of
all centers; and it implies, or is the expression of, complete control over
this working.

"What is necessary to understand and what the 'table of hydrogens'
helps us to grasp, is the idea of the complete materiality of all the psychic,
intellectual, emotional, volitional, and other inner processes, including
the most exalted poetic inspirations, religious ecstasies, and mystical
revelations.

"The materiality of processes means their dependence upon the quality
of the material or substance used on them. One process demands the
expenditure, that is, as it were, the burning, of hydrogen 48; another
process cannot be obtained with the help of hydrogen 48; it requires a
finer, a *more combustible* substance—hydrogen 24. For a third process
hydrogen 24 is too weak; it requires hydrogen 12.

"Thus we see that our organism has the different kinds of fuel necessary for the different centers. The centers can be compared to machines
working on fuels of different qualities. One machine can be worked on
oil residue or crude oil. Another requires kerosene; a third will not work
with kerosene but requires gasoline. The fine substances of our organism can
be characterized as substances of different flash-points, while the organism
itself can be compared to a laboratory in which the combustibles of different strengths required by the different centers are prepared from various kinds of raw material. Unfortunately, however, there is something
wrong with the laboratory. The forces controlling the distribution of combustibles among the different centers often make mistakes and the centers
receive fuel that is either too weak or too easily inflammable. Moreover, a
great quantity of all the combustibles produced is spent quite uselessly; it
simply runs out; is lost. Besides, explosions often take place in the laboratory which at one stroke destroy all the fuel prepared for the next day and
possibly for even a longer period, and are able to cause irreparable dam-
age to the whole factory.

"It must be noted that the organism usually produces in the course of one day all the substances necessary for the following day. And it very often happens that all these substances are spent or consumed upon some unnecessary and, as a rule, unpleasant emotion. Bad moods, worry, the expectation of something unpleasant, doubt, fear, a feeling of injury, irritation, each of these emotions in reaching a certain degree of intensity may, in half an hour, or even half a minute, consume all the substances prepared for the next day; while a single flash of anger, or some other violent emotion, can at once explode all the substances prepared in the laboratory and leave a man quite empty inwardly for a long time or even forever.

"All psychic processes are material. There is not a single process that does not require the expenditure of a certain substance corresponding to it. If this substance is present, the process goes on. When the substance is exhausted, the process comes to a stop."

Chapter Ten

ONCE there was a meeting with a large number of people who had not been at our meetings before. One of them asked: "From what does the way start?" The person who asked the question had not heard G.'s description of the four ways and he used the word "way" in the usual religious-mystical sense.

"The chief difficulty in understanding the idea of the way," said G., "consists in the fact that people usually think that the *way*" (he emphasized this word) "starts on the same level on which life is going. This is quite wrong. The way begins on another, much higher, level. This is exactly what people usually do not understand. The beginning of the way is thought to be easier or simpler than it is in reality. I will try to explain this in the following way.

"Man lives in life *under the law of accident* and under two kinds of influences again governed by accident.

"The first kind are influences created *in life itself* or by life itself. Influences of race, nation, country, climate, family, education, society, profession, manners and customs, wealth, poverty, current ideas, and so on. The second kind are influences created *outside this life*, influences of the inner circle, or esoteric influences—influences, that is, created under different laws, although also on the earth. These influences differ from the former, first of all in being *conscious* in their origin. This means that they have been created consciously by conscious men for a definite purpose. Influences of this kind are usually embodied in the form of religious systems and teachings, philosophical doctrines, works of art, and so on.

"They are let out into life for a definite purpose, and become mixed with influences of the first kind. But it must be borne in mind that these influences are conscious only in their origin. Coming into the general vortex of life they fall under the general law of accident and begin to act *mechanically*, that is, they may act on a certain definite man or may not act; they may reach him or they may not. In undergoing change and distortion in life through transmission and interpretation, influences of the second kind are transformed into influences of the first kind, that is, they become, as it were, merged into the influences of the first kind.

"If we think about this, we shall see that it is not difficult for us to distinguish influences created in life from influences whose source lies outside life. To enumerate them, to make up a catalogue of the one and the other, is impossible. It is necessary to *understand*; and the whole thing depends upon this understanding. We have spoken about the beginning of the way. The beginning of the way depends precisely upon this understanding or upon the capacity for discriminating between the two kinds of influences. Of course, their distribution is unequal. One man receives more of the influences whose source lies outside life, another less; a third is almost isolated from them. But this cannot be helped. This is already fate. Speaking in general and taking normal life under normal conditions and a normal man, conditions are more or less the same for everybody, that is, to put it more correctly, difficulties are equal for everybody. The difficulty lies in separating the two kinds of influences. If a man in receiving them does not separate them, that is, does not see or does not feel their difference, their action upon him also is not separated, that is, they act in the same way, on the same level, and produce the same results. But if a man in receiving these influences begins to discriminate between them and put on one side those which are not created in life itself, then gradually discrimination becomes easier and after a certain time a man can no longer confuse them with the ordinary influences of life.

"The results of the influences whose source lies outside life collect together within him, he *remembers* them together, *feels* them together. They begin to form within him a certain whole. He does not give a clear account to himself as to what, how, and why, or if he does give an account to himself, then he explains it wrongly. But the point is not in this, but in the fact that the results of these influences collect together within him and after a certain time they form within him a kind of *magnetic center*, which begins to attract to itself kindred influences and in this manner it grows. If the magnetic center receives sufficient nourishment, and if there is no strong resistance on the part of the other sides of a man's personality which are the result of influences created in life, the magnetic center begins to influence a man's orientation, obliging him to turn round and even to move in a certain direction. When the magnetic center attains sufficient force and development, a man already understands the idea of the way and he begins to look for the way. The search for the way may take many years and may lead to nothing. This depends upon conditions, upon circumstances, upon the power of the magnetic center, upon the power and the direction of inner tendencies which are not concerned with this search and which may divert a man at the very moment when the possibility of finding the way appears.

"If the magnetic center works rightly and if a man really searches, or even if he does not search actively yet feels rightly, he may meet *another man* who knows the way and who is connected directly or through other people with a center existing outside the law of accident, from which proceed the ideas which created the magnetic center.

"Here again there are many possibilities. But this will be spoken of later on. For the moment let us imagine that he has met a man who really knows the way and is ready to help him. The influence of this man upon him goes through his magnetic center. And then, *at this point,* the man frees himself from the law of accident. This is what must be understood. The influence of the man who knows the way upon the first man is a special kind of influence, differing from the former two, first of all in being a *direct* influence, and secondly in being a *conscious* influence. Influences of the second kind, which create magnetic center, are conscious in their origin but afterwards they are thrown into the general vortex of life, are intermixed with influences created in life itself, and are equally subject to the law of accident. Influences of the third kind can never be subject to the law of accident; they are themselves outside the law of accident and their action also is outside the law of accident. Influences of the second kind can proceed through books, through philosophical systems, through rituals. Influences of the third kind can proceed only from one person to another, directly, by means of oral transmission.

"The moment when the man who is looking for the way meets a man who knows the way is called the *first threshold* or the *first step.* From this first threshold the *stairway* begins. Between 'life' and the 'way' lies the 'stairway.' Only by passing along this 'stairway' can a man enter the 'way.' In addition, the man ascends this stairway with the help of the man who is his guide; he cannot go up the stairway by himself. The *way* begins only where the *stairway* ends, that is, after the *last threshold* on the stairway, on a level much higher than the ordinary level of life.

"Therefore it is impossible to answer the question, *from what does the way start?* The way starts with something that is not in life at all, and therefore it is impossible to say from what. Sometimes it is said: in ascending the stairway a man is not sure of anything, he may doubt everything, his own powers, whether what he is doing is right, *the guide,* his knowledge and his powers. At the same time, what he attains is very unstable; even if he has ascended fairly high on the stairway, he may fall down at any moment and have to begin again from the beginning. But when he has passed the last threshold and enters the way, all this changes. First of all, all doubts he may have about his guide disappear and at the same time the guide becomes far less necessary to him than before. In many respects he may even be independent and know where he is going. Secondly, he can no longer lose so easily the results of his work and he cannot find himself again in ordinary life. Even if he leaves the way, he will be unable to return where he started from.

"This is almost all that can be said in general about the 'stairway' and about the 'way,' because there are different ways. We have spoken of this before. And, for instance, on the fourth way there are special conditions which cannot be on the other ways. Thus the conditions for ascending the stairway on the fourth way are that a man cannot ascend to a higher step until he places another man upon his own step. The other, in his turn, must put in his place a third man in order to ascend higher. Thus, the higher a man ascends the more he depends upon those who are following him. If they stop he also stops. Such situations as this may also occur on the way. A man may attain something, for instance, some special powers, and may later on sacrifice these powers in order to raise other people to his level. If the people with whom he is working ascend to his level, he will receive back all that he has sacrificed. But if they do not ascend, he may lose it altogether.

"There are also various possibilities as regards the teacher's situation in relation to the esoteric center, namely, he may know more or he may know less about the esoteric center, he may know exactly where this center is and how knowledge and help was or is received from it; or he may know nothing of this and may only know the man from whom he himself received his knowledge. In most cases people start precisely from the point that they know only one step higher than themselves. And only in proportion to their own development do they begin to see further and to recognize where what they know came from.

"The results of the work of a man who takes on himself the role of teacher do not depend on whether or not he knows exactly the origin of what he teaches, but very much depends on whether or not his ideas come *in actual fact* from the esoteric center and whether he himself understands and can distinguish *esoteric ideas*, that is, ideas of objective knowledge, from subjective, scientific, and philosophical ideas.

"So far I have spoken of the right magnetic center, of the right guide, and of the right way. But a situation is possible in which the magnetic center has been wrongly formed. It may be divided in itself, that is, it may include contradictions. In it, moreover, may enter influences of the first kind, that is, those created in life, under the guise of influences of the second kind, or the traces of influences of the second kind but distorted to such an extent that they have become their own opposite. Such a wrongly formed magnetic center cannot give a right orientation. A man with a wrong magnetic center of this kind may also look for the way and he may meet another man who will call himself a teacher and will say that he knows the way and that he is connected with a center standing outside the law of accident. But in reality he may not know the way and may not be connected with such a center. Moreover here again there are many possibilities:

"1. He may be genuinely mistaken and think that he knows something, when in reality he knows nothing.

"2. He may believe another man, who in his turn may be mistaken.

"3. He may deceive consciously.

"Then if the man who is seeking the way believes him, he may lead him in a quite different direction and not where he promises; he may lead him very far from the right way and bring him to results directly opposite to the results of the right way.

"But fortunately this happens very rarely, that is, wrong ways are very numerous but in the majority of cases they do not lead anywhere. And a man simply turns circles on the same spot and thinks that he is going somewhere."

"How can a wrong way be recognized?" asked somebody.

"How can it be recognized?" said G. "It is impossible to recognize a wrong way without knowing the right way. This means that it is no use troubling oneself how to recognize a wrong way. One must think of how to find the right way. This is what we are speaking about all the time. It cannot be said in two words. But from what I have said you can draw many useful conclusions if you remember everything that has been said and everything which follows from it. For example, you can see that the teacher always corresponds to the level of the pupil. The higher the pupil, the higher can be the teacher. But a pupil of a level which is not particularly high cannot count on a teacher of a very high level. Actually a pupil can never see the level of the teacher. This is a law. No one can see higher than his own level. But usually people not only do not know this, but, on the contrary, the lower they are themselves, the higher the teacher they demand. The right understanding of this point is already a very considerable understanding. But it occurs very seldom. Usually the man himself is not worth a brass farthing but he must have as teacher no other than Jesus Christ. To less he will not agree. And it never enters his head that even if he were to meet such a teacher as Jesus Christ, taking him as he is described in the Gospels, he would never be able to follow him because it would be necessary to be on the level of an apostle in order to be a pupil of Jesus Christ. Here is a definite law. The higher the teacher, the more difficult for the pupil. And if the difference in the levels of the teacher and pupil go beyond a certain limit, then the difficulties in the path of the pupil become insuperable. It is exactly in connection with this law that there occurs one of the fundamental rules of the fourth way. On the fourth way there is not *one* teacher. Whoever is the elder, he is the teacher. And as the teacher is indispensable to the pupil, so also is the pupil indispensable to the teacher. The pupil cannot go on without the teacher, and the teacher cannot go on without the pupil or pupils. And this is not a general consideration but an indispensable and quite concrete rule on which is based the law of a man's ascending. As has been said before, *no one can ascend onto a higher step until he places another man in his own place.* What a man has received he must immediately give back; only then can he receive more. Otherwise from him will be taken even what he has already been given."

At one of the following meetings, in the presence of G., when he made me repeat what he had said about the way and about magnetic center, I embodied his idea in the following diagram:

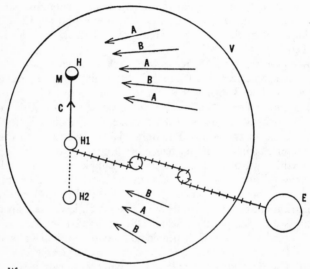

V ... life

H ... an individual man

A ... influences created in life, that is, in life itself—the first kind of influences

B ... influences created outside life but thrown into the general vortex of life—the second kind of influences

H1 ... a man, connected by means of succession with the esoteric center or pretending to it

E ... esoteric center, standing outside the general laws of life

M ... magnetic center in man

C ... influence of man *h1* on man *h*; in the event of his actually being connected with the esoteric center, directly or by succession, this is the third kind of influences. This influence is conscious, and under its action at the point *m*, that is, in the magnetic center, a man becomes free from the law of accident

H2 ... a man, deceiving himself or deceiving others and having no connection, either directly or by succession, with the esoteric center

Fig. 40

At one of the following meetings, after a fairly long talk on knowledge and being, G. said:

"Strictly speaking, you cannot as yet speak of knowledge because you do not know with what knowledge begins.

"Knowledge begins with the teaching of the cosmoses.

"You know the expressions 'macrocosm' and 'microcosm.' This means 'large cosmos' and 'small cosmos,' 'large world' and 'small world.' The universe is regarded as a 'large cosmos' and man as a 'small cosmos,' analogous to the large one. This establishes, as it were, the idea of the unity and the similarity of the world and man.

"The teaching of the two cosmoses is known from the Cabala and other more ancient systems. But this teaching is *incomplete* and nothing can be derived from it, nothing can be built on it. Nothing can be derived from it because this teaching is merely a fragment split off from another, much fuller, ancient esoteric teaching about cosmoses or worlds, included one within another and created in the image and the likeness of the greatest of them, including in itself all the others. "As above, so below," is an expression which refers to cosmoses.

"But it is essential to know that the *full* teaching on cosmoses speaks not of two, but of seven cosmoses, included one within another.

"Seven cosmoses, taken together in their relation to one another, alone represent a complete picture of the universe. The idea of two analogous cosmoses, accidentally preserved from a great and complete teaching, is so incomplete that it can give no idea whatever of the analogy between man and the world.

"The teaching on cosmoses examines seven cosmoses:

"The first cosmos is the *Protocosmos*—the first cosmos.

"The second cosmos is the *Ayocosmos*, the holy cosmos, or the *Megalocosmos*, the 'great cosmos.'

"The third cosmos is the *Macrocosmos*—the 'large cosmos.'

"The fourth cosmos is the *Deuterocosmos*—the 'second cosmos.'

"The fifth cosmos is the *Mesocosmos*—the 'middle cosmos.'

"The sixth cosmos is the *Tritocosmos*—the 'third cosmos.'

"The seventh cosmos is the *Microcosmos*—the 'small cosmos.'

"The *Protocosmos* is the Absolute in the ray of creation, or world 1. The *Ayocosmos* is world 3 ('all worlds' in the ray of creation). The *Macrocosmos* is our starry world or the Milky Way (world 6 in the ray of creation). The *Deuterocosmos* is the sun, the solar system (world 12). The *Mesocosmos* is 'all planets' (world 24), or the earth as the representative of the planetary world. The *Tritocosmos* is man. The *Microcosmos* is the 'atom.'

"As I have already explained before," said G., "what is called 'atom' is the smallest amount of any substance in which the substance retains all its properties, physical, chemical, psychical, and cosmic. From this point of view there can, for instance, be an 'atom of water.'

"You see that in the general order of the seven cosmoses the Microcosm and the Macrocosm stand so far apart from each other that it is impossible to see or establish any direct analogy between them.

"Each cosmos is a living being which lives, breathes, thinks, feels, is born, and dies.

"All cosmoses result from the action of the same forces and the same laws. Laws are the same everywhere. But they manifest themselves in a different, or at least, in not quite the same way on different planes of the universe, that is, on different levels. Consequently cosmoses are not quite analogous one to another. If the law of octaves did not exist, the analogy between them would have been complete, but owing to the law of octaves there is no complete analogy between them, just as there is no complete analogy between the different notes of the octave. It is only *three* cosmoses, taken together, that are similar and analogous to any other three.

"The conditions of the action of laws on each plane, that is, in each cosmos, are determined by the two adjoining cosmoses, the one above and the one below. Three cosmoses standing next to one another give a complete picture of the manifestation of the laws of the universe. One cosmos cannot give a complete picture. Thus in order to know one cosmos, it is necessary to know the two adjoining cosmoses, the one above and the one below the first, that is, one larger and one smaller. Taken together, these two cosmoses determine the one that lies between them. Thus the Mesocosmos and the Microcosmos, taken together, determine the Tritocosmos. The Deuterocosmos and the Tritocosmos determine the Mesocosmos, and so on.

"The relation of one cosmos to another is different from the relation of one world to another in the astronomical ray of creation. In the ray of creation worlds are taken in the actual relation in which they exist in the universe for us, from our point of view: the moon, the earth, the planets, the sun, the Milky Way, and so on. Therefore the quantitative interrelation of the worlds one to another in the ray of creation is not permanent. In one case or on one level it is greater, for instance, the relation of 'all suns' to our sun; in another case, on another level, it is less, for instance, the relation of the earth to the moon. But the interrelation of the cosmoses is permanent and always the same. That is to say, one cosmos is related to another as *zero to infinity*. This means that the relation of the Microcosmos to the Tritocosmos is the same as that of zero to infinity; the relation of the Tritocosmos to the Mesocosmos is that of zero to infinity; the relation of the Mesocosmos to the Deuterocosmos is that of zero to infinity; and so on.

"In order to understand the meaning of the division into cosmoses and the relation of cosmoses to each other, it is necessary to understand what the relation of zero to infinity means. If we understand what this means, the principle of the division of the universe into cosmoses, the necessity of such a division, and the impossibility of drawing for ourselves a more or less lucid picture of the world without this division will immediately become clear to us.

"The idea of cosmoses helps us to understand our place in the world; and it solves many problems, as for instance, those connected with space, with time, and so on. And above all this idea serves to establish exactly the *principle of relativity*. The latter is especially important for it is quite impossible to have an exact conception of the world without having established the principle of relativity.

"The idea of cosmoses enables us to put the study of relativity on a firm basis. At the first glance there is much that seems paradoxical in the system of cosmoses. In reality, however, this apparent paradox is simply relativity.

"The idea of the possibility of broadening man's consciousness and increasing his capacities for knowledge stands in direct relation to the teaching on cosmoses. In his ordinary state a man is conscious of himself in *one cosmos*, and all the other cosmoses he looks at from the point of view of one cosmos. The broadening of his consciousness and the intensifying of his psychic functions lead him into the sphere of activity and life of *two other* cosmoses simultaneously, the one above and the one below, that is, one larger and one smaller. The broadening of consciousness does not proceed in one direction only, that is, in the direction of the higher cosmoses; in going above, at the same time it goes below.

"This last idea will, perhaps, explain to you some expressions you may have met with in occult literature; for instance, the saying that 'the way up is at the same time the way down.' As a rule this expression is quite wrongly interpreted.

"In reality this means that if, for instance, a man begins to feel the life of the planets, or if his consciousness passes to the level of the planetary world, he begins at the same time to feel the life of atoms, or his consciousness passes to their level. In this way the broadening of consciousness proceeds simultaneously in two directions, towards the greater and towards the lesser. Both the great and the small require for their cognition a like change in man. In looking for parallels and analogies between the cosmoses we may take each cosmos in three relations:

"1. in its relation to itself,

"2. in its relation to a higher or a larger cosmos, and

"3. in its relation to a lower, or a smaller cosmos.

"The manifestation of the laws of one cosmos in another cosmos constitutes what we call a *miracle*. There can be no other kind of miracle. A miracle is not a breaking of laws, nor is it a phenomenon outside laws.

It is a phenomenon which takes place according to the laws of another cosmos. These laws are incomprehensible and unknown to us, and are therefore *miraculous*.

"In order to understand the laws of relativity, it is very useful to examine the life and phenomena of one cosmos as though looking at them from another cosmos, that is, to examine them from the point of view of the laws of another cosmos. All the phenomena of the life of a given cosmos, examined from another cosmos, assume a completely different aspect and have a completely different meaning. Many new phenomena appear and many other phenomena disappear. This in general completely changes the picture of the world and of things.

"As has been said before, the idea of cosmoses alone can provide a firm basis for the establishment of the laws of relativity. Real science and real philosophy ought to be founded on the understanding of the laws of relativity. *Consequently it is possible to say that science and philosophy, in the true meaning of these terms, begin with the idea of cosmoses.*"

Having said these words, after a fairly long silence, G. turned to me and added:

"Try to discuss all I have said just now, from the point of view of your dimensions."

"All that you have said," I said, "refers without doubt to the problems of dimensions. But before I pass to them, I should like to elucidate one point, which is not quite clear to me. It is what you said about the Microcosmos. We are accustomed to connect the idea of the Microcosmos with man. This means that man represents a world in himself. A world analogous to the large world, the Macrocosmos. But you give man the name of Tritocosmos, that is, the third cosmos. Why third? The first is Protocosmos; the second, the sun or Deuterocosmos. Why is man the third cosmos?"

"It is difficult to explain at present," said G.; "you will understand this later."

"But do you really mean that the concept Microcosmos cannot be used in relation to man?" asked one of the audience. "This creates a strange difference in terminology."

"Yes, yes," said G. "Man is the Tritocosmos. The Microcosmos is the atom or rather"—he paused as though looking for a word—"the microbe.

"But do not stop over this question. All that will be explained later." [1]

Then he again turned to me.

"See what you can say from your point of view, taking everything just as I said it."

"First of all we must examine what the ratio of zero to infinity means," I said. "If we understand this, we shall understand the relation of one

[1] I mention this here because later G. changed this.

cosmos to another. In the world accessible to our study we have a perfectly clear example of the relation of zero to infinity. In geometry this
is the relation of one unit of a certain number of dimensions to another
unit of a greater number of dimensions. The relation of a point to a line,
of a line to a plane, of a plane to a solid, of a solid, that is, of a three-
dimensional body to a four-dimensional body, and so on.

"If we adopt this point of view, we shall have to admit that the relation of one cosmos to another is the relation of two bodies of different
dimensions. If one cosmos is three-dimensional then the next cosmos, that
is, the one above it, must be four-dimensional, the next—five-dimensional,
and so on. If we take the 'atom' or 'microbe,' as you say, that is, the
Microcosmos as a point, then relative to this point man will be a line,
that is, a figure of one dimension. The next cosmos, the earth, will be a
plane relative to man, that is, it will have two dimensions, as is actually
the case for direct perception. The sun, the solar system, will be three-
dimensional for the earth. The starry world will be four-dimensional for
the sun. 'All worlds' are five-dimensional, and the Absolute or Protocosmos
is six-dimensional.

"What personally interests me most in this system of cosmoses is that
I see in them the full 'period of dimensions,' of my *New Model of the
Universe*. It is not merely a coincidence of details—it is absolutely identical. I do not know how it has come about; I have never heard of seven
cosmoses related to one another in the ratio of zero to infinity. Nevertheless my 'period of dimensions' coincides with this absolutely exactly.

"The 'period of dimensions' contains within itself seven dimensions:
The zero-dimension, the first, the second, and so on up to the sixth
dimension. The zero-dimension or the point is a *limit*. This means that
we see something as a point, but we do not know what is concealed
behind this point. It may actually be a point, that is, a body having no
dimensions and it may also be a whole world, but a world so far removed
from us or so small that it appears to us as a point. The movement of this
point in space will appear to us as a line. In the same way the point itself
will see the space along which it moves as a line. The movement of the
line in a direction perpendicular to itself will be a plane and the line itself
will see the space along which it moves in the shape of a plane.

"Up to now I have examined the line from the point of view of the
point, and the plane from the point of view of the line, but the point,
the line, and the plane can also be taken from the point of view of a
three-dimensional body. In this case the plane will be the boundary of the
body, or its side, or its section. The line will be the boundary limiting the
plane, or the section of the plane. The point will be the limit or the
section of the line.

"A three-dimensional body differs from the point, the line, and the
plane by the fact that it has a real physical existence for our perception.

"The plane is in fact only a projection of a body, the line is a projection of a plane, and the point is a projection of a line.

"A 'body' has an independent physical existence, that is, it possesses a number of different physical properties.

"But when we say a thing 'exists,' we mean by this existence in time. But there is no time in three-dimensional space. Time lies outside the three-dimensional space. Time, as we feel it, is the fourth dimension. Existence is for us existence in time. Existence in time is movement or extension along the fourth dimension. If we take existence as an extension along the fourth dimension, if we think of life as a four-dimensional body, then a three-dimensional body will be its section, its projection, or its limit.

"But existence in time does not embrace all the aspects of existence. Apart from existing in time, everything that exists, exists also in eternity.

"Eternity is the infinite existence of every moment of time. If we conceive time as a line, then this line will be crossed at every point by the lines of eternity. Every point of the line of time will be a line in eternity. The line of time will be a plane of eternity. Eternity has one dimension more than time. Therefore, if time is the fourth dimension, eternity is the fifth dimension. If the space of time is four-dimensional, then the space of eternity is five-dimensional.

"Further, in order to understand the idea of the fifth and the sixth dimensions, a certain view of time must be established.

"Every moment of time contains a certain number of possibilities, at times a small number, at others a great number, but never an infinite number. It is necessary to realize that there are possibilities and there are impossibilities. I can take from this table and throw on the floor a piece of paper, a pencil, or an ash-tray, but I cannot take from the table and throw on the floor an orange which is not on the table. This clearly defines the difference between possibility and impossibility. There are several combinations of possibilities in relation to things which can be thrown on the floor from this table. I can throw a pencil, or a piece of paper, or an ash-tray, or else a pencil and a piece of paper, or a pencil and an ash-tray, or a piece of paper and an ash-tray, or all three together, or nothing at all. There are only these possibilities. If we take as a moment of time the moment when these possibilities exist, then the next moment will be a moment of the actualization of one of the possibilities. A pencil is thrown on the floor. This is the actualization of one of the possibilities. Then a new moment comes. This moment also has a certain number of possibilities in a certain definite sense. And the moment after it will again be a moment of the actualization of one of the possibilities. The consecutiveness of these moments of actualization of one possibility constitutes the line of time. But each moment of time has an infinite existence in eternity. The possibilities which have been actualized con-

tinue to be endlessly actualized in eternity, while the non-actualized possibilities continue to remain non-actualized and non-actualizable.

"But all the possibilities that have been created or have originated in
the world must be actualized. The actualization of all the possibilities
created or originated constitutes the world's being. At the same time there
is no place for the actualization of these possibilities within the limits of
eternity. In eternity everything that has been actualized continues to be
actualized and everything non-actualized continues to remain non-actualized. Eternity, however, is only a plane crossed by the line of time. At
every point of this line there remains a certain number of non-actualized
possibilities. If we imagine the line of the actualization of these possibilities, they will proceed along radii issuing from one point at different
angles to the line of time and the line of eternity. These lines will proceed
outside eternity, outside the five-dimensional space, in 'higher eternity' or
in six-dimensional space, in the sixth dimension.

"The sixth dimension is the line of the actualization of all possibilities.

"The fifth dimension is the line of the eternal existence or repetition of
the actualized possibilities.

"The fourth dimension is the sequence of the moments of the actualization of one possibility.

"As I have said, seven dimensions, from zero-dimension to the sixth
dimension, constitute the full period of dimensions. Beyond this period
there is either nothing or the same period may repeat itself on another
scale.

"As I have already said, the system of cosmoses, the exposition of which
we have just heard, strikes me above all by the fact that it fully corresponds to the 'period of dimension' which is the basis of my *New Model
of the Universe*, only this system of cosmoses goes still further and explains many things which were not clear in my *model of the universe*.

"Thus, if we take the Microcosmos, that is, the 'atom' or 'microbe,' as
G. has defined it, then the Tritocosmos for it will be four-dimensional
space, the Mesocosmos will be five-dimensional space, and the Deuterocosmos six-dimensional space.

"This means that all the possibilities of the 'atom' or 'microbe' are
realized within the limits of the solar system.

"If we take man as the Tritocosmos, then, for him, the Mesocosmos
will be four-dimensional space, the Deuterocosmos five-dimensional space,
and the Macrocosmos six-dimensional space. This means that all the possibilities of the Tritocosmos are realized in the Macrocosmos.

"Therefore parallel with this, all the possibilities of the Mesocosmos are
realized in the Ayocosmos and all the possibilities of the Deuterocosmos,
or the sun, are realized in the Protocosmos or the Absolute.

"As every cosmos has a real physical existence, every cosmos therefore
is three-dimensional for itself or in itself. In relation to a lower cosmos it

is four-dimensional, in relation to a higher cosmos it is a point. To put it differently, it is, itself, three-dimensional, but the fourth dimension lies for it in the cosmos above and the cosmos below. This last point is perhaps the most paradoxical, but nevertheless it is exactly as it should be. For a three-dimensional body, such as is a cosmos, the fourth dimension lies as much in the realm of very large magnitudes as in the realm of very small magnitudes; as much in the realm of what is actually infinity as in the realm of what is actually zero.

"Further we must understand that the three-dimensionality of even one and the same body can be different. Only a six-dimensional body can be completely real. A five-dimensional body is only an incomplete view of a six-dimensional body, a four-dimensional body is an incomplete view of a five-dimensional body, a three-dimensional body is an incomplete view of a four-dimensional body. And of course, a plane is an incomplete view of a three-dimensional body, that is to say, a view of one side of it. In the same way a line is an incomplete view of a plane and a point is an incomplete view of a line.

"Moreover, though we do not know how, a six-dimensional body can see itself as three-dimensional. Somebody looking at it from outside may possibly also see it as a three-dimensional body, but in a completely different kind of three-dimensionality. For instance, we represent the earth to ourselves as three-dimensional. This three-dimensionality is only imaginary. As a three-dimensional body the earth is something quite different for itself from what it is for us. Our view of it is incomplete, we see it as a section of a section of a section of its complete being. The 'earthly globe' is an imaginary body. It is the section of a section of a section of the six-dimensional earth. But this six-dimensional earth can also be three-dimensional for itself, only we do not know and we can have no conception of the form in which the earth sees itself.

"The possibilities of the earth are actualized in the Ayocosmos; this means that in the Ayocosmos the earth is a six-dimensional body. And actually we can to a certain extent see in what way the form of the earth must change. In the Deuterocosmos, that is, in relation to the sun, the earth is no longer a point (taking a point as a scale reduction of a three-dimensional body), but a line which we trace as the path of the earth around the sun. If we take the sun in the Macrocosmos, that is, if we visualize the line of the sun's motion, then the line of the motion of the earth will become a spiral encircling the line of the sun's motion. If we conceive a lateral motion of this spiral, then this motion will construct a figure which we cannot imagine because we do not know the nature of its motion, but which, nevertheless, will be the six-dimensional figure of the earth, which the earth itself can see as a three-dimensional figure. It is necessary to establish and to understand this because otherwise the idea of the three-dimensionality of the cosmoses will become linked with our idea of three-dimensional bodies. *The three-dimensionality even of one and the same body can be different.*

"And this last point seems to me to be connected with what G. calls the 'principle of relativity.' His principle of relativity has nothing in common with the principle of relativity in mechanics or with Einstein's principle of relativity. It is the same again as in the *New Model of the Universe*; it is the principle of the relativity of existence."

At this point I ended my survey of the system of cosmoses from the point of view of the theory of many dimensions.

"There is a great deal of material in what you have just said," said G., "but this material must be elaborated. If you can find out how to elaborate the material that you have now, you will understand a great deal that has not occurred to you till now. For example, take note that *time* is different in different cosmoses. And it can be calculated exactly, that is, it is possible to establish exactly how time in one cosmos is related to the time of another cosmos.

"I will add only one thing more:

"Time is breath—try to understand this."

He said nothing further.

Later on one of G.'s Moscow pupils added to this that, speaking with them once of cosmoses and of different time in different cosmoses, G. had said that the *sleep and waking* of living beings and plants, that is, twenty-four hours or a day and night, constitute the "breath of organic life."

G.'s lecture on cosmoses and the talk following it greatly aroused my curiosity. This was a direct transition from the "three-dimensional universe" with which we had begun, to the problems which I had elaborated in the *New Model of the Universe*, that is, to the problems of space and time and higher dimensions, on which I had been working for several years.

For over a year G. added nothing to what he had said about cosmoses.

Several of us tried to approach these problems from many different sides and, although all of us felt a great deal of potential energy in the idea of cosmoses, for a long time we got no results. We were especially confused by the "Microcosmos."

"If it were possible to take man as the Microcosmos and the Tritocosmos as the human race, or rather as organic life, it would be much easier to establish the relation of man to other cosmoses," one of us, Z., said in this connection, who with me had attempted to understand and to develop further the idea of the cosmoses.

But on the one or two occasions that we began to speak to G. about it he persisted in his definitions.

I remember once when he was leaving Petersburg, it was possibly even his final departure in 1917, one of us asked him at the station something relating to cosmoses.

"Try to understand what the Microcosmos means," answered G. "If you succeed in understanding this, then all the rest about which you ask now will become clear to you."

I remember that when we talked about it later the question was quite easy to solve when we took the "Microcosmos" as man.

It was certainly conditional, but nevertheless it was in complete accord with the whole system which studied the world and man. Every individual living being—a dog, a cat, a tree—could be taken as a Microcosmos; the combination of all living beings constituted the Tritocosmos or organic life on earth. These definitions seemed to me the only ones that were logically possible. And I could not understand why G. objected to them.

At any rate, some time later when I returned again to the problem of cosmoses I decided to take man as the Microcosmos, and to take the Tritocosmos as organic life on earth.

With such a construction a great number of things began to be much more connected. And once, looking through a manuscript of "Glimpses of Truth" given me by G., that is, the beginning of the story that was read at the Moscow group the first time I went there, I found in it the expressions "Macrocosmos" and "Microcosmos"; moreover "Microcosmos" meant man.

Now you have some idea of the laws governing the life of the Macrocosmos and have returned to the Earth. Recall to yourself: "As above, so below." I think that already, without any further explanation, you will not dispute the statement that the life of individual man—the Microcosmos—is governed by the same laws.

—"Glimpses of Truth"

This still further strengthened us in our decision to understand "Microcosmos" as applying to man. Later it became clear to us why G. wished to make us apply the concept "Microcosmos" to small magnitudes as compared with man, and to what he wished to direct our thought by this.

I remember one conversation on this subject.

"If we want to represent graphically the interrelation of the cosmoses," I said, "we must take the Microcosmos, that is, man, as a point, that is to say, we must take him on a very small scale and, as it were, at a very great distance from ourselves. Then his life in the Tritocosmos, that is, among other people and in the midst of nature, will be the line which he traces on the surface of the earthly globe in moving from place to place. In the Mesocosmos, that is, taken in connection with the twenty-four hours' motion of the earth around its axis, this line will become a plane, whereas taken in relation to the sun, that is, taking into consideration the motion of the earth around the sun, it will become a three-dimensional body, or, in other words, it will be something really existing, something realized. But as the fundamental point, that is, the man or the Microcosmos, was also a three-dimensional body, we have consequently two three-dimensionalities.

"In this case all the possibilities of man are actualized in the sun. This corresponds to what has been said before, namely, that man number seven *becomes immortal within the limits of the solar system.*

"Beyond the sun, that is, beyond the solar system, he has not and cannot have any existence, or in other words, from the point of view of the next cosmos he does not exist at all. A man does not exist at all in the Macrocosmos. The Macrocosmos is the cosmos in which the possibilities of the Tritocosmos are realized and man can exist in the Macrocosmos only as an atom of the Tritocosmos. The possibilities of the earth are actualized in the Megalocosmos and the possibilities of the sun are actualized in the Protocosmos.

"If the Microcosmos, or man, is a three-dimensional body, then the Tritocosmos—organic life on earth—is a four-dimensional body. The earth has five dimensions and the sun—six.

"The usual scientific view takes man as a three-dimensional body; it takes organic life on earth as a whole, more as a phenomenon than a three-dimensional body; it takes the earth as a three-dimensional body; the sun as a three-dimensional body; the solar system as a three-dimensional body; and the Milky Way as a three-dimensional body.

"The inexactitude of this view becomes evident if we try to conceive the existence of one cosmos within the other, that is, of a lower cosmos in a higher, of a smaller cosmos in a greater, such as, for instance, the existence of man in organic life or in relation to organic life. In this case organic life must inevitably be taken in time. Existence in time is an extension along the fourth dimension.

"Neither can the earth be regarded as a three-dimensional body. It would be three-dimensional if it were stationary. Its motion around its axis makes man a five-dimensional being, whereas its motion around the sun makes the earth itself four-dimensional. The earth is not a sphere but a spiral encircling the sun, and the sun is not a sphere but a kind of spindle inside this spiral. The spiral and the spindle, taken together, must have a lateral motion in the next cosmos, but what results from this motion we cannot know, for we know neither the nature nor the direction of the motion.

"Further, seven cosmoses represent a 'period of dimensions,' but this does not mean that the chain of cosmoses comes to an end with the Microcosmos. If man is a Microcosmos, that is, a cosmos in himself, then the microscopic cells composing his body will stand towards him in about the same relation as he himself stands to organic life on earth. A microscopic cell which is on the boundary line of microscopic vision is composed of milliards of molecules comprising the next step, the next cosmos. Going still further, we can say that the next cosmos will be the electron. Thus we have obtained a second Microcosmos—the cell; a third Microcosmos—the molecule; and a fourth Microcosmos—the electron. These divisions and definitions, namely 'cells,' 'molecules,' and 'electrons,' are possibly very imperfect; it may be that with time science will establish others, but the principle will remain always the same and lower cosmoses will always be in precisely such relation to the Microcosmos."

It is difficult to reconstruct all the conversations which we had at that time about cosmoses.

I returned particularly often to G.'s words about the difference of time in different cosmoses. I felt that here was a riddle which I could and must solve.

Finally having decided to try to put together everything I thought on the subject, I took man as the Microcosmos. The next cosmos in relation to man I took as "organic life on earth," which I called "Tritocosmos" although I did not understand this name, because I would have been unable to answer the question why organic life on earth was the "third" cosmos. But the name is immaterial. After that everything was in accordance with G.'s system. Below man, that is, as the next smaller cosmos, was the "cell." Not any cell and not a cell under any conditions, but a fairly large cell, such as for instance the embryo-cell of the human organism. As the next cosmos one could take a small, *ultramicroscopic* cell. The idea of two cosmoses in the microscopic world, that is, the idea of two microscopic individuals differing one from the other as much as does "man" from a "large cell," is perfectly clear in bacteriology.

The next cosmos was the molecule, and the next the electron. Neither "molecule" nor "electron" appeared to me to be very sound or reliable definitions, but for the lack of others these could be taken.

Such a succession undoubtedly introduced or maintained a complete incommensurability between the cosmoses, that is, it preserved the ratio of zero to infinity. And later this system made possible many very interesting constructions.

The idea of cosmoses received a further development only a year after we heard it for the first time, that is, in the spring of 1917, when I succeeded for the first time in constructing a "table of time in different cosmoses." But I will speak of this table further on. I will only add that G. never explained, as he promised, the names of the cosmoses and the origin of these names.

Chapter Eleven

"I AM often asked questions in connection with various texts, parables, and so on, from the Gospels," said G., on one occasion. "In my opinion the time has not yet come for us to speak about the Gospels. This requires much more knowledge. But from time to time we will take certain Gospel texts as points of departure for our discussions. This will teach you to treat them in the right way, and, above all, to realize that in the texts known to us the most essential points are usually missing.

"To begin with, let us take the well-known text about the seed which must die in order to be born. 'Except a corn of wheat fall into the ground and die, it abideth alone; but, if it die, it bringeth forth much fruit.'

"This text has many different meanings and we shall often return to it. But first of all it is necessary to know the principle contained in this text in its full measure as applied to man.

"There is a book of aphorisms which has never been published and probably never will be published. I have mentioned this book before in connection with the question of the meaning of knowledge and I quoted then one aphorism from this book.

"In relation to what we are speaking of now this book says the following:

"'A man may be born, but in order to be born he must first die, and in order to die he must first awake.'

"In another place it says:

"'When a man awakes he can die; when he dies he can be born.'

"We must find out what this means.

"'To awake,' 'to die,' 'to be born.' These are three successive stages. If you study the Gospels attentively you will see that references are often made to the possibility of being born, several references are made to the necessity of 'dying,' and there are very many references to the necessity of 'awakening'—'watch, for ye know not the day and hour . . .' and so on. But these three possibilities of man, to awake or not to sleep, to die, and to be born, are not set down in connection with one another. Nevertheless this is the whole point. If a man dies without having awakened he cannot be born. If a man is born without having died he may become an 'immortal thing.' Thus the fact that he has not 'died' prevents a man from being 'born'; the fact of his not having awakened prevents him from 'dying'; and should he be born without having died he is prevented from 'being.'

"We have already spoken enough about the meaning of being 'born.' This relates to the beginning of a new growth of essence, the beginning of the formation of individuality, the beginning of the appearance of one indivisible I.

"But in order to be able to attain this or at least begin to attain it, a man must die, that is, he must free himself from a thousand petty attachments and identifications which hold him in the position in which he is. He is attached to everything in his life, attached to his imagination, attached to his stupidity, attached even to his sufferings, possibly to his sufferings more than to anything else. He must free himself from this attachment. Attachment to things, identification with things, keep alive a thousand useless I's in a man. These I's must die in order that the big I may be born. But how can they be made to die? They do not want to die. It is at this point that the possibility of awakening comes to the rescue. To awaken means to realize one's nothingness, that is to realize one's complete and absolute mechanicalness and one's complete and absolute helplessness. And it is not sufficient to realize it philosophically in words. It is necessary to realize it in clear, simple, and concrete facts, in one's own facts. When a man begins to know himself a little he will see in himself many things that are bound to horrify him. So long as a man is not horrified at himself he knows nothing about himself. A man has seen in himself something that horrifies him. He decides to throw it off, stop it, put an end to it. But however many efforts he makes, he feels that he cannot do this, that everything remains as it was. Here he will see his impotence, his helplessness, and his nothingness; or again, when he begins to know himself a man sees that he has nothing that is his own, that is, that all that he has regarded as his own, his views, thoughts, convictions, tastes, habits, even faults and vices, all these are not his own, but have been either formed through imitation or borrowed from somewhere ready-made. In feeling this a man may feel his nothingness. And in feeling his nothingness a man should see himself as he really is, not for a second, not for a moment, but constantly, never forgetting it.

"This continual consciousness of his nothingness and of his helplessness will eventually give a man the courage to 'die,' that is, to die, not merely mentally or in his consciousness, but to die in fact and to renounce actually and forever those aspects of himself which are either unnecessary from the point of view of his inner growth or which hinder it. These aspects are first of all his 'false I,' and then all the fantastic ideas about his 'individuality,' 'will,' 'consciousness,' 'capacity to do,' his powers, initiative, determination, and so on.

"But in order to see a thing *always*, one must first of all see it even if only for a second. All new powers and capacities of realization come always in one and the same way. At first they appear in the form of flashes at rare and short moments; afterwards they appear more often and last longer until, finally, after very long work they become permanent. The same thing applies to awakening. It is impossible to awaken completely all at once. One must first begin to awaken for short moments. *But one must die all at once and forever* after having made a certain effort, having surmounted a certain obstacle, having taken a certain decision from which there is no going back. This would be difficult, even impossible, for a man, were it not for the slow and gradual awakening which precedes it.

"But there are a thousand things which prevent a man from awakening, which keep him in the power of his dreams. In order to act consciously with the intention of awakening, it is necessary to know the nature of the forces which keep man in a state of sleep.

"First of all it must be realized that the sleep in which man exists is not normal but hypnotic sleep. Man is hypnotized and this hypnotic state is continually maintained and strengthened in him. One would think that there are forces for whom it is useful and profitable to keep man in a hypnotic state and prevent him from seeing the truth and understanding his position.

"There is an Eastern tale which speaks about a very rich magician who had a great many sheep. But at the same time this magician was very mean. He did not want to hire shepherds, nor did he want to erect a fence about the pasture where his sheep were grazing. The sheep consequently often wandered into the forest, fell into ravines, and so on, and above all they ran away, for they knew that the magician wanted their flesh and skins and this they did not like.

"At last the magician found a remedy. He *hypnotized* his sheep and suggested to them first of all that they were immortal and that no harm was being done to them when they were skinned, that, on the contrary, it would be very good for them and even pleasant; secondly he suggested that the magician was a *good master* who loved his flock so much that he was ready to do anything in the world for them; and in the third place he suggested to them that if anything at all were going to happen to them it was not going to happen just then, at any rate not that day, and *therefore* they had no need to think about it. Further the magician suggested to his sheep that they were not sheep at all; to some of them he suggested that they were *lions*, to others that they were *eagles*, to others that they were *men*, and to others that they were *magicians*.

"And after this all his cares and worries about the sheep came to an end. They never ran away again but quietly awaited the time when the magician would require their flesh and skins.

"This tale is a very good illustration of man's position.

"In so-called 'occult' literature you have probably met with the expression 'Kundalini,' 'the fire of Kundalini,' or the 'serpent of Kundalini.' This expression is often used to designate some kind of strange force which is present in man and which can be awakened. But none of the known theories gives the right explanation of the force of Kundalini. Sometimes it is connected with sex, with sex energy, that is with the idea of the possibility of using sex energy for other purposes. This latter is entirely wrong because Kundalini can be in anything. And above all, Kundalini is not anything desirable or useful for man's development. It is very curious how these occultists have got hold of the word from somewhere but have completely altered its meaning and from a very dangerous and terrible thing have made something to be hoped for and to be awaited as some blessing.

"In reality Kundalini is the power of imagination, the power of fantasy, *which takes the place of a real function.* When a man dreams instead of acting, when his dreams take the place of reality, when a man imagines himself to be an eagle, a lion, or a magician, it is the force of Kundalini acting in him. Kundalini can act in all centers and with its help all the centers can be satisfied with the imaginary instead of the real. A sheep which considers itself a lion or a magician lives under the power of Kundalini.

"Kundalini is a force put into men in order to keep them in their present state. If men could really see their true position and could understand all the horror of it, they would be unable to remain where they are even for one second. They would begin to seek a way out and they would quickly find it, *because there is a way out*; but men fail to see it simply because they are hypnotized. Kundalini is the force that keeps them in a hypnotic state. 'To awaken' for man means to be 'dehypnotized.' In this lies the chief difficulty and in this also lies the guarantee of its possibility, for there is no organic reason for sleep and man *can* awaken.

"Theoretically he can, but practically it is almost impossible because as soon as a man awakens for a moment and opens his eyes, all the forces that caused him to fall asleep begin to act upon him with tenfold energy and he immediately falls asleep again, very often *dreaming* that he is awake or is awakening.

"There are certain states in ordinary sleep in which a man wants to awaken but cannot. He tells himself that he is awake but, in reality, he continues to sleep—and this can happen several times before he finally awakes. But in ordinary sleep, once he is awake, he is in a different state; in hypnotic sleep the case is otherwise; there are no objective characteristics, at any rate not at the beginning of awakening; a man cannot pinch himself in order to make sure that he is not asleep. And if, which God forbid, a man has heard anything about *objective characteristics*, Kundalini at once transforms it all into imagination and dreams.

"Only a man who fully realizes the difficulty of awakening can understand the necessity of long and hard work in order to awake.

"Speaking in general, what is necessary to awake a sleeping man? A good shock is necessary. But when a man is fast asleep one shock is not enough. A long period of continual shocks is needed. Consequently there must be somebody to administer these shocks. I have said before that if a man wants to awaken he must hire somebody who will keep on shaking him for a long time. But whom can he hire if everyone is asleep? A man will hire somebody to wake him up but this one also falls asleep. What is the use of such a man? And a man who can really keep awake will probably refuse to waste his time in waking others up: he may have his own much more important work to do.

"There is also the possibility of being awakened by mechanical means. A man may be awakened by an alarm clock. But the trouble is that a man gets accustomed to the alarm clock far too quickly, he ceases to hear it. Many alarm clocks are necessary and always new ones. Otherwise a man must surround himself with alarm clocks which will prevent him sleeping. But here again there are certain difficulties. Alarm clocks must be wound up; in order to wind them up one must remember about them; in order to remember one must wake up often. But what is still worse, a man gets used to all alarm clocks and after a certain time he only sleeps the better for them. Therefore alarm clocks must be constantly changed, new ones must be continually invented. In the course of time this may help a man to awaken. But there is very little chance of a man doing all the work of winding up, inventing, and changing clocks all by himself, without outside help. It is much more likely that he will begin this work and that it will afterwards pass into sleep, and in sleep he will dream of inventing alarm clocks, of winding them up and changing them, and simply sleep all the sounder for it.

"Therefore, in order to awaken, a combination of efforts is needed. It is necessary that somebody should wake the man up; it is necessary that somebody should look after the man who wakes him; it is necessary to have alarm clocks and it is also necessary continually to invent new alarm clocks.

"But in order to achieve all this and to obtain results a certain number of people must work together.

"One man can do nothing.

"Before anything else he needs help. But help cannot come to one man alone. Those who are able to help put a great value on their time. And, of course, they would prefer to help, say, twenty or thirty people who want to awake rather than one man. Moreover, as has been said earlier, one man can easily deceive himself about his awakening and take for awakening simply a new dream. If several people decide to struggle together against sleep, they will wake each other. It may often happen that twenty of them will sleep but the twenty-first will be awake and he will wake up the rest. It is exactly the same thing with alarm clocks. One man will invent one alarm clock, another man will invent another, afterwards they can make an exchange. Altogether they can be of very great help one to another, and without this help no one can attain anything.

"Therefore a man who wants to awake must look for other people who also want to awake and work together with them. This, however, is easier said than done because to start such work and to organize it requires a knowledge which an ordinary man cannot possess. The work must be organized and it must have a leader. Only then can it produce the results expected of it. Without these conditions no efforts can result in anything whatever. Men may torture themselves but these tortures will not make them awake. This is the most difficult of all for certain people to understand. By themselves and on their own initiative they may be capable of great efforts and great sacrifices. But because their first effort and their first sacrifice ought to be obedience nothing on earth will induce them to obey another. And they do not want to reconcile themselves to the thought that all their efforts and all their sacrifices are useless.

"Work must be organized. And it can be organized only by a man who knows its problems and its aims, who knows its methods; by a man who has in his time passed through such organized work himself.

"A man usually begins his studies in a small group. This group is generally connected with a whole series of similar groups on different levels which, taken together, constitute what may be called a 'preparatory school.'

"The first and most important feature of groups is the fact that groups are not constituted according to the wish and choice of their members. Groups are constituted by the teacher, who selects types which, from the point of view of his aims, can be useful to one another.

"No work of groups is possible without a teacher. The work of groups with a wrong teacher can produce only negative results.

"The next important feature of group work is that groups may be connected with some *aim* of which those who are beginning work in them have no idea whatever and which cannot even be explained to them until they understand the essence and the principles of the work and the ideas connected with it. But this aim towards which without knowing it they are going, and which they are serving, is the necessary balancing principle in their own work. Their first task is to understand this aim, that is, the aim of the teacher. When they have understood this aim, although at first not fully, their own work becomes more conscious and consequently can give better results. But, as I have already said, it often happens that the aim of the teacher cannot be explained at the beginning.

"Therefore, the first aim of a man beginning work in a group should be *self-study*. The work of self-study can proceed only in properly organized groups. One man alone cannot see himself. But when a certain number of people unite together for this purpose they will even involuntarily help one another. It is a common characteristic of human nature that a man sees the faults of others more easily than he sees his own. At the same time on the path of self-study he learns that he himself possesses all the faults that he finds in others. But there are many things that he does not see in himself, whereas in other people he begins to see them. But, as I have just said, in this case he knows that these features are his own. Thus other members of the group serve him as mirrors in which he sees himself. But, of course, in order to see himself in other people's faults and not merely to see the faults of others, a man must be very much on his guard against and be very sincere with himself.

"He must remember that he is not one; that one part of him is the man who wants to awaken and that the other part is 'Ivanov,' 'Petrov,' or 'Zakharov,' who has no desire whatever to awaken and who has to be awakened by force.

"A group is usually a pact concluded between the I's of a certain group of people to make a common struggle against 'Ivanov,' 'Petrov,' and 'Zakharov,' that is, against their own 'false personalities.'

"Let us take Petrov. Petrov consists of two parts—'I' and 'Petrov.' But 'I' is powerless against 'Petrov.' 'Petrov' is the master. Suppose there are twenty people; twenty 'I's' now begin to struggle against one 'Petrov.' They may now prove to be stronger than he is. At any rate they can spoil his sleep; he will no longer be able to sleep as peacefully as he did before. And this is the whole aim.

"Furthermore, in the work of self-study one man begins to accumulate material resulting from self-observation. Twenty people will have twenty times as much material. And every one of them will be able to use the whole of this material because the exchange of observations is one of the purposes of the group's existence.

"When a group is being organized its members have certain conditions put before them; in the first place, conditions general for all members, and secondly, individual conditions for individual members.

"General conditions at the beginning of the work are usually of the following kind. First of all it is explained to all the members of a group that they must keep secret everything they hear or learn in the group and not only while they are members of it but forever afterwards.

"This is an indispensable condition whose idea should be clear to them from the very beginning. In other words, it should be clear to them that in this there is no attempt whatever to make a secret of what is not essentially a secret, neither is there any deliberate intention to deprive them of the right to exchange views with those near to them or with their friends.

"The idea of this restriction consists in the fact that *they are unable* to transmit correctly what is said in the groups. They very soon begin to learn *from their own personal experience* how much effort, how much time, and how much explaining is necessary in order to grasp what is said in groups. It becomes clear to them that they are unable to give their friends a right idea of what they have learned themselves. At the same time also they begin to understand that by giving their friends *wrong ideas* they shut them off from any possibility of approaching the work at any time or of understanding anything in connection with the work, to say nothing of the fact that in this way they are creating very many difficulties and even very much unpleasantness for themselves in the future. If a man in spite of this tries to transmit what he hears in groups to his friends he will very quickly be convinced that attempts in this direction give entirely unexpected and undesirable results. Either people begin to argue with him and without wanting to listen to him expect him to listen to *their* theories, or they misinterpret everything he tells them, attach an entirely different meaning to everything they hear from him. In seeing this and understanding the uselessness of such attempts a man begins to see one aspect of this restriction.

"The other and no less important side consists in the fact that it is very difficult for a man to keep silent about things that interest him. He would like to speak about them to everyone with whom he is accustomed to share his thoughts, as he calls it. This is the most mechanical of all desires and in this case silence is the most difficult abstinence of all. But if a man understands this or, at least, if he follows this rule, it will constitute for him the best exercise possible for self-remembering and for the development of will. Only a man who can be silent when it is necessary can be master of himself.

"But for many people it is very difficult to reconcile themselves to the thought that one of their chief characteristics consists in undue talkativeness, especially for people who are accustomed to regard themselves as serious or sound persons, or for those who regard themselves as silent persons who are fond of solitude and reflection. And for this reason this demand is especially important. In remembering about this and in carrying it out, a man begins to see sides of himself which he never noticed before.

"The next demand which is made of the members of a group is that they must tell the *teacher* of the group the whole truth.

"This also must be clearly and properly understood. People do not realize what a big place in their lives is occupied by lying or even if only by *the suppression of the truth.* People are unable to be sincere either with themselves or with others. They do not even understand that to learn to be sincere *when it is necessary* is one of the most difficult things on earth. They imagine that to speak or not to speak the truth, to be or not to be sincere, depends upon them. Therefore they have to learn this and learn it first of all in relation to the *teacher* of the work. Telling the teacher a deliberate lie, or being insincere with him, or suppressing something, makes their presence in the group completely useless and is even worse than being rude or uncivil to him or in his presence.

"The next demand made of members of a group is that they must *remember why they came to the group.* They came to learn and to work on themselves and to learn and to work not as they understand it themselves but as they are told to. If, therefore, once they are in the group, they begin to feel or to express mistrust towards the teacher, to criticize his actions, to find that they understand better how the group should be conducted and especially if they show lack of external considering in relation to the teacher, lack of respect for him, asperity, impatience, tendency to argument, this at once puts an end to any possibility of work, for work is possible only as long as people remember that they have come to learn and not to teach.

"If a man begins to distrust the teacher, the teacher becomes unnecessary to him and he becomes unnecessary to the teacher. And in this event it is better for him to go and look for another teacher or try to work without one. This will do him no good, but in any case it will do less harm than lying, suppression, or resistance, or mistrust of the teacher.

"In addition to these fundamental demands it is of course presumed that the members of the group must work. If they merely frequent the group and do no work but merely imagine that they are working, or if they regard as work their mere presence in the group, or, as often happens, if they look upon their presence in the group as a pastime, if they make pleasant acquaintances, and so on, then their presence in the group likewise becomes completely useless. And the sooner they are sent away or leave of their own accord the better it will be for them and for the others.

"The fundamental demands which have been enumerated provide the material for rules which are obligatory for all members of a group. In the first place rules help everyone who wants to work to avoid everything that may hinder him or do harm to his work, and secondly *they help him to remember himself.*

"It very often happens that at the beginning of the work the members of a group do not like some or other of the rules. And they even ask: *Can we not work without rules?* Rules seem to them to be an unnecessary constraint on their freedom or a tiresome formality, and to be reminded about rules seems to them to be ill will or dissatisfaction on the part of the teacher.

"In reality rules are the chief and the first *help* that they get from the work. It stands to reason that rules do not pursue the object of affording them amusement or satisfaction or of making things more easy for them. Rules pursue a definite aim: to make them behave as they would behave '*if they were,*' that is, if they remembered themselves and realized how they ought to behave with regard to people outside the work, to people in the work, and to the teacher. If they remembered themselves and realized this, rules would not be necessary for them. But they are not able to remember themselves and understand this at the beginning of work, so that rules are indispensable, although rules can never be either easy, pleasant, or comfortable. On the contrary, they ought to be difficult, unpleasant, and uncomfortable; otherwise they would not answer their purpose. Rules are the alarm clocks which wake the sleeping man. But the man, opening his eyes for a second, is indignant with the alarm clock and asks: *Can one not awaken without alarm clocks?*

"Besides these general rules there are certain individual conditions which are given to each person separately and which are generally connected with his 'chief fault,' or chief feature.

"This requires some explanation.

"Every man has a certain feature in his character which is central. It is like an axle round which all his 'false personality' revolves. Every man's personal work must consist in struggling against this chief fault. This explains why there can be no general rules of work and why all systems that attempt to evolve such rules either lead to nothing or cause harm. How can there be general rules? What is useful for one is harmful for another. One man talks too much; he must learn to keep silent. Another man is silent when he ought to talk and he must learn to talk; and so it is always and in everything. General rules for the work of groups refer to everyone. Personal directions can only be individual. In this connection again a man cannot find his own chief feature, his chief fault, by himself. This is practically a law. The teacher has to point out this feature to him and show him how to fight against it. No one else but the teacher can do this.

"The study of the chief fault and the struggle against it constitute, as it were, each man's individual path, but the aim must be the same for all. This aim is the realization of one's nothingness. Only when a man has truly and sincerely arrived at the conviction of his own helplessness and nothingness and only when he feels it constantly, *will he be ready for the next and much more difficult stages of the work.*

"All that has been said up till now refers to real groups connected with real concrete work which in its turn is connected with what has been called the 'fourth way.' But there are many imitation ways, imitation groups, and imitation work. These are not even 'black magic.'

"Questions have often been asked at these lectures as to what is 'black magic' and I have replied that there is neither red, green, nor yellow magic. There is mechanics, that is, what 'happens,' and there is 'doing.' 'Doing' is magic and 'doing' can be only of one kind. There cannot be two kinds of 'doing.' But there can be a falsification, an imitation of the outward appearance of 'doing,' which cannot give any objective results

but which can deceive naïve people and produce in them faith, infatuation, enthusiasm, and even fanaticism.

"This is why in true work, that is, in true 'doing,' the producing of
infatuation in people is not allowed. What you call black magic is based
on infatuation and on playing upon human weaknesses. Black magic does
not in any way mean magic of evil. I have already said earlier that no
one ever does anything for the sake of evil, in the interests of evil. Everyone always does everything in the interests of good *as he understands it*.
In the same way it is quite wrong to assert that black magic must necessarily be *egoistical*, that in black magic a man strives after some results
for himself. This is quite wrong. Black magic may be quite altruistic, may
strive after the good of humanity or after the salvation of humanity from
real or imaginary evils. But what can be called black magic has always
one definite characteristic. This characteristic is the tendency to use people
for some, even the best of aims, *without their knowledge and understanding,* either by producing in them faith and infatuation or by acting upon
them through fear.

"But it must be remembered in this connection that a 'black magician,'
whether good or evil, has at all events been at a school. He has learned
something, has heard something, knows something. He is simply a 'half-
educated man' who has either been turned out of a school or who has
himself left a school having decided that he already knows enough, that
he does not want to be in subordination any longer, and that he can work
independently and even direct the work of others. All 'work' of this kind
can produce only subjective results, that is to say, it can only increase
deception and increase sleep instead of decreasing them. Nevertheless
something can be learned from a 'black magician' although in the wrong
way. He can sometimes by accident even tell the truth. That is why I say
that there are many things worse than 'black magic.' Such are various
'occult' and theosophical societies and groups. Not only have their teachers
never been at a school but they have never even met anyone who has
been near a school. Their work simply consists in aping. But imitation
work of this kind gives a great deal of self-satisfaction. One man feels
himself to be a 'teacher,' others feel that they are 'pupils,' and everyone
is satisfied. No realization of one's nothingness can be got here and if
people affirm that they have it, it is all illusion and self-deception, if not
plain deceit. On the contrary, instead of realizing their own nothingness
the members of such circles acquire a realization of their own importance
and a growth of false personality.

"At first it is very difficult to verify whether the work is right or wrong,
whether the directions received are correct or incorrect. The theoretical
part of the work may prove useful in this respect, because a man can
judge more easily from this aspect of it. He knows what he knows and
what he does not know. He knows what can be learned by ordinary means

and what cannot. And if he learns something new, something that cannot be learned in the ordinary way from books and so on, this, to a certain extent, is a guarantee that the other, the practical side, may also be right. But this of course is far from being a full guarantee because here also mistakes are possible. All occult and spiritualistic societies and circles assert that they possess a new knowledge. And there are people who believe it.

"In properly organized groups no faith is required; what is required is simply a little trust and even that only for a little while, for the sooner a man begins to verify all he hears the better it is for him.

"The struggle against the 'false I,' against one's chief feature or chief fault, is the most important part of the work, and it must proceed in deeds, not in words. For this purpose the teacher gives each man definite tasks which require, in order to carry them out, the conquest of his chief feature. When a man carries out these tasks he struggles with himself, works on himself. If he avoids the tasks, tries not to carry them out, it means that either he does not want to or that he cannot work.

"As a rule only very easy tasks are given at the beginning which the teacher does not even call tasks, and he does not say much about them but gives them in the form of hints. If he sees that he is understood and that the tasks are carried out he passes on to more and more difficult ones.

"More difficult tasks, although they are only subjectively difficult, are called 'barriers.' The peculiarity of barriers consists in the fact that, having surmounted a serious barrier, a man can no longer return to ordinary sleep, to ordinary life. And if, having passed the first barrier, he feels afraid of those that follow and does not go on, he stops so to speak between two barriers and is unable to move either backwards or forwards. This is the worst thing that can happen to a man. Therefore the teacher is usually very careful in the choice of tasks and barriers, in other words, he takes the risk of giving definite tasks requiring the conquest of inner barriers only to those people who have already shown themselves sufficiently strong on small barriers.

"It often happens that, having stopped before some barrier, usually the smallest and the most simple, people turn against the work, against the teacher, and against other members of the group, and accuse them of the very thing that is becoming revealed to them in themselves.

"Sometimes they repent later and blame themselves, then they again blame others, then they repent once more, and so on. But there is nothing that shows up a man better than his attitude towards the work and the teacher *after he has left it*. Sometimes such tests are arranged intentionally. A man is placed in such a position that he is *obliged* to leave and he is fully justified in having a grievance either against the teacher or against some other person. And then he is watched to see how he will behave. A decent man will behave decently even if he thinks that he has been treated unjustly or wrongly. But many people in such circumstances show a side of their nature which otherwise they would never show. And at times it is a necessary means for exposing a man's nature. So long as you are good to a man he is good to you. But what will he be like if you scratch him a little?

"But this is not the chief thing; the chief thing is his own personal attitude, his own *valuation* of the ideas which he receives or has received, and his keeping or losing this valuation. A man may think for a long time and quite sincerely that he wants to work and even make great efforts, and then he may throw up everything and even definitely go against the work; justify himself, invent various fabrications, deliberately ascribe a wrong meaning to what he has heard, and so on."

"What happens to them for this?" asked one of the audience.

"Nothing—what could happen to them?" said G. "*They are their own punishment.* And what punishment could be worse?

"It is impossible to describe in full the way work in a group is conducted," continued G. "One must go through it. All that has been said up to now are only hints, the true meaning of which will only be revealed to those who go on with the work and learn from experience what 'barriers' mean and what difficulties they represent.

"Speaking in general the most difficult barrier is the conquest of lying. A man lies so much and so constantly both to himself and to others that he ceases to notice it. Nevertheless lying must be conquered. And the first effort required of a man is to conquer lying in relation to the teacher. A man must either decide at once to tell him nothing but the truth, or at once give up the whole thing.

"You must realize that the teacher takes a very difficult task upon himself, the cleaning and the repair of human machines. Of course he accepts only those machines that are within his power to mend. If something essential is broken or put out of order in the machine, then he refuses to take it. But even such machines, which by their nature could still be cleaned, become quite hopeless if they begin to tell lies. A lie to the teacher, even the most insignificant, concealment of any kind such as the concealment of something another has asked to be kept secret, or of something the man himself has said to another, at once puts an end to the work of that man, especially if he has previously made any efforts.

"Here is something you must bear in mind. Every effort a man makes increases the demands made upon him. So long as a man has not made any serious efforts the demands made upon him are very small, but his efforts immediately increase the demands made upon him. And the greater the efforts that are made, the greater the new demands.

"At this stage people very often make a mistake that is constantly made. They think that the efforts they have previously made, their former merits, so to speak, give them some kind of rights or advantages, *diminish* the demands to be made upon them, and constitute as it were an excuse should they not work or should they afterwards do something wrong. This, of course, is most profoundly false. Nothing that a man did yesterday excuses him today. Quite the reverse, if a man did nothing yesterday, no demands are made upon him today; if he did anything yesterday, it means that he must do more today. This certainly does not mean that it is better to do nothing. Whoever does nothing receives nothing.

"As I have said already, one of the first demands is sincerity. But there are different kinds of sincerity. There is clever sincerity and there is stupid sincerity, just as there is clever insincerity and stupid insincerity. Both stupid sincerity and stupid insincerity are equally mechanical. But if a man wishes to learn to be *cleverly sincere,* he must be sincere first of all with his teacher and with people who are senior to him in the work. This will be 'clever sincerity.' But here it is necessary to note that sincerity must not become 'lack of considering.' Lack of considering in relation to the teacher or in relation to those whom the teacher has appointed, as I have said already, destroys all possibility of any work. If he wishes to learn to be *cleverly insincere* he must be insincere about the work and he must learn to be silent when he ought to be silent with people outside it, who can neither understand nor appreciate it. But sincerity in the group is an absolute demand, because, if a man continues to lie in the group in the same way as he lies to himself and to others in life, he will never learn to distinguish the truth from a lie.

"The second barrier is very often the conquest of fear. A man usually has many unnecessary, imaginary fears. Lies and fears—this is the atmosphere in which an ordinary man lives. Just as the conquest of lying is individual, so also is the conquest of fear. Every man has fears of his own which are peculiar to him alone. These fears must first be found and then destroyed. The fears of which I speak are usually connected with the lies among which a man lives. You must realize that they have nothing in common with the fear of spiders or of mice or of a dark room, or with unaccountable nervous fears.

"The struggle against lying in oneself and the struggle against fears is the first positive work which a man begins to do.

"One must realize in general that positive efforts and even sacrifices in the work do not justify or excuse mistakes which may follow. On the contrary, things that could be forgiven in a man who has made no efforts and who has sacrificed nothing will not be forgiven in another who has already made great sacrifices.

"This seems to be unjust, but one must understand the law. There is, as it were, a separate account kept for every man. His efforts and sacrifices are written down on one side of the book and his mistakes and misdeeds on the other side. What is written down on the positive side can never atone for what is written down on the negative side. What is recorded on the negative side can only be wiped out by the truth, that is to say, by an instant and complete confession to himself and to others and above all to the teacher. If a man sees his fault but continues to justify himself, a small offense may destroy the result of whole years of work and effort. In the work, therefore, it is often better to admit one's guilt even when one is not guilty. But this again is a delicate matter and it must not be exaggerated. Otherwise the result will again be lying, and lying prompted by fear."

On another occasion, speaking of groups, G. said:

"Do not think that we can begin straight away by forming a group. A group is a big thing. A group is begun for definite *concerted* work, for a definite aim. I should have to trust you in this work and you would have to trust me and one another. Then it would be a group. Until there is general work it will only be a preparatory group. We shall prepare ourselves so as in the course of time to become a group. And it is only possible to prepare ourselves to become a group by trying to imitate a group such as it ought to be, imitating it inwardly of course, not outwardly.

"What is necessary for this? First of all you must understand that in a group all are responsible for one another. A mistake on the part of one is considered as a mistake on the part of all. This is a law. And this law is well founded for, as you will see later, what one acquires is acquired also by all.

"The rule of common responsibility must be borne well in mind. It has another side also. Members of a group are responsible not only for the mistakes of others, but also for their failures. The success of one is the success of all. The failure of one is the failure of all. A grave mistake on the part of one, such as for instance the breaking of a fundamental rule, inevitably leads to the dissolution of the whole group.

"A group must work as one machine. The parts of the machine must know one another and help one another. In a group there can be no personal interests opposed to the interests of others, or opposed to the interests of the work, there can be no personal sympathies or antipathies which hinder the work. All the members of a group are friends and brothers, but if one of them leaves, and especially if he is sent away by the teacher, he ceases to be a friend and a brother and at once becomes a stranger, as one who is cut off. It often becomes a very hard rule, but nevertheless it is necessary. People may be lifelong friends and may enter a group together. Afterwards one of them leaves. The other then has no right to speak to him about the work of the group. The man who has left feels hurt, he does not understand this, and they quarrel. In order to avoid this where relations, such as husband and wife, mother and daughter, and so on, are concerned, we count them as one, that is, husband and wife are counted as one member of the group. Thus if one of them cannot go on with the work and leaves, the other is considered guilty and must also leave.

"Furthermore, you must remember that I can help you only to the extent that you help me. Moreover your help, especially at the beginning, will be reckoned not by actual results which are almost certain to be nil, but by the number and the magnitude of your efforts."

After this G. passed to individual tasks and to the definition of our "chief faults." Then he gave us several definite tasks with which the work of our group began.

Later, in 1917, when we were in the Caucasus, G. once added several interesting observations to the general principles of the formation of groups. I think I must quote them here.

"You take it all too theoretically," he said. "You ought to have known more by now. There is no particular benefit in the existence of groups in themselves and there is no particular merit in belonging to groups. The benefit or usefulness of groups is determined by their results.

"The work of every man can proceed in three directions. He can be useful to the *work*. He can be useful to *me*. And he can be useful to *himself*. Of course it is desirable that a man's work should produce results in all three directions. Failing this, one can be reconciled to two. For instance, if a man is useful to me, by this very fact he is useful also to the work. Or if he is useful to the work, he is useful also to me. But if, let us say, a man is useful to the work and useful to me, but is not able to be useful to himself, this is much worse because it cannot last long. If a man takes nothing for himself and does not change, if he remains such as he was before, then the fact of his having by chance been useful for a short time is not placed to his credit, and, what is more important, his usefulness does not last for long. The work grows and changes. If a man himself does not grow or change he cannot keep up with the work. The work leaves him behind and then the very thing that was useful may begin to be harmful."

I return to St. Petersburg, in the summer of 1916.

Soon after our group, or "preparatory group," had been formed, G. spoke to us about efforts in connection with the tasks he set before us.

"You must understand," he said, "that ordinary efforts do not count. *Only super-efforts count*. And so it is always and in everything. Those who do not wish to make super-efforts had better give up everything and take care of their health."

"Can not super-efforts be dangerous?" asked one of the audience who was usually particularly careful about his health.

"Of course they can," said G., "but it is better to die making efforts to awaken than to live in sleep. That's one thing. For another thing it is not so easy to die from efforts. We have much more strength than we think. But we never make use of it. You must understand one feature of the organization of the human machine.

"A very important role in the human machine is played by a certain kind of accumulator. There are two small accumulators near each center filled with the particular substance necessary for the work of the given center.

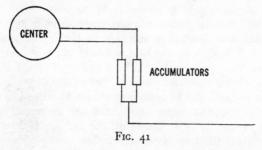

FIG. 41

"In addition, there is in the organism a large accumulator which feeds the small ones. The small accumulators are connected together, and further, each of them is connected with the center next to which it stands, as well as with the large accumulator."

G. drew a general diagram of the "human machine" and pointed out the positions of the large and small accumulators and the connections between them.

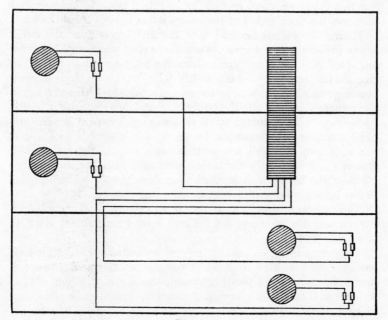

FIG. 42

"Accumulators work in the following way," he said. "Let us suppose that a man is working or is reading a difficult book and trying to understand it, in which case several 'rolls' revolve in the thinking apparatus in his head. Or let us suppose that he is walking up a hill and is getting tired, in which case the 'rolls' revolve in the moving center.

"In the first instance the intellectual center, and in the second the moving center, draw the energy necessary for their work from the small accumulators. When an accumulator is nearly empty a man feels tired. He would like to stop, to sit down if he is walking, to think of something else if he is solving a difficult problem. But quite unexpectedly he feels an inflow of strength, and he is once more able to walk or to work. This means that the center has become connected with the second accumulator and is taking energy from it. Meanwhile the first accumulator is refilling with energy from the large accumulator. The work of the center goes on. The man continues to walk or to work. Sometimes a short rest is required to insure this connection. Sometimes a shock, sometimes an effort. Anyway, the work goes on. After a certain time the store of energy in the second accumulator also becomes exhausted. The man again feels tired.

"Again an external shock, or a short rest, or a cigarette, or an effort, and he is connected with the first accumulator. But it may easily happen that the center has drawn energy from the second accumulator so quickly that the first one has had no time to refill itself from the large accumulator, and has taken only half the energy it can hold; it is only half full.

"Having become reconnected with the first accumulator the center begins to draw energy from it, while the second accumulator becomes connected with and draws energy from the large accumulator. But this time the first accumulator was only half full. The center quickly exhausts its energy, and in the meantime the second accumulator has succeeded in getting only a quarter full. The center becomes connected with it, swiftly exhausts all its energy, and connects once more with the first accumulator, and so on. After a certain time the organism is brought to such a state that neither of the small accumulators has a drop of energy left. This time the man feels really tired. He almost falls down, he almost drops asleep, or else his organism becomes affected, he starts a headache, palpitations begin, or he feels sick.

"Then suddenly, again a short rest, or an external shock, or an effort, brings a new flow of energy and the man is once more able to think, to walk, or to work.

"This means that the center has become connected directly to the large accumulator. The large accumulator contains an enormous amount of energy. Connected with the large accumulator a man is literally able to perform miracles. But of course, if the 'rolls' continue to turn and energy which is made from air, food, and impressions continues to pour out of the large accumulator faster than it pours in, then there comes a moment when the large accumulator is drained of all energy and the organism dies. But this happens very seldom. Usually the organism automatically stops working long before this. Special conditions are necessary to cause the organism to die exhausted of all its energy. In ordinary conditions a man will fall asleep or he will faint or he will develop some internal complication which will stop the work a long time before the real danger.

"One need not, therefore, be afraid of efforts; the danger of dying from them is not at all great. It is much easier to die from inaction, from laziness, and from the fear of making efforts.

"Our aim, on the contrary, is to learn to connect the necessary center with the large accumulator. So long as we are unable to do this, all our work will be wasted because we shall fall asleep before our efforts can give any kind of results.

"Small accumulators suffice for the ordinary, everyday work of life. But for work on oneself, for inner growth, and for the efforts which are required of a man who enters the way, the energy from these small accumulators is not enough.

"We must learn how to draw energy straight from the large accumulator.

"This however is possible only with the help of the emotional center. It is essential that this be understood. The connection with the large accumulator can be effected only through the emotional center. The instinctive, moving, and intellectual centers, by themselves, can feed only on the small accumulators.

"This is precisely what people do not understand. Therefore their aim must be the development of the activity of the emotional center. The emotional center is an apparatus much more subtle than the intellectual center, particularly if we take into consideration the fact that in the whole of the intellectual center the only part that works is the formatory apparatus and that many things are quite inaccessible to the intellectual center. If anyone desires to know and to understand more than he actually knows and understands, he must remember that this new knowledge and this new understanding will come through the emotional center and not through the intellectual center."

In addition to what he had said about accumulators G. made some very interesting remarks about *yawning* and about *laughter*.

"There are two incomprehensible functions of our organism inexplicable from the scientific point of view," he said, "although naturally science does not admit them to be inexplicable; these are yawning and laughter. Neither the one nor the other can be rightly understood and explained without knowing about accumulators and their role in the organism.

"You have noticed that you yawn when you are tired. This is especially noticeable, for instance, in the mountains, when a man who is unaccustomed to them yawns almost continually while he is ascending a mountain. Yawning is the pumping of energy into the small accumulators. When they empty too quickly, that is, when one of them has no time to fill up while the other is being emptied, yawning becomes almost continuous. There are certain diseased conditions which can cause stoppage of the heart when a man wishes but is not able to yawn, and other conditions are known when something goes wrong with the pump, causing it to work without effect, when a man yawns the whole time, but does not pump in any energy.

"The study and the observation of yawning from this point of view may reveal much that is new and interesting.

"Laughter is also directly connected with accumulators. But laughter is the opposite function to yawning. It is not pumping in, but pumping out, that is, the pumping out and the discarding of superfluous energy collected in the accumulators. Laughter does not exist in all centers, but only in centers divided into two halves—positive and negative. If I have not yet spoken of this in detail, I shall do so when we come to a more detailed study of the centers. At present we shall take only the intellectual center. There can be impressions which fall at once on two halves of the center and produce at once a sharp 'yes' and 'no.' Such a simultaneous 'yes' and 'no' produces a kind of convulsion in the center and, being unable to harmonize and digest these two opposite impressions of one fact, the center begins to throw out in the form of laughter the energy which flows into it from the accumulator whose turn it is to supply it. In another instance it happens that in the accumulator there has collected too much energy which the center cannot manage to use up. Then every, the most ordinary, impression can be received as double, that is, it may fall at once on the two halves of the center and produce laughter, that is, the discarding of energy.

"You must understand that I am only giving you an outline. You must remember that both yawning and laughter are very contagious. This shows that they are essentially functions of the instinctive and the moving centers."

"Why is laughter so pleasant?" asked someone.

"Because," G. answered, "laughter relieves us of superfluous energy, which, if it remained unused, might become negative, that is, poison. We always have plenty of this poison in us. Laughter is the antidote. But this antidote is necessary only so long as we are unable to use all the energy for useful work. It is said of Christ that he never laughed. And indeed you will find in the Gospels no indication or mention of the fact that at any time Christ laughed. But there are different ways of *not laughing.* There are people who do not laugh because they are completely immersed in negative emotions, in malice, in fear, in hatred, in suspicion. And there may be others who do not laugh because they cannot have negative emotions. Understand one thing. In the higher centers there can be no laughter, because in higher centers there is no division, and no 'yes' and 'no.' "

Chapter Twelve

B Y THAT time, midsummer 1916, work in our groups began to
take new and more intensive forms. G. spent most of the time in
St. Petersburg, only going to Moscow for a few days and coming
back again generally with two or three of his Moscow pupils. Our lectures and meetings had by that time already lost their formal character;
we had all begun to know one another better and, though there was a
little friction, we represented on the whole a very compact group united
by interest in the new ideas we were learning and the new possibilities of
knowledge and self-knowledge which had been opened out before us. At
that time there were about thirty of us. We met almost every evening.
Several times, on arriving from Moscow, G. arranged excursions into
the country for large parties, and picnics where we had *shashlik*, which
were somehow totally out of keeping with St. Petersburg. There remains
in my memory a trip to Ostrovki up the river Neva, more particularly
because I suddenly realized on this trip why G. arranged these seemingly
quite aimless amusements. I realized that he was all the time observing
and that many of us on these occasions showed entirely new aspects of
ourselves which had remained well hidden at the formal meetings in St.
Petersburg.

My meetings with G.'s Moscow pupils were at that time quite unlike
my first meeting with them in the spring of the preceding year. They
did not appear to me now to be either artificial or to be playing a role
which had been learned by heart. On the contrary, I always eagerly
awaited their coming and tried to find out from them what their work
consisted of in Moscow and what G. had said to them that we did not
know. And I found out from them a great deal which came in very useful
to me later in my work. In my new talks with them I saw the development
of a very definite plan. We were not only learning from G. but we had
also to learn one from another. I was beginning to see G.'s groups as a
"school" of some medieval painter whose pupils lived with him and
worked with him and, while learning from him, taught one another. At
the same time I understood why G.'s Moscow pupils could not answer
my questions at our first meeting. I realized how utterly naïve my questions had been: "On what is based their work on themselves?" "What

238

constitutes the system which they study?" "What is the origin of this system?" And so on.

I understood now that these questions could not be answered. One must *learn* in order to begin to understand this. And at that time, a little over a year ago, I had thought I had the right to ask such questions just as the new people who now came to us began with precisely the same kind of questions and were surprised we did not answer them, and, as we were already able to see, regarded us as artificial or as playing a part which we had learned.

But new people appeared only at large meetings at which G. took part. Meetings of the original group were at that time held separately. And it was quite clear why this should have been so. We were already beginning to get free from the self-confidence and the knowing of everything with which people approach the work and we could already understand G. better than before.

But at general meetings it was extraordinarily interesting for us to hear how new people asked the same questions we used to ask in the beginning and how they did not understand the same elementary, simple things that we had been unable to understand. These meetings with new people gave us a certain amount of self-satisfaction.

But when we were alone again with G. he often with one word destroyed everything that we had built up for ourselves and forced us to see that actually we did not as yet know anything or understand anything, either in ourselves or in others.

"The whole trouble is that you are quite sure that you are always one and the same," he said. "But I see you quite differently. For instance, I see that today one Ouspensky has come here, whereas yesterday there was another. Or the doctor—before you came we were sitting and talking here together; he was one person. Then you all came. I happened to glance at him and I see quite another doctor sitting there. And the one I see when I am alone with him you very seldom see.

"You must realize that each man has a definite repertoire of roles which he plays in ordinary circumstances," said G. in this connection. "He has a role for every kind of circumstance in which he ordinarily finds himself in life; but put him into even only slightly different circumstances and he is unable to find a suitable role and *for a short time he becomes himself*. The study of the roles a man plays represents a very necessary part of self-knowledge. Each man's repertoire is very limited. And if a man simply says 'I' and 'Ivan Ivanich,' he will not see the whole of himself because 'Ivan Ivanich' also is not one; a man has at least five or six of them. One or two for his family, one or two at his office (one for his subordinates and another for his superiors), one for friends in a restaurant, and perhaps one who is interested in exalted ideas and likes intellectual conversation. And at different times the man is fully identified with one of them and is unable to separate himself from it. To see the roles, to know one's repertoire, particularly to know its limitedness, is to know a great deal. But the point is that, outside his repertoire, a man feels very uncomfortable should something push him if only temporarily out of his rut, and he tries his hardest to return to any one of his usual roles. Directly he falls back into the rut everything at once goes smoothly again and the feeling of awkwardness and tension disappears. This is how it is in life; but in the work, in order to observe oneself, one must become reconciled to this awkwardness and tension and to the feeling of discomfort and helplessness. Only by experiencing this discomfort can a man really observe himself. And it is clear why this is so. When a man is not playing any of his usual roles, when he cannot find a suitable role in his repertoire, he feels that he is undressed. He is cold and ashamed and wants to run away from everybody. But the question arises: What does he want? A quiet life or to work on himself? If he wants a quiet life, he must certainly first of all never move out of his repertoire. In his usual roles he feels comfortable and at peace. But if he wants to work on himself, he must destroy his peace. To have them both together is in no way possible. A man must make a choice. But when choosing the result is very often deceit, that is to say, a man tries to deceive himself. In words he chooses *work* but in reality he does not want to lose his *peace*. The result is that he sits between two stools. This is the most uncomfortable position of all. He does no work at all and he gets no comfort whatever. But it is very difficult for a man to decide to throw everything to the devil and begin real work. And why is it difficult? Principally because *his life is too easy* and even if he considers it bad he is already accustomed to it. It is better for it to be bad, yet known. But here there is something new and unknown. He does not even know whether any result can be got from it or not. And besides, the most difficult thing here is that it is necessary to obey someone, to submit to someone. If a man could invent difficulties and sacrifices for himself, he would sometimes go very far. But the point here is that this is not possible. It is necessary to obey another or to follow the direction of general work, the control of which can belong only to one person. Such submission is the most difficult thing that there can be for a man who thinks that he is capable of deciding anything or of doing anything. Of course, when he gets rid of these fantasies and sees what he really is, the difficulty disappears. This, however, can only take place in the course of work. But to begin to work and particularly to continue to work is very difficult and it is difficult because life runs too smoothly."

On one occasion, continuing this talk about the work of groups, G. said:

"Later on you will see that everyone in the work is given his own individual tasks corresponding to his type and his chief feature or his chief fault, that is, something that will give him an opportunity of struggling more intensively against his chief fault. But besides individual tasks there are general tasks which are given to the group as a whole, in which case the whole group is responsible for their execution or their non-execution, although in some cases the group is also responsible for individual tasks. But first we will take general tasks. For instance, you ought by now to have some understanding as to the nature of the system and its principal methods, and you ought to be able to pass these ideas on to others. You will remember that at the beginning I was against your talking about the ideas of the system outside the groups. On the contrary there was a definite rule that none of you, excepting those whom I specially instructed to do so, should talk to anyone either about the groups or the lectures or the ideas. And I explained then why this was necessary. You would not have been able to give a correct picture, a correct impression. Instead of giving people the possibility of coming to these ideas you would have repelled them for ever; you would have even deprived them of the possibility of coming to them at any later time. But now the situation is different. You have already heard enough. And if you really have made efforts to understand what you have heard, then you should be able to pass it on to others. Therefore I give you all a definite task.

"Try to lead conversations with your friends and acquaintances up to these subjects, try to prepare those who show interest and, if they ask you to, bring them to the meetings. But everyone must realize that this is his own task and not expect others to do it for him. The proper performance of this task by each of you will show first, that you have already assimilated something, understood something, and second, that you are able to appraise people, to understand with whom it is worth while talking and with whom it is not worth while, because the majority of people cannot take in any of these ideas and it is perfectly useless to talk to them. But at the same time there are people who are able to take in these ideas and with whom it is worth while talking."

The next meeting after this was very interesting. Everyone was full of impressions of talks with friends; everyone had a great many questions; everyone was somewhat discouraged and disappointed.

It proved that friends and acquaintances asked very shrewd questions to which most of our people had no answers. They asked for instance what we had got from the work and openly expressed doubts as to our "remembering ourselves." On the other hand others had themselves no doubt whatever that *they* "remembered themselves." Others found the "ray of creation" and the "seven cosmoses" ridiculous and useless; "What has 'geography' to do with this?" very wittily asked one of my friends parodying a sentence from an amusing play which had been running shortly before this; others asked who had seen the centers and how they could be seen; others found absurd the idea that we could not "do." Others found the idea of esotericism "entertaining but not convincing." Others said that this idea in general was a "new invention." Others were not prepared to sacrifice their descent from apes. Others found that there was no idea of the "love of mankind" in the system. Others said that our ideas were thorough-going materialism, that we wanted to make people machines, that there was no idea of the miraculous, no idealism, and so on, and so on.

G. laughed when we recounted to him our conversations with our friends.

"This is nothing," he said. "If you were to put together everything that people are able to say about this system, you would not believe in it yourselves. This system has a wonderful property: even a mere contact with it calls forth either the best or the worst in people. You may know a man all your life and think that he is not a bad fellow, that he is even rather intelligent. Try speaking to him about these ideas and you will see at once that he is an utter fool. Another man, on the other hand, might appear to have nothing in him, but speak to him on these subjects and you find that he thinks, and thinks very seriously."

"How can we recognize people who are able to come to the work?" asked one of those present.

"How to *recognize* them is another question," said G. "To do this it is necessary to a certain extent 'to be.' But before speaking of this we must establish what kind of people are able to come to the work and what kind are not able.

"You must understand that a man should have, first, a certain preparation, certain luggage. He should know what it is possible to know through *ordinary channels* about the ideas of esotericism, about hidden knowledge, about possibilities of the inner evolution of man, and so on. What I mean is that these ideas ought not to appear to him as something entirely new. Otherwise it is difficult to speak to him. It is useful also if he has at least some scientific or philosophical preparation. If a man has a good knowledge of religion, this can also be useful. But if he is tied to religious forms and has no understanding of their essence, he will find it very difficult. In general, if a man knows but little, has read but little, has thought but little, it is difficult to talk to him. If he has a good essence there is another way for him without any talks at all, but in this case he has to be obedient, he has to give up his will. And he has to come to this also in some way or other. It can be said that there is one general rule for everybody. In order to approach this system seriously, people must be *disappointed*, first of all in themselves, that is to say, in their powers, and secondly in all the old ways. A man cannot feel what is most valuable in the system unless he is disappointed in what he has been doing, disappointed in what he has been searching for. If he is a scientist he should be disappointed in his science. If he is a religious man he should be disappointed in his religion. If he is a politician he should be disappointed in politics. If he is a philosopher he should be disappointed in philosophy. If he is a theosophist he should be disappointed in theosophy. If he is an occultist he should be disappointed in occultism. And so on. But you must understand what this means. I say for instance that a religious man should be disappointed in religion. This does not mean that he should lose his faith. On the contrary, it means being 'disappointed' *in the teaching and the methods only*, realizing that the religious teaching he knows is not enough for him, can lead him nowhere. All religious teachings, excepting of course the completely degenerated religions of savages and the invented religions and sects of modern times, consist of two parts, the visible and the hidden. To be disappointed in religion means being disappointed in the visible, and to feel the necessity for finding the hidden and unknown part of religion. To be disappointed in science does not mean losing interest in knowledge. It means being convinced that the usual scientific methods are not only useless but lead to the construction of absurd and self-contradictory theories, and, having become convinced of this, to begin to search for others. To be disappointed in philosophy means being convinced that ordinary philosophy is merely —as it is said in the Russian proverb—pouring from one empty vessel into another, and that people do not even know what philosophy means although true philosophy also can and should exist. To be disappointed in occultism does not mean losing faith in the miraculous, it is merely being convinced that ordinary, accessible, and even advertised occultism, under whatever name it may pass, is simply charlatanism and self-deception and that, although *somewhere something* does exist, everything that man knows or is able to learn in the ordinary way is not what he needs.

"So that, no matter what he used to do before, no matter what used to interest him, if a man has arrived at this state of disappointment in ways that are possible and accessible, it is worth while speaking to him about our system and then he may come to the work. But if he continues to think that he is able to find anything on his former way, or that he has not as yet tried all the ways, or that he can, by himself, find anything or do anything, it means that he is not ready. I do not mean that he must throw up everything he used to do before. This is entirely unnecessary. On the contrary, it is often even better if he continues to do what he used to do. But he must realize that it is only a profession, or a habit, or a necessity. In this case it is another matter; he will then be able not to 'identify.'

"There is only one thing incompatible with work and that is 'professional occultism,' in other words, professional charlatanism. All these spiritualists, healers, clairvoyants, and so on, or even people closely connected with them, are none of them any good to us. And you must always remember this and take care not to tell them much because everything they learn from you they might use for their own purposes, that is, to make fools of other people.

"There are still other categories which are no good but we will speak of them later. In the meantime remember one thing only: A man must be sufficiently disappointed in ordinary ways and he must at the same time think or be able to accept the idea that there may be something—somewhere. If you should speak to such a man, he might discern the flavor of truth in what you say no matter how clumsily you might speak. But if you should speak to a man who is convinced about something else, everything you say will sound absurd to him and he will never even listen to you seriously. It is not worth while wasting time on him. This system is for those who have already sought and have burned themselves. Those who have not sought and who are not seeking do not need it. And those who have not yet burned themselves do not need it either."

"But this is not what people begin with," said one of our company. "They ask: Do we admit the existence of the ether? Or how do we look on evolution? Or why do we not believe in progress? Or why do we not think that people can and should organize life on the basis of justice and the common good? And things of this sort."

"All questions are good," said G., "and you can begin from any question *if only it is sincere*. You understand that what I mean is that this very question about ether or about progress or about the common good could be asked by a man simply in order to say something, or to repeat what someone else has said or what he has read in some book, and on the other hand he could ask it because this is the question with which he aches. If it is an aching question for him you can give him an answer and you can bring him to the system through any question whatever. But it is necessary for the question to be an aching one."

Our talks about people who could be interested in the system and able to work, involuntarily led us towards a valuation of our friends from an entirely new point of view. In this respect we all experienced bitter disappointment. Even before G. had formally requested us to speak of the system to our friends we had of course all tried in one way or another to talk about it at any rate with those of them whom we met most often. And in most cases our enthusiasm in regard to the ideas of the system met with a very cold reception. They did not understand us; the ideas which seemed to us new and original seemed to our friends to be old and tedious, leading nowhere, and even repellent. This astonished us more than anything else. We were amazed that people with whom we had felt an inner intimacy, with whom in former times we had been able to talk about all questions that worried us, and in whom we had found a response, could fail to see what we saw and above all that they could see something quite opposite. I have to say that, in regard to my own personal experience, it gave me a very strange even painful impression. I speak of the absolute impossibility of making people understand us. We are of course accustomed to this in ordinary life, in the realm of ordinary questions, and we know that people who are hostile to us at heart or narrow-minded or incapable of thought can misunderstand us, twist and distort anything we say, can ascribe to us thoughts we never had, words which we never uttered, and so on. But now when we saw that all this was being done by those whom we used to regard *as our kind of people*, with whom we used to spend very much of our time, and who formerly had seem to us to understand us better than anyone else, it produced on us a discouraging impression. Such cases of course constituted the exceptions; most of our friends were merely indifferent, and all our attempts to infect them with our interest in G.'s system led to nothing. But sometimes they got a very curious impression of us. I do not remember now who was the first to notice that our friends found we had begun to change for the worse. They found us less interesting than we had been before; they told us we were becoming colorless, as though we were fading, were losing our former spontaneity, our former responsiveness to everything, that we were becoming "machines," were ceasing to think originally, were ceasing to feel, that we were merely repeating like parrots what we heard from G.

G. laughed a great deal when we told him about this.

"Wait, there is worse to come," he said. "Do you understand what this really means? It means that you have stopped lying; at any rate you don't lie so well, that is, you can no longer lie in so interesting a way as before. He is an interesting man who lies well. But you are already ashamed of lying. You are now able to acknowledge to yourselves sometimes that there is something you do not know or do not understand, and you cannot talk as if you knew all about everything. It means of course that you have become less interesting, less original, and less, as they say, *responsive*. So now you are really able to see what sort of people your friends are. And on their part they are sorry for you. And in their own way they are right. You have already begun to *die*." He emphasized this word. "It is a long way yet to complete death but still a certain amount of silliness is going out of you. You can no longer deceive yourselves as sincerely as you did before. You have now got the taste of truth."

"Why does it seem to me sometimes now that I understand absolutely nothing?" said one of those present. "Formerly I used to think that sometimes at any rate there were some things I understood but now I do not understand anything."

"It means you have begun to understand," said G. "When you understood nothing you thought you understood everything or at any rate that you were able to understand everything. Now, when you have begun to understand, you think you do not understand. This comes about because the *taste of understanding* was quite unknown to you before. And now the taste of understanding seems to you to be a lack of understanding."

In our talks we often returned to the impressions our friends had of us and to our new impressions of our friends. And we began to realize that, more than anything else, these ideas could either unite people or separate them.

There was once a very long and interesting talk about "types." G. repeated everything he had said before about this together with many additions and indications for personal work.

"Each of you," he said, "has probably met in life people of one and the same type. Such people often even look like one another, and their inner reactions to things are exactly the same. What one likes the other will like. What one does not like the other will not like. You must remember such occasions because you can study the *science of types* only by meeting types. There is no other method. Everything else is imagination. You must understand that in the conditions in which you live you cannot meet with more than six or seven types although there are in life a greater number of fundamental types. The rest are all combinations of these fundamental types."

"How many fundamental types are there in all?" asked someone.

"Some people say twelve," said G. "According to the legend the twelve apostles represented the twelve types. Others say more."

He paused.

"May we know these twelve types, that is, their definitions and characteristics?" asked one of those present.

"I was expecting this question," said G. "There has never been an occasion when I have spoken of types when some clever person has not asked this question. How is it you do not understand that if it could be explained it would have been explained long ago. But the whole thing is that types and their differences cannot be defined in ordinary language, and the language in which they could be defined you do not as yet know and will not know for a long time. It is exactly the same as with the 'forty-eight laws.' Someone invariably asks whether he may not know these forty-eight laws. As if it were possible. Understand that you are being given everything that can be given. With the help of what is given to you, you must find the rest. But I know that I am wasting time now in saying this. You still do not understand me and will not understand for a long time yet. Think of the difference between knowledge and being. There are things for the understanding of which a different being is necessary."

"But if there are no more than seven types around us, why can we not know them, that is, know what is the chief difference between them, and, when meeting them, be able to recognize and distinguish them?" said one of us.

"You must begin with yourself and with the observations of which I have already spoken," said G., "otherwise it would be knowledge of which you would be able to make no use. Some of you think you can see types but they are not types at all that you see. In order to see types one must know one's own type and be able to 'depart' from it. In order to know one's own type one must make a good study of one's life, one's whole life from the very beginning; one must know why, and how, things have happened. I want to give you all a task. It will be a general and an individual task at one and the same time. Let every one of you in the group tell about his life. Everything must be told in detail without embellishment, and without suppressing anything. Emphasize the principal and essential things without dwelling on trifles and details. You must be sincere and not be afraid that others will take anything in a wrong way, because everyone is in the same position; everyone must strip himself; everyone must show himself as he is. This task will once more show you why nothing must be taken outside the groups. Nobody would dare to speak if he thought or suspected that what he said in the group would be repeated outside. But he ought to be fully and firmly convinced that nothing will be repeated. And then he will be able to speak without fear with the understanding that others must do the same."

Soon afterwards G. went to Moscow and in his absence we tried in various ways to carry out the tasks allotted to us. First of all, in order to put G.'s task more easily into practice, some of us, at my suggestion, tried telling the story of our lives not at the general group meeting but in small groups composed of people they knew best.

I am bound to say that all these attempts came to nothing. Some said too much, others said too little. Some went into unnecessary details or into descriptions of what they considered were their particular and original characteristics; others concentrated on their "sins" and errors. But everything taken together failed to produce what G. evidently expected. The result was anecdotes, or chronological memoirs which interested nobody, and family recollections which made people yawn. Something was wrong, but what exactly was wrong even those who had tried to be as sincere as they could were unable to determine. I remember my own attempts. In the first place I tried to convey certain early childhood impressions which seemed to me psychologically interesting because I remembered myself as I was at a very early age and was always myself astonished by some of these early impressions. But nobody was interested in this and I quickly saw that this was certainly not what was required of us. I proceeded further *but almost immediately I felt a certainty that there were many things that I had no intention whatever of telling.* This was a quite unexpected realization. I had accepted G.'s idea without any opposition and I thought I would be able to tell the story of my life without any particular difficulty. But in reality it turned out to be quite impossible. Something in me registered such a vehement protest against it that I did not even attempt to struggle and in speaking of certain periods of my life I tried to give only the general idea and the significance of the facts which I did not want to relate. In this connection I noted that my voice and intonations changed when I talked in this way. This helped me to understand other people. I began to hear that, in speaking of themselves and their lives, they also spoke in different voices and different intonations. And there were intonations of a particular kind which I had first heard in myself and which showed me that people wanted to hide something in what they were talking about. But intonations gave them away. Observation of intonations afterwards made it possible for me to understand many other things.

When G. next came to St. Petersburg (he had been in Moscow this time for two or three weeks) we told him of our attempts; he listened to everything and merely said that we did not know how to separate "personality" from "essence."

"Personality hides behind essence," he said, "and essence hides behind personality and they mutually screen each other."

"How can essence be separated from personality?" asked one of those present.

"How would you separate your own from what is not your own?" G. replied. "It is necessary to think, it is necessary to know where one or another of your characteristics has come from. And it is necessary to realize that most people, especially in your circle of society, have very little of their own. Everything they have is not their own and is mostly stolen; everything that they call ideas, convictions, views, conceptions of the world, has all been pilfered from various sources. And all of it together makes up personality and must be cast aside."

"But you yourself said that work begins with personality," said someone there.

"Quite true," replied G. "Therefore we must first of all establish of what precisely we are speaking—of what moment in a man's development and of what level of being. Just now I was simply speaking of a man in life who had no connection whatever with the work. Such a man, particularly if he belongs to the 'intellectual' classes, is almost entirely composed of personality. In most cases his essence ceases to develop at a very early age. I know respected fathers of families, professors full of various ideas, well-known authors, important officials who were almost ministers, whose essence had stopped developing approximately at the age of twelve. And that is not so bad. It sometimes happens that certain aspects of essence stop at five or six years of age and then everything ends; all the rest is not their own; it is repertoire, or taken from books; or it has been created by imitating ready-made models."

After this there were many conversations, in which G. took part, during which we tried to find out the reason for our failure to fulfill the task set by G. But the more we talked the less we understood what he actually wanted from us.

"This only shows to what extent you do not know yourselves," said G. "I do not doubt that at least some of you sincerely wished to do what I said, that is, to relate the story of their lives. At the same time they see that they cannot do it and do not even know how to begin. But remember that sooner or later you will have to go through this. This is, as it is called, one of the first tests on the way. Without going through this no one can go further."

"What is it we do not understand?" asked someone.

"You do not understand what it means to be sincere," said G. "You are so used to lying both to yourselves and to others that you can find neither words nor thoughts when you wish to speak the truth. To tell the complete truth about oneself is very difficult. But before telling it one must know it. And you do not even know what the truth about yourselves consists of. Some day I will tell every one of you his chief feature or chief fault. We shall then see whether you will understand me or not."

One very interesting conversation took place at this time. I felt very strongly everything that took place at that time; especially strongly did I feel that in spite of every effort I was unable to remember myself for any length of time. At first something seemed to be successful, but later it all went and I felt without any doubt the deep sleep in which I was immersed. Failures in attempts to relate the story of my life, and especially the fact that I even failed to understand clearly what G. wanted, still further increased my bad mood which, however, as always with me, expressed itself not in depression, but in irritation.

In this state I came once to lunch with G. in a restaurant on the Sadovaya opposite the Gostinoy Dvor. I was probably very curt or on the contrary very silent.

"What is the matter with you today?" asked G.

"I myself do not know," said I, "only I am beginning to feel that with us nothing is being achieved, or rather, that I am achieving nothing. I cannot speak about others. But I cease to understand you and you no longer explain anything as you used to explain it in the beginning. And I feel that in this way nothing will be achieved."

"Wait a little," said G. "Soon conversations will start. Try to understand me; up to now we have been trying to find each thing's place. Soon we shall begin to call things by their proper names."

G.'s words remained in my memory, but I did not go into them, and continued my own thoughts.

"What does it matter," I said, "how we shall call things when I can connect nothing together? You never answer any questions I ask."

"Very well," said G., laughing. "I promise to answer now any question you care to ask, as it happens in fairy tales."

I felt that he wanted to draw me out of my bad mood and I was inwardly grateful to him, although something in me refused to be mollified.

And suddenly I remembered that I wanted above all to know what G. thought about "eternal recurrence," about the repetition of lives, as I understood it. I had many times tried to start a conversation about this and to tell G. my views. But these conversations had always remained almost monologues. G. had listened in silence and then begun to talk of something else.

"Very well," I said, "tell me what you think of recurrence. Is there any truth in this, or none at all. What I mean is: Do we live only this once and then disappear, or does everything repeat and repeat itself, perhaps an endless number of times, only we do not know and do not remember it?"

"This idea of repetition," said G., "is not the full and absolute truth, but it is the nearest possible approximation of the truth. In this case truth cannot be expressed in words. But what you say is very near to it. And if you understand why I do not speak of this, you will be still nearer to it. What is the use of a man knowing about recurrence if he is not conscious of it and if he himself does not change? One can say even that if a man does not change, repetition does not exist for him. If you tell him about repetition, it will only increase his sleep. Why should he make any efforts today when there is so much time and so many possibilities ahead—the whole of eternity? Why should he bother today? This is exactly why the system does not say anything about repetition and takes only this one life which we know. The system has neither meaning nor sense without striving for self-change. And work on self-change must begin today, immediately. All laws can be seen in one life. Knowledge about the repetition of lives will add nothing for a man if he does not see how everything repeats itself in one life, that is, in this life, and if he does not strive to change himself in order to escape this repetition. But if he changes something essential in himself, that is, if he attains something, this cannot be lost."

"Is the conclusion right that all the tendencies that are created or formed must grow?" I asked.

"Yes and no," said G. "This is true in most cases, just as it is true in one life. But on a big scale new forces may enter. I shall not explain this now; but think about what I am going to say: Planetary influences also can change. They are not permanent. Besides this, tendencies themselves can be different; there are tendencies which, once they have appeared, continue and develop by themselves mechanically, and there are others which need constant pushing and which immediately weaken and may vanish altogether or turn into dreaming if a man ceases to work on them. Moreover there is a *definite* time, a definite term, for everything. Possibilities *for everything*" (he emphasized these words) "exist only for a definite time."

I was extremely interested in everything G. said. Much of this I had "guessed" before. But the fact that he recognized my fundamental premises and all that he brought into them had for me a tremendous importance. Everything began immediately to become connected. I felt that I saw the outline of the "majestic building" which was spoken of in the "Glimpses of Truth." My bad mood vanished, I did not even notice when.

G. sat there smiling.

"You see how easy it is to *turn* you; but perhaps I was merely *romancing* to you, perhaps there is no recurrence at all. What pleasure is it when a sulky Ouspensky sits there, does not eat, does not drink. 'Let us try to cheer him up,' I think to myself. And how is one to cheer a person up? One likes funny stories. For another you must find his hobby. And I know that Ouspensky has this hobby—'eternal recurrence.' So I offered to answer any question of his. I knew what he would ask."

But G.'s chaff did not affect me. He had given me something very substantial and could not take it back. I did not believe his jokes and did not believe that he could have invented what he had said about recurrence. I also learned to understand his intonations. The future showed that I was right, for although G. did not introduce the idea of recurrence into his exposition of the system, he referred several times to the idea of recurrence, chiefly in speaking of the lost possibilities of people who had approached the system and then had drawn away from it.

Conversations in groups continued as usual. Once G. said that he wanted to carry out an experiment on the separation of personality from essence. We were all very interested because he had promised "experiments" for a long time but till then we had seen nothing. I will not describe his methods, I will merely describe the people whom he chose that first evening for the experiment. One was no longer young and was a man who occupied a fairly prominent position in society. At our meetings he spoke much and often about himself, his family, about Christianity, and about the events of the moment connected with the war and with all possible kinds of "scandal" that had very much disgusted him. The other was younger. Many of us did not consider him to be a serious person. Very often he played what is called the fool; or, on the other hand, entered into endless formal arguments about some or other details of the system without any relation whatever to the whole. It was very difficult to understand him. He spoke in a confused and intricate manner even of the most simple things, mixing up in a most impossible way different points of view and words belonging to different categories and levels.

I pass over the beginning of the experiment.

We were sitting in the big drawing room.

The conversation went on as usual.

"Now observe," G. whispered to us.

The older of the two who was speaking heatedly about something suddenly became silent in the middle of a sentence and seemed to sink into his chair looking straight in front of him. At a sign from G. we continued to talk without looking at him. The younger one began to listen to the talk and then spoke himself. All of us looked at one another. His voice had become different. He told us some observations about himself in a clear, simple, and intelligible manner without superfluous words, without extravagances, and without buffoonery. Then he became silent; he smoked a cigarette and was obviously thinking of something. The first one sat still without moving, as though shrunken into a ball.

"Ask him what he is thinking about," said G. quietly.

"I?" He lifted his head as though waking up when he was questioned. "About nothing." He smiled weakly as though apologizing or as though he were surprised at anyone asking him what he was thinking about.

"Well, you were talking about the war just now," said one of us, "about what would happen if we made peace with the Germans; do you still think as you did then?"

"I don't know really," he said in an uncertain voice. "Did I say that?"

"Yes, certainly, you just said that everyone was obliged to think about it, that no one had the right not to think about it, and that no one had the right to forget the war; everyone ought to have a definite opinion; yes or no—for or against the war."

He listened as though he did not grasp what the questioner was saying.

"Yes?" he said. "How odd. I do not remember anything about it."

"But aren't you interested in it?"

"No, it does not interest me at all."

"Are you not thinking of the consequences of all that is now taking place, of the results for Russia, for the whole of civilization?"

He shook his head as though with regret.

"I do not understand what you are talking about," he said, "it does not interest me at all and I know nothing about it."

"Well then, you spoke before of your family. Would it not be very much easier for you if they became interested in our ideas and joined the work?"

"Yes, perhaps," again in an uncertain voice. "But why should I think about it?"

"Well, you said you were afraid of the gulf, as you expressed it, which was growing between you and them."

No reply.

"But what do you think about it now?"

"I am not thinking about it at all."

"If you were asked what you would like, what would you say?"

Again a wondering glance—"I do not want anything."

"But think, what would you like?"

On the small table beside him there stood an unfinished glass of tea. He gazed at it for a long time as though considering something. He glanced around him twice, then again looked at the glass, and said in such a serious voice and with such serious intonations that we all looked at one another:

"*I think I should like some raspberry jam.*"

"Why are you questioning him?" said a voice from the corner which we hardly recognized.

This was the second "experiment."

"Can you not see that he is asleep?"

"And you yourself?" asked one of us.

"I, on the contrary, have woken up."

"Why has he gone to sleep while you have woken up?"

"I do not know."

With this the experiment ended.

Neither of them remembered anything the next day. G. explained to us that with the first man everything that constituted the subject of his ordinary conversation, of his alarms and agitation, was in personality. And when his personality was asleep practically nothing remained. In the personality of the other there was also a great deal of undue talkativeness but behind the personality there was an essence which knew as much as the personality and knew it better, and when personality went to sleep essence took its place to which it had a much greater right.

"Note that contrary to his custom he spoke very little," said G. "But he was observing all of you and everything that was taking place, and nothing escaped him."

"But of what use is it to him if he also does not remember?" said one of us.

"Essence remembers," said G., "personality has forgotten. And this was necessary because otherwise personality would have perverted everything and would have ascribed all this to itself."

"But this is a kind of black magic," said one of us.

"Worse," said G. "Wait and you will see worse than that."

When speaking of "types" G. once said:

"Have you noticed what a tremendous part 'type' plays in the relationship between man and woman?"

"I have noticed," I said, "that throughout his whole life every man comes into contact with women of a definite type and every woman comes into contact with men of a definite type. As though the type of woman for every man had been predetermined and the type of man predetermined for every woman."

"There is a good deal of truth in that," said G. "But in that form it is, of course, much too general. Actually you did not see types of men and women but types of events. What I speak of refers to the real type, that is to say, to essence. If people were to live in essence one type would always find the other type and wrong types would never come together. But people live in personality. Personality has its own interests and its own tastes which have nothing in common with the interests and the tastes of essence. Personality in our case is the result of the wrong work of centers. For this reason personality can dislike precisely what essence likes—and like what essence does not like. Here is where the struggle between essence and personality begins. Essence knows what it wants but cannot explain it. Personality does not want to hear of it and takes no account of it. It has its own desires. And it acts in its own way. But its power does not continue beyond that moment. After that, in some way or other, the two essences have to live together. And they hate one another. No sort of acting can help here. In one way or another essence or type gains the upper hand and decides.

"In this case nothing can be done by reason or by calculation. Neither can so-called love help because, in the real meaning of the word, mechanical man cannot love—with him *it loves* or *it does not love.*

"At the same time sex plays a tremendous role in maintaining the mechanicalness of life. Everything that people do is connected with 'sex': politics, religion, art, the theater, music, is all 'sex.' Do you think people go to the theater or to church to pray or to see some new play? That is only for the sake of appearances. The principal thing, in the theater as well as in church, is that there will be a lot of women or a lot of men. This is the center of gravity of all gatherings. What do you think brings people to cafés, to restaurants, to various fêtes? One thing only. *Sex:* it is the principal motive force of all mechanicalness. All sleep, all hypnosis, depends upon it.

"You must try to understand what I mean. Mechanicalness is especially dangerous when people try to explain it by something else and not by what it really is. When sex is clearly conscious of itself and does not cover itself up by anything else it is not the mechanicalness about which I am speaking. On the contrary sex which exists by itself and is not dependent on anything else is already a great achievement. But the evil lies in this constant self-deception!"

"What then is the deduction; should it be so or should it be changed?" asked someone.

G. smiled.

"That is something people always ask," he said. "Whatever they may be speaking about, they ask: Ought it to be like that and how can it be changed, that is, what ought to be done in such a case? As though it were possible to change anything, as though it were possible to do anything. You at least ought to have realized by now how naïve such questions are. Cosmic forces have created this state of affairs and cosmic forces control this state of affairs. And you ask: Can it be left like that or should it be changed! God himself could change nothing. Do you remember what was said about the forty-eight laws? They cannot be changed, but liberation from a considerable portion of them is possible, that is to say, there is a possibility of changing the state of affairs *for oneself*, it is possible to escape from the general law. You should understand that in this case as well as in all others the general law cannot be changed. But one can change one's own position in relation to this law; one can escape from the general law. The more so since in this law about which I speak, that is, in the power of sex over people, are included many different possibilities. It includes the chief form of slavery and it is also the chief possibility of liberation. This is what you must understand.

" 'New birth,' of which we have spoken before, depends as much upon sex energy as do physical birth and the propagation of species.

" 'Hydrogen' si 12 is the 'hydrogen' which represents the final product of the transformation of food in the human organism. This is the matter with which sex works and which sex manufactures. It is 'seed' or 'fruit.'

" 'Hydrogen' si 12 can pass into do of the next octave with the help of an 'additional shock.' But this 'shock' can be of a dual nature and different octaves can begin, one outside the organism which has produced si, and the other in the organism itself. The union of male and female si 12 and all that accompanies it constitutes the 'shock' of the first kind and the new octave begun with its help develops independently as a new organism or a new life.

"This is the normal and natural way to use the energy of si 12. But in the same organism there is a further possibility. And this is the possibility of creating a new life within the actual organism, in which the si 12 has been manufactured, without the union of the two principles, the male and the female. A new octave then develops within the organism, not outside it. This is the birth of the 'astral body.' You must understand that the 'astral body' is born of the same material, of the same matter, as the physical body, only the process is different. The whole of the physical body, all its cells, are, so to speak, permeated by emanations of the matter si 12. And when they have become sufficiently saturated the matter si 12 begins to crystallize. The crystallization of this matter constitutes the formation of the 'astral body.'

"The transition of matter si 12 into emanations and the gradual saturation of the whole organism by it is what alchemy calls 'transmutation' or transformation. It is just this transformation of the physical body into the astral that alchemy called the transformation of the 'coarse' into the 'fine' or the transformation of base metals into gold.

"Completed transmutation, that is to say, the formation of the 'astral body,' is possible only in a healthy, normally functioning organism. In a sick, or a perverted, or a crippled organism, no transmutation is possible."

"Is complete sexual abstinence necessary for transmutation and is sexual abstinence, in general, useful for work on oneself?" we asked him.

"Here there is not one but a number of questions," said G. "In the first place sexual abstinence is necessary for transmutation only in certain cases, that is, for certain types of people. For others it is not at all necessary. And with yet others it comes by itself when transmutation begins. I will explain this more clearly. For certain types a long and complete sexual abstinence is necessary for transmutation *to begin*; this means in other words that without a long and complete sexual abstinence transmutation will not begin. But once it has begun abstinence is no longer necessary. In other cases, that is, with other types, transmutation can begin in a normal sexual life—and on the contrary, can begin sooner and proceed better with a very great outward expenditure of sex energy. In the third case the beginning of transmutation does not require abstinence, but, having begun, transmutation takes the whole of sexual energy and puts an end to normal sexual life or the outward expenditure of sex energy.

"Then the other question—'Is sexual abstinence useful for the work or not?'

"It is useful if there is abstinence in all centers. If there is abstinence in one center and full liberty of imagination in the others, then there could be nothing worse. And still more, abstinence can be useful if a man knows what to do with the energy which he saves in this way. If he does not know what to do with it, nothing whatever can be gained by abstinence."

"Speaking in general, what is the most correct form of life in this connection from the point of view of the work?"

"It is impossible to say. I repeat that while a man *does not know* it is better for him not to attempt anything. Until he has new and *exact* knowledge it will be quite enough if his life is guided by the usual rules and principles. If a man begins to theorize and invent in this sphere, it will lead to nothing except psychopathy. But it must again be remembered that only a person who is completely normal as regards sex has any chance in the work. Any kind of 'originality,' strange tastes, strange desires, or, on the other hand, fears, constantly working 'buffers,' must be destroyed from the very beginning. Modern education and modern life create an enormous number of sexual psychopaths. They have no chance at all in the work.

"Speaking in general, there are only two correct ways of expending sexual energy—normal sexual life and transmutation. All inventions in this sphere are very dangerous.

"People have tried abstinence from times beyond memory. Sometimes, very rarely, it has led to something but in most cases what is called abstinence is simply exchanging normal sensations for abnormal, because the abnormal are more easily hidden. But it is not about this that I wish to speak. You must understand where lies the chief evil and what makes for slavery. It is not in sex itself but in the *abuse of sex*. But what the abuse of sex means is again misunderstood. People usually take this to be either excess or perversion. But these are comparatively innocent forms of abuse of sex. And it is necessary to know the human machine very well in order to grasp what abuse of sex in the real meaning of these words is. It means the wrong work of centers in relation to sex, that is, the action of the sex center through other centers, and the action of other centers through the sex center; or, to be still more precise, the functioning of the sex center with energy borrowed from other centers and the functioning of other centers with energy borrowed from the sex center."

"Can sex be regarded as an independent center?" asked one of those present.

"It can," said G. "At the same time if all the lower story is taken as one whole, then sex can be regarded as the neutralizing part of the moving center."

"With what 'hydrogen' does the sex center work?" asked another.

This question had interested us for a long time but we had not previously been able to answer it. And G., when he had been asked before, had never given a direct reply.

"The sex center works with 'hydrogen' 12," he said on this occasion, "that is to say, it ought to work with it. This is si 12. But the fact is that it very rarely works with its proper hydrogen. Abnormalities in the working of the sex center require special study.

"In the first place it must be noted that *normally* in the sex center as well as in the higher emotional and the higher thinking centers, there is no negative side. In all the other centers except the higher ones, in the thinking, in the emotional, in the moving, in the instinctive, in all of them there are, so to speak, two halves—the positive and the negative; affirmation and negation, or 'yes' and 'no,' in the thinking center, pleasant and unpleasant sensations in the moving and instinctive centers. There is no such division in the sex center. There are no positive and negative sides in it. There are no unpleasant sensations or unpleasant feelings in it; there is either a pleasant sensation, a pleasant feeling, or there is nothing, an absence of any sensation, complete indifference. But in consequence of the wrong work of centers it often happens that the sex center unites with the negative part of the emotional center or with the negative part of the instinctive center. And then, stimulation of a certain kind of the sex center, or even any stimulation at all of the sex center, calls forth unpleasant feelings and unpleasant sensations. People who experience unpleasant feelings and sensations which have been evoked in them through ideas and imagination connected with sex are inclined to regard them as a great virtue or as something original; in actual fact it is simply disease. Everything connected with sex should be either pleasant or indifferent. Unpleasant feelings and sensations all come from the emotional center or the instinctive center.

"This is the 'abuse of sex.' It is necessary, further, to remember that the sex center works with 'hydrogen' 12. This means that it is stronger and quicker than all other centers. Sex, in fact, governs all other centers. The only thing in ordinary circumstances, that is, when man has neither consciousness nor will, that holds the sex center in submission is 'buffers.' 'Buffers' can entirely bring it to nought, that is, they can stop its normal manifestation. But they cannot destroy its energy. The energy remains and passes over to other centers, finding expression for itself through them; in other words, the other centers rob the sex center of the energy which it does not use itself. The energy of the sex center in the work of the thinking, emotional, and moving centers can be recognized by a particular 'taste,' by a particular fervor, by a vehemence which the nature of the affair concerned does not call for. The thinking center writes books, but in making use of the energy of the sex center it does not simply occupy itself with philosophy, science, or politics—it is always fighting something, disputing, criticizing, creating new subjective theories. The emotional center preaches Christianity, abstinence, asceticism, or the fear and horror of sin, hell, the torment of sinners, eternal fire, all this with the energy of the sex center. . . . Or on the other hand it works up revolutions, robs, burns, kills, again with the same energy. The moving center occupies itself with sport, creates various records, climbs mountains, jumps, fences, wrestles, fights, and so on. In all these instances, that is, in the work of the thinking center as well as in the work of the emotional and the moving centers, when they work with the energy of the sex center, there is always one general characteristic and this is a certain particular vehemence and, together with it, the *uselessness* of the work in question. Neither the thinking nor the emotional nor the moving centers can ever create anything *useful* with the energy of the sex center. This is an example of the 'abuse of sex.'

"But this is only one aspect of it. Another aspect consists in the fact that, when the energy of the sex center is plundered by the other centers and spent on useless work, it has nothing left for itself and has to steal the energy of other centers which is much lower and coarser than its own. And yet the sex center is very important for the general activity, and particularly for the inner growth of the organism, because, working with 'hydrogen' 12, it can receive a very fine *food of impressions*, such as none of the ordinary centers can receive. The fine food of impressions is very important for the manufacture of the higher 'hydrogens.' But when the sex center works with energy that is not its own, that is, with the comparatively low 'hydrogens' 48 and 24, its impressions become much coarser and it ceases to play the role in the organism which it could play. At the same time union with, and the use of its energy by, the thinking center creates far too great an imagination on the subject of sex, and in addition *a tendency to be satisfied with this imagination.* Union with the emotional center creates sentimentality or, on the contrary, jealousy, cruelty. This is again a picture of the 'abuse of sex.' "

"What must be done to struggle against the 'abuse of sex'?" asked somebody present.

G. laughed.

"I was just waiting for that question," he said. "But you already ought to understand that it is just as impossible to explain to a man who has not yet begun to work on himself and does not know the structure of the machine what the 'abuse of sex' means, as it is to say what must be done to avoid these abuses. Right work on oneself begins with the creation of a *permanent center of gravity.* When a permanent center of gravity has been created everything else begins to be disposed and distributed in subordination to it. The question comes to this: From what and how can a permanent center of gravity be created? And to this may be replied that only a man's attitude to the work, to school, his valuation of the work, and his realization of the mechanicalness and aimlessness of everything else can create in him a permanent center of gravity.

"The role of the sex center in creating a general equilibrium and a permanent center of gravity can be very big. According to its energy, that is to say, if it uses its own energy, the sex center stands on a level with the higher emotional center. And all the other centers are subordinate to it. Therefore it would be a great thing if it worked with its own energy. This alone would indicate a comparatively very high level of being. And in this case, that is, if the sex center worked with its own energy and in its own place, all other centers could work correctly in their places and with their own energies."

Chapter Thirteen

THIS period, the middle of the summer of 1916, has remained in the memory of all the members of our groups as a time of very great inner intensity in our work. We all felt that we had to hurry, that we were doing too little compared with the immensity of the task we had set ourselves. We realized that our chance of knowing more might go just as suddenly as it had come and we tried to increase the pressure of work in ourselves and to do all that we could while conditions were favorable.

I began a series of experiments or exercises, making use of a certain experience in this direction that I had acquired earlier. I carried out a series of short but very intensive fasts. I call them "intensive" because I did not take them at all from the hygienic point of view but tried, on the contrary, to give the strongest possible shocks to the organism. In addition to this I began to "breathe" according to a definite system which, together with fasting, had given me interesting psychological results before; and also "repetition" on the method of the *prayer of the mind* which had helped me very much before to concentrate my attention and to observe myself. And also a series of mental exercises of a rather complicated kind for the concentration of the attention. I do not describe these experiments and exercises in detail because they were, after all, attempts to feel my way, without having exact knowledge of possible results.

But all these things taken together, as well as our talks and meetings, kept me in a state of unusual tension and to a great extent, of course, prepared me for the series of extraordinary experiences which I had to go through in August, 1916, because G. kept his word and I saw *facts* and at the same time understood what G. meant when he said that many other things are necessary before facts.[1]

These other things consisted in preparation, in understanding certain ideas, and in being in a certain state. This state, which is emotional, is exactly what we do not understand, .hat is, we do not understand that it is indispensable and that facts are not possible without it.

[1] Chap. I, page 23.

I now come to a most difficult thing because there is no possibility whatever of describing the facts themselves.

Why?

I have often put this question to myself. And I could only answer that there was far too much in them of what was personal for them to be made common property. And I think that it was so not only in my case *but that it always is so.*

I remember that assertions of this kind always made me indignant when I came across them in the memoirs or the notes of people who had passed through any sort of extraordinary experiences and afterwards refused to describe them. They had sought the miraculous and, in one form or another, they thought they had found it. But when they had found what they sought they invariably said: "I have found it. But I cannot describe what I have found."—It always seemed to me to be artificial and invented.

And now I found myself in exactly the same position. I had found what I sought. I saw and observed facts that entirely transcended the sphere of what we consider possible, acknowledged, or admissible, and I can say nothing about them.

The principal part of these experiences was in their inner content and in the new knowledge which came with them. But even the outer aspect could be described only very approximately. As I have already said, after all my fasts and other experiments I was in a rather excited and nervous state and physically less steady than usual. I arrived at the country house of E. N. M. in Finland, at whose house in St. Petersburg we had of late often had our meetings. G. and about eight of our people were there. In the evening the talk went on our attempts to tell about our lives. G. was very harsh and sarcastic, as though he was trying to provoke now one, now another of us, and in particular he emphasized our cowardice and the laziness of our thought.

I was particularly affected when he began to repeat in front of everyone something I had told him in absolute confidence, what I thought of Dr. S. What he said was very unpleasant for me principally because I had always condemned such talk in others.

I think it was at about ten o'clock that he called me, Dr. S., and Z. into a small separate room. We sat on the floor "Turkish fashion" and G. began to explain and to show us certain postures and physical movements. I could not help noticing that there was an astonishing assurance and precision in all his movements although the movements and postures themselves did not present any particular problem and a good gymnast could have done them without exceptional difficulty. I had never had any pretensions to the role of an athlete but I could imitate them outwardly. G. explained that although a gymnast could of course do these movements the gymnast would do them in a different way from him and that he did them in a special way with muscles relaxed.

Afterwards G. again passed to the question why we could not tell the story of our lives.

And with this the miracle began.

I can say with complete assurance that G. did not use any kind of external methods, that is, he gave me no narcotics nor did he hypnotize me by any of the known methods.

It all started with my beginning to *hear his thoughts*. We were sitting in a small room with a carpetless wooden floor as it happens in country houses. I sat opposite G., and Dr. S. and Z. at either side. G. spoke of our "features," of our inability to see or to speak the truth. His words perturbed me very much. And suddenly I noticed that among the words which he was saying to us all there were "thoughts" which were intended for me. I caught one of these thoughts and replied to it, speaking aloud in the ordinary way. G. nodded to me and stopped speaking. There was a fairly long pause. He sat still saying nothing. After a while I heard his voice inside me as it were in the chest near the heart. He put a definite question to me. I looked at him; he was sitting and smiling. His question provoked in me a very strong emotion. But I answered him in the affirmative.

"Why did he say that?" asked G., looking in turn at Z. and Dr. S. "Did I ask him anything?"

And he at once put another still more difficult question to me in the same way as before. And I again answered it in a natural voice. Z. and S. were visibly astonished at what was taking place, especially Z. This conversation, if it can be called a conversation, proceeded in this fashion for not less than half an hour. G. put questions to me without words and I answered them speaking in the usual way. I was very agitated by the things G. said to me and the things he asked me which I cannot transmit. The matter was concerned with certain conditions which I had either to accept or *leave the work*. G. gave me a month's time. I refused the time and said that no matter how difficult what he demanded was I would carry it out at once. But G. insisted on the month's time.

At length he got up and we went out on the veranda. On the other side of the house was another large veranda where the rest of our people were sitting.

What transpired after this I can say very little about, although the chief things happened after. G. was speaking with Z. and S. Then something he said about me affected me very strongly and I sprang up from my chair and went into the garden. From there I went into the forest. I walked about there for a long time in the dark, wholly in the power of the most extraordinary thoughts and feelings. Sometimes it seemed to me that I had found something, at other times I lost it again.

This went on for one or two hours. Finally, at the moment of what felt like the climax of contradictions and of inner turmoil, there flashed through my mind a thought following which I very quickly came to a clear and right understanding of all G. had said and of my own position. I saw that G. was right; that what I had considered to be firm and reliable in myself in reality did not exist. But I had found something else. I knew that he would not believe me and that he would laugh at me if I showed him this other thing. But for myself it was indubitable and what happened later showed that I was right.

For a long time I sat and smoked in some kind of glade. When I returned to the house it was already dark on the small veranda. Thinking that everyone had gone to bed I went to my own room and went to bed myself. As a matter of fact G. and the others were at that time having supper on the large veranda. A little while after I had gone to bed a strange excitement again began in me, my pulse began to beat forcibly, and I again heard G.'s voice in my chest. On this occasion I not only heard *but I replied mentally* and G. heard me and answered me. There was something very strange in this conversation. I tried to find something that would confirm it as a fact but could find nothing. And after all it could have been "imagination" or a waking dream, because although I tried to ask G. something of a concrete nature that would have left no doubt about the conversation or his participation in it, I could not invent anything weighty enough. And certain questions I asked him and which he answered I could have asked and answered myself. I even had the impression that he avoided concrete answers which later might serve as "proofs," and to one or two of my questions he intentionally gave indefinite answers. But the *feeling that it was a conversation* was very strong and entirely new and unlike anything else.

After one long pause G. asked me something that at once put me all on the alert, then stopped as if waiting for an answer.

What he said suddenly put a stop to all my thoughts and feelings. It was not fear, at least not a conscious fear when one knows that one is afraid, but I was all shivering and something literally paralyzed me completely so that I could not articulate a single word although I made terrible efforts, wishing to give an affirmative reply.

I felt that G. was waiting and that he would not wait long.

"Well, you are tired now," he said at last, "we will leave it till another time."

I began to say something, I think I asked him to wait, to give me a little time to get accustomed to this thought.

"Another time," said his voice. "Sleep." And his voice stopped.

I could not go to sleep for a long time. In the morning as I came out onto the little terrace where we had sat the evening before, G. was sitting in the garden twenty yards away near a round table; there were three of our people with him.

"Ask him what happened last night," said G.

For some reason this made me angry. I turned and walked towards the terrace. As I reached it I again heard G.'s voice in my chest.

"Stop!"

I stopped and turned towards G. He was smiling.

"Where are you going, sit down here," he said in his ordinary voice.

I sat with him but I could say nothing, nor did I want to talk. At the same time I felt a kind of extraordinary clarity of thought and I decided to try to concentrate on certain problems which had seemed to me to be particularly difficult. The thought came to my mind that in this unusual state I might perhaps find answers to questions which I could not find in the ordinary way.

I began to think about the first triad of the ray of creation, about the three forces which made one force. What could they mean? Can we define them? Can we realize their meaning? Something began to formulate itself in my head but just as I tried to translate this into words everything disappeared.—*Will, consciousness* . . . and what was the third? I asked myself. It seemed to me that if I could name the *third* I would at once understand everything else.

"Leave it," said G. aloud.

I turned my eyes towards him and he looked at me.

"That is a very long way away yet," he said. "You cannot find the answer now. Better think of yourself, of your work."

The people sitting with us looked at us in perplexity. G. had answered my thoughts.

Then something very strange began that lasted the whole day and afterwards. We stayed in Finland three days longer. During these three days there were very many talks about the most varied subjects. And I was in an unusual emotional state all the time which sometimes began to be burdensome.

"How can this be got rid of? I cannot bear it any more," I asked G.

"Do you want to go to sleep?" said G.

"Certainly not," I said.

"Then what are you asking about? This is what you wanted, make use of it. *You are not asleep at this moment!*"

I do not think that this was altogether true. I undoubtedly "slept" at some moments.

Many things that I said at that time must have surprised my companions in this strange adventure very much. And I was surprised at many things myself. Many things were like sleep, many things had no relation whatever to reality. Undoubtedly I invented a lot. Afterwards it was very strange for me to remember the things I had said.

At length we went to St. Petersburg. G. went to Moscow and we went to the Nikolaievsky Station straight from the Finland Station.

A fairly large company had met together to see him off. He went.

But the miraculous was still far from ended. There were new and very strange phenomena again late in the evening of that day and I "conversed" with him *while seeing* him in the compartment of the train going to Moscow.

After this there followed a strange period of time. It lasted about three weeks. And during this period from time to time I saw "sleeping people." This requires a particular explanation.

Two or three days after G.'s departure I was walking along the Troitsky street and suddenly I saw that the man who was walking towards me was *asleep*. There could be no doubt whatever about this. Although his eyes were open, he was walking along obviously immersed in dreams which ran like clouds across his face. It entered my mind that if I could look at him long enough I should see his dreams, that is, I should understand what he was seeing in his dreams. But he passed on. After him came another also sleeping. A sleeping *izvostchik* went by with two sleeping passengers. Suddenly I found myself in the position of the prince in the "Sleeping Princess." Everyone around me was asleep. It was an indubitable and distinct sensation. I realized what it meant that many things could be *seen* with our eyes which we do not usually see. These sensations lasted for several minutes. Then they were repeated very weakly on the following day. But I at once made the discovery that *by trying to remember myself* I was able to intensify and prolong these sensations for so long as I had energy enough not to be diverted, that is, not to allow things and everything around me to attract my attention. When attention was diverted I ceased to see "sleeping people" because I had obviously gone to sleep myself. I told only a few of our people of these experiments and two of them when they tried to remember themselves had similar experiences.

Afterwards everything became normal. I could not give myself a clear account of what exactly had taken place. But everything in me had been turned upside down. And there is no doubt that in the things I said and thought during these three weeks there was a good deal of fantasy.

But I had seen myself, that is, I had seen things in myself that I had never seen before. There could be no doubt about it and although I afterwards became the same as I had been before I could not help *knowing* that this had been and I could forget nothing.

One thing I understood even then with undoubted clarity, that no phenomena of a higher order, that is, transcending the category of ordinary things observable every day, or phenomena which are sometimes called "metaphysical," can be observed or investigated by *ordinary means*, in an ordinary state of consciousness, like physical phenomena. It is a complete absurdity to think that it is possible to study phenomena of a higher order like "telepathy," "clairvoyance," foreseeing the future, mediumistic phenomena, and so on, in the same way as electrical, chemical, or meteorological phenomena are studied. There is something in phenomena of a higher order which requires a particular emotional state *for their observation and study.* And this excludes any possibility of "properly conducted" laboratory experiments and observations.

I had previously arrived at the same conclusions after experiments of my own described in the *New Model of the Universe* in the chapter "Experimental Mysticism," but now I understood the reason why this was impossible.

The second interesting conclusion that I came to is much more difficult to describe. It relates to a change which I noticed in certain of my views, in certain formulations of my aims, desires, and aspirations. Many aspects of this became clear to me only afterwards. And afterwards I saw clearly that it was at this time that certain very definite changes began in my views on myself, on those around me, and particularly on "methods of action," if this can be said without more precise definition. To describe the changes themselves is very difficult. I can only say that they were not in any way connected with what *was said* in Finland but that they had come as a result of the emotions which I had experienced there. The first thing I could record was the weakening in me of that extreme individualism which up to that time had been the fundamental feature in my attitude to life. I began to see people more, to feel my community with them more. And the second thing was that somewhere very deep down inside me I understood the esoteric principle of the impossibility of violence, that is, the uselessness of violent means to attain no matter what. I saw with undoubted clarity, and never afterwards did I wholly lose this feeling, that violent means and methods *in anything whatever* would unfailingly produce negative results, that is to say, results opposed to those aims for which they were applied. What I arrived at was like Tolstoi's non-resistance in appearance but it was not at all non-resistance because I had reached it not from an ethical but from a practical point of view; not from the standpoint of what is *better* or what is *worse* but from the standpoint of what is more effective and expedient.

The next time G. came to St. Petersburg was in the beginning of September. I tried to question him about what had actually occurred in Finland—was it true that he had said something that had frightened me, and why had I been frightened?

"If that was the case it means you were not ready," said G.

He explained nothing further.

On this visit the center of gravity of the talks was in the "chief feature" or "chief fault" of each one of us.

G. was very ingenious in the definition of features. I realized on this occasion that not everyone's chief feature could be defined. With some people this feature can be so hidden beneath different formal manifestations as to be almost impossible to find. And then a man can consider *himself* as his chief feature just as I could call my chief feature "Ouspensky" or, as G. always called it, "Piotr Demianovich." Mistakes there cannot be because the "Piotr Demianovich" of each person forms so to speak "round his chief feature."

Whenever anyone disagreed with the definition of his chief feature given by G. he always said that the fact that the person disagreed with him showed that he was right.

"I disagree only with what you say is actually my *chief feature*," said one of our people. "The chief feature which I know in myself is very much worse. But I do not dispute that people may see me as you describe."

"You know nothing in yourself," G. told him; "if you knew you would not have that feature. And people certainly see you in the way I told you. But you do not see how they see you. If you accept what I told you as your chief feature you will understand how people see you. And if you find a way to struggle with this feature and to destroy it, that is, to destroy its *involuntary manifestation*" (G. emphasized these words), "you will produce on people not the impression that you do now but any impression you like."

With this began long talks about the impressions that a man produces on other people and how he can produce a desirable or an undesirable impression.

Those around him see a man's chief feature however hidden it may be. Of course they cannot always define it. But their definitions are often very good and very near. Take nicknames. Nicknames sometimes define chief features very well.

The talk about impressions brought us once more to "inner" and "outward considering."

"There cannot be proper outward considering while a man is seated in his chief feature," said G. "For instance So-and-So" (he named one of our party). "His feature is that he is *never at home*. How can he consider anything or anybody?"

I was astonished at the artistic finish of the feature that was represented by G. It was not psychology even, it was art.

"And psychology ought to be art," G. replied, "psychology can never be simply a science."

To another of our party he said on the question of feature that his feature was *that he did not exist at all*.

"You understand, *I do not see you*," said G. "It does not mean that you are always like that. But when you are like you are now, you do not exist at all."

He said to another that his chief feature was a tendency always to argue with everybody about everything.

"*But then I never argue*," the man very heatedly at once replied.

Nobody could help laughing.

G. told another of our party—it was the middle-aged man on whom he had carried out the experiment of dividing personality from essence and who asked for raspberry jam—that his feature was that he had *no conscience*.

The following day the man came and said that he had been in the public library and had looked through the encyclopedic dictionaries of four languages for the meaning of the word "conscience."

G. merely waved his hand.

To the other man, his companion in the experiment, G. said that he had *no shame*, and he at once cracked a rather amusing joke against himself.

On this occasion G. stopped in quarters on the Liteiny near the Nevsky. He had caught a severe chill and we met at his place in small groups.

He said once that there was no sense in our going on any further in this way and that we ought to make a definite decision whether we wanted to go on with him, wanted to work, or whether it was better to abandon all attempts in this direction, because a half-serious attitude could give no results whatever. He added that he would continue the work only with those who would make a definite and serious decision to struggle with mechanicalness in themselves and with sleep.

"You already know by this time," he said, "that nothing terrible is demanded of you. But there is no sense in sitting between two stools. Whoever does not want to wake up, at any rate let him sleep well."

He said that he would talk to each of us separately and that each of us must show him sufficient reason why he, that is, G., should trouble about him.

"You think perhaps that this affords me a great deal of satisfaction," he said. "Or perhaps you think that there is nothing else that I could do. If so you are very gravely mistaken in both cases. There are very many other things that I could do. And if I give my time *to this* it is only because I have a definite aim. By now you ought better to understand in what my aim consists and by now you ought to see whether you are on the same road as I am or not. I will say nothing more. But in the future I shall work only with those who can be useful to me in attaining my aim. And only those people can be useful to me who have firmly decided to struggle with themselves, that is, to struggle with mechanicalness."

With this the talk ended. G.'s talks with members of the group lasted about a week. With some he spoke for a very long time, with others not so long. Finally almost everybody stayed on.

P., the middle-aged man whom I have mentioned in connection with experiments in dividing personality from essence, came out of the situation with honor and quickly became a very active member of our group, only on occasions going astray into a formal attitude or in "literal understanding."

Only two people dropped off who, exactly as though through some kind of magic as it seemed to us, suddenly ceased to understand anything and saw in everything that G. said *misunderstanding on his part*, and, on the part of the rest, a lack of sympathy and feeling.

This attitude, at first mistrustful and suspicious and then openly hostile to almost all of us, coming from nobody knew where and full of strange and quite unexpected accusations, astonished us very much.

"We made everything a secret"; we failed to tell them what G. had spoken of in their absence. We told tales about them to G., trying to make him distrust them. We recounted to him all talks with them, leading him constantly into error by distorting all the facts and striving to present everything in a false light. *We had given G. wrong impressions about them*, making him see everything far from as it was.

At the same time G. himself had "completely changed," had become altogether different from what he used to be before, had become harsh, requiring, had lost all feeling and all interest for individual people, had ceased to demand the truth from people; that he preferred to have round him people such as were afraid to tell him the truth, who were hypocrites, who threw flowers at one another and at the same time spied on the others.

We were amazed at all these and similar talks. They brought with them immediately a kind of entirely new atmosphere which up to this time we had not had. And it was particularly strange because precisely at this time most of us were in a very emotional state and were particularly well disposed towards these two protesting members of our group.

We tried many times to talk to G. about them. He laughed very much when we told him that in their opinion we always gave him "wrong impressions" of them.

"How they value the work," he said, "and what a miserable idiot I am from their point of view; how easily I am deceived! You see that they have ceased to understand the most important thing. In the work the teacher of the work cannot be deceived. This is a law which proceeds from what has been said about knowledge and being. I may deceive you if I want to. But you cannot deceive me. If it were otherwise you would not learn from me and I would have to learn from you."

"How must we speak to them and how can we help them to come back to the group?" some of us asked G.

"Not only can you do nothing," G. said to them, "but you ought not to try because by such attempts you will destroy the last chance they have of understanding and seeing themselves. *It is always very difficult to come back.* And it must be an absolutely voluntary decision without any sort of persuasion or constraint. You should understand that everything you have heard about me and yourselves are attempts at self-justification, endeavors to blame others in order to feel that they are in the right. It means more and more lying. It must be destroyed and it can only be destroyed through suffering. If it was difficult for them to see themselves before, it will be ten times more difficult now."

"How could this have happened?" others asked him. "Why did their attitude towards all of us and towards you change so abruptly and unexpectedly?"

"It is the first case for you," said G., "and therefore it appears strange to you, but later on you will see that it happens very often and you will see that it always takes place in the same way. The principal reason for it is that it is impossible to sit between two stools. And people usually think that they can sit between two stools, that is, that they can acquire the new and preserve the old; they do not think this consciously of course but it comes to the same thing.

"And what is it that they most of all desire to preserve? First the right to have their own valuation of ideas and of people, that is, that which is more harmful for them than anything else. They are fools and they already know it, that is to say, they realized it at one time. For this reason they came to learn. But they forget all about this the next moment; they are already bringing into the work their own paltry and subjective attitude; they begin to pass judgment on me and on everyone else as though they were able to pass judgment on anything. And this is immediately reflected in their attitude towards the ideas and towards what I say. Already 'they accept one thing' and 'they do not accept another thing'; with one thing they agree, with another they disagree; they trust me in one thing, in another thing they do not trust me.

"And the most amusing part is that they imagine they are able 'to work' under such conditions, that is, without trusting me in everything and without accepting everything. In actual fact this is absolutely impossible. By not accepting something or mistrusting something they immediately invent something of their own in its place. 'Gagging' begins —new theories and new explanations which have nothing in common either with the work or with what I have said. Then they begin to find faults and inaccuracies in everything that I say or do and in everything that others say or do. From this moment I now begin to speak of things about which I have no knowledge and even of things of which I have no conception, but which *they* know and understand much better than I do; all the other members of the group are fools, idiots. And so on, and so on, like a barrel organ. When a man says something on these lines I already know all he will say later on. And you also will know by the consequences. And it is amusing that people can see this in relation to others. But when they themselves do crazy things they at once cease to see it in relation to themselves. This is a law. It is difficult to climb the hill but very easy to slide down it. They even feel no embarrassment in talking in such a manner either with me or with other people. And chiefly they think that this can be combined with some kind of 'work.' They do not even want to understand that when a man reaches this notch his little song has been sung.

"And note one thing more. They are a pair. If they were separate, each one by himself, it would be easier for them to see their situation and come back. But they are a pair, they are friends, and one supports the other precisely in his weaknesses. Now one cannot return without the other. And even if they wanted to come back, I would just take one of them and not take the other."

"Why?" asked one of those present.

"That is another question entirely," said G., "in the present case simply in order to enable the other to ask himself who is the most important for him, I or his friend. If he is the most important, then there is nothing to talk about, but if I am the most important, then he must leave his friend and come back alone. And then, afterwards, the other may come back. But I tell you that they cling to one another and hinder one another. This is an exact example of how people do the very worst thing they possibly can for themselves when they depart from what is good in them."

In October I was with G. in Moscow.

His small apartment on the Bolshaia Dmitrovka, all the floors and walls of which were covered in the Eastern style with carpets and the ceilings hung with silk shawls, astonished me by its special atmosphere. First of all the people who came there—who were all G.'s pupils—*were not afraid to keep silent*. This alone was something unusual. They came, sat down, smoked, they often did not speak a single word for hours. And there was nothing oppressive or unpleasant in this silence; on the contrary, there was a feeling of assurance and of freedom from the necessity of playing a forced and invented role. But on chance and curious visitors this silence produced an extraordinarily strange impression. They began to talk and they talked without stopping as if they were afraid of stopping and feeling something. On the other hand others were offended, they thought that the "silence" was directed against them in order to show them how much superior G.'s pupils were and to make them understand that it was not worth while even talking to them; others found it stupid, amusing, "unnatural," and that it showed our worst features, particularly our weakness and our complete subordination to G. who was "oppressing us."

P. even decided to make notes of the reactions of various types of people to the "silence." I realized in this place that people feared silence more than anything else, that our tendency to talk arises from self-defense and is always based upon a reluctance to see something, a reluctance to confess something to oneself.

I quickly noticed a still stranger property of G.'s apartment. *It was not possible to tell lies there.* A lie at once became apparent, obvious, tangible, indubitable. Once there came an acquaintance of G.'s whom I had met before and who sometimes came to G.'s groups. Besides myself there were two or three people in the apartment. G. himself was not there. And having sat a while in silence our guest began to tell how he had just met a man who had told him some extraordinarily interesting things about the war, about possibilities of peace and so on. And suddenly quite unexpectedly for me I felt *that he was lying.* He had not met anybody and nobody had told him anything. He was making it all up on the spot simply because he could not endure the silence.

I felt awkward looking at him. It seemed to me that if I looked at him he would realize that I saw that he was lying. I glanced at the others and saw that they felt as I did and were barely able to repress their smiles. I then looked at the one who was talking and I saw that he alone noticed nothing and he continued to talk very rapidly, becoming more and more carried away by his subject and not at all noticing the glances that we unintentionally exchanged with one another.

This was not the only case. I suddenly remembered the attempts we made in the summer to describe our lives and the "intonations" with which we spoke when we tried to hide facts. I realized that here also the whole thing was in the intonations. When a man is chattering or simply waiting for an opportunity to begin he does not notice the intonations of others and is unable to distinguish lies from the truth. But directly he is quiet himself, that is, awakes a little, he hears the different intonations and begins to distinguish other people's lies.

We spoke several times with G.'s pupils on this subject. I told them what had happened in Finland and about the "sleeping people" I had seen on the streets of St. Petersburg. The feeling of mechanical lying people here in G.'s apartment reminded me very much of the feeling of "sleeping people."

I wanted very much to introduce some of my Moscow friends to G., but from among all those whom I met during these days only one, my old newspaper friend V. A. A., produced the impression of being sufficiently alive, although he was as usual overloaded with work and rushing from one place to another. But he was very interested when I told him about G. and with G.'s permission I invited him to have lunch at G.'s place.—

G. summoned about fifteen of his people and arranged a lunch which, at that time, was luxurious, with *zakuski*, pies, *shashlik*, Khaghetia wine, and so on, in a word it was one of those Caucasian lunches that begin at midday and last until the evening.—He seated A. near him, was very kind to him, entertained him all the time, and poured out wine for him. My heart suddenly fell when I realized to what a test I had brought my old friend. The fact was that everyone kept silence. A. held out for five minutes. Then he began to talk. He spoke of the war, of all our allies and enemies together and separately; he communicated the opinions of all the public men of Moscow and St. Petersburg upon all possible subjects; then he talked about the desiccation of vegetables for the army (with which he was then occupied in addition to his journalistic work), particularly the desiccation of onions, then about artificial manures, agricultural chemistry, and chemistry in general; about "melioration"; about spiritism, the "materialization of hands," and about what else I do not remember now. Neither G. nor anyone else spoke a single word. I was on the point of speaking fearing that A. would be offended, but G. looked at me so fiercely that I stopped short. Besides, my fears were in vain. Poor A. noticed nothing, he was so carried away by his own talk and his own eloquence that he sat on happily at the table and talked without stopping for a moment until four o'clock. Then with great feeling he shook hands with G. and thanked him for his "very interesting conversation." G., looking at me, laughed slyly.

I felt very ashamed. They had made a fool of poor A. He certainly could not have expected anything of the kind, so he was caught. I realized that G. had given a demonstration to his people.

"There, you see," he said, when A. had gone. "He is called a clever man. But he would not have noticed it even if I had taken his trousers off him. Only let him talk. He wants nothing else. And everybody is like that. This one was much better than many others. He told no lies. And he really knew what he talked about, in his own way of course. But think, what use is he? He is no longer young. And perhaps this was the one time in his life when there was an opportunity of hearing the truth. And he talked himself all the time."

Of the Moscow talks with G. I remember one which is connected with another talk in St. Petersburg I have already given.

This time G. himself began to speak.

"What do you find is the most important thing of all you have learned up to now?" he asked me.

"The experiences, of course, which I had in August," I said. "If I were able to evoke them at will and use them, it would be all that I could wish for because I think that then I should be able to find all the rest. But at the same time I know that these 'experiences,' I choose this word only because there is no other, but you understand of what I speak"—he nodded—"depended on the emotional state I was in then. And I know that they will always depend on this. If I could create such an emotional state in myself I should very quickly come to these experiences. But I feel infinitely far from this emotional state, as though I were asleep. This is 'sleep,' that was being awake.—How can this emotional state be created? Tell me."

"There are three ways," said G. "First, this state can come by itself, accidentally. Second, someone else can create it in you. And third, you can create it yourself. Which do you prefer?"

I confess that for a second I had a very strong desire to say that I preferred someone else, that is, him, to create in me the emotional state of which I was speaking. But I at once realized that he would say that he had already done it once and that now I ought either to wait until *this* came itself or that I ought to do something myself to get it.

"I want of course to create it myself," I said. "But how can it be done?"

"I have already said before that sacrifice is necessary," said G. "Without sacrifice nothing can be attained. But if there is anything in the world that people do not understand it is the idea of sacrifice. They think they have to sacrifice something that they have. For example, I once said that they must sacrifice 'faith,' 'tranquillity,' 'health.' They understand this literally. But then the point is that they have not got either faith, or tranquillity, or health. All these words must be taken in quotation marks. In actual fact they have to sacrifice only what they imagine they have and which in reality they do not have. They must sacrifice their fantasies. But this is difficult for them, very difficult. It is much easier to sacrifice real things.

"Another thing that people must sacrifice *is their suffering*. It is very difficult also to sacrifice one's suffering. A man will renounce any pleasures you like but he will not give up his suffering. Man is made in such a way that he is never so much attached to anything as he is to his suffering. And it is necessary to be free from suffering. No one who is not free from suffering, who has not sacrificed his suffering, can work. Later on a great deal must be said about suffering. Nothing can be attained without suffering but at the same time one must begin by sacrificing suffering. Now, decipher what this means."

I stayed in Moscow about a week and returned to St. Petersburg with a fresh store of ideas and impressions. Here a very interesting occurrence took place which explained many things to me in the system and in G.'s methods of instruction.

During the period of my stay in Moscow G.'s pupils had explained to me various laws relating to man and the world; among others they showed me again the "table of hydrogens," as we called it in St. Petersburg, but in a considerably expanded form. Namely, besides the three scales of "hydrogens" which G. had worked out for us before, they had taken the reduction further and had made in all twelve scales. (See Table 4.)

In such a form the table was scarcely comprehensible. I was not able to convince myself of the necessity of reduced scales.

"Let us take for instance the seventh scale," said P. "The Absolute here is 'hydrogen' 96. Fire can serve as an example of 'hydrogen' 96. Fire then is the Absolute for a piece of wood. Let us take the ninth scale. Here the Absolute is 'hydrogen' 384 or *water*. Water will be the Absolute for a piece of sugar."

But I was unable to grasp the principle on the basis of which it would be possible to determine exactly when to make use of such a scale. P. showed me a table made up to the fifth scale and relating to parallel levels in different worlds. But I got nothing from it. I began to think whether it was not possible to unite all these various scales with the various cosmoses. And having dwelt on this thought I went in an absolutely wrong direction because the cosmoses of course had no relation whatever to the division of the scale. It seemed to me at the same time that I had in general ceased to understand anything in the "three octaves of radiations" from which the first scale of "hydrogens" was deduced. The principal stumbling block here was the relation of the three forces 1, 2, 3 and 1, 3, 2 and the relations between "carbon," "oxygen," and "nitrogen."

At the same time I realized that this contained something important. And I left Moscow with the unpleasant feeling that not only had I not acquired anything new but that I seemed to have lost the old, that is, what I thought I had already understood.

We had an agreement in our group that whoever went to Moscow and heard any new explanations or lectures must, on his arrival in St. Petersburg, communicate it all to the others. But on the way to St. Petersburg while going carefully in my head through the Moscow talks, I felt that I would not be able to communicate the principal thing because I did not understand it myself. This irritated me and I did not know what I was to do. In this state I arrived at St. Petersburg and on the following day I went to our meeting.

Trying to draw out as much as possible the beginning of the "diagrams," as we called a part of G.'s system, dealing with general questions and laws, I began to convey the general impressions of my journey. And all the time I was saying one thing, in my head another thing was running: How shall I begin—what does the transition 1, 2, 3 into 1, 3, 2 mean? Can an example of such a transition be found in the phenomena we know?

I felt that I must find something now, immediately, because unless I found something myself first I could say nothing to the others.

H1	H6											
H1	H6	H12										
H1	H6	H12	H24									
H1	H6	H12	H24	H48								
H1	H6	H12	H24	H48	H96							
H1	H6	H12	H24	H48	H96	H192						
H1	H6	H12	H24	H48	H96	H192	H384					
H1	H6	H12	H24	H48	H96	H192	H384	H768				
H1	H6	H12	H24	H48	H96	H192	H384	H768	H1536			
H1	H6	H12	H24	H48	H96	H192	H384	H768	H1536	H3072		
H1	H6	H12	H24	H48	H96	H192	H384	H768	H1536	H3072	H6144	
	H6	H12	H24	H48	H96	H192	H384	H768	H1536	H3072	H6144	H12288

TABLE 4

I began to draw the diagram on the board. It was the diagram of radiations in three octaves: *Absolute–sun–earth–moon*. We were already accustomed to this terminology and to G.'s form of exposition. But I did not know at all what I would say beyond what they knew already.

And suddenly a single word, which came into my head and *which no one had pronounced in Moscow*, connected and explained everything: "a moving diagram." I realized that it was necessary to imagine this diagram as a *moving one*, all the links in the chain changing places as in some mystical dance.

I felt so much in this word that for some time I did not hear myself what I was saying. But after I had collected my thoughts I saw that they were listening to me and that I had explained everything I had not understood myself on the way to the meeting. This gave me an extraordinarily strong and clear sensation as though I had discovered for myself new possibilities, a new method of perception and understanding *by giving explanations to other people*. And under the impetus of this sensation, as soon as I had said that examples or analogies of the transition of the forces 1, 2, 3 and 1, 3, 2 must be found in the real world, I at once saw these examples both in the human organism and in the astronomical world and in mechanics in the movements of waves.

I afterwards had a talk with G. about various scales, the purpose of which I did not understand.

"We waste time on guessing riddles," I said. "Would it not be simpler to help us to solve these more quickly? You know that before us there are many other difficulties, we shall never even reach them going at this pace. You yourself have said, and very often, that we have very little time."

"It is precisely because there is little time and because there are many difficulties ahead that it is necessary to do as I am doing," said G. "If you are afraid of these difficulties, what will it be like later on? Do you think that anything is given in a completed form in schools? You look at this very naïvely. You must be cunning, you must pretend, lead up to things in conversation. Sometimes things are learned from jokes, from stories. And you want everything to be very simple. This never happens. You must know how to take when it is not given, to *steal* if necessary, but not to wait for somebody to come and give it to you."

Chapter Fourteen

THERE were certain points to which G. invariably used to return in all his talks with us after the formal lectures, to which outside people were admitted, were over. The first was the question of self-remembering and the necessity of constant work on oneself in order to attain this, and the second was the question of the imperfection of our language and of the difficulty of conveying "objective truths" in our words.

As I have already mentioned before, G. used the expressions "objective" and "subjective" in a special sense, taking as a basis the divisions of "subjective" and "objective" states of consciousness. All our ordinary knowledge which is based on ordinary methods of observation and verification of observations, all scientific theories deduced from the observation of facts accessible to us in subjective states of consciousness, he called *subjective*. Knowledge based upon ancient methods and principles of observation, knowledge of things in themselves, knowledge accompanying "an objective state of consciousness," *knowledge of the All*, was for him *objective* knowledge.

I will try to convey what followed as far as I remember it, making use partly of notes made by some of G.'s Moscow pupils and partly of notes of my own on the Petersburg talks.

"One of the most central of the ideas of objective knowledge," said G., "is the idea of the unity of everything, of unity in diversity. From ancient times people who have understood the content and the meaning of this idea, and have seen in it the basis of objective knowledge, have endeavored to find a way of transmitting this idea in a form comprehensible to others. The successive transmission of the ideas of objective knowledge has always been a part of the task of those possessing this knowledge. In such cases the idea of the unity of everything, as the fundamental and central idea of this knowledge, had to be transmitted first and transmitted with adequate completeness and exactitude. And to do this the idea had to be put into such forms as would insure its proper perception by others and avoid in its transmission the possibility of distortion and corruption. For this purpose the people to whom the idea was being transmitted were required to undergo a proper preparation, and the idea itself was put either into a logical form, as for instance in philosophical systems which endeavored to give a definition of the 'fundamental principle' or ἀρχή from which everything else was derived, or into religious teachings which endeavored to create an element of faith and to evoke a wave of emotion carrying people up to the level of 'objective consciousness.' The attempts of both the one and the other, sometimes more sometimes less successful, run through the whole history of mankind from the most ancient times up to our own time and they have taken the form of religious and philosophical creeds which have remained like monuments on the paths of these attempts to unite the thought of mankind and esoteric thought.

"But objective knowledge, the idea of unity included, belongs to objective consciousness. The forms which express this knowledge when perceived by subjective consciousness are inevitably distorted and, instead of truth, they create more and more delusions. With objective consciousness it is possible to see and feel the unity of everything. But for subjective consciousness the world is split up into millions of separate and unconnected phenomena. Attempts to connect these phenomena into some sort of system in a scientific or a philosophical way lead to nothing because man cannot reconstruct the idea of the whole starting from separate facts and they cannot divine the principles of the division of the whole without knowing the laws upon which this division is based.

"None the less the idea of the unity of everything exists also in intellectual thought but in its exact relation to diversity it can never be clearly expressed in words or in logical forms. There remains always the insurmountable difficulty of language. A language which has been constructed through expressing impressions of plurality and diversity in subjective states of consciousness can never transmit with sufficient completeness and clarity the idea of unity which is intelligible and obvious for the objective state of consciousness.

"Realizing the imperfection and weakness of ordinary language the people who have possessed objective knowledge have tried to express the idea of unity in 'myths,' in 'symbols,' and in particular 'verbal formulas' which, having been transmitted without alteration, have carried on the idea from one school to another, often from one epoch to another.

"It has already been said that the higher psychic centers work in man's higher states of consciousness: the 'higher emotional' and the 'higher mental.' The aim of 'myths' and 'symbols' was to reach man's higher centers, to transmit to him ideas inaccessible to the intellect and to transmit them in such forms as would exclude the possibility of false interpretations. 'Myths' were destined for the higher emotional center; 'symbols' for the higher thinking center. By virtue of this all attempts to understand or explain 'myths' and 'symbols' with the mind, or the formulas and the expressions which give a summary of their content, are doomed beforehand to failure. It is always possible to understand anything but only with the appropriate center. But the preparation for receiving ideas belonging to objective knowledge has to proceed by way of the mind, for only a mind properly prepared can transmit these ideas to the higher centers without introducing elements foreign to them.

"The symbols that were used to transmit ideas belonging to objective knowledge included diagrams of the fundamental laws of the universe and they not only transmitted the knowledge itself but showed also the way to it. The study of symbols, their construction and meaning, formed a very important part of the preparation for receiving objective knowledge and it was in itself a test because a literal or formal understanding of symbols at once made it impossible to receive any further knowledge.

"Symbols were divided into the fundamental and the subordinate; the first included the principles of separate domains of knowledge; the second expressed the essential nature of phenomena in their relation to unity.

"Among the formulas giving a summary of the content of many symbols there was one which had a particular significance, namely the formula 'As above, so below,' from the 'Emerald Tablets of Hermes Trismegistus.' This formula stated that all the laws of the cosmos could be found in the atom or in any other phenomenon which exists as something completed according to certain laws. This same meaning was contained in the analogy drawn between the *microcosm*—man, and the *macrocosm*— the universe. The fundamental laws of triads and octaves penetrate everything and should be studied simultaneously both in the world and in man. But in relation to himself man is a nearer and a more accessible object of study and knowledge than the world of phenomena outside him. Therefore, in striving towards a knowledge of the universe, man should begin with the study of himself and with the realization of the fundamental laws within him.

"From this point of view another formula, *Know thyself,* is full of particularly deep meaning and is one of the symbols leading to the knowledge of truth. The study of the world and the study of man will assist one another. In studying the world and its laws a man studies himself, and in studying himself he studies the world. In this sense every symbol teaches us something about ourselves.

"The understanding of symbols can be approached in the following way: In studying the world of phenomena a man first of all sees in everything the manifestation of two principles, one opposed to the other, which, in conjunction or in opposition, give one result or another, that is, reflect the essential nature of the principles which have created them. This manifestation of the great laws of *duality* and *trinity* man sees simultaneously in the cosmos and in himself. But in relation to the cosmos he is merely a spectator and moreover one who sees only the surface of phenomena which are moving in various directions though seeming to him to move in one direction. But in relation to himself his understanding of the laws of duality and trinity can express itself in a practical form, namely, having understood these laws in himself, he can, so to speak, confine the manifestation of the laws of duality and trinity to the permanent line of struggle with himself on the way to self-knowledge. In this way he will introduce the *line of will* first into the circle of time and afterwards into the cycle of eternity, the accomplishing of which will create in him the great symbol known by the name of the *Seal of Solomon*.

"The transmission of the meaning of symbols to a man who has not reached an understanding of them in himself is impossible. This sounds like a paradox, but the meaning of a symbol and the disclosure of its essence can only be given to, and can only be understood by, one who, so to speak, already knows what is comprised in this symbol. And then a symbol becomes for him a synthesis of his knowledge and serves him for the expression and transmission of his knowledge just as it served the man who constructed it.

"The more simple symbols:

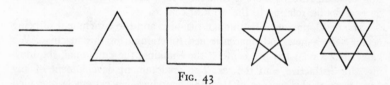

FIG. 43

or the numbers 2, 3, 4, 5, 6, which express them, possess a definite meaning in relation to the inner development of man; they show different stages on the path of man's self-perfection and of the growth of his being.

"Man, in the normal state natural to him, is taken as a *duality*. He consists entirely of dualities or 'pairs of opposites.' All man's sensations, impressions, feelings, thoughts, are divided into positive and negative, useful and harmful, necessary and unnecessary, good and bad, pleasant and unpleasant. The work of centers proceeds under the sign of this division. Thoughts oppose feelings. Moving impulses oppose instinctive craving for quiet. This is the duality in which proceed all the perceptions, all the reactions, the whole life of man. Any man who observes himself, however little, can see this duality in himself.

"But this duality would seem to alternate; what is victor today is the vanquished tomorrow; what guides us today becomes secondary and subordinate tomorrow. And everything is equally mechanical, equally independent of will, and leads equally to no aim of any kind. The understanding of duality in oneself begins with the realization of mechanicalness and the realization of the difference between what is mechanical and what is conscious. This understanding must be preceded by the destruction of the self-deceit in which a man lives who considers even his most mechanical actions to be volitional and conscious and himself to be single and whole.

"When self-deceit is destroyed and a man begins to see the difference between the mechanical and the conscious in himself, there begins a struggle for the realization of consciousness in life and for the subordination of the mechanical to the conscious. For this purpose a man begins with endeavors to set a definite *decision*, coming from conscious motives, against mechanical processes proceeding according to the laws of duality. The creation of a permanent third principle is for man the *transformation of the duality into the trinity*.

"Strengthening this decision and bringing it constantly and infallibly into all those events where formerly accidental neutralizing 'shocks' used to act and give accidental results, gives a permanent line of results in time and is the *transformation of trinity into quaternity*. The next stage, the transformation of quaternity into quinternity and the *construction of the pentagram* has not one but many different meanings even in relation to man. And of these is learned, first of all, one, which is the most beyond doubt, relating to the work of centers.

"The development of the human machine and the enrichment of being begins with a new and unaccustomed functioning of this machine. We know that a man has five centers: the thinking, the emotional, the moving, the instinctive, and the sex. The predominant development of any one center at the expense of the others produces an extremely one-sided type of man, incapable of further development. But if a man brings the work of the five centers within him into harmonious accord, he then 'locks the pentagram within him' and becomes a finished type of the physically perfect man. The full and proper functioning of five centers brings them into union with the higher centers which introduce the missing principle and put man into direct and permanent connection with objective consciousness and objective knowledge.

"And then man becomes the *six-pointed star*, that is, by becoming locked within a circle of life independent and complete in itself, he becomes isolated from foreign influences or accidental shocks; he embodies in himself the *Seal of Solomon*.

"In the present instance the series of symbols given—2, 3, 4, 5, and 6 —is interpreted as applicable to one process. But even this interpretation is incomplete, because a symbol can never be fully interpreted. It can only be experienced, in the same way, for instance, as the idea of *self-knowledge* must be experienced.

"This same process of the harmonious development of man can be examined from the point of view of the law of octaves. The law of octaves gives another system of symbols. In the sense of the law of octaves every completed process is a transition of the note do through a series of successive tones to the do of the next octave. The seven fundamental tones of the octave express the law of seven. The addition to it of the do of the next octave, that is to say, the crowning of the process, gives the eighth step. The seven fundamental tones together with the two 'intervals' and 'additional shocks' give nine steps. By incorporating in it the do of the next octave we have ten steps. The last, the tenth, step is the end of the preceding and the beginning of the next cycle. In this way the law of octaves and the process of development it expresses, include the numbers 1 to 10. At this point we come to what may be termed the *symbolism of numbers*. The symbolism of numbers cannot be understood without the law of octaves or without a clear conception of how octaves are expressed in the *decimal system* and vice versa.

"In Western systems of occultism there is a method known by the name of 'theosophical addition,' that is, the definition of numbers consisting of two or more digits by the sum of those digits. To people who do not understand the symbolism of numbers this method of synthesizing numbers seems to be absolutely arbitrary and to lead nowhere. But for a man who understands the unity of everything existing and who has the key to this unity the method of theosophical addition has a profound meaning, for it resolves all diversity into the fundamental laws which govern it and which are expressed in the numbers 1 to 10.

"As was mentioned earlier, in symbology, as represented, *numbers* are connected with definite *geometrical figures*, and are mutually complementary one to another. In the Cabala a *symbology of letters* is also used and in combination with the symbology of letters a *symbology of words*. A combination of the four methods of symbolism by numbers, geometrical figures, letters, and words, gives a complicated but more perfect method.

"Then there exists also a *symbology of magic*, a *symbology of alchemy*, and a *symbology of astrology* as well as the system of the *symbols of the Tarot* which unites them into one whole.

"Each one of these systems can serve as a means for *transmitting* the idea of unity. But in the hands of the incompetent and the ignorant, however full of good intentions, the same symbol becomes an 'instrument of delusion.' The reason for this consists in the fact that a *symbol* can never be taken in a final and definite meaning. In expressing the laws of the unity of endless diversity a symbol itself possesses an endless number of aspects from which it can be examined and it demands from a man approaching it the ability to see it simultaneously from different points of view. Symbols which are transposed into the words of ordinary language become rigid in them, they grow dim and very easily become 'their own opposites,' confining the meaning within narrow dogmatic frames, without giving it even the very relative freedom of a *logical* examination of a subject. The cause of this is in the literal understanding of symbols, in attributing to a symbol a single meaning. The truth is again veiled by an outer covering of lies and to discover it requires immense efforts of negation in which the idea of the symbol itself is lost. It is well known what delusions have arisen from the symbols of religion, of alchemy, and particularly of magic, in those who have taken them literally and only in one meaning.

"At the same time the right understanding of symbols cannot lead to dispute. It deepens knowledge, and it cannot remain theoretical because it intensifies the striving towards real results, towards the union of knowledge and being, that is, to *Great Doing*. Pure knowledge cannot be transmitted, but by being expressed in symbols it is covered by them as by a veil, although at the same time for those who desire and who know how to look this veil becomes transparent.

"And in this sense it is possible to speak of the symbolism of speech although this symbolism is not understood by everyone. To understand the inner meaning of what is said is possible only on a certain level of development and when accompanied by the corresponding efforts and state of the listener. But on hearing things which are new for him, instead of making efforts to understand them, a man begins to dispute them, or refute them, maintaining against them an opinion which he considers to be right and which as a rule has no relation whatever to them. In this way he loses all chance of acquiring anything new. To be able to understand speech when it becomes symbolical it is essential to have learned before and to know already how to listen. Any attempt to understand literally, where speech deals with objective knowledge and with the union of diversity and unity, is doomed to failure beforehand and leads in most cases to further delusions.

"It is necessary to dwell upon this because the intellectualism of contemporary education imbues people with a propensity and a tendency to look for logical definitions and for logical arguments against everything they hear and, without noticing it, people unconsciously fetter themselves with their desire, as it were, for exactitude in those spheres where exact definitions, by their very nature, imply inexactitude in meaning.

"Therefore, because of the tendency referred to in our thinking, it often happens that exact knowledge concerning details, communicated to a man before he has acquired an understanding of the essential nature of a thing, makes it difficult for him to understand this essential nature. This does not mean that exact definitions do not exist on the way of true knowledge, on the contrary, only there do they exist; but they differ very greatly from what we usually think them to be. And if anyone supposes that he can go along the way of self-knowledge guided by an exact knowledge of all details, and if he expects to have such knowledge without first having given himself the trouble to assimilate the indications he has received concerning his own work, then he should first of all understand that he will not attain knowledge until he makes the necessary efforts and that only of himself and only by his own efforts can he attain what he seeks. No one can ever give him what he did not possess before; no one can do for him the work he should do for himself. All that another can do for him is to give him the impetus to work and from this point of view symbolism, properly perceived, plays the part of an impetus of this kind for our knowledge.

"We have spoken earlier of the law of octaves, of the fact that every process, no matter upon what scale it takes place, is completely determined in its gradual development by the law of the structure of the seven-tone scale. In connection with this it has been pointed out that every note, every tone, if taken on another scale is again a whole octave. The 'intervals' between mi and fa and between si and do which cannot be filled by the intensity of the energy of the process in operation, and which require an outside 'shock,' outside help so to speak, connect by this very fact one process with other processes. From this it follows that the law of octaves connects all processes of the universe and, to one who knows the scales of the passage and the laws of the structure of the octave, it presents the possibility of an exact cognition of everything and every phenomenon in its essential nature and of all its interrelations with phenomena and things connected with it.

"For uniting into one whole all knowledge connected with the law of the structure of the octave there is a certain symbol which takes the form of a circle divided into nine parts with lines connecting the nine points on the circumference in a certain order.

"Before passing on to the study of the symbol itself it is essential to understand certain aspects of the teaching which makes use of this symbol, as well as the relation of this teaching to other systems which make use of symbolical methods for the transmission of knowledge.

"In order to understand the interrelation of these teachings it must always be remembered that the ways which lead to the cognition of unity approach it like the radii of a circle moving towards the center; the closer they come to the center, the closer they approach one another.

"As a result of this the theoretical statements which form the basis of one line can sometimes be explained from the point of view of statements of another line and vice versa. For this reason it is sometimes possible to form a certain intermediate line between two adjacent lines. But in the absence of a complete knowledge and understanding of the fundamental lines, such intermediate ways may easily lead to a mixing of lines, to confusion and error.

"Of the principal lines, more or less known, four can be named:

1) The Hebraic
2) The Egyptian
3) The Persian
4) The Hindu

"Moreover of the last we know only its philosophy, and of the first three, parts of their theory.

"In addition to these there are two lines known in Europe, namely *theosophy* and so-called *Western occultism*, which have resulted from a mixture of the fundamental lines. Both lines bear in themselves grains of truth, but neither of them possesses full knowledge and therefore attempts to bring them to practical realization give only negative results.

"The teaching whose theory is here being set out is completely self-supporting and independent of other lines and it has been completely unknown up to the present time. Like other lines it makes use of the symbolical method and one of its principal symbols is the figure which has been mentioned, that is, the circle divided into nine parts:

"This symbol takes the following form:

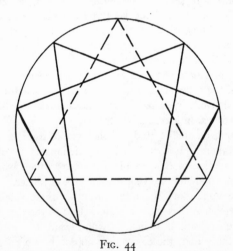

FIG. 44

"The circle is divided into nine equal parts. Six points are connected by a figure which is symmetrical in relation to a diameter passing through the uppermost point of the divisions of the circumference. Further, the uppermost point of the divisions is the apex of an equilateral triangle linking together the points of the divisions which do not enter into the construction of the original complicated figure.

"This symbol cannot be met with anywhere in the study of 'occultism,' either in books or in oral transmission. It was given such significance by those who knew, that they considered it necessary to keep the knowledge of it secret.

"Only some hints and partial representations of it can be met with in literature.[1] Thus it is possible to meet with a drawing of it like this:

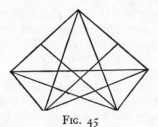

FIG. 45

"And another like this:

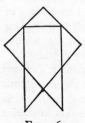

FIG. 46

"The symbol which takes the form of a circle divided into nine parts with lines connecting them together expresses the law of seven in its union with the law of three.

"The octave possesses seven tones and the eighth is a repetition of the

[1] In the book *Etude sur les origines de la nature du Zohar* by S. Karppe, Paris, 1901, pp. 200-201, there is a drawing of a circle divided into nine parts:

with the following description of this circle:

"If we multiply 9×9 the result is shown in the number 8 on the left side and the number 1 on the right side; in the same way 9×8 gives the product shown in number 7 on the left and in number 2 on the right; exactly in the same way with 9×6. Beginning with 9×5 the order becomes reversed, that is, the number representing the units takes the left side and the number representing the tens takes the right."

first. Together with the two 'additional shocks' which fill the 'intervals' mi–fa and si–do, there are nine elements.

"The complete construction of this symbol which connects it with a complete expression of the law of octaves is more complicated than the construction shown. But even this construction shows the inner laws of *one octave* and it points out a method of cognizing the essential nature of a thing examined in itself.

"The isolated existence of a thing or phenomenon under examination is the closed circle of an eternally returning and uninterruptedly flowing process. The circle symbolizes this process. The separate points in the division of the circumference symbolize the steps of the process. The symbol as a whole is *do*, that is, something with an orderly and complete existence. It is a circle—a completed cycle. It is the *zero* of our decimal system; in its inscription it represents a closed cycle. It contains within itself everything necessary for its own existence. It is isolated from its surroundings. The succession of stages in the process must be connected with the succession of the remaining numbers from 1 to 9. The presence of the ninth step filling up the 'interval' si–do, completes the cycle, that is, it closes the circle, which begins anew at this point. The apex of the triangle closes the duality of its base, making possible the manifold forms of its manifestation in the most diverse triangles, in the same way as the point of the apex of the triangle multiplies itself infinitely in the line of its base. Therefore every beginning and completion of the cycle is situated in the apex of the triangle, in the point where the beginning and the end merge, where the circle is closed, and which sounds in the endlessly flowing cycle as the two do's in the octave. But it is the ninth step that closes and again begins a cycle. Therefore in the upper point of the triangle corresponding to do stands the number 9, and among the remaining points are disposed the numbers 1 to 8.

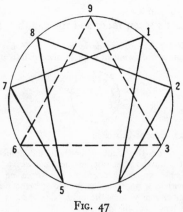

FIG. 47

"Passing on to the examination of the complicated figure inside the circle we should understand the laws of its construction. The laws of unity are reflected in all phenomena. The decimal system is constructed on the basis of the same laws. Taking a unit as one note containing within itself a whole octave we must divide this unit into seven unequal parts in order to arrive at the seven notes of this octave. But in the graphic representation the inequality of the parts is not taken into account and for the construction of the diagram there is taken first a seventh part, then two-sevenths, then three-sevenths, four-sevenths, five-sevenths, six-sevenths, and seven-sevenths. Calculating these parts in decimals we get:

$$\tfrac{1}{7} - 0.142857 \ldots$$
$$\tfrac{2}{7} - 0.285714 \ldots$$
$$\tfrac{3}{7} - 0.428571 \ldots$$
$$\tfrac{4}{7} - 0.571428 \ldots$$
$$\tfrac{5}{7} - 0.714285 \ldots$$
$$\tfrac{6}{7} - 0.857142 \ldots$$
$$\tfrac{7}{7} - 0.999999 \ldots$$

"In examining the series of periodic decimals obtained we at once see that in all except the last the periods consist of exactly the same six digits which run in a definite sequence, so that, knowing the first digit of the period, it is possible to reconstruct the whole period in full.

"If we now place on the circumference all the nine numbers from 1 to 9 and connect those numbers which are included in the period by straight lines in the same sequence in which the numbers stand in the period, according to which number we start from, we shall obtain the figure found inside the circle. The numbers 3, 6, and 9 are not included in the period. They form the separate triangle—the free trinity of the symbol.

"Making use of 'theosophical addition' and taking the sum of the numbers of the period, we obtain *nine*, that is, a whole octave. Again in each separate note there will be included a whole octave subject to the same laws as the first. The positions of the notes will correspond to the numbers of the period and the drawing of an octave will look like the following:

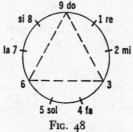

Fig. 48

"The triangle 9–3–6, which unites into one whole the three points on the circumference not included in the period, connects together the law of seven and the law of three. The numbers 3–6–9 are not included in the period; two of them, 3 and 6, correspond to the two 'intervals' in the octave, the third is, so to speak, superfluous and at the same time it replaces the fundamental note which does not enter the period. Moreover, any phenomenon which is able to act reciprocally with a phenomenon similar to it sounds as the note do in a corresponding octave. Therefore do can emerge from its circle and enter into orderly correlation with another circle, that is, play that role in another cycle which, in the cycle under consideration, is played by the 'shocks' filling the 'intervals' in the octave. Therefore, here also, by having this possibility do is connected by the triangle 3–6–9 with those places in the octave where the shocks from outside sources occur, where the octave can be penetrated to make connection with what exists outside it. The law of three stands out, so to speak, from the law of seven, the triangle penetrates through the period and these two figures in combination give the inner structure of the octave and its notes.

"At this point in our reasoning it would be entirely right to raise the question: Why is one of the 'intervals' which is designated by the number 3 found in its right place between the notes mi and fa, and the other, which is designated by the number 6, found between sol and la, when its right place is between si and do.

"If the conditions had been observed as to the appearance of the second interval (6) in its own place, we should have had the following circle:

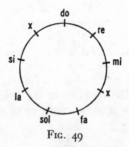

Fig. 49

And the nine elements of the closed cycle would have been grouped symmetrically together in the following way:

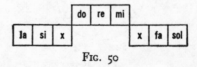

Fig. 50

"The distribution we do get:

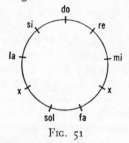

FIG. 51

can only give the following grouping:

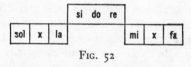

FIG. 52

that is, in one case x between mi and fa, and in the other between sol and la, where it is not necessary.

"The apparent placing of the interval in *its wrong place* itself shows to those who are able to read the symbol what kind of 'shock' is required for the passage of si to do.

"In order to understand this, it is essential to recollect what was said about the role of 'shocks' in the processes proceeding in man and in the universe.

"When we examined the application of the law of octaves to the cosmos then the step 'sun–earth' was represented in this way:

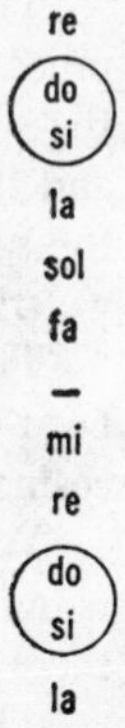

"In relation to the three octaves of radiation it was pointed out that the passage of do to si, the filling of the interval, takes place within the organism of the sun. It was pointed out in the cosmic octave in relation to the 'interval' do–si that this passage is accomplished by the will of the Absolute. The passage fa–mi in the cosmic octave is accomplished mechanically with the help of a special machine which makes it possible for fa, which enters it, to acquire by a series of inner processes the characteristics of sol standing above it, without changing its note, that is, to accumulate, as it were, the inner energy for passing independently into the next note, into mi.

"Exactly the same relationship is repeated in all completed processes. In examining the processes of nutrition in the human organism and the transformation of the substances taken into the organism, we find in these processes exactly the same 'intervals' and 'shocks.'

re
do
si
la
sol
fa
—
mi
re
do
si
la

FIG. 53

"As we pointed out before, man takes in three kinds of food. Each one of them is the beginning of a new octave. The second octave, that is, the air octave, joins up with the first, that is, the octave of food and drink, at the point where the first octave comes to a stop in its development at the note mi. And the third octave joins up with the second at the point where the second octave comes to a stop in its development at the note mi.

"But it must be understood that, just as in many chemical processes, only definite *quantities* of substances, exactly determined by nature, give compounds of the required quality, so in the human organism the 'three kinds of food' must be mixed in definite proportions.

"The final substance in the process of the food octave is the substance si ('hydrogen' 12 in the third scale), which needs an 'additional shock' in order to pass into a new do. But as three octaves have taken part in the production of this substance their influence is also reflected in the final result by determining its quality. The quality and quantity can be regulated by regulating the three kinds of food received by the organism. Only in the presence of a full and harmonious conformity between all three kinds of food, by a strengthening or weakening of the different parts of the process, is the required result obtained.

"But it is essential to remember that no arbitrary attempts to regulate food, in the literal sense of the word, or breathing can lead to the desired end unless one knows exactly what one is doing and why, and what kind of result it will give.

"And furthermore, even if a man were to succeed in regulating two components of the process, food and breathing, again this would not be enough, because it is still more important to know how to regulate the food of the third story—'impressions.'

"Therefore before even thinking of influencing practically the inner processes it is essential to understand the exact mutual relationship of the substances entering the organism, the nature of the possible 'shocks,' and the laws governing the transition of notes. These laws are everywhere the same. In studying man we study the cosmos, in studying the cosmos we study man.

"The cosmic octave 'Absolute–moon' has, according to the law of three, been broken into three subordinate octaves. In these three octaves the cosmos is like man; the same 'three stories,' the same three shocks.

"Where, in the cosmic octaves of radiation, the place of the interval fa–mi appears, in the diagram are marked the 'machines' which are found there in the same way as in the human body.

"The process of the transition fa–mi can be represented in the most schematic way thus: the cosmic fa enters this machine like the food of the lower story and begins its cycle of changes. Therefore in the beginning it sounds in the machine as do. The substance sol of the cosmic octave serves as the substance which enters the middle story like the air in breathing, which helps the note fa inside the machine to pass into the note mi. This sol on entering the machine also sounds as do. The matter which has now been obtained is joined in the upper story by the substance of the cosmic la, which enters the upper story of the machine, also as do.

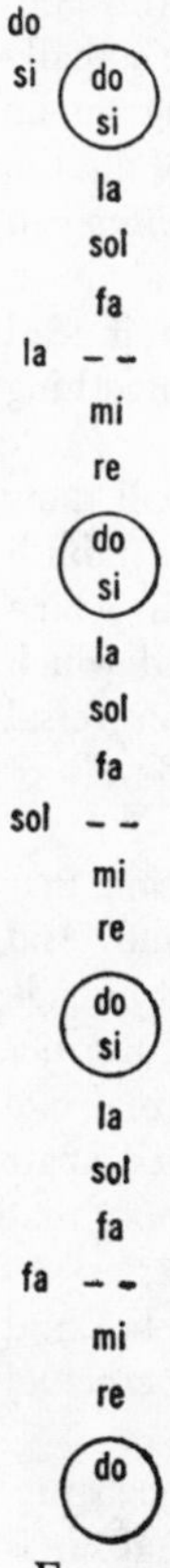

"As we see from this the following notes la, sol, fa serve as food for the machine. In the order of their succession, according to the law of three, la will be the active element, sol the neutralizing, and fa the passive. The active principle reacting with the passive (that is, becoming connected with it by the help of the neutralizing principle) gives a certain definite result. This is represented symbolically thus:

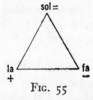

Fig. 55

"This symbol points out that the substance fa in being mixed with the substance la gives as a result the substance sol. And as this process proceeds in the octave, developing as it were inside the note fa, it is therefore possible to say that fa without changing its pitch acquires the properties of sol.

"All that has been said about the octaves of radiation and about the food octaves in the human organism has a direct connection with the symbol consisting of a circle divided into nine parts. This symbol, as the expression of a perfect synthesis, contains within itself all the elements of the laws it represents, and from it can be extracted, and by its help transmitted, everything that is connected with these octaves and much else besides."

G. returned to the enneagram many times and in various connections. "Each completed whole, each cosmos, each organism, *each plant*, is an enneagram," he said. "But not each of these enneagrams has an inner triangle. The inner triangle stands for the presence of higher elements, according to the scale of 'hydrogens,' in a given organism. This inner triangle is possessed by such plants, for example, as hemp, poppy, hops, tea, coffee, tobacco, and many other plants which play a definite role in the life of man. The study of these plants can reveal much for us in regard to the enneagram.

do
si (do si)
la
sol
fa
la − −
mi
re
(do si)
la
sol
fa
sol − −
mi
re
(do si)
la
sol
fa
fa − −
mi
re
(do)

Fig. 54

"Speaking in general it must be understood that the enneagram is a *universal symbol.* All knowledge can be included in the enneagram and with the help of the enneagram it can be interpreted. And in this connection only what a man is able to put into the enneagram does he actually *know,* that is, understand. What he cannot put into the enneagram he does not understand. For the man who is able to make use of it, the enneagram makes books and libraries entirely unnecessary. *Everything* can be included and read in the enneagram. A man may be quite alone in the desert and he can trace the enneagram in the sand and in it read the eternal laws of the universe. And every time he can learn something new, something he did not know before.

"If two men who have been in different schools meet, they will draw the enneagram and with its help they will be able at once to establish which of them knows more and which, consequently, stands upon which step, that is to say, which is the elder, which is the teacher and which the pupil. The enneagram is the fundamental hieroglyph of a universal language which has as many different meanings as there are levels of men.

"The enneagram is *perpetual motion,* the same *perpetual motion* that men have sought since the remotest antiquity and could never find. And it is clear why they could not find *perpetual motion.* They sought outside themselves that which was within them; and they attempted to *construct* perpetual motion as a machine is constructed, whereas real perpetual motion is a part of another perpetual motion and cannot be created apart from it. The enneagram is a schematic diagram of *perpetual motion,* that is, of a machine of eternal movement. But of course it is necessary to know how to read this diagram. The understanding of this symbol and the ability to make use of it give man very great power. It is *perpetual motion* and it is also the *philosopher's stone* of the alchemists.

"The knowledge of the enneagram has for a very long time been preserved in secret and if it now is, so to speak, made available to all, it is only in an incomplete and theoretical form of which nobody could make any practical use without instruction from a man who knows.

"In order to understand the enneagram it must be thought of as in motion, as moving. A motionless enneagram is a dead symbol; the living symbol is in motion."

Much later—it was in the year 1922—when G. organized his Institute in France and when his pupils were studying dances and dervish exercises, G. showed them exercises connected with the "movement of the enneagram." On the floor of the hall where the exercises took place a large enneagram was drawn and the pupils who took part in the exercises stood on the spots marked by the numbers 1 to 9. Then they began to move in the direction of the numbers of the period in a very interesting movement, turning round one another at the points of meeting, that is, at the points where the lines intersect in the enneagram.

G. said at that time that exercises of moving according to the enneagram would occupy an important place in his ballet the "Struggle of the Magicians." And he said also that, without taking part in these exercises, without occupying some kind of place in them, it was almost impossible to understand the enneagram.

"It is possible to experience the enneagram by movement," he said. "The rhythm itself of these movements would suggest the necessary ideas and maintain the necessary tension; without them it is not possible to feel what is most important."

There was yet another drawing of the enneagram which was made under his direction in Constantinople in the year 1920. In this drawing inside the enneagram were shown the four beasts of the Apocalypse—the bull, the lion, the man, and the eagle—and with them a dove. These additional symbols were connected with "centers."

In connection with talks about the meaning of the enneagram as a universal symbol G. again spoke of the existence of a universal "philosophical" language.

"Men have tried for a long time to invent a universal language," he said. "And in this instance, as in many others, they seek something which has long since been found and try to think of and *invent* something which has been known and in existence a long time. I said before that there exist not one but three universal languages, to speak more exactly, three degrees. The first degree of this language already makes it possible for people to express their own thoughts and to understand the thoughts of others in relation to things concerning which ordinary language is powerless."

"In what relation do these languages stand to art?" someone asked. "And does not art itself represent that 'philosophical language' which others seek intellectually?"

"I do not know of which art you speak," said G. "There is art and art. You have doubtless noticed that during our lectures and talks I have often been asked various questions by those present relating to art but I have always avoided talks on this subject. This was because I consider all ordinary talks about art as absolutely meaningless. People speak of one thing while they imply something quite different and they have no idea whatever what they are implying. At the same time it is quite useless to try to explain the real relationship of things to a man who does not know the A B C about himself, that is to say, about man. We have talked together now for some time and by now you ought to know this A B C, so that I can perhaps talk to you now even about art.

"You must first of all remember that there are two kinds of art, one quite different from the other—objective art and subjective art. All that you know, all that you call art, is subjective art, that is, something that I do not call art at all because it is only objective art that I call art.

"To define what I call objective art is difficult first of all because you ascribe to subjective art the characteristics of objective art, and secondly because when you happen upon objective works of art you take them as being on the same level as subjective works of art.

"I will try to make my idea clear. You say—an artist creates. I say this only in connection with objective art. In relation to subjective art I say that with him 'it is created.' You do not differentiate between these, but this is where the whole difference lies. Further you ascribe to subjective art an invariable action, that is, you expect works of subjective art to have the same reaction on everybody. You think, for instance, that a funeral march should provoke in everyone sad and solemn thoughts and that any dance music, a *komarinsky* for instance, will provoke happy thoughts. But in actual fact this is not so at all. Everything depends upon association. If on a day that a great misfortune happens to me I hear some lively tune for the first time this tune will evoke in me sad and oppressive thoughts for my whole life afterwards. And if on a day when I am particularly happy I hear a sad tune, this tune will always evoke happy thoughts. And so with everything else.

"The difference between objective art and subjective art is that in objective art the artist really does 'create,' that is, he makes what he intended, he puts into his work whatever ideas and feelings he wants to put into it. And the action of this work upon men is absolutely definite; they will, of course each according to his own level, receive the same ideas and the same feelings that the artist wanted to transmit to them. There can be nothing accidental either in the creation or in the impressions of objective art.

"In subjective art everything is accidental. The artist, as I have already said, does not create; with him 'it creates itself.' This means that he is in the power of ideas, thoughts, and moods which he himself does not understand and over which he has no control whatever. They rule him and they express themselves in one form or another. And when they have accidentally taken this or that form, this form just as accidentally produces on man this or that action according to his mood, tastes, habits, the nature of the hypnosis under which he lives, and so on. There is nothing invariable; nothing is definite here. In objective art there is nothing indefinite."

"Would not art disappear in being definite in this way?" asked one of us. "And is not a certain indefiniteness, elusiveness, exactly what distinguishes art from, let us say, science? If this indefiniteness is taken away, if you take away the fact that the artist himself does not know what he will obtain or what impression his work will produce on people, it will then be a 'book' and not art."

"I do not know what you are talking about," said G. "We have different standards: I measure the merit of art by its *consciousness* and you measure it by its *unconsciousness*. We cannot understand one another. A work of objective art ought to be a 'book' as you call it; the only difference is that the artist transmits his ideas not directly through words or signs or hieroglyphs, but through certain feelings which he excites consciously and in an orderly way, knowing what he is doing and why he does it."

"Legends," said one of those present, "have been preserved of statues of gods in ancient Greek temples, for example the statue of Zeus at Olympia, which produced upon everybody a definite and always identical impression."

"Quite true," said G., "and even the fact that such stories exist shows that people understood that the difference between real and unreal art lay precisely in this, an invariable or else an accidental action."

"Can you not indicate other works of objective art?" "Is there anything that it is possible to call objective in contemporary art?" "When was the last objective work of art created?" Nearly everyone present began to put these and similar questions to G.

"Before speaking of this," said G., "principles must be understood. If you grasp the principles you will be able to answer these questions yourselves. But if you do not grasp them nothing that I may say will explain anything to you. It was exactly about this that it was said—they will see with their eyes and will not perceive, they will hear with their ears and will not understand.

"I will cite you one example only—music. Objective music is all based on 'inner octaves.' And it can obtain not only definite psychological results but definite physical results. There can be such music as would freeze water. There can be such music as would kill a man instantaneously. The Biblical legend of the destruction of the walls of Jericho by music is precisely a legend of objective music. Plain music, no matter of what kind, will not destroy walls, but objective music indeed can do so. And not only can it destroy but it can also build up. In the legend of Orpheus there are hints of objective music, for Orpheus used to impart knowledge by music. Snake charmers' music in the East is an approach to objective music, of course very primitive. Very often it is simply one note which is long drawn out, rising and falling only very little; but in this single note 'inner octaves' are going on all the time and melodies of 'inner octaves' which are inaudible to the ears but felt by the emotional center. And the snake hears this music or, more strictly speaking, he feels it, and he obeys it. The same music, only a little more complicated, and men would obey it.

"So you see that art is not merely a language but something much bigger. And if you connect what I have just said with what I said earlier about the different levels of man's being, you will understand what is said about art. Mechanical humanity consists of men number one, number two, and number three and they, of course, can have subjective art only. Objective art requires at least flashes of objective consciousness; in order to understand these flashes properly and to make proper use of them a great inner unity is necessary and a great control of oneself."

Chapter Fifteen

AMONG the talks of the period I am describing, that is, the end of 1916, G. several times touched upon questions of religion. And when anyone asked him anything connected with religion G. invariably began by emphasizing the fact that there is something very wrong at the basis of our usual attitude towards problems of religion.

"In the first place," he always said, "religion is a relative concept; it corresponds to the level of a man's being; and one man's religion might not be at all suitable for another man, that is to say, the religion of a man of one level of being is not suitable for a man of another level of being.

"It must be understood that the religion of man number one is of one kind; the religion of man number two is of another kind; and the religion of man number three is of a third kind. The religion of man number four, number five, and further is something of a kind totally different from the religion of man number one, number two, and number three.

"In the second place religion is doing; a man does not merely *think* his religion or feel it, he 'lives' his religion as much as he is able, otherwise it is not religion but fantasy or philosophy. Whether he likes it or not he shows his attitude towards religion by his actions and he can show his attitude *only by his actions*. Therefore if his actions are opposed to those which are demanded by a given religion he cannot assert that he belongs to that religion. The vast majority of people who call themselves Christians have no right whatever to do so, because they not only fail to carry out the demands of their religion but they do not even think that these demands ought to be carried out.

"Christianity forbids murder. Yet all that the whole of our progress comes to is progress in the technique of murder and progress in warfare. How can we call ourselves Christians?

"No one has a right to call himself a Christian who does not carry out Christ's precepts. A man can say that he *desires* to be a Christian if he tries to carry out these precepts. If he does not think of them at all, or laughs at them, or substitutes for them some inventions of his own, or simply forgets about them, he has no right whatever to call himself a Christian.

"I took the example of war as it is the most striking example. But even without war the whole of life is exactly the same. People call themselves Christians but they do not realize that not only do they not want, but they are unable, to be Christians, because in order to be a Christian it is necessary not only to desire, but *to be able,* to be one.

"Man in himself is not one, he is not 'I,' he is 'we,' or to speak more correctly, he is 'they.' Everything arises from this. Let us suppose that a man decides according to the Gospels to turn the left cheek if somebody strikes him on the right cheek. But one 'I' decides this either in the mind or in the emotional center. One 'I' knows of it, one 'I' remembers it—the others do not. Let us imagine that it actually happens, that some-body strikes this man. Do you think he will turn the left cheek? Never. He will not even have time to think about it. He will either strike the face of the man who struck him, or he will begin to call a policeman, or he will simply take to flight. His moving center will react in its customary way, or as it has been taught to react, before the man realizes what he is doing.

"Prolonged instruction, prolonged training, is necessary to be able to turn the cheek. And if this training is mechanical—it is again worth nothing because in this case it means that a man will turn his cheek because he cannot do anything else."

"Cannot prayer help a man to live like a Christian?" asked someone.

"It depends upon whose prayer," said G. "The prayer of subjective man, that is, of man number one, number two, and number three, can give only subjective results, namely, self-consolation, self-suggestion, self-hyp-nosis. It cannot give objective results."

"But cannot prayer in general give objective results?" asked one of those present.

"I have already said, it depends upon whose prayer," G. replied.

"One must learn to pray, just as one must learn everything else. Who-ever knows how to pray and is able to concentrate in the proper way, his prayer can give results. But it must be understood that there are different prayers and that their results are different. This is known even from or-dinary divine service. But when we speak of prayer or of the results of prayer we always imply only one kind of prayer—petition, or we think that petition can be united with all other kinds of prayers. This of course is not true. Most prayers have nothing in common with petitions. I speak of ancient prayers; many of them are much older than Christianity. These prayers are, so to speak, *recapitulations*; by repeating them aloud or to him-self a man endeavors to experience what is in them, their whole content, with his mind and his feeling. And a man can always make new prayers for himself. For example a man says—'I want to be serious.' But the whole point is in how he says it. If he repeats it even ten thousand times a day and is thinking of how soon he will finish and what will there be for dinner and the like, then it is not prayer but simply self-deceit. But it can become a prayer if a man recites the prayer in this way: He says 'I' and tries at the same time to think of everything he knows about 'I.' It does not exist, there is no single 'I,' there is a multitude of petty, clamorous, quarrelsome 'I's. But he wants to be one 'I'—the master; he recalls the carriage, the horse, the driver, and the master. 'I' is master. 'Want'—he thinks of the meaning of 'I want.' Is he able to want? With him 'it wants' or 'it does not want' all the time. But to this 'it wants' and 'it does not want' he strives to oppose his own 'I want' which is connected with the aims of work on himself, that is, to introduce the third force into the customary combination of the two forces, 'it wants' and 'it does not want.' 'To be'—the man thinks of what to be, what 'being,' means. The being of a mechanical man with whom everything happens. The being of a man who can do. It is possible 'to be' in different ways. He wants 'to be' not merely in the sense of existence but in the sense of greatness of power. The words 'to be' acquire weight, a new meaning for him. 'Serious' —the man thinks what it means to be serious. How he answers himself is very important. If he understands what this means, if he defines correctly for himself what it means to be serious, and feels that he truly desires it, then his prayer can give a result in the sense that strength can be added to him, that he will more often notice when he is not serious, that he will overcome himself more easily, make himself be serious. In exactly the same way a man can 'pray'—'I want to remember myself.' 'To remember'—what does 'to remember' mean? The man must think about memory. How little he remembers! How often he forgets what he has decided, what he has seen, what he knows! His whole life would be different if he could remember. All ills come because he does not remember. 'Myself'—again he returns to himself. Which self does he want to remember? Is it worth while remembering the whole of himself? How can he distinguish what he wants to remember? The idea of work! How can he connect himself with the idea of the work, and so on, and so on.

"In Christian worship there are very many prayers exactly like this, where it is necessary to reflect upon each word. But they lose all sense and all meaning when they are repeated or sung mechanically.

"Take the ordinary *God have mercy upon me!* What does it mean? A man is appealing to God. He should think a little, he should make a comparison and ask himself what God is and what he is. Then he is asking God to have *mercy* upon him. But for this God must first of all *think of him, take notice of him.* But is it worth while taking notice of him? What is there in him that is worth thinking about? And who is to think about him? God himself. You see, all these thoughts and yet many others should pass through his mind when he utters this simple prayer. *And then it is precisely these thoughts which could do for him what he asks God to do.* But what can he be thinking of and what result can a prayer give if he merely repeats like a parrot: 'God have mercy! God have mercy! God have mercy!' You know yourselves that this can give no result whatever.

"Generally speaking we know very little about Christianity and the form of Christian worship; we know nothing at all of the history and origin of a number of things. For instance, the church, the temple in which gather the faithful and in which services are carried out according to special rites; where was this taken from? Many people do not think about this at all. Many people think that the outward form of worship, the rites, the singing of canticles, and so on, were invented by the fathers of the church. Others think that this outward form has been taken partly from pagan religions and partly from the Hebrews. But all of it is untrue. The question of the origin of the Christian church, that is, of the Christian temple, is much more interesting than we think. To begin with, the church and worship in the form which they took in the first centuries of Christianity could not have been borrowed from paganism because there was nothing like it either in the Greek or Roman cults or in Judaism. The Jewish synagogue, the Jewish temple, Greek and Roman temples of various gods, were something quite different from the Christian church which made its appearance in the first and second centuries. The Christian church is—a school concerning which people have forgotten that it is a school. Imagine a school where the teachers give lectures and perform explanatory demonstrations without knowing that these are lectures and demonstrations; and where the pupils or simply the people who come to the school take these lectures and demonstrations for ceremonies, or rites, or 'sacraments,' i.e., magic. This would approximate to the Christian church of our times.

"The Christian church, the Christian form of worship, was not invented by the fathers of the church. It was all taken in a ready-made form from Egypt, only not from the Egypt that we know but from one which we do not know. This Egypt was in the same place as the other but it existed much earlier. Only small bits of it survived in historical times, and these bits have been preserved in secret and so well that we do not even know where they have been preserved.

"It will seem strange to many people when I say that this prehistoric Egypt was Christian many thousands of years before the birth of Christ, that is to say, that its religion was composed of the same principles and ideas that constitute true Christianity. Special schools existed in this prehistoric Egypt which were called 'schools of repetition.' In these schools a public repetition was given on definite days, and in some schools perhaps even every day, of the entire course in a condensed form of the sciences that could be learned at these schools. Sometimes this repetition lasted a week or a month. Thanks to these repetitions people who had passed through this course did not lose their connection with the school and retained in their memory all they had learned. Sometimes they came from very far away simply in order to listen to the repetition and went away feeling their connection with the school. There were special days of the year when the repetitions were particularly complete, when they were carried out with particular solemnity—and these days themselves possessed a symbolical meaning.

"These 'schools of repetition' were taken as a model for Christian churches—the form of worship in Christian churches almost entirely represents the course of repetition of the science dealing with the universe and man. Individual prayers, hymns, responses, all had their own meaning in this repetition as well as holidays and all religious symbols, though their meaning has been forgotten long ago."

Continuing, G. quoted some very interesting examples of the explanations of various parts of orthodox liturgy. Unfortunately no notes were made at the time and I will not undertake to reconstruct them from memory.

The idea was that, beginning with the first words, the liturgy so to speak goes through the process of creation, recording all its stages and transitions. What particularly astonished me in G.'s explanations was the extent to which so much has been preserved in its pure form and how little we understand of all this. His explanations differed very greatly from the usual theological and even from mystical interpretations. And the principal difference was that he did away with a great many allegories. I mean to say that it became obvious from his explanations that we take many things for allegories in which there is no allegory whatever and which ought to be understood much more simply and psychologically. What he said before about the Last Supper serves as a good example of this.

"Every ceremony or rite has a value if it is performed without alteration," he said. "A ceremony is a book in which a great deal is written. Anyone who understands can read it. One rite often contains more than a hundred books."

Indicating what had been preserved up to our time, G. at the same time pointed out what had been lost and forgotten. He spoke of sacred dances which accompanied the "services" in the "temples of repetition" and which were not included in the Christian form of worship. He also spoke of various exercises, and of special postures for different prayers, that is, for different kinds of meditation; about acquiring control over the breathing and of the necessity of being able to tense or relax any group of muscles, or the muscles of the whole body at will; and about many other things having relation, so to speak, to the "technique" of religion.

On one occasion, in connection with the description of exercises in concentration and bringing the attention from one part of the body to another, G. asked:

"When you pronounce the word 'I' aloud, have you noticed where *this word sounds* in you?"

We did not at once understand what he meant. But we very soon began to notice that when pronouncing the word 'I' some of us definitely felt as if this word *sounded* in the head, others felt it in the chest, and others over the head—outside the body.

I must mention here that personally I was entirely unable to evoke this sensation in myself and that I have to rely on others.

G. listened to all these remarks and said that there was an exercise connected with this which, according to him, had been preserved up to our time in the monasteries of Mount Athos.

A monk kneels or stands in a certain position and, lifting his arms, which are bent at the elbows, he says—*Ego* aloud and drawn out while listening at the same time where the word "Ego" sounds.

The purpose of this exercise is to feel "I" every moment a man thinks of himself and to bring "I" from one center to another.

G. many times pointed out the necessity of studying this forgotten "technique" as well as the impossibility of attaining results of any kind on the way of religion without it, excepting purely subjective results.

"You must understand," he said, "that every real religion, that is, one that has been created by learned people for a definite aim, consists of two parts. One part teaches *what* is to be done. This part becomes common knowledge and in the course of time is distorted and departs from the original. The other part teaches *how* to do what the first part teaches. This part is preserved in secret in special schools and with its help it is always possible to rectify what has been distorted in the first part or to restore what has been forgotten.

"Without this second part there can be no knowledge of religion or in any case such knowledge would be incomplete and very subjective.

"This secret part exists in Christianity also as well as in other religions and it teaches *how* to carry out the precepts of Christ and what they really mean."

I must quote here still one more talk with G., once again in connection with cosmoses.

"This is connected with Kant's ideas of phenomena and noumena," I said. "But after all this is the whole point.—The earth as a three-dimensional body is the 'phenomenon,' as a six-dimensional body, the 'noumenon.' "

"Perfectly true," said G., "only add here also the idea of scale. If Kant had introduced the idea of scale into his arguments many things he wrote would be very valuable. This was the only thing he lacked."

I thought while listening to G. that Kant would have been very surprised at this pronouncement. But the idea of scale was very near to me. And I realized that with this as a starting point it was possible to find very much that is new and unexpected in things which we think we know.

About a year afterwards while developing the ideas of the cosmoses in connection with problems of time I obtained a table of time in different cosmoses of which I will speak later on.

On one occasion when speaking of the orderly connectedness of everything in the universe, G. dwelt on "organic life on earth."

"To ordinary knowledge," he said, "organic life is a kind of accidental appendage violating the integrity of a mechanical system. Ordinary knowledge does not connect it with anything and draws no conclusions from the fact of its existence. But you should already understand that there is nothing accidental or unnecessary in nature and that there can be nothing; everything has a definite function; everything serves a definite purpose. Thus organic life is an indispensable link in the chain of the worlds which cannot exist without it just as it cannot exist without them. It has been said before that organic life transmits planetary influences of various kinds to the earth and that it serves to feed the moon and to enable it to grow and strengthen. But the earth also is growing; not in the sense of size but in the sense of greater consciousness, greater receptivity. The planetary influences which were sufficient for her at one period of her existence become insufficient, she needs the reception of finer influences. To receive finer influences a finer, more sensitive receptive apparatus is necessary. Organic life, therefore, has to evolve, to adapt itself to the needs of the planets and the earth. Likewise also the moon can be satisfied at one period with the food which is given her by organic life of a certain quality, but afterwards the time comes when she ceases to be satisfied with this food, cannot grow on it, and begins to get hungry. Organic life must be able to satisfy this hunger, otherwise it does not fulfill its function, does not answer its purpose. This means that in order to answer its purpose organic life must evolve and stand on the level of the needs of the planets, the earth, and the moon.

"We must remember that the ray of creation, as we have taken it, from the Absolute to the moon, is like a branch of a tree—a growing branch. The end of this branch, the end out of which come new shoots, is the moon. If the moon does not grow, if it neither gives nor promises to give new shoots, it means that either the growth of the whole ray of creation will stop or that it must find another path for its growth, give out some kind of lateral branch. At the same time from what has been said before we see that the growth of the moon depends on organic life on earth. It follows that the growth of the ray of creation depends on organic life on earth. If this organic life disappears or dies the whole branch will immediately wither, in any case all that part of the branch which lies beyond organic life. The same thing must happen, only more slowly, if organic life is arrested in its development, in its evolution, and fails to respond to the demands made upon it. The branch may wither. This must be remembered. To the ray of creation, or let us say to its part earth–moon, exactly the same possibility of development and growth has been given as is given to each separate branch of a big tree. But the accomplishment of this growth is not at all guaranteed, it depends upon the harmonious and right action of its own tissues. The development of one tissue stops and all the others stop. Everything that can be said of the ray of creation or of its part earth–moon equally refers to organic life on earth. Organic life on earth is a complex phenomenon in which the separate parts depend upon one another. General growth is possible only on the condition that the 'end of the branch' grows. Or, speaking more precisely, there are in organic life tissues which are evolving, and there are tissues which serve as food and medium for those which are evolving. Then there are evolving cells within the evolving tissues, and cells which serve as food and medium for those which are evolving. In each separate evolving cell there are evolving parts and there are parts which serve as food for those which are evolving. But always and in everything it must be remembered that evolution is never guaranteed, it is possible only and it can stop at any moment and in any place.

"The evolving part of organic life is humanity. Humanity also has its evolving part but we will speak of this later; in the meantime we will take humanity as a whole. If humanity does not evolve it means that the evolution of organic life will stop and this in its turn will cause the growth of the ray of creation to stop. At the same time if humanity ceases to evolve it becomes useless from the point of view of the aims for which it was created and as such it may be destroyed. In this way the cessation of evolution may mean the destruction of humanity.

"We have no clues from which we are able to tell in what period of planetary evolution we exist and whether the moon and the earth have time to await the corresponding evolution of organic life or not. But people who know may, of course, have exact information about it, that is, they may know at what stage in their possible evolution are the earth, the moon, and humanity. We cannot know this but we should bear in mind that the number of possibilities is never infinite.

"At the same time in examining the life of humanity as we know it historically we are bound to acknowledge that humanity is moving in a circle. In one century it destroys everything it creates in another and the progress in mechanical things of the past hundred years has proceeded at the cost of losing many other things which perhaps were much more important for it. Speaking in general there is every reason to think and to assert that humanity is at a standstill and from a standstill there is a straight path to downfall and degeneration. A standstill means that a process has become balanced. The appearance of any one quality immediately evokes the appearance of another quality opposed to it. The growth of knowledge in one domain evokes the growth of ignorance in another; refinement on the one hand evokes vulgarity on the other; freedom in one connection evokes slavery in another; the disappearance of some superstitions evokes the appearance and the growth of others; and so on.

"Now if we recall the law of octaves we shall see that a balanced process proceeding in a certain way cannot be changed at any moment it is desired. It can be changed and set on a new path only at certain 'crossroads.' In between the 'crossroads' nothing can be done. At the same time if a process passes by a 'crossroad' and nothing happens, nothing is done, then nothing can be done afterwards and the process will continue and develop according to mechanical laws; and even if people taking part in this process foresee the inevitable destruction of everything, they will be unable to do anything. I repeat that something can be done only at certain moments which I have just called 'crossroads' and which in octaves we have called the 'intervals' mi–fa and si–do.

"Of course there are very many people who consider that the life of humanity is not proceeding in the way in which according to their views it ought to go. And they invent various theories which in their opinion ought to change the whole life of humanity. One invents one theory. Another immediately invents a contradictory theory. And both expect everyone to believe them. And many people indeed do believe either one or the other. Life naturally takes its own course but people do not stop believing in their own or other people's theories and they believe that it is possible to do something. All these theories are certainly quite fantastic, chiefly because they do not take into account the most important thing, namely, the subordinate part which humanity and organic life play in the world process. Intellectual theories put man in the center of everything; everything exists for him, the sun, the stars, the moon, the earth. They even forget man's relative size, his nothingness, his transient existence, and other things. They assert that a man if he wishes is able to change his whole life, that is, to organize his life on rational principles. And all the time new theories appear evoking in their turn opposing theories; and all these theories and the struggle between them undoubtedly constitute one of the forces which keep humanity in the state in which it is at present. Besides, all these theories for general welfare and general equality are not only unrealizable, but they would be fatal if they were realized. Everything in nature has its aim and its purpose, both the inequality of man and his suffering. To destroy inequality would mean destroying the possibility of evolution. To destroy suffering would mean, first, destroying a whole series of perceptions for which man exists, and second, the destruction of the 'shock,' that is to say, the force which alone can change the situation. And thus it is with all intellectual theories.

"The process of evolution, of that evolution which is possible for humanity as a whole, is completely analogous to the process of evolution possible for the individual man. And it begins with the same thing, namely, a certain group of cells gradually becomes conscious; then it attracts to itself other cells, subordinates others, and gradually makes the whole organism serve its aims and not merely eat, drink, and sleep. This is evolution and there can be no other kind of evolution. In humanity as in individual man everything begins with the formation of a conscious nucleus. All the mechanical forces of life fight against the formation of this conscious nucleus in humanity, in just the same way as all mechanical habits, tastes and weaknesses fight against conscious self-remembering in man."

"Can it be said that there is a *conscious force* which fights against the evolution of humanity?" I asked.

"From a certain point of view it can be said," said G.

I am putting this on record because it would seem to contradict what he said before, namely, that there are only two forces struggling in the world—"consciousness" and "mechanicalness."

"Where can this force come from?" I asked.

"It would take a long time to explain," said G., "and it cannot have a practical significance for us at the present moment. There are two processes which are sometimes called 'involutionary' and 'evolutionary.' The difference between them is the following: An involutionary process begins consciously in the Absolute but at the next step it already becomes mechanical—and it becomes more and more mechanical as it develops; an evolutionary process begins half-consciously but it becomes more and more conscious as its develops. But consciousness and conscious opposition to the evolutionary process can also appear at certain moments in the involutionary process. From where does this consciousness come? From the evolutionary process of course. The evolutionary process must proceed without interruption. Any stop causes a separation from the fundamental process. Such separate fragments of consciousnesses which have been stopped in their development can also unite and at any rate for a certain time can live by struggling against the evolutionary process. After all it merely makes the evolutionary process more interesting. Instead of struggling against mechanical forces there may, at certain moments, be a struggle against the intentional opposition of fairly powerful forces though they are not of course comparable with those which direct the evolutionary process. These opposing forces may sometimes even conquer. The reason for this consists in the fact that the forces guiding evolution have a more limited choice of means; in other words, they can only make use of certain means and certain methods. The opposing forces are not limited in their choice of means and they are able to make use of every means, even those which only give rise to a temporary success, and in the final result they destroy both evolution and involution at the point in question.

"But as I have said already, this question has no practical significance for us. It is only important for us to establish the indications of evolution beginning and the indications of evolution proceeding. And if we remember the full analogy between humanity and man it will not be difficult to establish whether humanity can be regarded as evolving.

"Are we able to say for instance that life is governed by a group of conscious people? Where are they? Who are they? We see exactly the opposite: that life is governed by those who are the least conscious, by those who are most asleep.

"Are we able to say that we observe in life a preponderance of the best, the strongest, and the most courageous elements? Nothing of the sort. On the contrary we see a preponderance of vulgarity and stupidity of all kinds.

"Are we able to say that aspirations towards unity, towards unification, can be observed in life? Nothing of the kind of course. We only see new divisions, new hostility, new misunderstandings.

"So that in the actual situation of humanity there is nothing that points to evolution proceeding. On the contrary when we compare humanity with a man we quite clearly see a growth of personality at the cost of essence, that is, a growth of the artificial, the unreal, and what is foreign, at the cost of the natural, the real, and what is one's own.

"Together with this we see a growth of automatism.

"Contemporary culture requires automatons. And people are undoubtedly losing their acquired habits of independence and turning into automatons, into parts of machines. It is impossible to say where is the end of all this and where the way out—or whether there is an end and a way out. One thing alone is certain, that man's slavery grows and increases. Man is becoming a willing slave. He no longer needs chains. He begins to grow fond of his slavery, to be proud of it. And this is the most terrible thing that can happen to a man.

"Everything I have said till now I have said about the whole of humanity. But as I pointed out before, the evolution of humanity can proceed only through the evolution of a certain group, which, in its turn, will influence and lead the rest of humanity.

"Are we able to say that such a group exists? Perhaps we can on the basis of certain signs, but in any event we have to acknowledge that it is a very small group, quite insufficient, at any rate, to subjugate the rest of humanity. Or, looking at it from another point of view, we can say that humanity is in such a state that it is unable to accept the guidance of a conscious group."

"How many people could there be in this conscious group?" someone asked.

"Only they themselves know this," said G.

"Does it mean that they all know each other?" asked the same person again.

"How could it be otherwise?" asked G. "Imagine that there are two or three people who are awake in the midst of a multitude of sleeping people. They will certainly know each other. But those who are asleep cannot know them. How many are they? We do not know and we cannot know until we become like them. It has been clearly said before that each man can only see on the level of his own being. But *two hundred conscious people*, if they existed and if they found it necessary and legitimate, could change the whole of life on the earth. But either there are not enough of them, or they do not want to, or perhaps the time has not yet come, or perhaps other people are sleeping too soundly.

"We have approached the problems of esotericism.

"It was pointed out before when we spoke about the history of humanity that the life of humanity to which we belong is governed by forces proceeding from two different sources: first, planetary influences which act entirely mechanically and are received by the human masses as well as by individual people quite involuntarily and unconsciously; and then, influences proceeding from inner circles of humanity whose existence and significance the vast majority of people do not suspect any more than they suspect planetary influences.

"The humanity to which we belong, namely, the whole of historic and prehistoric humanity known to science and civilization, in reality constitutes only the *outer circle of humanity*, within which there are several other circles.

"So that we can imagine the whole of humanity, known as well as unknown to us, as consisting so to speak of several concentric circles.

"The inner circle is called the 'esoteric'; this circle consists of people who have attained the highest development possible for man, each one of whom possesses individuality in the fullest degree, that is to say, an indivisible 'I,' all forms of consciousness possible for man, full control over these states of consciousness, the whole of knowledge possible for man, and a free and independent will. They cannot perform actions opposed to their understanding or have an understanding which is not expressed by actions. At the same time there can be no discords among them, no differences of understanding. Therefore their activity is entirely co-ordinated and leads to one common aim without any kind of compulsion because it is based upon a common and identical understanding.

"The next circle is called the 'mesoteric,' that is to say, the middle. People who belong to this circle possess all the qualities possessed by the members of the esoteric circle with the sole difference that their knowledge is of a more theoretical character. This refers, of course, to knowledge of a cosmic character. They know and understand many things which have not yet found expression in their actions. They know more than they do. But their understanding is precisely as exact as, and therefore precisely identical with, the understanding of the people of the esoteric circle. Between them there can be no discord, there can be no misunderstanding. One understands in the way they all understand, and all understand in the way one understands. But as was said before, this understanding compared with the understanding of the esoteric circle is somewhat more theoretical.

"The third circle is called the 'exoteric,' that is, the outer, because it is the outer circle of the inner part of humanity. The people who belong to this circle possess much of that which belongs to people of the esoteric and mesoteric circles but their cosmic knowledge is of a more philosophical character, that is to say, it is more abstract than the knowledge of the mesoteric circle. A member of the *mesoteric* circle *calculates,* a member of the exoteric circle *contemplates.* Their understanding may not be expressed in actions. But there cannot be differences in understanding between them. What one understands all the others understand.

"In literature which acknowledges the existence of esotericism humanity is usually divided into two circles only and the 'exoteric circle' as opposed to the 'esoteric,' is called ordinary life. In reality, as we see, the 'exoteric circle' is something very far from us and very high. For ordinary man this is already 'esotericism.'

" 'The outer circle' is the circle of mechanical humanity to which we belong and which alone we know. The first sign of this circle is that among people who belong to it there is not and there cannot be a common understanding. Everybody understands in his own way and all differently. This circle is sometimes called the circle of the 'confusion of tongues,' that is, the circle in which each one speaks in his own particular language, where no one understands another and takes no trouble to be understood. In this circle mutual understanding between people is impossible excepting in rare exceptional moments or in matters having no great significance, and which are confined to the limits of the given *being.* If people belonging to this circle become *conscious of this general lack of understanding* and acquire a desire to understand and to be understood, then it means they have an unconscious tendency towards the inner circle because mutual understanding begins only in the exoteric circle and is possible only there. But the consciousness of the lack of understanding usually comes to people in an altogether different form.

"So that the possibility for people to understand depends on the possibility of penetrating into the exoteric circle where understanding begins.

"If we imagine humanity in the form of four concentric circles we can imagine four gates on the circumference of the third inner circle, that is, the exoteric circle, through which people of the mechanical circle can penetrate.

"These four gates correspond to the four ways described before.

"The first way is the way of the fakir, the way of people number one, of people of the physical body, instinctive-moving-sensory people without much mind and without much heart.

"The second way is the way of the monk, the religious way, the way of people number two, that is, of emotional people. The mind and the body should not be too strong.

"The third way is the way of the yogi. This is the way of the mind, the way of people number three. The heart and the body must not be particularly strong, otherwise they may be a hindrance on this way.

"Besides these three ways yet a fourth way exists by which can go those who cannot go by any of the first three ways.

"The fundamental difference between the first three ways, that is, the way of the fakir, the way of the monk, and the way of the yogi, and the fourth way consists in the fact that they are tied to permanent forms which have existed throughout long periods of history almost without change. At the basis of these institutions is religion. Where schools of yogis exist they differ little outwardly from religious schools. And in different periods of history various societies or orders of fakirs have existed in different countries and they still exist. These three traditional ways are *permanent* ways within the limits of our historical period.

"Two or three thousand years ago there were yet other ways which no longer exist and the ways now in existence were not so divided, they stood much closer to one another.

"The fourth way differs from the old and the new ways by the fact that it is never a permanent way. It has no definite forms and there are no institutions connected with it. It appears and disappears governed by some particular laws of its own.

"The fourth way is never without some *work* of a definite significance, is never without some *undertaking* around which and in connection with which it can alone exist. When this work is finished, that is to say, when the aim set before it has been accomplished, the fourth way disappears, that is, it disappears from the given place, disappears in its given form, continuing perhaps in another place in another form. Schools of the fourth way exist for the needs of the work which is being carried out in connection with the proposed undertaking. They never exist by themselves as schools for the purpose of education and instruction.

"Mechanical help cannot be required in any work of the fourth way. Only conscious work can be useful in all the undertakings of the fourth way. Mechanical man cannot give conscious work so that the first task of the people who begin such a work is to create conscious assistants.

"The work itself of schools of the fourth way can have very many forms and many meanings. In the midst of the ordinary conditions of life the only chance a man has of finding a 'way' is in the possibility of meeting with the beginning of work of this kind. But the chance of meeting with such work as well as the possibility of profiting by this chance depends upon many circumstances and conditions.

"The quicker a man grasps the aim of the work which is being executed, the quicker can he become useful to it and the more will he be able to get from it for himself.

"But no matter what the fundamental aim of the work is, the schools continue to exist only while this work is going on. When the work is done the schools close. The people who began the work leave the stage. Those who have learned from them what was possible to learn and have reached the possibility of continuing on the way independently begin in one form or another their own personal work.

"But it happens sometimes that when the school closes a number of people are left who were *round about* the work, who saw the outward aspect of it, *and saw the whole of the work in this outward aspect.*

"Having no doubts whatever of themselves or in the correctness of their conclusions and understanding they decide to continue the work. To continue this work they form new schools, teach people what they have themselves learned, and give them the same promises that they themselves received. All this naturally can only be outward imitation. But when we look back on history it is almost impossible for us to distinguish where the real ends and where the imitation begins. Strictly speaking almost everything we know about various kinds of occult, masonic, and alchemical schools refers to such imitation. We know practically nothing about real schools excepting the results of their work and even that only if we are able to distinguish the results of real work from counterfeits and imitations.

"But such pseudo-esoteric systems also play their part in the work and activities of esoteric circles. Namely, they are the intermediaries between humanity which is entirely immersed in the materialistic life and schools which are interested in the education of a certain number of people, as much for the purposes of their own existences as for the purposes of the work of a *cosmic* character which they may be carrying out. The very idea of esotericism, the idea of initiation, reaches people in most cases through pseudo-esoteric systems and schools; and if there were not these pseudo-esoteric schools the vast majority of humanity would have no possibility whatever of hearing and learning of the existence of anything greater than life because the truth in its pure form would be inaccessible for them. By reason of the many characteristics of man's being, particularly of the contemporary being, truth can only come to people *in the form of a lie*—only in this form are they able to accept it; only in this form are they able to digest and assimilate it. Truth undefiled would be, for them, indigestible food.

"Besides, a grain of truth in an unaltered form is sometimes found in pseudo-esoteric movements, in church religions, in occult and theosophical schools. It may be preserved in their writings, their rituals, their traditions, their conceptions of the hierarchy, their dogmas, and their rules.

"Esoteric schools, that is, *not pseudo-esoteric schools*, which perhaps exist in some countries of the East, are difficult to find because they exist there in the guise of ordinary monasteries and temples. Tibetan monasteries are usually built in the form of four concentric circles or four concentric courts divided by high walls. Indian temples, especially those in Southern India, are built on the same plan but in the form of squares, one contained within the other. Worshipers usually have access to the first outer court, and sometimes, as an exception, persons of another religion and Europeans; access to the second court is for people of a certain caste only or for those having special permission; access to the third court is only for persons belonging to the temple; and access to the fourth is only for Brahmins and priests. Organizations of this kind which, with minor variations, are everywhere in existence, enable esoteric schools to exist without being recognized. Out of dozens of monasteries one is a school. But how is it to be recognized? If you get inside it you will only be inside the first court; to the second court only pupils have access. But this you do not know, you are told they belong to a special caste. As regards the third and fourth courts you cannot even know anything about them. And you can, in fact, observe the same order in all temples and until you are told you cannot distinguish an esoteric temple or monastery from an ordinary one.

"The idea of initiation, which reaches us through pseudo-esoteric systems, is also transmitted to us in a completely wrong form. The legends concerning the outward rites of initiation have been created out of the scraps of information we possess in regard to the ancient Mysteries. The Mysteries represented a special kind of way in which, side by side with a difficult and prolonged period of study, theatrical representations of a special kind were given which depicted in allegorical forms the whole path of the evolution of man and the world.

"Transitions from one level of being to another were marked by ceremonies of presentation of a special kind, that is, initiation. But a change of being cannot be brought about by any rites. Rites can only mark an accomplished transition. And it is only in pseudo-esoteric systems in which there is nothing else except these rites, that they begin to attribute to the rites an independent meaning. It is supposed that a rite, in being transformed into a sacrament, transmits or communicates certain forces to the initiate. This again relates to the psychology of an imitation way. There is not, nor can there be, any outward initiation. In reality only self-initiation, self-presentation exist. Systems and schools can indicate methods and ways, but no system or school whatever can do for a man the work that he must do himself. Inner growth, a change of being, depend entirely upon the work which a man must do on himself."

Chapter Sixteen

B Y THIS time, that is, by November, 1916, the position of affairs in Russia had begun to assume a very gloomy aspect. Up to this time we, at any rate most of us, had by some miracle kept clear of "events." Now "events" were drawing nearer to us, that is to say, they were drawing nearer to each one of us personally, and we could no longer fail to notice them.

It in no way enters into my task either to describe or to analyze what was taking place. At the same time it was such an exceptional period that I cannot altogether avoid all mention of what was going on around us, otherwise I should have to admit that I had been both blind and deaf. Besides, nothing could have given such material for the study of the "mechanicalness" of events, that is, of the entire and complete absence of any element of will, as the observation of events at this period. Some things appeared or might have appeared to be dependent on somebody's will, but even this was illusion and in reality it had never been so clear that everything *happens*, that no one *does* anything.

In the first place it was clear to everyone who was able and who wanted to see it that the war was coming to an end and that it was coming to an end by itself through some deep inner weariness and from the realization, though dull and obscure yet firmly rooted, of the senselessness of all this horror. No one believed now in words of any kind. No attempts of any kind to galvanize the war were able to lead to anything. At the same time it was impossible to stop anything and all talk about the necessity of continuing the war or of the necessity of stopping the war merely showed the helplessness of the human mind which was even incapable of realizing its own helplessness. In the second place it was clear that the crash was approaching. And it was clear that nobody could stop anything nor could they avert events or direct them into some safe channel. Everything was going in the only way it could go and it could go in no other way. I was particularly struck at this time by the position of professional politicians of the left who, up to this time, had played a passive role but were now preparing to pass into an active one. To be precise they showed themselves to be the blindest, the most unprepared, and the most incapable of understanding what they were really doing, where they were going to, what they were preparing, even for themselves.

I remember Petersburg so well during the last winter of its life. Who could have known then, even assuming the very worst, that this was its last winter? But too many people hated this city and too many feared it and its last days were numbered.

Our meetings continued. During the last months of 1916 G. did not come to Petersburg but some of the members of our group went to Moscow and brought back new diagrams and some notes which had been made by G.'s Moscow pupils under his instruction.

Many new people made their appearance in our groups at this time, and although it was clear that everything must come to some unknown end, G.'s system gave us a certain feeling of confidence and security. We often spoke at this time of how we should feel in the midst of all this chaos if we had not got the system which was becoming more and more our own. Now we could not imagine how we could live without it and find our way in the labyrinth of all existing contradictions.

This period marks the beginning of talks about Noah's Ark. I had always considered the myth of Noah's Ark to be an esoteric allegory. Many of our company had now begun to see that this myth was not merely an allegory of the general idea of esotericism but was, at the same time, a plan of any esoteric work, our own included. The system itself was an "ark" in which we could hope to save ourselves at the time of the "flood."

G. arrived only at the beginning of February, 1917. At one of the first talks he showed us an entirely new side to everything he had spoken about up till then.

"So far," he said, "we have looked upon the 'table of hydrogens' as a table of vibrations and of the densities of matter which are in an inverse proportion to them. We must now realize that the density of vibrations and the density of matter express many other properties of matter. For instance, till now we have said nothing about the *intelligence* or the consciousness of matter. Meanwhile the speed of vibrations of a matter shows the degree of intelligence of the given matter. You must remember that there is nothing dead or inanimate in nature. Everything in its own way is alive, everything in its own way is intelligent and conscious. Only this consciousness and intelligence is expressed in a different way on different levels of being—that is, on different scales. But you must understand once and for all that nothing is dead or inanimate in nature, there are simply different degrees of animation and different scales.

"The 'table of hydrogens,' while serving to determine the density of matter and the speed of vibrations, serves at the same time to determine the degree of intelligence and consciousness because the degree of consciousness corresponds to the degree of density or the speed of vibrations. This means that the denser the *matter* the less conscious it is, the less intelligent. And the denser the *vibrations*, the more conscious and the more intelligent the matter.

"Really dead matter begins where vibrations cease. But under ordinary conditions of life on the earth's surface we have no concern with *dead matter*. And science cannot procure it. All the matter we know is living matter and in its own way it is intelligent.

"In determining the degree of density of matter the 'table of hydrogens' also determines by this the degree of intelligence. This means that in making comparisons between the matters which occupy different places in the 'table of hydrogens,' we determine not only their density but also their intelligence. And not only can we say how many times this or that 'hydrogen' is denser or lighter than another, but we can say how many times one 'hydrogen' is more intelligent than another.

"The application of the 'table of hydrogens' for the determination of the different properties of things and of living creatures which consist of many 'hydrogens' is based on the principle that in each living creature and in each thing there is one definite 'hydrogen' which is the center of gravity; it is, so to speak, the 'average hydrogen' of all the 'hydrogens' constituting the given creature or thing. To find this 'average hydrogen' we will, to begin with, speak about living creatures. First of all it is necessary to know the level of being of the creature in question. The level of being is primarily determined by the number of stories in the given machine. So far we have spoken only about man. And we have taken man as a three-story structure. We cannot speak about animals and man at one and the same time because animals differ in a radical way from man. The highest animals we know consist of two stories and the lowest of only one story."

G. made a drawing.

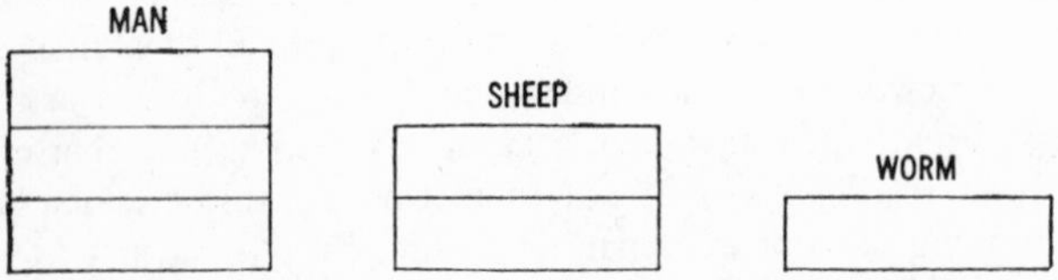

Fig. 56

"A man consists of three stories.

"A sheep consists of two stories.

"A worm consists of only one story.

"At the same time the lower and middle stories of a man are, so to speak, equivalent to the sheep, and the lower story—to the worm. So that it can be said that a man consists of a man, a sheep, and a worm, and that a sheep consists of a sheep and a worm. Man is a complex creature; the level of his being is determined by the level of being of the creatures of which he is composed. The sheep and the worm may play a bigger or a smaller part in man. Thus the worm plays the chief part in man number one; in man number two—the sheep; and in man number three—man. But these definitions are important only in individual cases. In a general sense 'man' is determined by the center of gravity of the middle story.

"The center of gravity of the middle story of man is 'hydrogen' 96. The intelligence of 'hydrogen' 96 determines the average intelligence of 'man,' that is, the physical body of man. The center of gravity of the 'astral body' will be 'hydrogen' 48. The center of gravity of the third body will be 'hydrogen' 24, and the center of gravity of the fourth body will be 'hydrogen' 12.

"If you remember the diagram of the four bodies of man which has been previously given and in which the 'average hydrogens' of the upper story were shown, it will be easier for you to understand what I am now saying."

G. drew this diagram:

48	24	12	6
96	48	24	12
192	96	48	24.

Fig. 57

"The center of gravity of the upper story is only one 'hydrogen' higher than the center of gravity of the middle story. And the center of gravity of the middle story is one 'hydrogen' higher than the center of gravity of the lower story.

"But, as I have already said, to determine the level of being by the 'table of hydrogens' it is usual to take the middle story.

"With this as a point of departure it is possible for example to solve such problems:

"Let us suppose Jesus Christ to be man number eight, how many times is Jesus Christ more intelligent than a table?

"A table has no stories. It lies wholly between 'hydrogen' 1536 and 'hydrogen' 3072 according to the third scale of the 'table of hydrogens.' Man number eight is 'hydrogen' 6. This is the center of gravity of the middle story of man number eight. If we are able to calculate how many times 'hydrogen' 6 is more intelligent than 'hydrogen' 1536 we shall know how many times man number eight is more intelligent than a table. But, in this connection, it must be remembered that 'intelligence' is determined not by the density of matter but by the density of vibrations. The density of vibrations, however, increases not by doubling as in the octaves of 'hydrogens' but in an entirely different progression which many times outnumbers the first. If you know the exact coefficient of this increase you will be in a position to solve this problem. I only want to show that, however strange it looks, the problem can be solved.

"Partly in connection with what I have just said it is imperative that you should understand the principles of the classification and the definition of living beings from the cosmic point of view, from the point of view of their cosmic existence. In ordinary science classification is made according to external traits—bones, teeth, functions; mammals, vertebrates, rodents, and so on; in *exact knowledge* classification is made according to cosmic traits. As a matter of fact there are exact traits, identical for everything living, which allows us to establish the class and the species of a given creature with the utmost exactitude, both in relation to other creatures as well as to its own place in the universe.

"These traits are the traits of being. The cosmic level of being of every living creature is determined:

"First of all by what this creature eats,

"Secondly by what he breathes, and

"Thirdly by the medium in which it lives.

"These are the three cosmic traits of being.

"Take for instance man. He feeds on 'hydrogen' 768, breathes 'hydrogen' 192, and lives in 'hydrogen' 192. There is no other being like him on our planet. Although there are beings higher than he is. Animals such as the dog *can* feed on 'hydrogen' 768 but they can also feed on a lower 'hydrogen' not 768 but approaching 1536, food of a kind impossible for man. A bee feeds on a 'hydrogen' much higher than 768, even higher than 384, but it lives in a hive in an atmosphere where man could not live. From an outward point of view man is an animal. But he is an animal of a different order from all other animals.

"Let us take another example—a flour worm. It feeds on flour, a 'hydrogen' far coarser than 'hydrogen' 768 because the worm can also live on rotten flour. Let us say that this also is 1536. It breathes 'hydrogen' 192 and lives in 'hydrogen' 1536.

"A fish feeds on 'hydrogen' 1536, lives in 'hydrogen' 384, and breathes 'hydrogen' 192.

"A tree feeds on 'hydrogen' 1536, breathes only partly 'hydrogen' 192 and partly 'hydrogen' 96, and lives partly in 'hydrogen' 192 and partly in 'hydrogen' 3072 (soil).

"If you try to continue these definitions you will see that this plan, so simple at the first glance, makes it possible to determine the most subtle distinctions between classes of living beings, especially if you bear in mind that 'hydrogens,' taking them as we have by octaves, are very broad concepts. For example, we took it that a dog, a fish, and a flour worm alike feed on 'hydrogen' 1536, implying by this 'hydrogen' substances of organic origin which are not good for human food. Now, if we realize that these substances in their turn can be divided into definite classes, we shall see the possibility of very exact definitions. It is exactly the same with air and exactly the same with the medium.

"These cosmic traits of being are immediately connected with the definition of intelligence according to the 'table of hydrogens.'

"The intelligence of a *matter* is determined by the creature for whom it can serve as food. For example, which is more intelligent from this point of view, a raw potato or a baked potato? A raw potato can serve as food for pigs and a baked potato as food for man. A baked potato is more intelligent than a raw potato.

"If these principles of classification and definition are understood in the right way, many things become clear and comprehensible. No living being can change its food at will, or the air it breathes, or the medium in which it lives. The cosmic order of each being determines its food as well as the air it breathes and the medium in which it lives.

"When we talked before about the octaves of food in the three-story factory we saw that all the finer 'hydrogens' needed for the working, the growth, and the evolution of the organism were prepared from three kinds of food, that is, from *food* in the strict meaning of the word—eatables and drink, from *air* which we breathe, and from *impressions*. Now let us suppose that we could improve the quality of food and air, feed, let us say, on 'hydrogen' 384 instead of 768 and breathe 'hydrogen' 96 instead of 192. How much simpler and easier the preparation of fine matters in the organism would be then. But the whole point is that this is impossible. The organism is adapted to transform precisely *these* coarse matters into fine matters, and if you give it fine matters instead of coarse matters it will not be in a position to transform them and it will very soon die. Neither air nor food can be changed. But impressions, that is, the quality of the impressions possible to man, are not subject to any cosmic law. Man cannot improve his food, he cannot improve the air. *Improvement* in this case would be actually *making things worse*. For instance 'hydrogen' 96 instead of 192 would be either very rarefied air or very hot incandescent gases which man cannot possibly breathe; *fire* is 'hydrogen' 96. It is exactly the same with food. 'Hydrogen' 384 is water. If man could improve his food, that is, make it finer, he would have to feed on water and breathe fire. It is clear that this is impossible. But while it is not possible for him to improve his food and air he can improve his impressions to a very high degree and in this way introduce fine 'hydrogens' into the organism. It is precisely on this that the possibility of evolution is based. A man is not at all obliged to feed on the dull impressions of $H48$, he can have both $H24$, $H12$, and $H6$, and even $H3$. This changes the whole picture and a man who makes higher 'hydrogens' the food for the upper story of his machine will certainly differ from one who feeds on the lower 'hydrogens.' "

In one of the following conversations G. again returned to the subject of classification according to cosmic traits.

"There is still another system of classification," he said, "which you also ought to understand. This is a classification in an altogether different ratio of octaves. The first classification by 'food,' 'air,' and medium definitely refers to 'living beings' as we know them, including plants, that is to say, to individuals. The other classification of which I shall now speak leads us far beyond the limits of what we call 'living beings' both upwards, higher than living beings, as well as downwards, lower than living beings, and it deals not with individuals but with classes in a very wide sense. Above all this classification shows that there are no jumps whatever in nature. In nature everything is connected and everything is alive. The diagram of this classification is called the 'Diagram of Everything Living.'

"According to this diagram every kind of creature, every degree of being, is defined *by what serves as food for this kind of creature or being of a given level and for what they themselves serve as food*, because in the cosmic order each class of creature feeds on a definite class of lower creature and is food for a definite class of higher creatures."

G. drew a diagram in the form of a ladder with eleven squares. And in each square excepting the two higher he put three circles with numbers. (See Fig. 58.)

"Each square denotes a level of being," he said. "The 'hydrogen' in the lower circle shows what the given class of creatures feeds on. The 'hydrogen' in the upper circle shows the class which feeds on these features. And the 'hydrogen' in the middle circle is the average 'hydrogen' of this class showing what these creatures are.

"The place of man is the seventh square from the bottom or the fifth square from the top. According to this diagram man *is* 'hydrogen' 24, he feeds on 'hydrogen' 96, and is himself food for 'hydrogen' 6. The square next below man will be 'vertebrates'; the next 'invertebrates.' Invertebrates are 'hydrogen' 96. Consequently man feeds on 'invertebrates.'

"Do not for the moment look for contradictions but try to understand what this may mean. And equally do not compare this diagram with others. According to the diagram of food man feeds on 'hydrogen' 768; according to this diagram on 'hydrogen' 96. Why? What does it mean? Both the one is right and the other is right. Later, when you grasp this you will piece everything together into one.

"The square next below is—plants. The next—minerals, the next— metals, which constitute a separate cosmic group among minerals; and the following square has no name in our language because we never meet

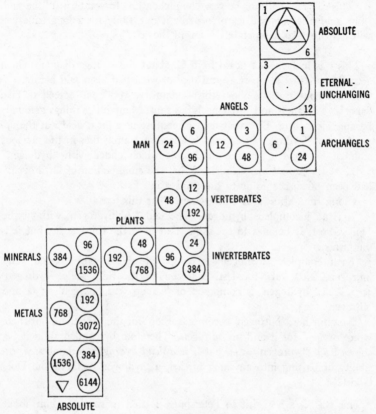

ABSOLUTE

ETERNAL-
UNCHANGING

ANGELS

MAN

ARCHANGELS

VERTEBRATES

PLANTS

MINERALS

INVERTEBRATES

METALS

ABSOLUTE

FIG. 58

with matter in this state on the earth's surface. This square comes into contact with the Absolute. You remember we spoke before about 'Holy the Firm.' This is 'Holy the Firm.' "

At the bottom of the last square he placed a small triangle with its apex below.

"Now, on the other side of man is square 3, 12, 48. This is a class of creatures which we do not know. Let us call them 'angels.' The next square—1, 6, 24; let us call these beings 'archangels.' "

In the following square he put figures 3 and 12 and two circles, each with a point at their centers, and called it the "Eternal Unchanging," and in the next square he put the figures 1 and 6; he put a circle in the middle and in this circle a triangle containing another circle with a point at its center and called it the "Absolute."

"This diagram will not be very comprehensible to you at first," he said. "But gradually you will learn to make it out. Only for a long time you will have to take it separately from all the rest."

This was in fact all I heard from G. about this strange diagram which actually appeared to upset a great deal of what had been said before.

In our conversations about this diagram we very soon agreed to take "angels" as planets and "archangels" as suns. Many other things gradually became clear to us. But what used to confuse us a great deal was the appearance of "hydrogen" 6144 which was absent altogether in the previous scale of "hydrogens" in the third scale which ended with "hydrogen" 3072. At the same time, G. insisted that the enumeration of "hydrogens" had been taken according to the third scale.

A long time afterwards I asked him what this meant.

"It is an incomplete 'hydrogen,'" he said. "A 'hydrogen' without the Holy Ghost. It belongs to the same, that is to the third, scale, but it is unfinished.

"Each complete 'hydrogen' is composed of 'carbon,' 'oxygen,' and 'nitrogen.' Now take the last 'hydrogen' of the third scale, 'hydrogen' 3072. This 'hydrogen' is composed of 'carbon' 512, 'oxygen' 1536, and 'nitrogen' 1024.

"Now further: 'Nitrogen' becomes 'carbon' for the next triad, but there is no 'oxygen' for it and no 'nitrogen.' Therefore by condensation it becomes itself 'hydrogen' 6144, but *it is a dead hydrogen* without any possibility of passing into anything further, a 'hydrogen' without the Holy Ghost."

This was G.'s last visit to Petersburg. I tried to speak to him about impending events. But he said nothing definite on which I could base my own actions.

A very interesting event took place in connection with his departure. This happened at the railway station. We were all seeing him off at the Nikolaevsky Station. G. was standing talking to us on the platform by the carriage. He was the usual G. we had always known. After the second bell he went into the carriage—his compartment was next to the door— and came to the window.

He was different! In the window we saw another man, not the one who had gone into the train. He had changed during those few seconds. It is very difficult to describe what the difference was, but on the platform he had been an ordinary man like anyone else, and from the carriage a man of quite a different order was looking at us, with a quite exceptional importance and dignity in every look and movement, as though he had sud-

denly become a ruling prince or a statesman of some unknown kingdom
to which he was traveling and to which we were seeing him off.

Some of our party could not at the time clearly realize what was happening but they felt and experienced in an emotional way something
that was outside the ordinary run of phenomena. All this lasted only a
few seconds. The third bell followed the second bell almost immediately, and the train moved out.

I do not remember who was the first to speak of this "transfiguration"
of G. when we were left alone, and then it appeared that we had all seen
it, though we had not all equally realized what it was while it was taking
place. But all, without exception, had felt something out of the ordinary.

G. had explained to us earlier that if one mastered the art of plastics
one could completely alter one's appearance. He had said that one could
become beautiful or hideous, one could compel people to notice one or
one could become *actually invisible*.

What was this? Perhaps it was a case of "plastics."

But the story is not yet over. In the carriage with G. there traveled
A. (a well-known journalist) who was at that time being sent away from
Petersburg (this was just before the revolution). We who were seeing
G. off, were standing at one end of the carriage while at the other end
stood a group seeing A. off.

I did not know A. personally, but among the people seeing him off
were several acquaintances of mine and even a few friends; two or three
of them had been at our meetings and these were going from one group
to the other.

A few days later the paper to which A. was contributing contained
an article "On the Road" in which A. described the thoughts and impressions he had on the way from Petersburg to Moscow. A strange
Oriental had traveled in the same carriage with him, who, among the
bustling crowd of speculators who filled the carriage, had struck him by
his extraordinary dignity and calm, exactly as though these people were
for him like small flies upon whom he was looking from inaccessible
heights. A. judged him to be an "oil king" from Baku, and in conversation with him several enigmatic phrases that he received still further
strengthened him in his conviction that here was a man whose millions
grew while he slept and who looked down from on high at bustling people
who were striving to earn a living and to make money.

My fellow traveler kept to himself also; he was a Persian or Tartar, a silent
man in a valuable astrakhan cap; he had a French novel under his arm. He was
drinking tea, carefully placing the glass to cool on the small window-sill table;
he occasionally looked with the utmost contempt at the bustle and noise of
those extraordinary, gesticulating people. And they on their part glanced at
him, so it seemed to me, with great attention, if not with respectful awe. What

interested me most was that he seemed to be of the same southern Oriental type as the rest of the group of speculators, a flock of vultures flying somewhere into Agrionian space in order to tear some carrion or other—he was swarthy, with jet-black eyes, and a mustache like Zelim-Khan. . . . Why does he so avoid and despise his own flesh and blood? But to my good fortune he began to speak to me.

"They worry themselves a great deal," he said, his face motionless and sallow, in which the black eyes, polite as in the Oriental, were faintly smiling.

He was silent and then continued:

"Yes, in Russia at present there is a great deal of business out of which a clever man could make a lot of money." And after another silence he explained:

"After all it is the war. Everyone wants to be a millionaire."

In his tone, which was cold and calm, I seemed to detect a kind of fatalistic and ruthless boasting which verged on cynicism, and I asked him somewhat bluntly:

"And you?"

"What?" he asked me back.

"Do not you also want this?"

He answered with an indefinite and slightly ironical gesture.

It seemed to me that he had not heard or had not understood and I repeated:

"Don't you make profits too?"

He smiled particularly quietly and said with gravity:

"We always make a profit. It does not refer to us. War or no war it is all the same to us. We always make a profit."

[G. of course meant esoteric work, "the collecting of knowledge" and the collecting of people. But A. understood that he was speaking about "oil."]

It would be curious to talk and become more closely acquainted with the psychology of a man whose capital depends entirely upon order in the solar system, which is hardly likely to be upset and whose interests for that reason prove to be higher than war and peace. . . .

In this way A. concluded the episode of the "oil king."

We were particularly surprised by G.'s "French novel." Either A. invented it, adding it to his own impressions, or G. actually made him "see," that is, presume, a French novel in some small volume in a yellow, or perhaps not even a yellow cover, because G. of course did not read French.

After G.'s departure up to the time of the revolution we only got news of him from Moscow once or twice.

All my plans had long since been upset. I had not succeeded in publishing the books I intended to publish; I had not succeeded in preparing anything for foreign editions, although right from the beginning of the war I saw that my literary work would have to be transferred abroad. During the past two years I had given up all my time to G.'s work, to his groups, to talks connected with this work, to journeys from Petersburg, and had completely neglected my own affairs.

Meanwhile the atmosphere was growing gloomier. One felt that something was bound to happen and that very soon. Only those upon whom the course of events still appeared to depend were unable to see and feel this. The marionettes failed to understand the danger that threatened them and did not understand that the very same wire which pulls the villain with a knife in his hand from behind a bush makes them turn and look at the moon. A marionette theater is worked in the same way.

Finally the storm broke. The "great bloodless revolution" took place— the most absurd and the most blatant lie that could have been thought of. But the most extraordinary thing of all was that people who were there on the spot, in the center of everything that was happening, could believe in this lie, and in the midst of all the murders could speak about a "bloodless" revolution.

I remember that we spoke at the time of the "power of theories." People who had been waiting for the revolution, who had put all their hopes in it, and who had seen in it liberation from something, could not and did not want to see what was *actually* happening and only saw what in their opinion ought to be happening.

When I read in a leaflet printed on one side only the news of the abdication of Nicholas II, I felt that in this lay the center of gravity of everything that took place.

"Ilovaisky may rise from the grave and write at the end of his books: 'March, 1917, the end of Russian history,'" I said to myself.

I had no feelings whatever for the dynasty, but I simply did not wish to deceive myself as many others were doing at that time.

I had always been interested in the person of the Emperor Nicholas II; he seemed to me to be a remarkable man in many ways; but he was completely misunderstood and did not understand his own self. That I was right is proved by the end of his diary which was published by the bolsheviks and which referred to the time when, betrayed and left by all, he showed wonderful strength and even greatness of mind.

But after all, the matter had nothing to do with him as a person but with the principle of the *unity of power* and the responsibility to this power which he represented in himself. It is true that this principle was denied by a considerable part of the Russian intelligentsia. And for the people the word "czar" had long lost all significance. But this word still had a very great significance for the army and for the bureaucratic machine which, though very imperfect, nevertheless worked and held everything together. The "czar" was the indispensable central part of this machine. The abdication of the "czar" at such a moment was bound to destroy the whole machine. *And we had nothing else.* The celebrated "public-co-operation," for the creation of which so many sacrifices had been made, proved, as was to be expected, to be bluff. To create anything "on the move" was impossible. Events were moving at a breathless speed. The army broke up in a few days. The war in reality had stopped earlier. But the new government did not wish to recognize this fact. A fresh lie was started. But what was most surprising in all this was that people should find something to be glad about. I do not speak of the soldiers who broke out of barracks or out of the trains which were ready to carry them to the slaughter. But I was surprised at our "intelligentsia" who from "patriots" immediately became "revolutionaries" and "socialists." Even the *Novoe Vremya* suddenly became a socialist paper. The famous Menshikov wrote one article "about freedom," but he evidently could not swallow it himself and gave it up.

I think it was about a week after the *revolution* that I collected the principal members of our group in the quarters of Dr. S. and put before them my views on the position of affairs. I said that in my opinion there was no sense whatever in staying in Russia and that we must go abroad; that in all probability there would be only a short period of comparative calm before everything began to break up and collapse. We could do nothing to help and our own work would be impossible.

I cannot say that my idea met with much approval. Most of them did not realize the gravity of the situation and to them it seemed possible that everything might yet calm down and become normal. Others were in the grip of the customary illusion that everything that happens is for the best. To them my words seemed to be exaggeration; at all events they saw no need for haste. For others the main difficulty was that we had heard nothing from G. and had had no news of him for a long time. Since the revolution there had only been one letter from Moscow and from this it was possible to gather that G. had gone away but no one knew where. Finally we decided to wait.

At that time there were two groups numbering about forty persons in all and there were also some separate groups which met at irregular intervals.

Soon after the meeting at Dr. S.'s house I received a postcard from G. written a month before in the train on the way from Moscow to the Caucasus which had been lying all that time at the post office owing to the prevailing disorders. It was evident from the postcard that G. had left Moscow before the revolution and as yet knew nothing of events when he wrote it. He wrote that he was going to Alexandropol; he asked me to continue the work of the groups until his arrival and he promised to return by Easter.

This communication faced me with a very difficult problem. I thought it senseless and stupid to stay in Russia. At the same time I did not want to leave without G.'s consent or, to speak more truthfully, without him. And he had gone to the Caucasus, and his card, written in February, that is, before the revolution, could have no relation to the present situation. At length I again decided to wait although I saw that what was possible today might become impossible tomorrow.

Easter came—there was no news whatever from G. A week after Easter came a telegram in which he said he was arriving in May. The first "provisional government" came to an end. It was already more difficult to get abroad. Our groups continued to meet and awaited G.

Our conversations used often to come back to the "diagrams," especially when we had to talk to new people in our groups. It seemed to me the whole time that in these "diagrams" which we had got from G. there was a good deal left unsaid and I often thought that perhaps gradually with a deeper study of the "diagrams," their inner meaning and significance would be revealed to us.

Once when looking through some notes, made the year before, I paused at the "cosmoses." I wrote earlier that the "cosmoses" particularly attracted me because they coincided completely with the "period of dimensions" of the *New Model of the Universe*. I mentioned also the difficulties which arose for us at one time in connection with the different understanding of the "Microcosmos" and the "Tritocosmos." But by this time we had already decided to understand "man" as the "Microcosmos" and *organic life on earth* as the "Tritocosmos." And in the last conversation G. silently approved of this. G.'s words about different time in different cosmoses intrigued me very much. And I tried to remember what P. had said to me about our "sleep and waking" and about the "breath of organic life." For a long time I could make nothing of it. Then I remembered G.'s words that "time is breath."

"'What is breath?' I asked myself.

"Three seconds. Man in a normal state takes about twenty full breaths, that is inhalations and exhalations, to the minute. Consequently a full breath takes about three seconds.

"Why are 'sleep and waking' the 'breath of organic life'? What are sleep and waking?

"For man and for all organisms commensurable with him and living in similar conditions to him, even for plants, this is *twenty-four hours*.

Besides this, sleep and waking *are breath*, as for instance plants when asleep, that is, at night, exhale, and when awake, that is, by day, inhale; in exactly the same way for all mammals as well as for man there is a difference in the absorption of oxygen and CO_2 by night and day, in sleep and waking."

Reasoning in this way I arranged the periods of breath and of sleep and waking in the following way:

Microcosmos	breath	3 seconds
	sleep and waking	24 hours
Tritocosmos	breath	24 hours
	sleep and waking	?

TABLE 5

I obtained a simple "rule of three." By dividing 24 hours by 3 seconds I got 28,800. By dividing 28,800 (days and nights) by 365 I got within a small fraction 79 years. This interested me. Seventy-nine years, continuing the former reasoning, made up the sleep and waking of "organic life." This did not correspond to anything that I could think of in organic life, but it represented the life of man.

"Could one not continue the parallel further?" I asked myself. I arranged the figures I had obtained in the following way:

Microcosmos *Man*	*Tritocosmos* *Organic Life*	*Mesocosmos* *Earth*
Breath: 3 secs.	Breath: 24 hours	Breath: 79 years
Day and Night: 24 hours	Day and Night: 79 years	
Life: 79 years		

TABLE 6

Again 79 years meant nothing in the life of the earth. I thereupon multiplied 79 years by 28,800 and got a little less than two and a half million years. By multiplying 2,500,000 years by 30,000 for shortness, I got a number of eleven figures, 75,000,000,000 years. This figure should signify the duration of life of the earth. So far these figures appear logically possible; two and a half million years for organic life and seventy-five milliards of years for the earth.

"But then there are cosmoses lower than man," I said to myself. "Let us try to see in what relation they will stand to this."

I decided to take two cosmoses *on the left* (on the diagram) from the Microcosmos, understanding by them first, comparatively large microscopic cells, and then the smallest (admissible), almost invisible cells.

Such a division of cells into two categories cannot be said to have been definitely accepted by science. But if we think of dimensions within the "micro-world," then it is impossible not to admit that this world consists of two worlds as distinct in themselves as is the world of people and the world of comparatively large micro-organisms and cells. I got the following picture:

	Small Cells	Large Cells	Micro-cosmos (Man)	Organic Life	Earth
Breath	—	—	3 secs.	24 hours	79 yrs.
Day and Night	—	3 secs.	24 hours	79 yrs.	2½ mn. yrs.
Life	3 secs.	24 hours	79 years	2½ mn. yrs.	75 milliard yrs.

TABLE 7

This was coming out very interestingly. Twenty-four hours made up the period of life of the cell. And although the period of life of individual cells can in no way be considered as established, many investigators have arrived at the fact that for a specialized cell such as a cell of the human organism the period of life appears to be *precisely 24 hours*. The breath of the cell equals 3 seconds. This told me nothing. But the 3 seconds of life of the small cell told me a great deal and it indicated above all why it is so difficult to see these cells, although from their size they should be accessible to vision in a good microscope.

I tried further to see what would be obtained if "breath," that is, 3 seconds, were divided by 30,000. *One ten-thousandth part of a second* was obtained. The period of duration of an electric spark and at the same time the *period of the shortest visual impression*. For convenience in calculating and for clarity I took 30,000 instead of 28,800. Four periods appeared to be connected with, or separated from, one another by one and the same coefficient of 30,000—the shortest visual impression, breath or the period of inhalation and exhalation, the period of sleep and waking, and the average maximum of life. At the same time each of these periods denoted a corresponding but lower period in a higher cosmos and a corresponding higher period in a lower cosmos. Without as yet drawing any conclusions I tried to make a fuller table, that is, to bring into it all the cosmoses and to add two more of the lower ones, the first of which I called the "molecule" and the second the "electron." Then, again for clarity when multiplying by 30,000, I took only round numbers and only two coefficients, 3 and 9; thus 2,400,000 I took as 3,000,000; 72,000,000,000 I took as 90,000,000,000; and 79 as 80, and so on.

I obtained the following table:

	ELECTRON	MOLECULE	SMALL CELLS	LARGE CELLS	MICRO-COSMOS (Man)	TRITO-COSMOS	MESO-COSMOS	DEUTERO-COSMOS	MACRO-COSMOS	AYO-COSMOS	PROTO-COSMOS
IMPRESSION					$\frac{1}{10,000}$ second	3 seconds	24 hours	80 years	3 million years	90 milliard years	3.10^{15} years (number of 16 figures)
BREATH				$\frac{1}{10,000}$ second	3 seconds	24 hours	80 years	3 million years	90 milliard years	3.10^{15} years (number of 16 figures)	9.10^{19} years (number of 20 figures)
DAY and NIGHT			$\frac{1}{10,000}$ second	3 seconds	24 hours	80 years	3 million years	90 milliard years	3.10^{15} years (number of 16 figures)	9.10^{19} years (number of 20 figures)	3.10^{23} years (number of 24 figures)
LIFE	$\frac{1}{300,000,000}$ second	$\frac{1}{10,000}$ second	3 seconds	24 hours	80 years	3 million years	90 milliard years	3.10^{15} years (number of 16 figures)	9.10^{19} years (number of 20 figures)	3.10^{23} years (number of 24 figures)	9.10^{28} years (number of 29 figures)

TABLE 8

This table at once aroused in me very many thoughts. Whether it was possible to look upon it as correct and as defining exactly the relation of one cosmos to another I was as yet unable to say. The coefficient 30,000 seemed too big. But at the same time I remembered that the relation of one cosmos to another is "as zero to infinity." And in the presence of such a relation no coefficient could be too big. "The relation of zero to infinity" was the relation of magnitudes of different dimensions.

G. said that every cosmos was three-dimensional for itself. This meant that the next cosmos above it was four-dimensional for it and the next cosmos below it—two-dimensional. The next one above that—five-dimensional, and the next one lower—one-dimensional. One cosmos in relation to another is a magnitude of a greater or smaller number of dimensions. But there could only be six dimensions or, with zero, seven, and by this table eleven cosmoses were obtained. At the first glance this seemed strange, but only at the first glance, because as soon as I took into account the period of existence of any cosmos in relation to higher cosmoses, the lower cosmoses disappeared long before reaching the seventh dimension. Take for example *man* in relation to the *sun*. The sun appeared as the fourth cosmos in relation to man, taking man as the first cosmos, but man's long life, eighty years, was equal in time to one electric spark for the sun, one shortest possible visual impression.

I tried to remember everything that G. had said about cosmoses.

"Each cosmos is an animate and intelligent being. Each cosmos is born, lives, and dies. In one cosmos it is impossible to understand all the laws of the universe, but *three cosmoses* taken together include in themselves all the laws of the universe, or two cosmoses, the one above and the other below, determine the cosmos which stands between them." "By passing in his consciousness to the level of a higher cosmos, a man by this very fact passes to a level of a lower cosmos."

I felt that here in each word was a clue to the understanding of the structure of the world, but there were too many clues; I did not know from which to start.

How would movement from one cosmos to another appear and where and when would the movement disappear? In what relation would the figures found by me stand to the more or less established figures of cosmic movements, as for instance the speed of movement of the heavenly bodies, the speed of movement of the electrons in an atom, the speed of light, and so on?

When I began to compare the movements of various cosmoses, I obtained some very startling correlations, for example, for the earth, the period of its rotation on its axis was equal to one ten-thousandth of a second, that is, the speed of an electric spark. It is very doubtful whether at such a speed the earth could notice its rotation on its axis. If man rotated, rotation round the sun should occupy about one twenty-fifth of a second, the speed of an instantaneous photograph. And taking into consideration the enormous distance which the earth has had to traverse in this time, the inevitable inference is that the earth could not be conscious of itself as we know it, that is, in the form of a sphere, but must be conscious of itself as a *ring* or as a *long spiral* of rings. The latter was the more probable on the basis of the definition of the *present* as the time of breath. This was by the way the first thought that came into my mind when, a year previously, after the first lecture on cosmoses, G., in adding to what he had said earlier, said that *time is breath*. I thought at the time that perhaps he meant that breath was the unit of time, that is to say, that for direct sensation the period of breath is felt as the *present*. Starting from this and supposing that the sensation of self, that is, of one's body, is connected with the sensation of the present, I came to the conclusion that for the earth, with one breath in eighty years, the sensation of itself should be connected with eighty rings of a spiral. I had obtained a completely unexpected confirmation of all the conclusions and inferences of the *New Model of the Universe*.

Passing to the lower cosmoses, that is, to the cosmoses in my table which stood *to the left* of man, I found already in the first of them the explanation of what had always appeared to me the most enigmatic and most inexplicable in the work of our organism, namely, the astonishing speed, which was almost instantaneous, of many inner processes. It had always seemed to me to be almost charlatanism on the part of physiologists that no due significance had been attributed to this fact. Science, of course, explains only what it can explain. But in this case it ought not, in my opinion, to conceal the fact and avoid it as if it did not exist, but should constantly draw attention to it, put it on record on every suitable occasion. A man who gives no thought to questions of physiology may not be astonished at the fact that the drinking of a cup of strong coffee or a glass of brandy, or inhaling the smoke of a cigarette is immediately felt in the whole body, changes all the inner correlation of forces and the form and character of the reactions, but it ought to be clear to a physiologist that in this quite imperceptible interval of time, approximately equal to one breath, a long series of complicated chemical and other processes are accomplished in the organism. The substance which has entered the organism is carefully analyzed, the smallest divergence from the usual is immediately noticed; in the process of analysis it passes through a series of laboratories; it is resolved into its component parts and mixed with other substances and in the form of these mixtures it is added to the fuel which nourishes the various nerve centers. All this must occupy a great deal of time. The seconds in our time in which this is accomplished make all this entirely fantastic and miraculous. But the fantastic side falls away when we realize that for the large cells which obviously govern the life of the organism, our one breath continues for over *twenty-four hours.* In twenty-four hours, even in half that time, even in a third, that is, in eight hours (which is equal to one second), it is possible to imagine all the processes which have been indicated being completed in an orderly way, exactly as they would be completed in a large and well-arranged "chemical factory" with various laboratories at its service.

Passing further to the cosmos of small cells, which stand on the border or beyond the border of microscopic vision, I again saw an explanation of the inexplicable. For example, cases of almost instantaneous infection by epidemic and infectious diseases in general, particularly those where the causes responsible for the infection have not yet been found. If three seconds is the limit of life for a small cell of this kind, and is equal to the long life of man, then what would be the speed at which these cells multiply when for them fifteen seconds would be equal to four centuries!

Further, passing to the world of molecules, I first of all came face to face with the fact that the brevity of the existence of a molecule is an almost unexpected idea. It is usually supposed that a molecule, although structurally very complicated, taken as the basic, so to speak, *living interior* of the bricks from which matter is built up, exists as long as the matter exists. We are obliged to part from this pleasant and soothing thought. The molecule, which is *alive inside* cannot be *dead outside* and in remaining alive it must, like everything living, be born, live, and die. The term of its life, equal to an electric spark or to one ten-thousandth part of a second, is too small for it to act directly on our imagination. Some comparison, some analogy, is necessary in order to understand what this means. The dying cells of our organism and their replacement by others bring us near to this idea. Dead matter, iron, copper, granite, must be renewed *from within* more quickly than our organism. In reality it changes under our eyes. If you look at a stone, shut your eyes, and immediately open them again, it will now not be the stone which you saw; in it not a single one of the molecules which you saw the first time now remain. But even then you did not see the molecules themselves, but only their traces. I came again to the *New Model of the Universe.* This explained also "why we cannot see molecules," about which I have written in Chapter II of the *New Model of the Universe.*

Further in the last cosmos, that is, in the world of the electron, I felt myself from the very beginning in the world of six dimensions. The question arose for me as to whether the relation of dimensions could not be worked out. The electron as a three-dimensional body is too unsatisfactory. To begin with it exists for one three-hundred-millionth part of a second. This is a quantity far beyond the limits of our possible imagination. It is considered that an electron within an atom moves in its orbit with the speed of one divided by a fifteen-figure number. And since the whole life of an electron in seconds is equal to one divided by a nine-figure number, it follows that during its lifetime an electron makes a number of revolutions round its "sun," equal to a six-figure, or taking into account the coefficient, a seven-figure number.

If we take the earth in its revolution round the sun, then according to my table it makes in the course of its lifetime a number of revolutions round the sun equal to an eleven-figure number. It looks as though there was an enormous difference between a seven-figure and an eleven-figure number but if we compare with the electron not the earth, but Neptune, then the difference will be considerably less, namely the difference between a seven-figure and a nine-figure number, that is, two figures in all instead of four. And besides the speed of revolution of an electron within the atom is a very approximate quantity. It should be remembered that the difference in the periods of revolution of the planets round the sun in our system represents a three-figure number because Mercury revolves 460 times faster than Neptune.

The relation of the life of an electron to our perception appears thus. Our quickest visual perception is equal to 1/10,000 second. The existence of an electron is equal to 1/30,000 of 1/10,000 second, that is, one three-hundred-millionth part of a second, and in that time it makes seven million revolutions round the proton. Consequently, if we were to see an electron as a flash in 1/10,000 second, we should not see the electron in the strict sense of the word, but the *trace* of the electron, consisting of seven million revolutions multiplied by thirty thousand, that is, a spiral with a thirteen-figure number of rings, or, expressed in the language of the *New Model of the Universe*, thirty thousand recurrences of the electron in eternity.

Time, according to the table which I had obtained, undoubtedly went beyond four dimensions. And I was interested by the thought whether it was not possible to apply to this table the Minkovski formula $\sqrt{-1}\ ct$, denoting time as the fourth "world" co-ordinate. The "world" of Minkovski in my opinion corresponded precisely to each of the cosmoses separately. I decided to begin with the "world of electrons" and to take as t the duration of the life of an electron. This coincided with one of the propositions in the *New Model of the Universe*, that *time is life*. The result should show the distance (in kilometers) that light travels during the life of an electron.

In the next cosmos this should be the distance that light travels during the life of a molecule; in the next—during the life of a small cell; then during the life of a large cell; then during the life of a man; and so on. The results for all cosmoses should be obtained in lineal measurements, that is, they should be expressed in fractions of a kilometer or in kilometers. The multiplication of a number of kilometers by $\sqrt{-1}$, that is, by the square root of minus one, ought to show that here we are not dealing with lineal measurements and that the figure obtained is a *measure of time.* The introduction of the square root of minus one into the formula, while it does not change the formula quantitatively, shows that the whole formula relates to another dimension.

In this way, in relation to the cosmos of electrons, the Minkovski formula takes the following form:

$$\sqrt{-1}. \quad 300,000. \quad 3.10^{-7}$$

that is, the square root of minus one, which has to be multiplied by the product of 300,000, that is c, or the speed of light, 300,000 kilometers per second, and 1/300,000,000 second, that is, the duration of the life of an electron. Multiplying 300,000 by 1/300,000,000 will give 1/1000 kilometer, which is one meter. "One meter" shows the distance which light traverses during the life of an electron, traveling at the speed of 300,000 kilometers a second. The square root of minus one, which makes "one meter" an imaginary quantity, shows that the lineal measurement of a meter in the case in question is a "measure of time," that is, of the fourth co-ordinate.

Passing to the "world of the molecule," we obtain the Minkovski formula in the following form:

$$\sqrt{-1}. \quad 300,000. \quad 1/10,000$$

One ten-thousandth part of a second, according to the table, is the duration of the life of a molecule. Multiplying 300,000 kilometers by 1/10,000 will give 30 kilometers. "Time" in the world of molecules is obtained in the form of the formula $\sqrt{-1}$. 30. Thirty kilometers represents the distance which light travels during the life of a molecule, or in 1/10,000 second.

Further, in the "world of small cells" the Minkovski formula takes the following form:

$$\sqrt{-1}. \quad 300,000. \quad 3 \text{ or}$$
$$\sqrt{-1}. \quad 900,000$$

that is, 900,000 kilometers multiplied by the square root of minus one. 900,000 kilometers represents the distance which light travels during the life of a small cell, that is in 3 seconds.

Continuing similar calculations for the further cosmoses, I obtained for "large cells" an *eleven-figure number,* showing the distance which light travels in 24 hours; for the "Microcosmos" a sixteen-figure number, showing the distance in kilometers which light travels in 80 years; for the "Tritocosmos" a twenty-figure number; for the "Mesocosmos" a twenty-five-figure number; for the "Deuterocosmos" a twenty-nine-figure number; for the "Macrocosmos" a thirty-four-figure number; for the "Ayocosmos" a thirty-eight-figure number; for the "Protocosmos" a forty-two-figure number or $\sqrt{-1}$. 9. 10^{41}; in other words it means that during the life of the "Protocosmos" a ray of light travels 900,000,000,000,000,000,000,- 000,000,000,000, 000,000,000 kilometers.[1]

The application of the Minkovski formula to the table of time, as I had obtained it, in my opinion showed very clearly that the "fourth co-ordinate" can be established only for one cosmos at a time, which then appears as the "four-dimensional world" of Minkovski. Two, three, or more cosmoses cannot be considered as a "four-dimensional" world and they require for their description five or six co-ordinates. At the same time Minkovski's consistent formula shows, for all cosmoses, the relation of the fourth co-ordinate of one cosmos to the fourth co-ordinate of another. And this relation is equal to thirty thousand, that is, the relation between the four chief periods of each cosmos and between one period of one cosmos and the corresponding, that is, the similarly named, period of another cosmos.

World of electrons	$\sqrt{-1}.\ ct = \sqrt{-1}.\ 300,000.$	$\dfrac{1}{300,000,000}$	$= \sqrt{-1}.\ \dfrac{1}{1000}$
World of molecules	$\sqrt{-1}.\ ct = \sqrt{-1}.\ 300,000.$	$\dfrac{1}{10,000}$	$= \sqrt{-1}.\ 30$
World of small cells	$\sqrt{-1}.\ ct = \sqrt{-1}.\ 300,000.$	3	$= \sqrt{-1}.\ 9.10^5$
World of large cells	$\sqrt{-1}.\ ct = \sqrt{-1}.\ 300,000.$	$30,000$	$= \sqrt{-1}.\ 3.10^{10}$
Microcosmos (man)	$\sqrt{-1}.\ ct = \sqrt{-1}.\ 300,000.$	9.10^8	$= \sqrt{-1}.\ 9.10^{14}$
Tritocosmos (organic life)	$\sqrt{-1}.\ ct = \sqrt{-1}.\ 300,000.$	3.10^{13}	$= \sqrt{-1}.\ 3.10^{19}$
Mesocosmos (planets)	$\sqrt{-1}.\ ct = \sqrt{-1}.\ 300,000.$	9.10^{17}	$= \sqrt{-1}.\ 9.10^{23}$
Deuterocosmos (sun)	$\sqrt{-1}.\ ct = \sqrt{-1}.\ 300,000.$	3.10^{22}	$= \sqrt{-1}.\ 3.10^{28}$
Macrocosmos (Milky Way)	$\sqrt{-1}.\ ct = \sqrt{-1}.\ 300,000.$	9.10^{26}	$= \sqrt{-1}.\ 9.10^{32}$
Ayocosmos (all worlds)	$\sqrt{-1}.\ ct = \sqrt{-1}.\ 300,000.$	3.10^{31}	$= \sqrt{-1}.\ 3.10^{37}$
Protocosmos (Absolute)	$\sqrt{-1}.\ ct = \sqrt{-1}.\ 300,000.$	9.10^{35}	$= \sqrt{-1}.\ 9.10^{41}$

TABLE 9

[1] But according to the latest scientific conclusions a ray of light travels in a curve and after going round the universe, returns to its source in approximately 1,000,000,000 light years. 1,000,000,000 light years represent in this case the circumference of the universe, although the opinions of various investigators differ widely and the figures relating to the circumference of the universe can in no way be considered as strictly established, even if all the considerations leading up to them as to the density of matter in the universe be accepted.

In any case, if we take the average figure indicated relating to the supposed circumference of the universe, then, by dividing 9.10^{28} by 10^8, we obtain a twenty-figure number, which will show how many times a ray of light will go round the universe during the life of the "Protocosmos."

The next thing that interested me in the "table of time in different cosmoses," as I called it, was the relation of cosmoses and of the time of different cosmoses to the *centers* of the human body.

G. spoke many times about the enormous difference in the speed of the different centers. The reasoning which I have cited above in regard to the speed of the inner work of the organism led me to the thought that this speed belongs to the *instinctive center*. With this as a basis I tried to proceed from the thinking center, taking as the unit of its work, for example, the time necessary for one full apperception, that is, for the reception of an outside impression, the classification and definition of this impression—and for the responding reaction. Then if the centers actually stand to one another in the relation of cosmoses, in exactly the same amount of time through the instinctive center there could pass 30,000 apperceptions, through the higher emotional and in the sex centers $30,000^2$ apperceptions and through the higher thinking $30,000^3$ apperceptions.

At the same time according to the law, pointed out by G., of the correlation of cosmoses, the instinctive center in relation to the head or thinking center should embrace *two cosmoses*, that is, the second Microcosmos and the Tritocosmos. Further, the higher emotional and the sex centers taken separately, should embrace the third Microcosmos and the Mesocosmos. And finally the higher thinking center should embrace the fourth Microcosmos and the Deuterocosmos.

But the latter refers to higher development, to that development of man which cannot be obtained accidentally or in a natural way. In man's normal state, an enormous advantage, in the sense of speed, over all the other centers should be possessed by the sex center, working 30,000 times faster than the instinctive or the moving and $30,000^2$ times faster than the intellectual.

In the relation of centers to cosmoses in general very many possibilities of study, from my point of view, had been opened up.

The next thing that caught my attention was the fact that my table coincided with some of the ideas and even the figures "of cosmic calculations of time," if it can be so expressed, which existed with the Gnostics and in India.

A day of light is a thousand years of the world, and thirty-six myriads of years and a half-myriad of years of the world (365,000) are a single year of Light.[1]

Here the figures do not coincide, but in Indian writings in some cases the correspondence was quite unquestionable. They speak of the "breath of Brahma," "days and nights of Brahma," "an age of Brahma."

If we take the figures for the years given in the Indian writings, then the Mahamanvantara, that is, the "age of Brahma," or 311,040,000,000,000

[1] *Pistis Sophia*, p. 203, English translation, 1921.

years (fifteen-figure number), almost coincides with the period of the existence of the *sun* (sixteen-figure number), and the "day and night of Brahma," 8,640,000,000 (ten-figure number), almost coincides with the "day and night of the sun" (eleven-figure number).

If we take Indian ideas of cosmic time without relation to figures, other interesting correspondences appear. Thus, if we take Brahma as the Protocosmos, then the expression "Brahma breathes in and breathes out the universe" coincides with the table, because the breath of Brahma (or the Protocosmos—a twenty-figure number) coincides with the life of the Macrocosmos, that is, our visible universe or the starry world.

I spoke a great deal with Z. about the "table of time" and it interested us very much as to what G. would say about it when we saw him.

Meanwhile time was passing. At last—it was already early in June—I received a telegram from Alexandropol: "If you want to rest come here to me."—That was G.!

In two days I left Petersburg. Russia with "no authorities" presented a very curious spectacle. It felt as though everything was existing and holding together simply by momentum. But the trains still ran regularly and at the stations the sentries turned a deeply indignant crowd of ticketless travelers out of the carriages. I was traveling for five days to Tiflis instead of the normal three.

The train arrived at Tiflis at night. It was not possible to walk about the town. I was obliged to await the morning in the station buffet. The whole station was crammed with soldiers who had returned from the Caucasian front on their own account. Many of them were drunk. "Meetings" were held throughout the night on the platform facing the windows of the buffet—and resolutions of some sort were carried. During the meetings there were three "courts-martial" and three men were shot there on the platform. A drunken "comrade" who appeared in the buffet explained to everyone that the first man had been shot for theft. The second was shot by mistake because he had been mistaken for the first; and the third was also shot by mistake because he had been mistaken for the second.

I was obliged to spend the day in Tiflis. The train to Alexandropol went in the evening only. The following morning I was there. I found G. setting up a dynamo for his brother.

And again I observed, as before, his remarkable capacity for adapting himself to any kind of work, to any kind of business.

I met his family, his father, and his mother. They were people of a very old and very peculiar culture. G.'s father was an amateur of local tales, legends, and traditions, something in the nature of a "bard"; and he knew by heart thousands and thousands of verses in the local idioms. They were Greeks from Asia Minor, but the language of the house, as of all the others in Alexandropol, was Armenian.

For the first few days after my arrival G. was so busy that I had no opportunity to ask him what he thought of the general situation or what he thought of doing. But when at length I spoke to him about it G. told me that he disagreed with me, that in his opinion everything would soon quiet down and that we would be able to work in Russia. He then added that in any case he wanted to go to Petersburg to see the Nevsky with hawkers selling sunflower seeds that I had told him about and to decide on the spot what had best be done. I could not take what he said seriously because I knew by now his manner of speaking and I waited for something further.

Indeed while saying this with apparent seriousness G. along with it said something altogether different, that it would be good to go to Persia or even further, that he knew a place in the Transcaucasian Mountains where one could live for several years without anyone knowing, and so on.

On the whole there remained with me a feeling of uncertainty, but all the same I hoped on the way to Petersburg to persuade him to go abroad if this were still possible.

G. was evidently waiting for something. The dynamo was working faultlessly but we made no move.

In the house there was an interesting portrait of G. which told me very many things about him. It was a big enlarged portrait of G. when he was quite young, dressed in a black frock coat with his curly hair brushed straight back.

G.'s portrait determined for me with undoubted accuracy what his profession was at the time the portrait was made—though G. never spoke of it. This discovery gave me many interesting ideas. But since this was my own personal discovery I shall keep it to myself.

Several times I tried to speak to G. about my "table of time in different cosmoses," but he dismissed all theoretical conversations.

I liked Alexandropol very much. It contained a great deal which was peculiar and original.

Outwardly the Armenian part of the town calls to mind a town in Egypt or northern India. The houses with their flat roofs upon which grass grows. There is a very ancient Armenian cemetery on a hill from which the snow-clad summit of Mount Ararat can be seen. There is a wonderful image of the Virgin in one of the Armenian churches. The center of the town calls to mind a Russian country town but alongside it is the bazaar which is entirely oriental, especially the coppersmiths' row where they work in open booths. There is also the Greek quarter, the least interesting of all outwardly, where G.'s house was situated, and a Tartar suburb in the ravines, a very picturesque but, according to those in the other parts of the town, a rather dangerous place.

I do not know what is left of Alexandropol after all these autonomies, republics, federations, and so on. I think one could only answer for the view of Mount Ararat.

I hardly saw G. alone and seldom succeeded in speaking to him. He spent a great deal of time with his father and mother. I very much liked his relationship with his father which was full of extraordinary consideration. G.'s father was still a robust old man, of medium height, with an inevitable pipe in his mouth and wearing an astrakhan cap. It was difficult to believe that he was over eighty. He spoke very little Russian. But with G. he used to speak for hours on end and I always liked to watch how G. listened to him, occasionally laughing a little, but evidently never for a second losing the line of the conversation and the whole time sustaining the conversation with questions and comments. The old man evidently enjoyed these conversations and G. devoted to him all his spare time, and not only did not evince the least impatience, but on the contrary the whole time showed a very great deal of interest in what the old man was saying. Even if this was partly acting it could not in any case have been all acting, otherwise there would have been no sense in it. I was very interested and attracted by this display of feeling on the part of G.

I spent in all about two weeks in Alexandropol. At length on one fine morning G. said that we would be going to Petersburg in two days and we set off.

In Tiflis we saw General S. who at one time used to come to our Petersburg group and it looked as though the talk with him gave G. a fresh view on the general situation and made him somewhat change his plans.

On the journey from Tiflis I remember an interesting talk with G. at one of the small stations between Baku and Derbent. Our train stood there a long time letting through trains with "comrades" from the Caucasian front. It was very hot, a quarter of a mile away the surface of the Caspian Sea was glittering, and all around us was nothing but fine shining flint with the outlines of two camels in the distance.

I tried to lead G. to talk about the immediate future of our work. I wanted to understand what he was going to do and what he wanted from us.

"Events are against us," I said. "It is by now clear that it is not possible to do anything in the midst of this mass madness."

"It is only now that it is possible," G. replied, "and events are not against us at all. They are merely moving too quickly. This is the whole trouble. But wait five years and you will see for yourself how what hinders today will prove useful to us."

I did not understand what G. meant by this. Neither after five years nor after fifteen years did this become any clearer. Looked at from the point of view of "facts," it was difficult to imagine in what way we could be helped by events in the nature of "civil war," "murder," epidemics, hunger, the whole of Russia becoming savage, and then the endless lying of European politics and the general crisis which was undoubtedly the result of this lying.

But if looked at, not from the point of view of "facts," but from the point of view of esoteric principles, then what G. meant becomes more comprehensible.

Why were there not these ideas earlier? Why did we not have them when Russia existed and when Europe was a comfortable and pleasant place "abroad"? It was here probably that lay the solution to G.'s enigmatic remark. Why were there not these ideas? Probably precisely because these ideas could come only in such a time when the attention of the majority is distracted in some other direction and when these ideas can reach only those who look for them. I was right from the point of view of "facts." Nothing could have hindered us more than "events." At the same time it is probable that precisely the "events" made it possible for us to receive what we had.

There remains in my memory one other conversation during this journey. Once when the train was standing a long time in some station and our fellow travelers were walking on the platform, I put one question to G. which I could not answer for myself. This was, in the division of oneself into "I" and "Ouspensky," how can one strengthen the feeling of "I" and strengthen the activity of "I"?

"You cannot do anything about it," said G. "This should come as a result of *all* your efforts" (he emphasized the word "all"). "Take for example yourself. By now you should have felt your 'I' differently. Try to ask yourself whether you notice the difference or not."

I tried to "feel myself" as G. had shown us, but I must say that I did not notice any difference from the way I felt before.

"That will come," said G. "And when it does come you will know. No doubt whatever is possible. It is quite a different feeling."

Later I understood about what he was speaking, that is, about which kind of feeling and which kind of change. But I began to notice this only two years after this conversation.

On the third day of our journey from Tiflis, while the train was waiting at Mozdok, G. said to us (there were four of us) that I was to go alone to Petersburg while he and the others would stop at Mineralni Vodi and go to Kislovodsk.

"You will stop at Moscow and go to Petersburg afterwards," he said to me, "and tell them in Moscow and Petersburg that I am beginning new work here. Those who want to work with me can come. And I advise you not to stay there long."

I said good-by to G. and his companions at Mineralni Vodi and traveled on alone.

It was clear that nothing remained of my plans for going abroad. But now this no longer troubled me. I did not doubt that we should have to live through a very difficult time but now it hardly mattered to me. I realized what I had been afraid of. I was not afraid of actual dangers, I was afraid of acting stupidly, that is, of not going away in time when I knew perfectly well what must be expected. Now all responsibility towards myself seemed to have been taken from me. I had not altered my opinions; I could say as before, that to stay in Russia was madness. But my attitude towards this was quite indifferent. It was not my decision.

I traveled still in the old way, alone in a first-class compartment, and near Moscow they charged me excess fare on my ticket because the reservation was issued for one direction and the ticket for another. In other words everything was as it ought to be. But the papers which I got on the way were full of news about shooting in the streets of Petersburg. Moreover it was now the bolsheviks who were shooting into the crowd; they were trying their strength.

The situation at this time was beginning to become defined. On the one side were the bolsheviks, as yet not fully realizing the incredible success which was awaiting them, but already beginning to feel the absence of resistance and to act more and more insolently. On the other side was the "second provisional government" with many serious people who understood the situation in the minor posts and with altogether insignificant babblers and theorists in the major posts; then there was the intelligentsia greatly decimated by the war; then the remains of former parties and the military circles. All these taken together were divided in their turn into two groups, one who, in the face of all the facts and common sense, accepted the possibility of peace parleys with the bolsheviks who very cleverly made use of this while gradually occupying one position after another; and the other who, while realizing the impossibility of any negotiations whatever with the bolsheviks, were at the same time not united and did not come out actively into the open.

The people were silent, although never perhaps in history has the will of the people been so clearly expressed—and that will was to *stop the war!*

Who could stop the war? This was the chief question of the moment. The provisional government did not dare. Naturally it could not come from the military circles. And yet power was bound to pass to whoever should be the first to pronounce the word: "*Peace.*" And as often happens in such cases the right word came from the wrong side. The bolsheviks pronounced the word "peace." First of all because it was a matter of complete indifference to them what they said. They had no intention of meeting their promissory notes, therefore they could issue as many of them as they liked. This was their chief advantage and chief strength.

There was something else here besides this. Destruction is always far easier than construction. How much easier it is to burn a house than to build one.

The bolsheviks were the agents of destruction. Neither then nor since could they or can they be anything else notwithstanding all their boasting and notwithstanding all the support of their open and their hidden friends. But they could and they can destroy very well, not so much by their own activity as by their very existence which corrupts and disintegrates everything around them. This special property of theirs explained their approaching victory and all that happened much later.

We who were looking at things from the point of view of the system could see not only the fact that everything *happens* but even *how* it happens, that is, how easily everything goes downhill and breaks up once a single impulse is given to it.

I did not stay in Moscow but I managed to see a few people while waiting for the evening train to Petersburg, and I passed on to them what G. had said. Then I went to Petersburg and passed on the same message to the members of our groups.

In twelve days time I was again in the Caucasus. In Pyatigorsk I learned that G. was not living at Kislovodsk but at Essentuki and in two hours time I was with him in a small country villa in Panteleimon Street.

G. asked me in detail about everyone I had seen, what each had said, who was going to come and who not, and so on. Next day three more people followed me from Petersburg, then two more, and so on. In all, excluding G. and myself, there forgathered twelve people.

Chapter Seventeen

I ALWAYS have a very strange feeling when I remember this period. On this occasion we spent about six weeks in Essentuki. But this now seems to be altogether incredible. Whenever I chance to speak with any one of those who were there they can hardly believe that it lasted only six weeks. It would be difficult even in six years to find room for everything that was connected with this time, to such an extent was it filled.

Half of our number, myself among them, lived throughout this period with G. in a small house on the outskirts of the village; the others came in in the morning and stayed late into the night. We went to bed very late and got up very early. We slept for four hours, at the most, five. We did all the housework; and the rest of the time was occupied with exercises of which I will speak later. G. several times arranged excursions to Kislovodsk, Jeleznovodsk, Pyatigorsk, Beshtau, and so on.

G. superintended the kitchen, and often prepared dinner himself. He proved to be a wonderful cook and knew hundreds of remarkable eastern dishes. Every day we had dinner in the style of some eastern country; we ate Tibetan, Persian, and other dishes.

I am not attempting to describe everything that took place in Essentuki; a whole book would have to be written in order to do this. G. led us at a fast pace without losing a single minute. He explained many things during our walks, while music was being played in the Essentuki park, and in the midst of housework.

In general, during the short period of our stay at Essentuki, G. unfolded to us the plan of the whole work. We saw the beginnings of all the methods, the beginnings of all the ideas, their links, their connections and direction. Many things remained obscure for us; many things we did not rightly understand, quite the contrary; but in any case we were given some general propositions by which I thought we could be guided later on.

All the ideas we had come to know up to that time brought us face to face with a whole series of questions connected with the practical realization of work on oneself, and, naturally, they evoked many discussions among the members of our group.

G. always took part in these discussions and explained different aspects of the organization of schools.

346

"Schools are imperative," he once said, "first of all because of the complexity of man's organization. A man is unable *to keep watch* on the *whole of himself*, that is, all his different sides. Only school can do this, school methods, school discipline—a man is much too lazy, he will do a great deal without the proper intensity, or he will do nothing at all while thinking that he is doing something; he will work with intensity on something that does not need intensity and will let those moments pass by when intensity is imperative. Then he spares himself; he is afraid of doing anything unpleasant. He will never attain the necessary intensity by himself. If you have observed yourselves in a proper way you will agree with this. If a man sets himself a task of some sort he very quickly begins to be indulgent with himself. He tries to accomplish his task in the easiest way possible and so on. This is not work. In work only *super-efforts* are counted, that is, beyond the normal, beyond the necessary; ordinary efforts are not counted."

"What is meant by a super-effort?" someone asked.

"It means an effort beyond the effort that is necessary to achieve a given purpose," said G. "Imagine that I have been walking all day and am very tired. The weather is bad, it is raining and cold. In the evening I arrive home. I have walked, perhaps, twenty-five miles. In the house there is supper; it is warm and pleasant. But, instead of sitting down to supper, I go out into the rain again and decide to walk another two miles along the road and then return home. This would be a super-effort. While I was going home it was simply an effort and this does not count. I was on my way home, the cold, hunger, the rain—all this made me walk. In the other case I walk because I myself decide to do so. This kind of super-effort becomes still more difficult when I do not decide upon it myself but obey a teacher who at an unexpected moment requires from me to make fresh efforts when I have decided that efforts for the day are over.

"Another form of super-effort is carrying out any kind of work at a faster rate than is called for by the nature of this work. You are doing something—well, let us say, you are washing up or chopping wood. You have an hour's work. Do it in half an hour—this will be a super-effort.

"But in actual practice a man can never bring himself to make super-efforts consecutively or for a long time; to do this another person's will is necessary which would have no pity and which would have method.

"If a man were able to work on himself everything would be very simple and schools would be unnecessary. But he cannot, and the reasons for this lie very deep in his nature. I will leave for the moment his insincerity with himself, the perpetual lies he tells himself, and so on, and take only the division of the centers. This alone makes independent work on himself impossible for a man. You must understand that the three principal centers, the thinking, the emotional, and the moving, are connected together and, in a normal man, they are always working in unison. This unison is what presents the chief difficulty in work on oneself. What is meant by this unison? It means that a definite work of the thinking center is connected with a definite work of the emotional and moving centers—that is to say, that a certain kind of thought is *inevitably* connected with a certain kind of emotion (or mental state) and with a certain kind of movement (or posture); and one evokes the other, that is, a certain kind of emotion (or mental state) evokes certain movements or postures and certain thoughts, and a certain kind of movement or posture evokes certain emotions or mental states, and so forth. Everything is connected and one thing cannot exist without another thing.

"Now imagine that a man decides *to think* in a new way. But he feels in the old way. Imagine that he dislikes R." He pointed to one of those present. "This dislike of R. immediately arouses old thoughts and he forgets his decision to think in a new way. Or let us suppose that he is accustomed to smoking cigarettes while he is thinking—this is a moving habit. He decides to think in a new way. He begins to smoke a cigarette and thinks in the old way without noticing it. The habitual movement of lighting a cigarette has turned his thoughts round to the old tune. You must remember that a man can never break this accordance by himself. Another man's will is necessary, and a stick is necessary. All that a man who wants to work on himself can do at a certain stage of his work is to obey. He can do nothing by himself.

"More than anything else he needs constant supervision and observation. He cannot observe himself *constantly*. Then he needs definite rules the fulfillment of which needs, in the first place, a certain kind of self-remembering and which, in the second place, helps in the struggle with habits. A man cannot do all this by himself. In life everything is always arranged far too comfortably for man to work. In a school a man finds himself among other people who are not of his own choosing and with whom perhaps it is very difficult to live and work, and usually in uncomfortable and unaccustomed conditions. This creates tension between him and the others. And this tension is also indispensable because it gradually chips away his sharp angles.

"Then work on moving center can only be properly organized in a school. As I have already said, the wrong, independent, or automatic work of the moving center deprives the other centers of support and they involuntarily follow the moving center. Often, therefore, the sole possibility of making the other centers work in a new way is to begin with the moving center; that is with the body. A body which is lazy, automatic, and full of stupid habits stops any kind of work."

"But theories exist," said one of us, "that a man ought to develop the spiritual and moral side of his nature and that if he attains results in this direction there will be no obstacles on the part of the body. Is this possible or not?"

"Both yes and no," said G. "The whole point is in the 'if.' If a man attains perfection of a moral and spiritual nature without hindrance on the part of the body, the body will not interfere with further achievements. But unfortunately this never occurs because the body interferes at the first step, interferes by its automatism, its attachment to habits, and chiefly by its wrong functioning. If the development of the moral and spiritual nature without interference on the part of the body is theoretically possible, it is possible only in the case of an ideal functioning of the body. And who is able to say that his body functions ideally?

"And besides there is deception in the very words 'moral' and 'spiritual' themselves. I have often enough explained before that in speaking of *machines* one cannot begin with their 'morality' or their 'spirituality,' but that one must begin with their mechanicalness and the laws governing this mechanicalness. The being of man number one, number two, and number three is the being of machines which are able to cease being machines but which have not ceased being machines."

"But is it not possible for man to be at once transposed to another stage of being by a wave of emotion?" someone asked.

"I do not know," said G., "we are again talking in different languages. A wave of emotion is indispensable, but it cannot change moving habits; it cannot of itself make centers work rightly which all their lives have been working wrongly. To change and repair this demands separate, special, and lengthy work. Then you say: transpose a man to another level of being. But from this point of view *a man* does not exist for me. There is a complex mechanism consisting of a whole series of complex parts. 'A wave of emotion' takes place in one part but the other parts may not be affected by it at all. No miracles are possible in a machine. It is miracle enough that a machine is able to change. But you want all laws to be violated."

"What of the robber on the cross?" asked one of those present. "Is there anything in this or not?"

"That is another thing entirely," said G., "and it illustrates an altogether different idea. In the first place it took place *on the cross*, that is, in the midst of terrible sufferings to which ordinary life holds nothing equal; secondly, it was at the moment of death. This refers to the idea of man's last thoughts and feelings at the moment of death. In life these pass by, they are replaced by other habitual thoughts. There can be no prolonged wave of emotion in life and therefore it cannot give rise to a change of being.

"And it must be further understood that we are not speaking of exceptions or accidents which may or may not occur, but of general principles, of what happens every day to everyone. Ordinary man, even if he comes to the conclusion that work on himself is indispensable—is the slave of his body. He is not only the slave of the recognized and visible activity of the body but the slave of the unrecognized and the invisible activities of the body, and it is precisely these which hold him in their power. Therefore when a man decides to struggle for freedom he has first of all to struggle with his own body.

"I will now point out to you only one aspect of the functioning of the body which it is indispensable to regulate in any event. So long as this functioning goes on in a wrong way no other kind of work, either moral or spiritual, can go on in a right way.

"You will remember that when we spoke of the work of the 'three-story factory,' I pointed out to you that most of the energy produced by the factory is wasted uselessly, among other things energy is wasted on unnecessary muscular tension. This unnecessary muscular tension eats up an enormous amount of energy. And with work on oneself attention must first be turned to this.

"In speaking of the work of the factory in general it is indispensable to establish that it is necessary to stop useless waste before there can be any sense in increasing the production. If production is increased while this useless waste remains unchecked and nothing is done to stop it, the new energy produced will merely increase this useless waste and may even give rise to phenomena of an unhealthy kind. Therefore one of the first things a man must learn previous to any physical work on himself is to observe and feel muscular tension and to be able to relax the muscles when it is necessary, that is to say, chiefly to relax unnecessary tension of the muscles."

In this connection G. showed us a number of different exercises for obtaining control over muscular tension and he showed us certain postures adopted in schools when praying or contemplating which a man can only adopt if he learns to relax unnecessary tension of the muscles. Among them was the so-called posture of Buddha with feet resting on the knees, and another still more difficult posture, which he could adopt to perfection, and which we were able to imitate only very approximately.

To adopt this posture G. kneeled down and then sat on his heels (without boots) with feet closely pressed together. It was very difficult even to sit on one's heels in this way for more than a minute or two. He then raised his arms and, holding them on a level with his shoulders, he slowly bent himself backwards and lay on the ground while his legs, bent at the knees, remained pressed beneath him. Having lain in this position for a certain time he just as slowly raised himself up with arms outstretched, then he again lay down, and so on.

He gave us many exercises for gradually relaxing the muscles *always beginning with the muscles of the face*, as well as exercises for "feeling" the hands, the feet, the fingers, and so on at will. The idea of the necessity of relaxing the muscles was not actually a new one, but G.'s explanation that relaxing the muscles of the body should begin with the muscles of the face was quite new to me; I had never come across this in books on "Yoga" or in literature on physiology.

Very interesting was the exercise with a "circular sensation," as G. called it. A man lies on his back on the floor. Trying to relax all his muscles, he then concentrates his attention on trying to sense his nose. When he begins to sense his nose the man then transfers his attention and tries to sense his ear; when this is achieved he transfers his attention to the right foot. From the right foot to the left; then to the left hand; then to the left ear and back again to the nose, and so on.

All this interested me particularly because certain experiments I had carried out had led me long ago to conclude that physical states, which are connected with new psychological experiences, begin *with feeling the pulse throughout the whole body,* which is what we do not feel in ordinary conditions; in this connection the pulse is felt at once in all parts of the body as one stroke. In my own personal experiments "feeling" the pulsation throughout the whole body was brought about, for instance, by certain breathing exercises connected with several days of fasting. I came to no definite results whatever in my own experiments but there remains with me the deep conviction that control over the body begins with acquiring control over the pulse. Acquiring for a short time the possibility of regulating, quickening, and slowing the pulse, I was able to slow down or quicken the heart beat and this in its turn gave me very interesting psychological results. I understood in a general way that control over the heart could not come from the heart muscles but that it depended upon controlling the pulse (the second stroke or the "big heart") and G. had explained a great deal to me in pointing out that control over the "second heart" depends upon controlling the tension of the muscles, because we do not possess this control chiefly in consequence of the wrong and irregular tension of various groups of muscles.

Exercises in relaxing the muscles which we began to perform gave very interesting results to some of our company. Thus one of us was suddenly able to stop a bad neuralgic pain in his arm by relaxing his muscles. Then relaxation of the muscles had an immense significance in proper sleep and whoever did exercises in relaxation seriously very quickly noticed that his sleep became sounder and that he needed fewer hours of sleep.

In this connection G. showed us an exercise that was quite new for us, without which, according to him, it was impossible to master moving nature. This was, as he called it, the "stop" exercise.

"Every race," he said, "every nation, every epoch, every country, every class, every profession, has its own definite number of postures and movements. These movements and postures, as things which are the most permanent and unchangeable in man, control his form of thought and his form of feeling. But a man never makes use of even all the postures and movements possible for him. In accordance with his individuality a man takes only a certain number of the postures and movements possible for him. So that each individual man's repertory of postures and movements is very limited.

"The character of the movements and postures in every epoch, in every race, and in every class is indissolubly connected with definite forms of thinking and feeling. A man is unable to change the form of his thinking or his feeling until he has changed his repertory of postures and movements. The forms of thinking and feeling can be called the postures and movements of thinking and feeling. Every man has a definite number of thinking and feeling postures and movements. Moreover moving, thinking, and feeling postures are connected with one another in man and he can never move out of his repertory of thinking and feeling postures unless he changes his moving postures. An analysis of man's thoughts and feelings and a study of his moving functions, arranged in a certain way, show that every one of our movements, voluntary or involuntary, is an unconscious transition from one posture to another, both equally mechanical.

"It is illusion to say our movements are voluntary. All our movements are automatic. Our thoughts and feelings are just as automatic. The automatism of thought and feeling is definitely connected with the automatism of movement. One cannot be changed without the other. So that if a man's attention is concentrated, let us say, on changing automatic thoughts, then habitual movements and habitual postures will interfere with this new course of thought by attaching to it old habitual associations.

"In ordinary conditions we have no conception how much our thinking, feeling, and moving functions depend upon one another, although we know, at the same time, how much our moods and our emotional states can depend upon our movements and postures. If a man takes a posture which with him corresponds to a feeling of sadness or despondency, then within a short time he is sure to feel sad or despondent. Fear, disgust, nervous agitation, or, on the other hand, calm, can be created by an intentional change of posture. But as each of man's functions, thinking, emotional, and moving, has its own definite repertory all of which are in constant interaction, a man can never get out of the charmed circle of his postures.

"Even if a man recognizes this and begins to struggle with it, his will is not sufficient. You must understand that a man's will can be sufficient to govern *one* center for a *short* time. But the other two centers prevent this. And a man's will can never be sufficient to govern three centers.

"In order to oppose this automatism and gradually to acquire control over postures and movements in different centers there is one special exercise. It consists in this—that at a word or sign, previously agreed upon, from the teacher, all the pupils who hear or see him have to arrest their movements at once, no matter what they are doing, and remain stock-still in the posture in which the signal has caught them. Moreover not only must they cease to move, but they must keep their eyes on the same spot at which they were looking at the moment of the signal, retain the smile on their faces, if there was one, keep the mouth open if a man was speaking, maintain the facial expression and the tension of all the muscles of the body exactly in the same position in which they were caught by the signal. In this 'stopped' state a man must also stop the flow of his thoughts and concentrate the whole of his attention on preserving the tension of the muscles in the various parts of the body exactly as it was, watching this tension all the time and leading so to speak his attention from one part of the body to another. And he must remain in this state and in this position until another agreed-upon signal allows him to adopt a customary posture or until he drops from fatigue through being unable to preserve the original posture any longer. But he has no right to change anything in it, neither his glance, points of support, nothing. If he cannot stand he must fall—but, again, he should fall like a sack without attempting to protect himself from a blow. In exactly the same way, if he was holding something in his hands he must hold it as long as he can and if his hands refuse to obey him and the object falls it is not his fault.

"It is the duty of the teacher to see that no personal injury occurs from falling or from unaccustomed postures, and in this connection the pupils must trust the teacher fully and not think of any danger.

"The idea of this exercise and its results differ very much. Let us take it first of all from the point of view of the study of movements and postures. This exercise affords a man the possibility of getting out of the circle of automatism and it cannot be dispensed with, especially at the beginning of work on oneself.

"A non-mechanical study of oneself is only possible with the help of the 'stop' exercise under the direction of a man who understands it.

"Let us try to follow what occurs. A man is walking, or sitting, or working. At that moment he hears a signal. A movement that has begun is interrupted by this sudden signal or command to stop. His body becomes immovable and arrested *in the midst of a transition from one posture to another, in a position in which he never stays in ordinary life.* Feeling himself in this state, that is, in an unaccustomed posture, a man involuntarily looks at himself from new points of view, sees and observes himself in a new way. In this unaccustomed posture he is able to think in a new way, feel in a new way, know himself in a new way. In this way the circle of old automatism is broken. The body tries in vain to adopt an ordinary comfortable posture. But the man's will, brought into action by the will of the teacher, prevents it. The struggle goes on not for life but till the death. But *in this case* will can conquer. This exercise taken together with all that has been said is an exercise for self-remembering. A man must remember himself so as not to miss the signal; he must remember himself so as not to take the most comfortable posture at the first moment; he must remember himself in order to watch the tension of the muscles in different parts of the body, the direction in which he is looking, the facial expression, and so on; he must remember himself in order to overcome very considerable pain sometimes from unaccustomed positions of the legs, arms, and back, so as not to be afraid of falling or dropping something heavy on his foot. It is enough to forget oneself for a single moment and the body will adopt, by itself and almost unnoticeably, a more comfortable position, it will transfer the weight from one foot to another, will slacken certain muscles, and so on. This exercise is a simultaneous exercise for the will, the attention, the thoughts, the feelings, and for moving center.

"But it must be understood that in order to bring into action a sufficient strength of will to keep a man in an unaccustomed position an order or command from the outside: '*stop*,' is indispensable. A man cannot give himself the command *stop*. His will will not obey this command. The reason for this, as I have said before, is that the combination of habitual thinking, feeling, and moving postures is stronger than a man's will. The command *stop* which, in relation to moving postures, comes from outside, takes the place of thinking and feeling postures. These postures and their influence are so to speak removed by the command *stop*—and *in this case* moving postures obey the will."

Soon after that G. began to put "stop," as we called this exercise, into practice in the most varied circumstances.

G. first of all showed us how to "stand stock-still" immediately at the command "stop," and to try not to move, not to look aside no matter what was happening, not to reply if anyone spoke, for instance if one were asked something or even unjustly accused of something.

"The 'stop' exercise is considered sacred in schools," he said. "Nobody except the principal teacher or the person he commissions has the right to command a 'stop.' 'Stop' cannot be the subject of play or exercise among the pupils. You never know the position a man can find himself in. If you cannot *feel for him*, you do not know what muscles are tensed or how much. Meanwhile if a difficult tension is continued it can cause the rupture of some important vessel and in some cases it can even cause immediate death. Therefore only he who is quite certain in himself that he knows what he is doing can allow himself to command a 'stop.'

"At the same time 'stop' demands unconditional obedience, without any hesitations or doubts. And this makes it the invariable method for studying school discipline. School discipline is something quite different from military discipline, for instance. In that discipline everything is mechanical and the more mechanical it is the better. In this everything should be conscious because the aim consists in awakening consciousness. And for many people school discipline is much more difficult than military discipline. There it is always one and the same, here it is always different.

"But very difficult cases occur. I will tell you of one case in my own life. It was many years ago in Central Asia. We had put up a tent by the side of an *arik*, that is, an irrigation canal. And three of us were carrying things from one side of the *arik* to the other where our tent was. The water in the *arik* came up to our waists. I and another man had just come out on the bank with some things and were preparing to dress; the third man was still in the water. He dropped something in the water, we afterwards found out that it was an ax, and he was feeling about on the bottom with a stick. At this moment we heard from the tent a voice which called 'Stop!' We both stood stock-still on the bank as we were. Our comrade in the water was just within our field of vision. He was standing bending down towards the water and when he heard 'stop' he remained in that posture. One or two minutes passed by and suddenly we saw that the water in the *arik* was rising. Someone perhaps a mile away had opened a sluice to let water into the small *arik*. The water rose very rapidly and soon reached the chin of the man in the water. We did not know if the man in the tent knew that the water was rising. We could not call out to him, we could not even turn our heads to see where he was, we could not look at each other. I could only hear my friend breathing. The water began to rise very rapidly and soon the head of the man in the water was completely covered. Only one hand was raised supported by a long staff. Only this hand was to be seen. It seemed to me that a very long time passed by. At length we heard: 'Enough!' We both sprang into the water and dragged our friend out of it. He had been almost suffocated."

We also very soon became convinced that the "stop" exercise was not at all a joke. In the first place it required us to be constantly on the alert, constantly ready to interrupt what we were saying or doing; and secondly it sometimes required endurance and determination of quite a special kind.

"Stop" occurred at any moment of the day. Once during tea P., who was sitting opposite me, had raised to his lips a glass of hot tea, just poured out, and he was blowing on it. At this moment we heard "Stop" from the next room. P.'s face, and his hand holding the glass, were just in front of my eyes. I saw him grow purple and I saw a little muscle near his eye quiver. But he held onto the glass. He said afterwards that his fingers only pained him during the first minute, the chief difficulty afterwards was with his arm which was bent awkwardly at the elbow, that is, stopped halfway through a movement. But he had large blisters on his fingers and they were painful for a long time.

Another time a stop caught Z. when he had just inhaled smoke from his cigarette. He said afterwards that never in his life had he experienced anything so unpleasant. He could not exhale the smoke and he sat with eyes full of tears and smoke slowly coming out of his mouth.

"Stop" had an immense influence on the whole of our life, on the understanding of our work and our attitude towards it. First of all, attitude towards "stop" showed with undoubted accuracy what anyone's attitude was to the work. People who had tried to evade work evaded "stop." That is, either they did not hear the command to "stop" or they said that it did not directly refer to them. Or, on the other hand, they were always prepared for a "stop," they made no careless movements, they took no glasses of hot tea in their hands, they sat down and got up very quickly and so on. To a certain extent it was even possible to cheat with the "stop." But of course this would be seen and would at once show who was sparing himself and who was able not to spare himself, able to take the work seriously, and who was trying to apply ordinary methods to it, to avoid difficulties, "to adapt themselves." In exactly the same way "stop" showed the people who were incapable and undesirous of submitting to school discipline and the people who were not taking it seriously. We saw quite clearly that without "stop" and other exercises which accompanied it, nothing whatever could be attained in a purely psychological way.

But later work showed us the methods of the psychological way.

The chief difficulty for most people, as it soon appeared, was the habit of talking. No one saw this habit in himself, no one could struggle with it because it was always connected with some characteristic which the man considered to be positive in himself. Either he wanted to be "sincere," or he wanted to know what another man thought, or he wanted to help someone by speaking of himself or of others, and so on, and so on.

I very soon saw that the struggle with the habit of talking, of speaking, in general, more than is necessary, could become the center of gravity of work on oneself because this habit touched everything, penetrated everything, and was for many people the least noticed. It was very curious to observe how this habit (I say "habit" simply for lack of another word, it would be more correct to say "this sin" or "this misfortune") at once took possession of everything no matter what a man might begin to do.

In Essentuki at that time G. made us, among other things, carry out a small experiment in fasting. I had carried out experiments of this kind before and a good deal was familiar to me. But for many others the feeling of days which were endlessly long, of complete emptiness, of a kind of futility of existence, was new.

"Well, now I clearly understand," said one of our people, "what we live for and the place that food occupies in our lives."

But I personally was particularly interested in observing the place that talk occupied in life. In my opinion our first fast consisted in everybody talking without stopping for several days about the fast, that is, everybody spoke about himself. In this respect I remember very early talks with a Moscow friend about the fact that voluntary silence could be the most severe discipline to which a man could subject himself. But at that time we meant absolute silence. Even into this G. brought that wonderfully practical element which distinguished his system and his methods from anything I had known previously.

"Complete silence is easier," he said, when I began once to tell him my ideas. "Complete silence is simply a way out of life. A man should be in the desert or in a monastery. We speak of work in life. And a man can keep silence in such a way that no one will even notice it. The whole point is that we say a good deal too much. If we limited ourselves to what is actually necessary, this alone would be keeping silence. And it is the same with everything else, with food, with pleasures, with sleep; with everything there is a limit to what is necessary. After this 'sin' begins. This is something that must be grasped, a 'sin' is something which is not necessary."

"But if people abstain from everything that is unnecessary now, at once, what will the whole of life become like?" I said. "And how can they know what is necessary and what is not necessary?"

"Again you speak in your own way," said G. "I was not talking of people at all. They are going nowhere and for them there are no sins. Sins are what keep a man on one spot if he has decided to move and if he is able to move. Sins exist only for people who are on the way or approaching the way. And then sin is what stops a man, helps him to deceive himself and to think that he is working when he is simply asleep. Sin is what puts a man to sleep when he has already decided to awaken. And what puts a man to sleep? Again everything that is unnecessary, everything that is not indispensable. The indispensable is always permitted. But beyond this hypnosis begins at once. But you must remember that this refers only to people in the work or to those who consider themselves in the work. And work consists in subjecting oneself voluntarily to temporary suffering in order to be free from eternal suffering. But people are afraid of suffering. They want pleasure now, at once and forever. They do not want to understand that pleasure is an *attribute of paradise* and that it must be earned. And this is necessary not by reason of any arbitrary or inner moral laws but because if man gets pleasure before he has earned it he will not be able to keep it and pleasure will be turned into suffering. But the whole point is to be able to get pleasure and be able to keep it. Whoever can do this has nothing to learn. But the way to it lies through suffering. Whoever thinks that as he is he can avail himself of pleasure is much mistaken, and if he is capable of being sincere with himself, then the moment will come when he will see this."

But I will return to the physical exercises we carried out at that time. G. showed us the different methods that were used in schools. Very interesting but unbelievably difficult were exercises in which a whole series of consecutive movements were performed in connection with taking the attention from one part of the body to another.

For instance, a man sits on the ground with knees bent and holding his arms, with the palms of the hands close together, between his feet. Then he has to lift one leg and during this time count: *om, om, om, om, om, om, om, om, om,* up to the tenth *om* and then nine times *om,* eight times *om,* seven times *om,* and so on, down to one and then again twice *om,* three times *om,* and so on, and at the same time "sense" his right eye. Then separate the thumb and "sense" his left ear and so on and so on.

It was necessary first to remember the order of the movements and "sensing," then not to go wrong in the counting, to remember the count of movements and sensing. This was very difficult but it did not end the affair. When a man had mastered this exercise and could do it, say, for about ten or fifteen minutes, he was given, in addition, a special form of breathing, namely, he must inhale while pronouncing *om* several times and exhale pronouncing *om* several times; moreover the count had to be made aloud. Beyond this there were still greater and greater complications of the exercise up to almost impossible things. And G. told us he had seen people who *for days* did exercises of this kind.

The short fast of which I spoke was also accompanied by special exercises. In the first place G. explained at the beginning of the fast that the difficulty in fasting consisted in not leaving unused the substances which are prepared in the organism for the digestion of food.

"These substances consist of very strong solutions," he said. "And if they are left without attention they will poison the organism. They must be used up. But how can they be used up if the organism gets no food? Only by an increase of work, an increase of perspiration. People make a tremendous mistake when they try to 'save their strength,' make fewer movements, and so on, when fasting. On the contrary it is necessary to expend as much energy as possible. Then fasting can be beneficial."

And when we began our fast we were not left in peace for a single second. G. made us run in the heat, doing a round of two miles, or stand with extended arms, or mark time at the double, or carry out a whole series of curious gymnastic exercises which he showed us.

And he, all the time, constantly said that these exercises we were doing were not real ones, but merely preliminary and preparatory exercises.

One experiment in connection with what G. said about breathing and fatigue explained many things to me and chiefly it explained why it is so difficult to attain anything in the ordinary conditions of life.

I had gone to a room where nobody could see me, and began to mark time at the double trying at the same time to breathe according to a particular count, that is, to inhale during a definite number of steps and exhale during a definite number. After a certain time when I had begun to tire I noticed, that is, to speak more correctly, I felt quite clearly, that my breathing was artificial and unreliable. I felt that in a very short time I would be unable to breathe in that way while continuing to mark time at the double and that ordinary normal breathing, very accelerated of course, without any count would gain the upper hand.

It became more and more difficult for me to breathe and to mark time, and to observe the count of breaths and steps. I was pouring with sweat, my head began to turn round, and I thought I should fall. I began to despair of obtaining results of any kind and I had almost stopped when suddenly something seemed to crack or move inside me and my breathing went on evenly and properly at the rate I wanted it to go, but without any effort on my part, while affording me all the amount of air I needed. It was an extraordinarily pleasant sensation. I shut my eyes and continued to mark time, breathing easily and freely and feeling exactly as though strength was increasing in me and that I was getting lighter and stronger. I thought that if I could continue to run in this way for a certain time I should get still more interesting results because waves of a sort of joyful trembling had already begun to go through my body which, as I knew from previous experiments, preceded what I called the opening of the inner consciousness.

But at this moment someone came into the room and I stopped.

Afterwards my heart beat strongly for a long time, but not unpleasantly. I had marked time and breathed for about half an hour. I do not recommend this exercise to people with weak hearts.

At all events this experiment showed me with accuracy that a given exercise could be transferred to the moving center, that is, that it was possible to make the moving center work in a new way. But at the same time I was convinced that the condition for this transition was extreme fatigue. A man begins any exercise with his mind; only when the last stage of fatigue is reached can the control pass to the moving center. This explained what G. had said about "super-efforts" and made many of his later requirements intelligible.

But afterwards, however much I tried I did not succeed in repeating the experiment, that is to say, in evoking the same sensations. It is true that the fast had come to an end and that the success of my experiment had been, to a considerable extent, connected with it.

When I told G. about this experiment he said that without general work, that is, without work on the whole organism, such things could only succeed by chance.

Later on I several times heard descriptions of experiences very similar to mine from people who were studying dances and dervish movements with G.

The more we saw and realized the complexity and the diversity of methods of work on oneself, the clearer became for us the difficulties of the way. We saw the indispensability of great knowledge, of immense efforts, and of help such as none of us either could or had the right to count upon. We saw that even to begin work on oneself in any serious form was an exceptional phenomenon needing thousands of favorable inner and outward conditions. And the beginning gave no guarantee for the future. Each step required an effort, each step needed help. The possibility of attaining anything seemed so small in comparison with the difficulties that many of us lost the desire to make efforts of any kind.

This was an inevitable stage through which everybody passes until they have learned to understand that it is useless to think of the possibility or impossibility of big and distant achievements, and that a man must value what he gets today without thinking of what he may get tomorrow.

But certainly the idea of the difficulty and the exclusiveness of the way was right. And at different times questions arose out of it which were put to G.:

"Can it be possible that there is any difference between us and those people who have no conception of this system?"—"Must we understand that people who are not passing along any of the ways are doomed to turn eternally in one and the same circle, that they are merely 'food for the moon,' that they have no escape and no possibilities?"—"Is it correct to think that there are no ways *outside the ways*; and how is it arranged that some people, much better people perhaps, do not come across a way, while others, weak and insignificant, come into contact with the possibilities of a way?"

On one occasion while talk was proceeding on these subjects, to which we were constantly returning, G. began to talk in a somewhat different way to what he had done before, because he had previously always insisted on the fact that *outside the ways* there was nothing.

"There is not and there cannot be any choice of the people who come into touch with the 'ways.' In other words, nobody selects them, they select themselves, partly by accident and partly by having a certain hunger. Whoever is without this hunger cannot be helped by accident. And whoever has this hunger very strongly can be brought by accident to the beginning of a way in spite of all unfavorable circumstances."

"But what of those who were killed and who died from disease in the war for instance?" someone asked. "Could not many of them have had this hunger? And how then could this hunger have helped?"

"That is an entirely different thing," said G. "These people came under a general law. We do not speak of them and we cannot. We can only speak of people who, thanks to chance, or fate, or their own cleverness, do not come under a general law, that is, who stay outside the action of any general law of destruction. For instance it is known through statistics that a certain definite number of people have to fall under trams in Moscow during the year. Then if a man, even one with a great hunger, falls under a tram and the tram crushes him we can no longer speak of him from the point of view of work on the ways. We can speak only of those who are alive and only while they are alive. Trams or war—they are exactly the same thing. One is merely larger, the other smaller. We are speaking of those who do not fall under trams.

"A man, if he is hungry, has a chance to come into contact with the beginning of a way. But besides hunger still other 'rolls' are necessary. Otherwise a man will not see the way. Imagine that an educated European, that is, a man who knows nothing about religion, comes into touch with the possibility of a religious way. He will see nothing and he will understand nothing. For him it will be stupidity and superstition. But at the same time he may have a great hunger though formulated intellectually. It is exactly the same thing for a man who has never heard of yoga methods, of the development of consciousness and so on. For him, if he comes into touch with a yoga way, everything he hears will be dead. The fourth way is still more difficult. In order to give the fourth way a right valuation a man must have thought and felt and been disappointed in many things beforehand. He ought, if not actually to have tried the way of the fakir, the way of the monk, and the way of the yogi previously, at least to have known and thought about them and to be convinced that they are no good for him. It is not necessary to understand what I say literally. This thinking process can be unknown to the man himself. But the results of this process must be in him and only they can help him to recognize the fourth way. Otherwise he can stand very near to it and not see it.

"But it is certainly wrong to say that unless a man enters one of these ways he has no more chances. 'Ways' are simply help; help given to people according to their type. At the same time the 'ways,' the accelerated ways, the ways of personal, individual evolution as distinct from general evolution, can precede it, can lead up to it, but in any case they are distinct from it.

"Whether general evolution is proceeding or not is again another question. It is enough for us to realize that it is possible, and therefore evolution for people outside the 'ways' is possible. Speaking more correctly there are two 'ways.' One we will call the 'subjective way.' It includes all four ways of which we have spoken. The other we will call the 'objective way.' This is the way of people in life. You must not take the names 'subjective' and 'objective' too literally. They express only one aspect. I take them only because there are no other words."

"Would it be possible to say 'individual' and 'general' ways?" asked someone.

"No," said G. "It would be more incorrect than 'subjective' and 'objective' because the subjective way is not individual in the general meaning of this word, because this way is a 'school way.' From this point of view the 'objective way' is much more individual because it admits of many more individual peculiarities. No, it is better to leave these names— 'subjective' and 'objective.' They are not altogether suitable but we will take them conditionally.

"People of the objective way simply live in life. They are those whom we call good people. Particular systems and methods are not necessary for them; making use of ordinary religious or intellectual teachings and ordinary morality, they live at the same time according to conscience. They do not of necessity do much good, but they do no evil. Sometimes they happen to be quite uneducated, simple people but they understand life very well, they have a right valuation of things and a right outlook. And they are of course perfecting themselves and evolving. Only their way can be very long with many unnecessary repetitions."

I had for a long time wanted to get G. to talk about repetition but he always avoided it. So it was on this occasion. Without answering my question about repetition he continued:

"It often seems to people of the 'way,' that is, of the subjective way, especially those who are just beginning, that other people, that is, people of the objective way, are not moving. But this is a great mistake. A simple *obyvatel* may sometimes do such work within him that he will overtake another, a monk or even a yogi.

"*Obyvatel* is a strange word in the Russian language. It is used in the sense of 'inhabitant,' without any particular shade. At the same time it is used to express contempt or derision—'*obyvatel*'—as though there could be nothing worse. But those who speak in this way do not understand that the *obyvatel* is the healthy kernel of life. And from the point of view of the possibility of evolution, a good *obyvatel* has many more chances than a 'lunatic' or a 'tramp.' Afterwards I will perhaps explain what I mean by these two words. In the meantime we will talk about the *obyvatel*. I do not at all wish to say that all *obyvatels* are people of the objective way. Nothing of the kind. Among them are thieves, rascals, and fools; but there are others. I merely wish to say that being a good *obyvatel* by itself does not hinder the 'way.' And finally there are different types of *obyvatel*. Imagine, for example, the type of *obyvatel* who lives all his life just as the other people round him, conspicuous in nothing, perhaps a good master, who makes money, and is perhaps even close-fisted. At the same time he dreams all his life of monasteries, for instance, and dreams that some time or other he will leave everything and go into a monastery. And such things happen in the East and in Russia. A man lives and works, then, when his children or his grandchildren are grown up, he gives everything to them and goes into a monastery. This is the *obyvatel* of which I speak. Perhaps he does not go into a monastery, perhaps he does not need this. His own life as an *obyvatel* can be his way.

"People who are definitely thinking about ways, particularly people of intellectual ways, very often look down on the *obyvatel* and in general despise the virtues of the *obyvatel*. But they only show by this their own personal unsuitability for any way whatever. Because no way can begin from a level lower than the *obyvatel*. This is very often lost sight of on people who are unable to organize their own personal lives, who are too weak to struggle with and conquer life, dream of the ways, or what they consider are ways, because they think it will be easier for them than life and because this, so to speak, justifies their weakness and their inadaptability. A man who can be a good *obyvatel* is much more helpful from the point of view of the way than a 'tramp' who thinks himself much higher than an *obyvatel*. I call 'tramps' all the so-called 'intelligentsia'—artists, poets, any kind of 'bohemian' in general, who despises the *obyvatel* and who at the same time would be unable to exist without him. Ability to orientate oneself in life is a very useful quality from the point of view of work. A good *obyvatel* should be able to support at least twenty persons by his own labor. What is a man worth who is unable to do this?"

"What does *obyvatel* actually mean?" asked somebody. "Can it be said that an *obyvatel* is a good citizen?"

"Ought an *obyvatel* to be patriotic?" someone else asked. "Let us suppose there is war. What attitude should an *obyvatel* have towards war?"

"There can be different wars and there can be different patriots," said G. "You all still believe in words. An *obyvatel*, if he is a good *obyvatel*, does not believe in words. He realizes how much idle talk is hidden behind them. People who shout about their patriotism are psychopaths for him and he looks upon them as such."

"And how would an *obyvatel* look upon pacifists or upon people who refuse to go to the war?"

"Equally as lunatics! They are probably still worse."

On another occasion in connection with the same question G. said:

"A good deal is incomprehensible to you because you do not take into account the meaning of some of the most simple words, for instance, you have never thought what *to be serious* means. Try to give yourselves an answer to the question what *being serious* means."

"To have a serious attitude towards things," someone said.

"That is exactly what everybody thinks, actually it is exactly the reverse," said G. "To have a serious attitude towards things does not at all mean being serious because the principal question is, *towards what things?* Very many people have a serious attitude towards trivial things. Can they be called serious? Of course not.

"The mistake is that the concept 'serious' is taken conditionally. One thing is serious for one man and another thing for another man. In reality seriousness is one of the concepts which can never and under no circumstances be taken conditionally. Only one thing is serious for all people at all times. A man may be more aware of it or less aware of it but the seriousness of things will not alter on this account.

"If a man could understand all the horror of the lives of ordinary people who are turning round in a circle of insignificant interests and insignificant aims, if he could understand what they are losing, he would understand that there can be only one thing that is serious for him—to escape from the general law, to be free. What can be serious for a man in prison who is condemned to death? Only one thing: How to save himself, how to escape: nothing else is serious.

"When I say that an *obyvatel* is more serious than a 'tramp' or a 'lunatic,' I mean by this that, accustomed to deal with real values, an *obyvatel* values the possibilities of the 'ways' and the possibilities of 'liberation' or 'salvation' better and quicker than a man who is accustomed all his life to a circle of imaginary values, imaginary interests, and imaginary possibilities.

"People who are not serious for the *obyvatel* are people who live by fantasies, chiefly by the fantasy that they are able to do something. The *obyvatel* knows that they only deceive people, promise them God knows what, and that actually they are simply arranging affairs for themselves—or they are lunatics, which is still worse, in other words they believe everything that people say."

"To what category do politicians belong who speak contemptuously about '*obyvatel*,' '*obyvatels*' opinions,' '*obyvatels*' interests'?" someone asked.

"They are the worst kind of *obyvatels*," said G., "that is, *obyvatels* without any positive redeeming features, or they are charlatans, lunatics, or knaves."

"But may there not be honest and decent people among politicians?" someone asked.

"Certainly there may be," said G., "but in this case they are not practical people, they are dreamers, and they will be used by other people as screens to cover their own obscure affairs.

"The *obyvatel* perhaps may not know it in a philosophical way, that is to say, he is not able to formulate it, but he knows that things 'do themselves' simply through his own practical shrewdness, therefore, in his heart, he laughs at people who think, or who want to assure him, that they signify anything, that anything depends on their decisions, that they can change or, in general, do anything. This for him is not being serious. And an understanding of what is not serious can help him to value that which is serious."

We often returned to questions on the difficulties of the way. Our own experience of communal life and work constantly threw us up against newer and newer difficulties that lay in ourselves.

"The whole thing is in being ready to sacrifice one's freedom," said G. "A man consciously and unconsciously struggles for freedom as he imagines it and this, more than anything else, prevents him from attaining real freedom. But a man who is capable of attaining anything comes sooner or later to the conclusion that his freedom is illusion and he agrees to sacrifice this illusion. He voluntarily becomes a slave. He does what he is told, says what he is told, and thinks what he is told. He is not afraid of losing anything because he knows that he has nothing. And in this way he acquires everything. Everything in him that was real in his understanding, in his sympathies, tastes, and desires, all comes back to him accompanied by new things which he did not have and could not have had before, together with a feeling of unity and will within him. But to arrive at this point, a man must pass through the hard way of slavery and obedience. And if he wants results he must obey not only outwardly but inwardly. This requires a great determination, and determination requires a great understanding of the fact that there is no other way, that a man can do nothing *himself*, but that at the same time, something has to be done.

"When a man comes to the conclusion that he cannot, and does not desire, to live any longer in the way he has lived till then; when he really sees everything that his life is made up of and decides to work, he must be truthful with himself in order not to fall into a still worse position. Because there is nothing worse than to begin work on oneself and then leave it and find oneself between two stools; it is much better not to begin. And in order not to begin in vain or risk being deceived on one's own account a man should test his decision many times. And principally he must know how far he is willing to go, what he is willing to sacrifice. There is nothing more easy to say than *everything*. A man can never sacrifice everything and this can never be required of him. But he must define exactly what he is willing to sacrifice and not bargain about it afterwards. Or it will be the same with him as with the wolf in the Armenian fairy tale.

"Do you know the Armenian fairy tale of the wolf and the sheep?

"Once there lived a wolf who slaughtered a great many sheep and reduced many people to tears.

"At length, I do not know why, he suddenly felt qualms of conscience and began to repent his life; so he decided to reform and to slaughter no more sheep.

"In order to do this seriously he went to a priest and asked him to hold a thanksgiving service.

"The priest began the service and the wolf stood weeping and praying in the church. The service was long. The wolf had slaughtered many of the priest's sheep, therefore the priest prayed earnestly that the wolf would indeed reform. Suddenly the wolf looked through a window and saw that sheep were being driven home. He began to fidget but the priest went on and on without end.

"At last the wolf could contain himself no longer and he shouted:

" 'Finish it, priest! Or all the sheep will be driven home and I shall be left without supper!'

"This is a very good fairy tale because it describes man very well. He is ready to sacrifice everything, but after all today's dinner is a different matter.

"A man always wishes to begin with something big. But this is impossible; there can be no choice, we must begin with the things of today."

I quote one talk as being a very characteristic example of G.'s methods. We were walking in the park. There were five of us besides G. One of us asked him what his views on astrology were, whether there was anything of value in the more or less known theories of astrology.

"Yes," said G., "it depends upon how they are understood. They can be of value and they can be without value. Astrology deals with only one part of man, *with his type,* his essence—it does not deal with personality, with acquired qualities. If you understand this you understand what is of value in astrology."

There had been talks in our groups about types before and it seemed to us that the science of types was the most difficult thing in the study of man because G. gave us very little material and required of us our own observations of ourselves and others.

We continued to walk and G. continued to speak trying to explain what there was in man that could depend upon planetary influences and what could not.

As we left the park G. stopped talking and was going a few steps ahead of us. We five walked behind him talking together. In going round a tree G. dropped the stick—ebony with a Caucasian silver handle —he was carrying and one of us bent down, picked it up, and gave it to him. G. walked on for a few steps, then turned to us and said:

"That was astrology. Do you understand? You all saw me drop the stick. Why did one of you pick it up? Let each of you speak for himself."

One said he had not seen G. drop the stick as he was looking another way. The second said he had noticed that G. had not dropped the stick accidentally as happens when a stick gets caught in something, but that he had intentionally loosened his hand and let the stick fall. This had excited his curiosity and he had waited to see what would happen next. The third said he saw G. drop the stick, but was very absorbed in thinking of astrology, particularly trying to remember what G. said once before, and did not pay sufficient attention to the stick. The fourth saw the stick fall and thought of picking it up, but at that moment the other picked up the stick and gave it to G. The fifth said he saw the stick fall and then he saw himself picking it up and giving it to G.

G. smiled as he listened to us.

"This is astrology," he said. "In the same situation one man sees and does one thing, another—another thing, a third—a third thing, and so on. And each one acted according to his type. Observe people and yourselves in this way and then perhaps we will afterwards talk of a different astrology."

The time passed by very quickly. The short Essentuki summer was drawing to a close. We had begun to think of the winter and to make a variety of plans.

And suddenly everything changed. For a reason that seemed to me to be accidental and which was the result of friction between certain members of our small group G. announced that he was dispersing the whole group and stopping all work. At first we simply did not believe him, thinking he was putting us to a test. And when he said he was going to the Black Sea coast with Z. alone, all excepting a few of us who had to return to Moscow or Petersburg announced that they would follow him wherever he went. G. consented to this but he said that we must look after ourselves and that there would be no work no matter how much we counted on it.

All this surprised me very much. I considered the moment most inappropriate for "acting," and if what G. said was serious, then why had the whole business been started? During this period nothing new had appeared in us. And if G. had started work with us such as we were, then why was he stopping it now? This altered nothing for me materially. I had decided to pass the winter in the Caucasus in any case. But it changed a good many things for some of the other members of our group who were still slightly uncertain and made the difficulty for them insuperable. And I have to confess that my confidence in G. began to waver from this moment. What the matter was and what particularly provoked me is difficult for me to define even now. But the fact is that from this moment there began to take place in me a separation between G. himself and his ideas. Until then I had not separated them.

At the end of August I at first followed G. to Tuapse and from there went to Petersburg with the intention of bringing back some things; unfortunately I had to leave behind all my books. I thought at the time that it would be risking very much to take them to the Caucasus. But in Petersburg, of course, everything was lost.

Chapter Eighteen

I WAS kept in St. Petersburg longer than I had thought to be and I only left there on the 15th of October, a week before the bolshevik revolution. It was quite impossible to stay there any longer. Something disgusting and clammy was drawing near. A sickly tension and the expectation of something inevitable could be felt in everything. Rumors were creeping about, each one more absurd and stupid than the other. Nobody understood anything. Nobody could imagine what was coming later on. The "temporary government," having vanquished Kornilov, conducted the most correct negotiations with the bolsheviks who openly showed they did not care a hang for the "socialist ministers" and tried only to gain time. The Germans for some reason did not march upon St. Petersburg although the front was open. People now thought of them as saviors both from the "temporary government" and from the bolsheviks. I did not share the hopes based upon the Germans because, in my opinion, what was taking place in Russia had to a considerable extent got out of hand.

In Tuapse there was still comparative calm. Some kind of soviet was sitting in the country house of the Shah of Persia but plunderings had not yet begun. G. settled down at a fair distance from Tuapse to the south a little over fifteen miles from Sochi. He hired a country house there overlooking the sea, bought a pair of horses, and lived with a small company of people. Altogether about ten persons were gathered there.

I went there too. It was a wonderful place, full of roses, with a view of the sea on one side and a chain of mountains already covered with snow on the other. I was very sorry for those of our people who had stayed in Moscow and St. Petersburg.

But even on the day following my arrival I noticed that there was something wrong. There was not a trace of the Essentuki atmosphere. I was particularly astonished at Z.'s position. When I had left for St. Petersburg in the beginning of September Z. was full of enthusiasm; he continually urged me not to stay in St. Petersburg since it might become so difficult to get through.

"Do you never intend to be in St. Petersburg any more?" I asked him then.

"One who flees to the mountains does not turn back," Z. replied.

And now, on the day following my arrival in Uch Dere, I heard that Z. intended to return to St. Petersburg.

"What can he be going back there for? He has left his employment, what is he going to do there?"

"I do not know," said Dr. S., who had told me about it. "G. is not pleased with him and says that he had better go."

It was difficult for me to get Z. himself into a talk. He obviously did not desire to explain but he said that he really intended to leave.

Gradually, by questioning others, I found out that a strange thing had happened. A very absurd quarrel between G. and some Letts, our neighbors, had occurred. Z. was present at it. G. had not liked something Z. had said or something, and from that day he had completely changed towards him, stopped speaking to him, and, in general, put him into such a position that Z. was obliged to announce his decision to leave.

I considered this to be pure idiocy. To go to St. Petersburg at this time seemed to me the height of absurdity. There was a real famine there, unruly crowds, robbery, and nothing else. At that time of course one could not yet have imagined that we should never see St. Petersburg again. I counted upon going there in the spring. I thought that by the spring there would be something definite. But now, in the winter, this was quite unreasonable. I could have understood it if Z. was interested in politics and was studying the events of the period, but as this was not the case I saw no motives for it whatever. I began to persuade Z. to wait, to decide nothing at once, to talk to G., and to try somehow to clarify the position. Z. promised me not to be in a hurry. But I saw that he was indeed in a very strange position. G. completely ignored him and this produced on Z. a most depressing impression. Two weeks passed in this way. My arguments had worked on Z. and he said that he would stay if G. agreed to let him. He went to speak to G., but came back very soon with a disturbed face.

"Well, what did he say to you?"

"Nothing in particular; he said that once I had decided to go I had better go."

Z. went. I could not understand it. I would not have let a dog go to St. Petersburg at that time.

G. intended to pass the winter at Uch Dere. We lived in several houses spread over a large plot of land. There was no kind of "work" in the sense of what had been at Essentuki. We chopped up trees for winter firewood; we collected wild pears; G. often went to Sochi where one of our people was in hospital, having contracted typhoid before my arrival from St. Petersburg.

Unexpectedly G. decided to go to another place. He found that here we might easily be cut off from all communication with the rest of Russia and be left without provisions.

G. went away with half of our company and afterwards sent Dr. S. for the rest. We again forgathered in Tuapse and from there we began to make excursions along the seashore to the north where there was no railway. During one of these trips S. found some of his St. Petersburg acquaintances who had a country house twenty-four miles north of Tuapse. We stayed the night with them and the next morning G. hired a house half a mile away from them. Here our small company again forgathered. Four went to Essentuki.

Here we lived for two months. It was a very interesting time. G., Dr. S., and I went to Tuapse every week for provisions for ourselves and fodder for the horses. These trips will always remain in my memory. They were full of the most improbable adventures and very interesting talks. Our house stood overlooking the sea three miles from the big village of Olghniki. I had hoped that we would live there a longer time. But in the second half of December there came the rumors that a part of the Caucasian Army was moving towards Russia on foot along the shores of the Black Sea. G. said that we would again go to Essentuki and begin fresh work. I went first. I took part of our belongings to Pyatigorsk and returned. It was possible to get through although there were bolsheviks in Armavir.

The bolsheviks, in general, had increased in the north Caucasus and friction began between them and the Cossacks. At Mineralni Vodi, when we all passed through there, everything was outwardly quiet, although murders of many persons whom the bolsheviks disliked had already occurred.

G. hired a large house in Essentuki and sent out a circular letter, dated the 12th of February, over my signature, to all the members of our Moscow and St. Petersburg groups inviting them to come with those near to them to live and to work with him.

There was already famine in St. Petersburg and Moscow but there was still an abundance of everything in the Caucasus. To get through now was not easy and several failed in spite of their desire to do so. But many came. Altogether about forty people assembled. With them came Z. to whom also a letter had been sent. He arrived quite ill.

In February while we were still waiting, G. once said, when he was showing me the house and everything he had arranged:

"Now do you understand why we collected money in Moscow and St. Petersburg? You said then that a thousand roubles was too much. And will even this money be enough? One and a half persons paid. I have now already spent more than was collected then."

G. intended to hire or buy a plot of land, arrange kitchen gardens, and in general to organize a colony. But he was prevented by the events which had begun during the summer.

When our people assembled in March, 1918, very strict rules were established in our house: it was forbidden to leave the grounds, day and night orderlies were established, and so on. And work of the most varied kind began.

In the organization of the house and of our lives there was very much of interest.

Exercises on this occasion were much more difficult and varied than during the preceding summer. We began rhythmic exercises to music, dervish dances, different kinds of mental exercises, the study of different ways of breathing, and so on. Particularly intensive were the exercises for studying various imitations of psychic phenomena, thought-reading, clairvoyance, mediumistic displays, and so forth. Before these exercises began G. explained to us that the study of these "tricks," as he called them, was an obligatory subject in all Eastern schools, because without having studied all possible counterfeits and imitations it was not possible to begin the study of phenomena of a supernormal character. A man is in a position to distinguish the real from the sham in this sphere only when he knows all the shams and is able to reproduce them himself. Besides this G. said that a practical study of these "psychic tricks" was in itself an exercise which could be replaced by nothing else, which was the best of all for developing certain special characteristics: keenness of observation, shrewdness, and more particularly for the enlargement of other characteristics for which there are no words in ordinary psychological language but which must certainly be developed.

But the principal part of the work which began at that time were the rhythmics to music and similar strange dances which afterwards led to the reproduction of the exercises of various dervishes. G. did not explain his aims and intentions but according to things he had said before, it was possible to think that the result of these exercises would be to bring under control the physical body.

In addition to exercises, dances, gymnastics, talks, lectures, and housework, special work was organized for those without means.

I remember that, when we were leaving Alexandropol the year before, G. took with him a box of skein silk which he told me he had bought cheaply at a sale. This silk always traveled with him. When our people assembled in Essentuki G. gave this silk to the women and children to wind onto star-shaped cards which were also made in our house. Then some of our people who possessed commercial talents sold this silk to shops in Pyatigorsk, Kislovodsk, and Essentuki itself. One must remember that time. There were absolutely no goods whatever, shops were empty, and the silk was snapped up at once because such things as silk, cotton, and so on were unbelievably difficult to obtain. This work continued for two months and gave a sure and regular income quite out of proportion with the original cost of the silk.

In normal times a colony like ours could not have existed in Essentuki nor probably anywhere else in Russia. We should have excited curiosity, we should have attracted attention, the police would have appeared, some kind of scandal would undoubtedly have arisen, all possible kinds of accusations would have made their appearance, political tendencies would certainly have been ascribed to us, or sectarian or anti-moral. People are made in such a way that they invariably make accusations against the things they fail to understand. But at that time, that is, in 1918, those who would have been curious about us were occupied in saving their own skins from the bolsheviks, and the bolsheviks were not yet strong enough to be interested in the lives of private people or private organizations having no direct political character. And, seeing that, among the intellectuals from the capital who found themselves by the will of fate at Mineralni Vodi at that time, a number of groups and working associations had just been organized, nobody paid any attention to us.

On one occasion during general conversation in the evening G. said that we must think of a name for our colony and in general legalize ourselves. This was at the time of the Pyatigorsk bolshevik government.

"Think out something like *Sodroojestvo*[1] and 'earned by work' or 'international' at the same time," said G. "In any case they will not understand. But it is necessary for them to be able to give us some kind of name."

We began in turn to propose various designations.

Public lectures were arranged in our house twice a week to which a fair number of people came and once or twice we gave demonstrations of imitation psychic phenomena which were not very successful since our public submitted very poorly to instruction.

But my personal position in G.'s work began to change. For a whole year something had been accumulating and I gradually began to see that there were many things I could not understand and that *I had to go*.

This may appear strange and unexpected after all I have written so far, but it had accumulated gradually. I wrote that I had for some time begun to separate G. and the *ideas*. I had no doubts about the ideas. On the contrary, the more I thought of them, the deeper I entered into them, the more I began to value them and realize their significance. But I began very strongly to doubt that it was possible for me, or even for the majority of our company, to continue to work under G.'s leadership. I do not in the least mean that I found any of G.'s actions or methods wrong or that they failed to respond to what I expected. This would be

[1] *Sodroojestvo:* approximately "Union of friends for common aim."

strange and completely out of place in connection with a leader in work, the esoteric nature of which I have admitted. The one excludes the other. In work of such a nature there can be no sort of criticism, no sort of "disagreement" with this or that person. On the contrary, all work consists in doing what the leader indicates, understanding in conformance with his opinions even those things that he does not say plainly, helping him in *everything* that he does. There can be no other attitude towards the work. And G. himself said several times that a most important thing in the work was *to remember that one came to learn* and to take no other role upon oneself.

At the same time this does not at all mean that a man has no choice or that he is obliged to follow something which does not respond to what he is seeking. G. himself said that there are no "general" schools, that each *"guru"* or leader of a school works at his own specialty, one is a sculptor, another is a musician, a third is again something else, and that all the pupils of such a *guru* have to study his specialty. And it stands to reason that here a choice is possible. A man has to wait until he meets a *guru* whose specialty *he is able* to study, a specialty which suits his tastes, his tendencies, and his abilities.

There is no doubt that there may be very interesting ways, like music and like sculpture. But it cannot be that every man should be required to learn music or sculpture. In school work there are undoubtedly *obligatory* subjects and there are, if it is possible to put it in this way, auxiliary subjects, the study of which is proposed merely as a means of studying the obligatory. Then the methods of the schools may differ very much. According to the three ways the methods of each *guru* may approximate either to the way of the fakir, the way of the monk, or the way of the yogi. And it is of course possible that a man who is beginning work will make a mistake, will follow a leader such as he cannot follow for any distance. It stands to reason that it is the task of the leader to see to it that people do not begin to work with him for whom his methods or his special subjects will always be alien, incomprehensible, and unattainable. But if this does happen and if a man had begun to work with a leader whom he cannot follow, then of course, having noticed and realized this, he ought to go and seek another leader or work independently, if he is able to do so.

In regard to my relations with G. I saw clearly at that time that I had been mistaken about many things that I had ascribed to G. and that by staying with him now I should not be going in the same direction I went at the beginning. And I thought that all the members of our small group, with very few exceptions, were in the same or in a similar situation.

This was a very strange "observation" but it was absolutely a right one. I had nothing to say against G.'s methods except that they did not suit me. A very clear example came to my mind then. I had never had a negative attitude towards the "way of the monk," to religious, mystical ways. At the same time I could never have thought for one moment that such a way was possible for me or suitable. And so, if after three years of work I perceived that G. was leading us in fact towards the way of religion, of the monastery, and required the observance of all religious forms and ceremonies, there would be of course a motive for disagreeing with this and for going away, even though at the risk of losing direct leadership. And certainly this would not, at the same time, mean that I considered the religious way a wrong way in general. It may even be a more correct way than my way *but it is not my way*.

The decision to leave G.'s work and leave him exacted from me a great inner struggle. I had built very much upon it and it was difficult for me now to reconstruct everything from the beginning. But there was nothing else to do. Of course, all that I had learned during those three years I retained. But a whole year passed by while I was going into all this and until I found it possible to continue to work in the same direction as G. but independently.

I went into a separate house and again began work abandoned in St. Petersburg, on my book which afterwards appeared under the title A *New Model of the Universe*.

In the "Home" lectures and demonstrations still continued for a certain time and then stopped.

Sometimes I met G. in the park or on the street, sometimes he came to my house. But I avoided going to the "Home."

At this time the position of affairs in the north Caucasus began to get very much worse. We were completely cut off from central Russia; what was going on there we did not know.

After the first Cossack raid on Essentuki the position quickly began to change for the worse and G. decided to leave Mineralni Vodi. Where he actually intended to go he did not say and it was difficult to say, having regard to the circumstances of the time.

The public who had left Mineralni Vodi at that time had tried to get through to Novorossiysk and I supposed that he would also go in that direction. I also decided to leave Essentuki. But I did not want to leave before he did. In this respect I had a strange kind of feeling. I wanted to wait until the end; to do everything that depended upon me so that afterwards I could tell myself that I had not let a single possibility escape me. It was very difficult for me to reject the idea of working with G.

In the beginning of August G. left Essentuki. Most of those living in the "Home" left with him. A few people had gone earlier. About ten persons were left in Essentuki.

I decided to go to Novorossiysk. But circumstances began to change swiftly. Within a week of G.'s departure communications even with places nearest to us came to a stop. Cossacks began to raid the branch line to

Mineralni Vodi and where we were, bolshevik robberies, "requisitions," and so on began. This was the time of the massacre of "hostages" in Pyatigorsk when General Russki, General Radko-Dimitriev, and Prince Ouroussov and many others perished.

I must confess that I felt very silly. I had not gone abroad when it was possible in order to work with G. and the final outcome was that I had parted from G. and stopped with the bolsheviks.

All of us who had stayed in Essentuki had to live through a very difficult time. For me and my family things turned out comparatively favorably. Only two people out of four got ill with typhoid. No one died. Not once were we robbed. And all the time I had work and earned money. Things were much worse for others. In January, 1919, we were set free by the Cossacks of Denikin's Army. But I was only able to leave Essentuki in the following summer of 1919.

The news we had of G. was very brief. He had traveled by railway to Maikop and from there the whole of the party with him went on foot by a very interesting but very difficult way, through the mountains to the sea at Sochi which had then been seized by the Georgians. Carrying with them the whole of their baggage they walked, with all possible kinds of adventures and dangers, over lofty passes where there were no roads and where hunters crossed but seldom. It was, apparently, only about a month after their departure from Essentuki that they reached Sochi.

But the inner situation had changed. In Sochi the greater part of the company, as I had foreseen, parted company with G. Among them were P. and Z. Only four people stayed with G. of whom Dr. S. alone belonged to the original St. Petersburg group. The others had only been in "young" groups.

In February P., who had established himself in Maikop after the rupture with G., came to Essentuki for his mother who had remained there, and from him we learned the details of everything that had taken place on the way to and on arrival at Sochi. Moscow people had gone to Kiev. G. with his four companions had gone to Tiflis. In the spring we learned that he was continuing work in Tiflis with new people and in a new direction, basing it principally on art, that is, on music, dances, and rhythmic exercises.

At the end of winter when conditions of living became slightly easier I began to look through my notes and drawings of G.'s diagrams which with G.'s permission I had preserved since St. Petersburg. My attention was particularly attracted by the *enneagram*. The explanation of the enneagram had clearly not been finished and I felt that there were in it hints at a possible continuation. I very soon saw that a continuation must be sought in connection with the wrong situation of the "shock" which came into the enneagram at the interval sol–la. Then I turned my attention to what the Moscow notes, in connection with commentaries on the enneagram, said about the influences of the three octaves on one another in the "food diagram." I drew the enneagram as it had been given to us and I saw that it represented up to a certain point the "food diagram."

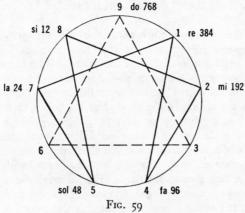

FIG. 59

The point 3, or the "interval" mi–fa, was the place where the "shock" came in which gave do 192 of the second octave. When I added the beginning of this octave to the enneagram I saw that the point 6 came at the "interval" mi–fa of the second octave and the "shock" in the form of the third octave do 48 which begins at this point. The completed drawing of the octaves came out as follows:

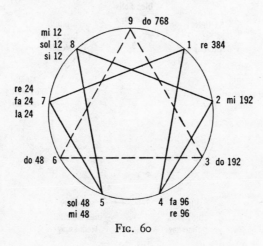

FIG. 60

This signified that there was no wrong place for a "shock" at all. Point 6 showed the entry of the "shock" in the second octave and the "shock" was the do which began the third octave. All three octaves reached H12. In one it was si, in the second sol, and in the third mi. The second octave which ended at 12 in the enneagram ought to have gone on further. But si 12 and mi 12 required an "additional shock." I thought a great deal about the nature of these "shocks" at that time but I will speak of them later.

I felt that there was very much material in the enneagram. Points 1, 2, 4, 5, 7, 8 represented, according to the "food diagram," different "systems" of the organism. 1—the digestive system; 2—the breathing system; 4—the blood stream; 5—the brain; 7—the spinal cord; 8—the sympathetic system and the sex organs. According to this the direction of the inner lines 1 4 2 8 5 7 1, that is, the content of fraction 7, showed the direction of the flow or distribution of arterial blood in the organism and then its return in the form of venous blood. It was particularly interesting that the *point of return* was not the heart but the digestive system which indeed is the case since venous blood is first of all mixed with the products of digestion, it then goes to the right auricle, through the right ventricle, then to the lungs to absorb oxygen, and from there goes to the left auricle and then the left ventricle and then through the aorta into the arterial system.

Examining the enneagram further I saw that the *seven points* could represent the *seven planets* of the ancient world; in other words the enneagram could be an astronomical symbol. And when I took the order of the planets in the order of the days of the week I obtained the following picture:

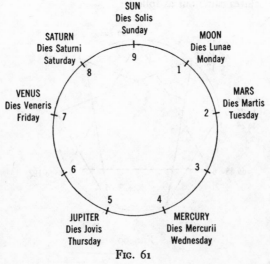

SUN
Dies Solis
Sunday

SATURN
Dies Saturni
Saturday

MOON
Dies Lunae
Monday

9

8

1

VENUS
Dies Veneris
Friday

MARS
Dies Martis
Tuesday

7

2

6

3

5

4

JUPITER
Dies Jovis
Thursday

MERCURY
Dies Mercurii
Wednesday

FIG. 61

I did not try to go any further as I did not have the necessary books to hand and there was very little time.

"Events" gave no time to go into philosophical speculations. One had to think about living, that is to say, simply and quite plainly to think about where one could live and work. The revolution and everything connected with it aroused in me deep physical disgust. At the same time, in spite of my sympathy with the "whites" I could not believe in their success. The bolsheviks did not hesitate to promise things that neither they nor anyone else could perform. In this was their principal strength. It was something in which nobody could compete with them. In addition to this they had the support of Germany, who saw in them a possibility of revenge in the future. The volunteer army, which had freed us from the bolsheviks, was able to fight them and conquer them. But it was not able to organize in a proper way the course of life in the liberated provinces. Its leaders had neither program, knowledge, nor experience in this direction. Of course this could not be demanded of them. But facts are facts. The situation was very unstable and the wave which was still rolling towards Moscow at the time could be rolled back again any day.

It was necessary to get abroad. I had marked down London as my final aim. First because I knew more people there and second because I thought that among the English I should find the greater response and a greater interest in the new ideas I now had, than anywhere else. Besides, when I was in London on my way to India before the war and on my return voyage at the beginning of the war I had decided to go there to write and publish my book, which had been begun in 1911, under the title of *The Wisdom of the Gods*, and which subsequently appeared under the title of *A New Model of the Universe*. As a matter of fact this book, in which I touched upon questions of religion and in particular upon methods for studying the New Testament, could not have been published in Russia.

So I decided to travel to London and to try to organize lectures and groups there like those at St. Petersburg. This only came to pass three and a half years later.

In the beginning of June, 1919, I at last succeeded in leaving Essentuki. At that time it had become quite calm there and life had been a little re-established. But I did not trust this calm. It was necessary to go abroad. At first I went to Rostov and then to Ekaterinodar and Novorossiysk and then returned again to Ekaterinodar. Ekaterinodar at that time was the capital of Russia. There I met some of our company who had left Essentuki before me as well as some friends and acquaintances from St. Petersburg.

There remains in my memory one of my first talks.

My friend from St. Petersburg asked me, when we had spoken of G.'s system and of work on oneself, whether I could indicate any practical results of this work.

Remembering all I had experienced during the preceding year, particularly after G.'s departure, I said that I had acquired a *strange confidence*, one which I could not define in one word but which I must describe.

"This is not self-confidence in the ordinary sense," I said, "quite the contrary, rather is it a confidence in the unimportance and the insignificance of *self*, that self which we usually know. But what I am confident about is that if something terrible happened to me like things that have happened to many of my friends during the past year, then it would be *not I* who would meet it, not this ordinary I, but another I within me who would be equal to the occasion. Two years ago G. asked me whether I felt a new I inside me and I had to answer that I felt no change whatever. Now I can speak otherwise. And I can explain how the change takes place. It does not take place at once, I mean that the change does not embrace every moment of life. All the ordinary life goes on in the ordinary way, all those very ordinary stupid small I's, excepting perhaps a few which have already become impossible. But if something big were to happen, something which would require the straining of every nerve, then I know that this big thing would be met not by the ordinary small I, which is now speaking, and which can be made afraid, nor by anything like it—but by another, a big I, which nothing can frighten and which would be equal to everything that happened. I cannot describe it better. But for me it is a fact. And this fact is definitely connected for me with this work. You know my life and you know that I was not afraid of many things, both inward and outward, that people are often afraid of. But this is something different, a different taste. Therefore I know, for myself, that this new confidence has not come simply as a result of a great experience of life. It is the result of that work on myself which I began four years ago."

In Ekaterinodar and afterwards in Rostov during the winter, I collected together a small group and, on a plan that I had worked out the preceding winter, I gave them lectures expounding G.'s system as well as the things from ordinary life which lead up to it.

During the summer and autumn of 1919 I received two letters from G. in Ekaterinodar and Novorossiysk. . . . He wrote that he had opened in Tiflis an "Institute for the Harmonious Development of Man" on a very broad program and enclosed a prospectus of this "Institute" which made me very thoughtful indeed. The prospectus began in this way:

With the permission of the Minister for National Education the Institute for the Harmonious Development of Man based on G. I. G.'s system is being opened in Tiflis. The Institute accepts children and adults of both sexes. Study will take place morning and evening. The subjects of study are: gymnastics of all kinds (rhythmical, medicinal, and others). Exercises for the development of will, memory, attention, hearing, thinking, emotion, instinct, and so on.

To this was added that G. I. G.'s system

was already in operation in a whole series of large cities such as Bombay, Alexandria, Cabul, New York, Chicago, Christiania, Stockholm, Moscow, Essentuki, and in all departments and homes of the true international and laboring fraternities.

At the end of the prospectus in a list of "specialist teachers" of the Institute for the Harmonious Development of Man I found my own name as well as the names of "Mechanical Engineer" P. and still another of our company, J., who was living at that time in Novorossiysk and had no intention whatever of going to Tiflis.

G. wrote in his letter that he was preparing his ballet "The Struggle of the Magicians" and without making any reference at all to past difficulties he invited me to go and work with him in Tiflis. This was very characteristic of him. But for various reasons I could not go there. In the first place there were very great material obstacles and secondly the difficulties which had arisen in Essentuki were for me very real ones. My decision to leave G. had cost me very dear and I could not give it up so easily, the more so as all his motives were to be seen. I must confess that I was not very enthusiastic about the program of the Institute for the Harmonious Development of Man. I realized, of course, that it meant that G. was obviously obliged to give some sort of outward form to his work having regard to outward conditions, as he had done at Essentuki, and that this outward form was somewhat in the nature of a caricature. But I also realized that behind this outward form stood the same thing as before and that *this* could not change. I was doubtful only of my own ability to adapt myself to this outward form. At the same time I was confident that I should soon have to meet G. again.

P. came to Ekaterinodar from Maikop and we spoke together a great deal about the system and G. P. was in a fairly negative frame of mind. But it seemed to me that my idea that it was imperative to make a distinction between the system and G. helped him to understand the position of affairs better.

I was beginning to get very interested in my groups. I saw a possibility of continuing the work. The ideas of the system found a response and obviously answered the needs of people who wanted to understand what was taking place both in them and around them. And around us was being concluded that brief little epilogue to Russian history which had frightened our friends and "allies" so much. Ahead of us everything was quite dark. I was in Rostov in the autumn and beginning of winter. There

I met another two or three of the St. Petersburg company as well as Z. who had arrived from Kiev. Z. like P. was in a very negative frame of mind in relation to all of the work. We settled down together in the same quarters and it seemed that talks with me made him revise many things and convince himself that the original valuations were right. He decided to try to get through to G. in Tiflis. But he was not fated to accomplish this. We left Rostov almost at the same time, Z. leaving one or two days after me, but he arrived in Novorossiysk already ill and in the first days of January, 1920, he died of the smallpox.

Soon afterwards I managed to leave for Constantinople.

At that time Constantinople was full of Russians. I met acquaintances from St. Petersburg and with their assistance I began to give lectures in the offices of the "Russki Miyak." I at once collected a fairly large audience mostly of young men. I continued to develop the ideas begun in Rostov and Ekaterinodar, connecting general ideas of psychology and philosophy with ideas of esotericism.

I got no further letters from G., but I was sure that he would come to Constantinople. He actually arrived in June with a fairly large company.

In former Russia, even in its distant outskirts, work had become impossible and we were gradually approaching the period which I had foreseen in St. Petersburg, that is, of working in Europe.

I was very glad to see G. and to me personally it seemed then that, in the interests of the work, all former difficulties could be set aside and that I could again work with him as in St. Petersburg. I brought G. to my lectures and handed over to him all the people who came to my lectures, particularly the small group of about thirty persons who met upstairs in the offices of the "Miyak."

G. gave to the ballet the central position of his work at that time. Besides this he wanted to organize a continuation of his Tiflis Institute in Constantinople, the principal place in which would be taken by dances and rhythmic exercises which would prepare people to take part in the ballet. According to his ideas the ballet should become a school. I worked out the scenario of the ballet for him and began to understand this idea better. The dances and all the other "numbers" of the ballet, or rather "revue," demanded a long and an entirely special preparation. The people who were being prepared for the ballet and who were taking part in it, would, in so doing, be obliged to study and to acquire control over themselves, in this way approaching the disclosure of the higher forms of consciousness. Into the ballet there entered, and as a necessary part of it, dances, exercises, and the ceremonies of various dervishes as well as many little known Eastern dances.

It was a very interesting time for me. G. often came to me in Prinkipo. We went together through the Constantinople bazaars. We went to the Mehlevi dervishes and he explained something to me that I had not been able to understand before. And this was that the whirling of the Mehlevi dervishes was an exercise for the brain based upon counting, like those exercises that he had shown to us in Essentuki. Sometimes I worked with him for entire days and nights. One such night in particular remains in my memory, when we "translated" a dervish song for "The Struggle of the Magicians." I saw G. the artist and G. the poet, whom he had so carefully hidden inside him, particularly the latter. This translation took the form of G. recalling the Persian verses, sometimes repeating them to himself in a quiet voice and then translating them for me into Russian. After a quarter of an hour, let us say, when I had completely disappeared beneath forms, symbols, and assimilations, he said: "There, now make *one line* out of that." I did not try to create any measure or to find a rhythm. This was quite impossible. G. continued and again after a quarter of an hour he said: "That is another line." We sat until the morning. This was in Koumbaradji Street a little below the former Russian consulate. At length the town began to wake. I had written, I think, five verses and had stopped at the last line of the fifth verse. No kind of effort could make my brain turn any more. G. laughed but he also was tired and could not go on. So the verse remained as it was, unfinished, because he never returned again to this song.

Two or three months passed by in this way. I helped G. all I could in organizing his Institute. But gradually the same difficulties arose before me as in Essentuki. So that, when the Institute was opened, I think in October, I was unable to join it. But in order not to hinder G. or to give rise to discord among those who came to my lectures, I put an end to my own lectures and ceased to visit Constantinople. A few of those who came to my lectures visited me in Prinkipo and there we continued the talks begun in Constantinople.

Two months later when G.'s work had already become consolidated I again started to give lectures at the "Miyak" in Constantinople and I continued them for another six months. I visited G.'s Institute from time to time and sometimes he came to me in Prinkipo. The inner relationship between us remained very good. In the spring he proposed that I should give lectures in his Institute and I began to give lectures there once a week in which G. himself took part, supplementing my explanations.

At the beginning of summer G. closed his Institute and went over to Prinkipo. Somewhere about this time I told him in detail of a plan I had drawn up for a book to expound his St. Petersburg lectures and talks with commentaries of my own. He agreed to this plan and authorized me to write and publish it. Up till then I had submitted to the general rule, obligatory for everyone, which concerned G.'s work. According to this rule nobody under any circumstances had the right to write even for his own use anything connected with him or his ideas, or any other participants in the work, or to keep letters, notes, and so on, still less to publish anything. During the first years G. insisted strongly upon the obligatory nature of this rule and it was supposed that everyone accepted in the work would give his word to write nothing (and it goes without saying to publish nothing) referring to G. without special permission, even in the event of his leaving the work and G.

This was one of the fundamental rules. Every new person who joined us heard about it and it was considered to be fundamental and obligatory. But afterwards G. accepted in his work people who paid no attention to this rule or who did not wish to consider it. This explains the subsequent appearance of descriptions of various moments in G.'s work.

I passed the summer of 1921 in Constantinople and in August left for London. Before my departure G. proposed that I should go with him to Germany where he once more intended to open his Institute and prepare his ballet. But in the first place I did not believe it was possible to organize work in Germany and secondly I did not believe that I could work with G.

Soon after my arrival in London I began to give lectures in continuation of the work at Constantinople and Ekaterinodar. I learned that G. had gone to Germany with his Tiflis company and with those of my Constantinople people who had joined him. He tried to organize work in Berlin and Dresden and intended to purchase the apartments of the former Institut Dalcroze in Helleran near Dresden. But nothing came out of it all and in connection with the proposed purchase some strange events took place which ended in legal proceedings. In February, 1922, G. came to London. I at once invited him, as a matter of course, to my lectures and introduced him to all who were coming to them. This time my attitude towards him was much more definite. I still expected a very great deal more from his work and I decided to do everything I could to help him to organize his Institute and the preparation of his ballet. But I did not believe it was possible for me to work with him. I saw again all the former obstacles which had begun to appear in Essentuki. This time they had appeared even before he arrived. The outward situation was that G. had done very much towards the accomplishment of his plans. The chief thing was that a certain cadre of people, about twenty, had been prepared, with whom it was possible to begin. The music for the ballet had almost all been prepared (with the co-operation of a well-known musician). The organization of the Institute had been worked out. But there was no money to put all this into practice. Soon after his arrival G. said that he thought of opening his Institute in England. Many of those who came to my lectures became interested in this idea and arranged a subscription among themselves to cover the material side of the business. A certain sum of money was immediately given to G. to prepare for the passage of the whole of his group to England. I continued my lectures, connecting them with what G. had said during his stay in London. But I had decided for myself that if the Institute opened in London I would go either to Paris or to America. The Institute was finally opened in London but for various reasons it failed. But my London friends and those who came to my lectures collected a considerable sum of money for him and with this G. bought the historic Château Prieuré in Avon near Fontainebleau, with an enormous neglected park, and in the autumn of 1922 he opened his Institute there. A very motley company assembled there. There were a certain number of people who remembered St. Petersburg. There were pupils of G.'s from Tiflis. There were people who had come to my lectures in Constantinople and London. The latter were divided into several groups. In my opinion some had been in far too great a hurry to give up their ordinary occupations in England in order to follow G. I could have said nothing to them because they had already made their decision when they spoke to me about it. I feared that they would meet with disappointment because G.'s work seemed to me not sufficiently rightly organized and therefore to be unstable. But at the same time I could not be sure of my own opinions and did not want to interfere with them because if everything went right and my fears proved to be false then they would undoubtedly have gained by their decision.

Others had tried to work with me but for some reason or other they had parted from me and now thought that it would be easier for them to work with G. They were particularly attracted by the idea of finding what they called *a short cut*. To this, when they asked my advice, I of course advised them to go to Fontainebleau and work with G. And there were others who came to G. temporarily, for two weeks, for a month. These were people who attended my lectures and who did not want to decide themselves, but on hearing about other people's decisions had come to me and asked whether they ought to "give up everything" and go to Fontainebleau and whether this was the only way to go on with the work. To this I said that they should wait until I was there.

I arrived at the Château Prieuré for the first time at the end of October or the beginning of November, 1922. Very interesting and animated work was proceeding there. A pavilion had been built for dances and exercises, housekeeping had been organized, the house had been finished off, and so on. And the atmosphere on the whole was very right and left a strong impression. I remember one talk with Miss Katherine Mansfield who was then living there. This was not more than three weeks before her death. I had given her G.'s address myself. She had been to two or three of my lectures and had then come to me to say that she was going to Paris. A Russian doctor was curing tuberculosis by treating the spleen with X-rays. I could not of course tell her anything about it. She already seemed to me to be halfway to death. And I thought that she was fully aware of it.

But with all this, one was struck by the striving in her to make the best use even of these last days, to find the truth whose presence she clearly felt but which she was unable to touch. I did not think that I should see her again. But I could not refuse when she asked me for the address of my friends in Paris, for the address of people with whom she would be able to talk about the same things she had talked about with me. And so I had met her again at the Prieuré. We sat in the evening in one of the salons and she spoke in a feeble voice which seemed to come from the void, but it was not unpleasant.

"I know that this is true and that there is no other truth. You know that I have long since looked upon all of us without exception as people who have suffered shipwreck and have been cast upon an uninhabited island, but who do not yet know of it. But these people here know it. The others, there, in life, still think that a steamer will come for them to-morrow and that everything will go on in the old way. These already know that there will be no more of the old way. I am so glad that I can be here."

Soon after my return to London I heard of her death. G. was very good to her, he did not insist upon her going although it was clear that she could not live. For this in the course of time he received the due amount of lies and slanders.

During the year 1923 I went fairly often to Fontainebleau, that is, to the Prieuré.

Soon after its opening the Institute attracted the attention of the press and for a month or two the French and English papers were active writing about it. G. and his pupils were called the "forest philosophers," they were interviewed, their photographs were published, and so on.

G.'s own work during this time, that is, from 1922, was dedicated chiefly to the development of methods of studying rhythm and plastics. He never stopped working the whole time on his ballet, bringing into it the dances of various dervishes and Sufis and recalling by memory the music he had listened to in Asia many years before. In this work was a very great deal that was new and interesting. Dervish dances and music were reproduced in Europe undoubtedly for the first time. And they produced a very great impression on all who were able to hear and see them.

In the Prieuré also they carried on very intensive mental exercises for the development of the memory, of attention, and of the imagination, and further, in connection with these exercises, in "imitation of psychic phenomena." Then there was a lot of obligatory work for everyone in the house and connected with the housekeeping which required great strenuousness, thanks to the speed of working and various other conditions.

From among the talks of that time I particularly remember one which related to the methods of breathing and although this talk as well as many other things that were done then passed unnoticed, it showed the possibility of an entirely fresh point of view on the subject in question.

"Right exercises," G. said once, "which lead direct to the aim of mastering the organism and subjecting its conscious and unconscious functions to the will, begin with breathing exercises. Without mastering breathing nothing can be mastered. At the same time to master breathing is not so easy.

"You must realize that there are three kinds of breathing. One is normal breathing. The second is 'inflation.' The third is breathing assisted by movements. What does this mean? It means that normal breathing goes on unconsciously, it is managed and controlled by the moving center. 'Inflation' is artificial breathing. If for instance a man says to himself that he will count ten inhaling and ten exhaling, or that he will inhale through the right nostril and exhale through the left—this is done by the formatory apparatus. And the breathing itself is different because the moving center and the formatory apparatus act through different groups of muscles. The group of muscles through which the moving center acts are neither accessible nor subordinate to the formatory apparatus. But in the event of a temporary stoppage of the moving center the formatory apparatus has been given a group of muscles which it can influence and with whose help it can set the breathing mechanism in motion. But its work will of course be worse than the work of the moving center and it cannot go on for long. You have read the book about 'yogi breathing,' you have heard or have also read about the special breathing connected with the 'mental prayer' in Orthodox monasteries. It is all one and the same thing. Breathing proceeding from the formatory apparatus is not breathing but 'inflation.' The idea is that if a man carries out this kind of breathing long enough and often enough through the formatory apparatus, the moving center which remains idle during this period can get tired of doing nothing and start working in 'imitation' of the formatory apparatus. And indeed this sometimes happens. But so that this should happen many conditions are necessary, fasting and prayer are necessary and little sleep and all kinds of difficulties and burdens for the body. If the body is well treated this cannot happen. You think there are no physical exercises in Orthodox monasteries? Well, you try to carry out one hundred prostrations according to all the rules. You will have an aching back that no kind of gymnastics could ever give.

"This all has one aim: to bring breathing into the right muscles, to hand it over to the moving center. And as I said, sometimes this is successful. But there is always a big risk that the moving center will lose its habit of working properly, and since the formatory apparatus cannot work all the time, as for instance during sleep, and the moving center does not want to, then the machine can find itself in a very sorry situation. A man may even die from breathing having stopped. The disorganization

of the functions of the machine through breathing exercises is almost inevitable when people try to do 'breathing exercises' from books by themselves without proper instruction. Many people used to come to me in
Moscow who had completely disorganized right functioning of their
machines by so-called 'yogi breathing' which they had learned from
books. Books which recommend such exercises represent a great danger.

"The transition of breathing from the control of the formatory apparatus into the control of the moving center can never be attained by
amateurs. For this transition to take place the organism must be brought
to the last stage of intensity, but a man himself can never do this.

"But as I have already said, there is a third way—breathing through
movements. This third way needs a great knowledge of the human machine and it is employed in schools directed by very learned people. In
comparison all other methods are 'home-made' and unreliable.

"The fundamental idea of this method consists in the fact that certain
movements and postures can call forth any kind of breathing you like
and it is also *normal* breathing, not 'inflation.' The difficulty is in knowing what movements and what postures will call forth certain kinds of
breathing in *what kind of people*. This latter is particularly important
because people from this point of view are divided into a certain number
of definite types and each type should have its own definite movements
to get one and the same breathing because the same movement produces
different breathing with different types. A man who knows the movement
which will produce in himself one or another kind of breathing is already
able to control his organism and is able at any moment he likes to set in
motion one or another center or cause that part which is working to stop.
Of course the knowledge of these movements and the ability to control
them like everything else in the world has its degrees. A man can know
more or less and make a better or a worse use of it. In the meantime it is
important only to understand the principle.

"And this is particularly important in connection with the study of the
divisions of centers in oneself. Mention has been made of this several
times before. You must understand that each center is divided into three
parts in conformity with the primary division of centers into 'thinking,'
'emotional,' and 'moving.' On the same principle each of these parts in
its turn is divided into three. In addition, from the very outset each center
is divided into two parts: positive and negative. And in all parts there
are groups of 'rolls' connected together, some in one direction and others
in another direction. This explains the differences between people, what is
called 'individuality.' Of course there is in this no individuality at all, but
simply a difference of 'rolls' and associations."

The talk took place in the big studio in the garden, decorated by G.
in the fashion of a dervish *tekkeh*.

Having explained the meaning of various kinds of breathing he began to divide those present into three groups according to type. About forty people were there. G.'s idea was to show how the same movements with different people produced different "moments of breathing," for instance, with some inhalation, with others exhalation, and how different movements and postures can produce one and the same moment of breathing—inhalation, exhalation, and holding the breath.

But this experiment was not completed. And, as far as I know, G. never afterwards returned to it again.

During this period G. invited me several times to go and live at the Prieuré. There was a good deal of temptation in this. But in spite of all my interest in G.'s work I could find no place for myself in this work nor did I understand its direction. At the same time I could not fail to see, as I had seen in Essentuki in 1918, that there were many destructive elements in the organization of the affair itself and that it had to fall to pieces.

In December, 1923, G. arranged demonstrations of dervish dances, rhythmic movements, and various exercises in Paris in the Theâtre des Champs Elysées.

Soon after these demonstrations in the beginning of January, 1924, G., together with a part of his pupils, went to America with the intention of arranging lectures and demonstrations there.

I was at the Prieuré on the day of his departure. And this departure reminded me very much of his departure from Essentuki in 1918 and all that was connected with it.

On returning to London I announced to those who came to my lectures that my work in the future would proceed quite independently *in the way it had been begun in London in 1921.*

Index